Achieving the Impossible Dream

The Asian American Experience

Series Editor
Roger Daniels, University of Cincinnati

*A list of books in the series appears at
the end of this book.*

Achieving the Impossible Dream

How Japanese Americans Obtained Redress

Mitchell T. Maki,

Harry H. L. Kitano,

and S. Megan Berthold

Forewords by

Representative Robert T. Matsui

and Roger Daniels

University of Illinois Press

Urbana and Chicago

D
769.8
.A6
M29
1999

© 1999 by the Board of Trustees of the University of Illinois
Manufactured in the United States of America
2 3 4 5 C P 5 4 3 2
⊗ This book is printed on acid-free paper.

Library of Congress Cataloging-in-Publication Data
Maki, Mitchell T. (Mitchell Takeshi)
Achieving the impossible dream : how Japanese Americans
obtained redress / Mitchell T. Maki, Harry H. L. Kitano,
and S. Megan Berthold ; forewords by Robert T. Matsui and
Roger Daniels.
p.   cm. — (The Asian American experience)
Includes bibliographical references (p.   ) and index.
ISBN 0-252-02458-3 (acid-free paper)
ISBN 0-252-06764-9 (paperback : acid-free paper)
1. Japanese Americans—Evacuation and relocation, 1942–1945.
2. Japanese Americans—Civil rights. 3. World War, 1939–1945—
Reparations. I. Kitano, Harry H. L. II. Berthold, S. Megan
(Sarah Megan) III. Title. IV. Series.
D769.8.A6M29   1999
940.53'089'956073—ddc21   98-58016
CIP

For those who suffered and endured
the exclusion and incarceration,

for those who contributed to the
struggle for justice,

and to our families, who supported us
in this labor of love

Contents

Illustrations follow page 50

Foreword

Representative Robert T. Matsui

The strength and character of the 120,000 Americans of Japanese ancestry who were incarcerated during World War II have been tested and proven many times over. They bore the indignity of losing their freedom and their material possessions when the war began. They persevered and endured through the depredations of life in the camps. When they returned to their homes after the war, they still faced an unfriendly, even hostile, world. Despite all this they reassembled their lives and livelihoods. With time, patience, and hard work they became successful professionals, community leaders, and parents. Hard work could overcome the material losses of seized property or the four years lost to camp, but it could not replace the dignity and self-respect lost when someone is ostracized and imprisoned without cause. For more than a generation Americans of Japanese ancestry bore this burden in silence and without remedy. This volume tells the stirring story of how the voices of Japanese Americans came to be heard again and how redress for the wrongs of the wartime years was won.

The events that unfold in this book touch great themes and carry many lessons. They tell of the strength and the character of the Issei and Nisei in grappling with the legacy of the war. They instruct us about the political awakening and education of younger Japanese Americans. They are a casebook in civics: the organization and championing of an important cause. Finally, this is the story of the vindication of American values—our ability as a nation to recognize injury and injustice and to set them right.

I am continually asked to address the tragic history of Japanese Americans during World War II. It is never an easy task because the issues run from grand and abstract constitutional principles to the searing personal stories of those who went to camp. It is a topic that makes us face fundamental questions.

How could a nation founded on principles of individual rights suddenly deny the due process rights of an entire group of people? How can a government protect itself and its citizens from its own overzealousness? How do individuals remain so loyal to a nation that questions their loyalty so completely? And long after you have been imprisoned without cause, how do you convince friends, children, and even yourself that you did nothing wrong?

The passage of redress legislation in 1988 responded to many of these issues. It was a meaningful gesture toward healing decades-old wounds: it acknowledged the agony of the survivors who suffered the harsh conditions, the social stigma, and the traumatic aftermath of the camps. It was also a victory for all Americans in that it removed any ambiguity about the rightful role of government, or perhaps more appropriately, the *wrongful* role of government. In sum it showed that a truly great nation is one that is so confident in itself and its citizens that it is willing to make an apology and provide redress for a grievous mistake.

But even great nations cannot come to the right conclusions without substantial effort. In the case of the Civil Liberties Act of 1988 the task was daunting: to create a national consensus that the government had erred in its harsh but not unpopular treatment of a small number of Americans more than forty-five years earlier and to create a willingness, if not an overwhelming demand, to amend a tarnished historical record. All of this occurred during the presidency of a conservative Republican and at a cost of nearly $1.5 billion.

As a member of Congress who was both an observer of and a participant in the battle for redress, I know that the effect of this legislation on my colleagues was powerful. Representatives and senators—many of whom had little or no knowledge of what occurred in 1942 and had few, if any, constituents who were incarcerated—told me that the passage of redress was one of the most important votes they ever cast. They were truly moved by the personal stories of heroic individuals, such as the many soldiers who fought for their country in Europe and the Pacific while back home their families were wrongfully confined by the government. Conservative Republicans, such as Newt Gingrich and Henry Hyde, joined with liberal Democrats, such as Barney Frank and Ron Dellums, to support the legislation, because it was the right thing to do and because it affirmed their own belief in the U.S. Constitution.

To be sure, the ultimate success of redress was the legislative version of David versus Goliath. When the battle began, most Americans did not know anything about the issue. There certainly were no monied interests to open the doors in Washington. Rather, the redress movement stands today, more than a decade after the passage of the act, as a textbook example of what it takes to enact a major statute through determination and perseverance: a motivated and energetic grass-roots constituency, voices that are eloquent simply because they tell powerful and affecting stories, committed public servants and elected officials, access to key lawmakers, and, most important, a powerful issue—a truly just cause.

When Mitchell Maki, Harry Kitano, and Megan Berthold approached me about this project—an authoritative documentation of the redress movement—I was truly delighted that such distinguished scholars were taking a methodological look at this extraordinary achievement. By conducting archival research and interviewing literally scores of individuals who affected the public policy process surrounding redress—proponents, opponents, elected officials, and community leaders—the authors have created a work of lasting value. It tracks the postwar history that led to redress: the effort that created a government commission to look into the wartime treatment of Japanese Americans, the hearings of the Commission on Wartime Relocation and Internment of Civilians that galvanized the Japanese American community, the pain and triumph of those who told their stories at the hearings, the publication of the commission's report, the victories of the *coram nobis* cases, the pioneering legal battles fought to quantify the losses suffered by those who were taken from their homes, and the long road the Civil Liberties Act of 1988 took through Congress and the White House to become law.

The value of this work lies in providing much needed perspective on an issue that was and continues to be controversial, even in the Japanese American community. It demonstrates in dramatic detail the importance of massive outside lobbying, individual insider relationships, and fortuitous twists of fate in passing important federal legislation. There was not one turning point in the success of redress but many. This is a story of not simply individual accomplishment but also what can be attained by many groups and individuals making the most of every resource at their disposal.

While the redress apology and symbolic compensation could in no way amount to full restitution to my parents' generation that lost everything during the prime of their lives, the drive for redress itself and the ultimate legislative success provided an emotional relief that few people could have predicted before the battle began. There was a literal absolution that took place when President Ronald Reagan signed the bill acknowledging for the first time in the history of our nation that our government had made a terrible mistake, admitting to the world that those who had been incarcerated had done nothing wrong.

There was also a catharsis in the community that grew from the very process of strategizing the redress legislation and seeing it through to fruition. Japanese Americans in their sixties, seventies, and eighties and some even older—many of whom had never even voted—got involved in testifying, letter writing, and lobbying. Many of them had never even been able to talk about their agonizing experiences, even with one another, let alone air their pain in public. But through the process of passing this landmark legislation, they were able to tell their powerful stories, move public opinion, influence members of Congress, and reclaim their civil and constitutional rights.

I was only six months old when my family was taken from our home in Sacramento to Tule Lake. I have no recollection of the experience of incarceration. As a result, I used to believe that I bore no scars from that time. With the passage of time, as I examined the lives of my parents and watched the development of my son, I have come to understand the effects, which were so acutely manifest in my parents and had almost entirely disappeared in my son, had in fact shaped my life.

My parents could not even bring themselves to talk about what happened for more than thirty years. Even though they were both native-born citizens of this country, they still carried themselves as exiles in their own nation long after their captivity. Why? Because their rights as citizens had been abrogated without cause or personal accusation and because their loyalty had been repaid by distrust and incarceration. More than forty years later the broken bonds of the social compact still had not healed or been repaired. Those anxieties and the wary uncertainty of one's surroundings had abated somewhat, but as a Sansei, I, too, feared that my peers would question my loyalties. I remember when I was in elementary school, I was asked to tell my fellow students about "being in the camps," and I denied that it had occurred. The effects have almost entirely vanished in my son. He has a confidence in who he is that could not have existed in previous generations, and he has none of the fear of his heritage that loomed over those who came before him.

Without the passage of redress the pain of the incarceration would have undoubtedly weakened over time. As survivors died and as their children and grandchildren made their own way in the world, the immediate force and sting of what occurred during World War II would have begun to abate naturally. But I know from personal experience the importance of this legislation in both righting a wrong for a generation of Japanese Americans and liberating future generations from the aftermath.

The power of the redress story surely lies in its telling and retelling of the great themes of the history of Japanese Americans and of the United States itself. Through this study and other historical endeavors a permanent record will be established that will chronicle not only what went wrong but also what went right so that future generations of Americans will know of the national victory and the personal triumphs achieved in the passage of the redress legislation.

Foreword

Roger Daniels

When Harry Kitano and I organized the first academic conference devoted to the wartime incarceration of Japanese Americans at UCLA in 1967 to mark the twenty-fifth anniversary of Executive Order 9066, we did not have the slightest notion that by the time the fiftieth anniversary rolled around in 1992 the complex process of what the Japanese American community came to call redress would be nearly complete. None of the participants in that conference even hinted at any kind of compensation. Most were simply concerned with drawing attention to the legal atrocity that had been inflicted on the Japanese American people.

In *Achieving the Impossible Dream* Mitchell Maki, Harry Kitano, and S. Megan Berthold have investigated how "redress," the passage of the Civil Liberties Act of 1988, came about. More important, they have delineated how the Japanese American community, at first highly skeptical, created a complex and eventually successful set of organizations that was able to bridge the not inconsiderable rifts within the community, rifts that had their roots in the wartime events of 1942–46 and the differing reactions to them. Although their interviews with key players in the redress struggle add depth and insight to their analysis, the true protagonist of this book is the community itself, for it was the community that made the dream come alive.

How did such an improbable event take place? The authors have provided helpful models of political behavior, but such models only indicate possibilities. The real story of this book is how those possibilities became political reality. It seems to me that once the presidential Commission on Wartime Relocation and Internment of Civilians made its report and recommendations in 1983, the eventual passage of some kind of meaningful monetary redress was ensured.[1] But there was a strong conservative tide flowing in the land, and the Congress and the executive branch were dominated by those opposed to new outlays of public money for anything other than military hardware. While everyone knew that the tide would turn again, time was clearly running out for the surviving victims of America's concentration camps. It was the particular genius of the Japanese American redress movement that its leadership managed to engage the consciences of not only such liberals as Barney Frank but also such conservatives as Warren Rudman. *Achieving the Impossible Dream* narrates and analyzes how, in just five years, the battle for redress was won while conservatism was still at high tide. Without the nuanced and knowing campaign, redress might have had to wait another five years, and, given the lack of harmony between Bill Clinton and the Congress, it might not have been ratified even then. Even after the Civil Liberties Act passed in August 1988, months of maneuvering and waiting went by before the necessary appropriations were made, and more months passed until the first redress checks were received by the aged survivors on October 9, 1990.

William Dean Howells once wrote that what the American people wanted was tragedies with a happy ending. Some would argue that the redress story meets that peculiar prescription. I think that it is a tragedy only slightly modified by a belated awareness of some of the evils done in the name of the "good war." No amount of repayment, not many times the $20,000 awarded to survivors, could properly redress the years of imprisonment and the decades of shame. And, of course, some 50,000 victims did not live to see redress achieved. An old axiom has it that justice delayed is justice denied. If that is true—and I believe it is—even the compensated survivors did not, could not, receive justice, although most appreciated the apology that the accompanying checks reified.

Note

1. This is not just hindsight. I made this point in a lecture given on March 10, 1983, which is printed in Roger Daniels, Sandra C. Taylor, and Harry H. L. Kitano, eds., *Japanese Americans: From Relocation to Redress* (Salt Lake City: University of Utah Press, 1986; rev. ed., Seattle: University of Washington Press, 1991).

Acknowledgments

The three of us came to this project from very different backgrounds. Harry, a Nisei and renowned Asian American scholar, was a former inmate of Topaz. Although he had written extensively about Japanese Americans, he had only lightly touched on this significant movement. On a personal level, both the incarceration and the redress movement had affected his life very deeply. Mitch, a Sansei, was born and reared in Los Angeles. His parents, however, were from Hawai'i, and no one in his family was directly affected by the exclusion and incarceration. Nonetheless, Mitch had long been interested in the redress movement, and as a college student, he had participated in candlelight marches, letter-writing campaigns, and lobbying for the California state redress bill. Megan, a white American from Vermont, came to the project with little knowledge of the history of the concentration camps or the redress movement. She was motivated by her deep commitment to civil and human rights. In some ways we were an unlikely trio. In other ways we were a microcosm of the redress movement, a collaboration of different generations, genders, regions, and ethnicities.

During the four years that we worked on the book, the process became truly a labor of love. Traveling, eating countless meals while editing the manuscript, and working long days together provided an incredible bonding experience. Harry would often share stories of the camps and his family's struggles before and after the war. His perspective as a Nisei provided us with a deep understanding of the emotional turmoil the community endured. Mitch would tell stories of his experiences with the redress movement. He also would share his admiration for those who made redress happen. As he constantly says, "These folks are my heroes." Megan initially brought an outsider's perspective and a freshness that prevented us from being too subjective. Her early unfamiliarity with the camp experience was quickly replaced by a drive to disseminate the redress story.

The legacy of the redress movement is composed of three elements. The first is the personal impact made by the apology and monetary payments given to the individuals who endured the exclusion and incarceration. The second is the transformation that occurred within the community. The community went from a point of saying "Shikata ga nai" (It can't be helped) to shouting "Justice delayed is justice denied." The third is the continuing education of all Americans that civic participation can affect national public policy.

The writing of this book has led to the development of a class on the Japanese American redress movement at UCLA. In 1997 we were also given the privilege of convening the Voices of Japanese American Redress Conference at UCLA. To each of us the redress movement is much more than simply a theme for a book. It has become a part of us, and we hope that this book becomes a part of the legacy of the movement.

We could not have completed this book without the cooperation, aid, and guidance of many people. The writing of this book, like the redress movement, was a community process. We thank all those who so graciously agreed to be interviewed. Many of these individuals also provided archival materials and personal notes from the redress movement. Their quotes are generously distributed throughout the book. Their words are the words of the redress movement. There were many powerful stories and moving moments during these interviews. We set out to gather information; we came back with meaningful friendships. We also thank the Japanese American National Museum, the Japanese American Citizens League, the National Coalition on Redress and Reparations, and the former National Council for Japanese American Redress for the archival material they provided.

A number of other individuals also provided invaluable assistance to this project. Susan Nakaoka, John Nakashima, Darleen Hirose Kuwahara, and Lisa Mochizuki all contributed to this project and in their own ways left their marks on the final product. The students in our redress class encouraged us through their thoughtful questions and interest in the subject. Supportive librarians, especially our friends at UCLA's "Gov Docs" helped us locate many sources for this work that were difficult to find. The staff at the University of Illinois Press, especially Karen Hewitt and Jane Mohraz, were instrumental in bringing the manuscript to fruition. We thank them all.

A work of this nature cannot be conducted without significant financial funding to offset related costs. This book could not have been completed without the generous support of the UCLA Japanese American Endowed Chair and the UCLA School of Public Policy and Social Research. Of particular note is the constant support we received from Don T. Nakanishi, director of the UCLA Asian American Studies Center. Not only did he provide financial support, but he believed in our efforts, even when we had moments of doubt.

Finally, a very special thank you to the series editor, Roger Daniels. His vast knowledge of the Japanese American experience, careful editing, and high standards were integral to the shaping of this manuscript. Roger inspired us. We thank him for this finished work and more important for the process of creating it.

The redress movement is not only a great Japanese American story but also a great American story. The stories of those who experienced the constitutional injustice and those who fought for the redressing of this wrong are full of lessons for us all. We feel very privileged to be able to tell this story.

Achieving the Impossible Dream

Introduction

The stress of going into camp, [the] poor diet and [the] worry
hastened the death of my mother. She was 52 years old. She had
to be cremated; there was no choice. My sorrow that I have to
this day is that I could not put a fresh flower on her grave. All
our flowers were made of Kleenex.

—Akiyo DeLoyd, Poston Camp, Commission on Wartime
    Relocation and Internment of Civilians Hearings

These are the words of a concentration camp survivor. A woman who was
imprisoned not by a hostile enemy nation or by a totalitarian regime. She,
and over 110,000 others like her, were imprisoned without charges or trial
by a country that prided itself in being the beacon of liberty and justice. She
was imprisoned in a concentration camp by her own nation, the United States
of America.

In 1942 the United States, engaged in World War II, abandoned the core
principles of its Constitution. Racism, wartime hysteria, and failed political
leadership resulted in the incarceration of U.S. citizens and legal residents in
concentration camps located in desolate and barren regions. How could this
happen in a land where citizens salute the flag and pledge to uphold the principles of "liberty and justice for all?" How could such a nation abandon these
ideals?

Forty-six years later, in 1988, the nation wrestled with the memory of its
actions. The country, however, was facing a variety of other critical challenges:
balancing the federal budget, containing welfare costs, stemming the crime
rate, ensuring social security solvency, and providing adequate medical care
and health coverage. In this political environment a relatively obscure but important event occurred on August 10. President Ronald W. Reagan signed the
Civil Liberties Act of 1988, which apologized and paid $20,000 to surviving
Japanese Americans excluded from the western region of the continental
United States and incarcerated in concentration camps during World War
II. Such legislation was unprecedented. The nation remembered and apolo-

gized for its denial of liberty and justice to Japanese Americans. The apology, however, was not only to the Japanese Americans whose constitutional rights were violated but also to the nation itself for forsaking its most cherished ideals.

In 1990 Japanese American survivors of the camps began to receive redress checks of $20,000 each and the following letter of apology from President George Bush:

> A monetary sum and words alone cannot restore lost years or erase painful memories; neither can they fully convey our Nation's resolve to rectify injustice and to uphold the rights of individuals. We can never fully right the wrongs of the past. But we can take a clear stand for justice and recognize that serious injustices were done to Japanese Americans during World War II.
>
> In enacting a law calling for restitution and offering a sincere apology, your fellow Americans have, in a very real sense, renewed their traditional commitment to the ideals of freedom, equality, and justice. You and your family have our best wishes for the future.
>
> > Sincerely,
> > [signed]
> > George Bush

The Question of Redress

How did the Japanese American community progress from incarceration in 1942 to an apology and redress payments in 1988? An examination of this process reveals the transformation of an idea, of a specific ethnic community, and of a nation. During the 1940s the idea of excluding men, women, and children of Japanese ancestry from the Pacific Coast of the United States and incarcerating them in concentration camps was popular. The proposal was formulated by powerful politicians and supported by Franklin Delano Roosevelt, one of the greatest American presidents.

The camps were billed as a military necessity and essential for the protection of the Japanese American community. A propaganda film produced by the federal government, *Japanese Relocation,* described the camps as "humane" and asserted that the Japanese American community "cheerfully" cooperated with the plan. Ultimately it would be proven that the Federal Bureau of Investigation (FBI) and the Office of Naval Intelligence (ONI) apprised the federal government that no military necessity existed. Many Japanese Americans felt no need for protection. It was clear that the rationale of "protection" was simply a guise for incarceration. Representative Norman Y. Mineta (Democrat from California), a second-generation Japanese American incarcerated as a ten-year-old in the Heart Mountain camp, was fond of stating, "Some say the internment was for our own protection.

But even as a boy of 10, I could see that the machine guns and the barbed wired faced inward."[1]

In 1988 the Japanese American community, the general American society, and the nation's government faced several obstacles when struggling with the concept of redress for Japanese Americans. First, the redress movement needed to overcome arguments that this was a different generation's action and too far in the past for a modern remedy.

Second, the redress movement demanded an admission by the federal government that the forced incarceration was a mistake. Third, the idea of redress involved monetary payments in an era of fiscal restraints. The supporters of redress would need to deal with three sources of opposition: those who refused to acknowledge any wrongdoing on the part of the United States, those who feared the possible precedent that redress would set for all the other wrongs the United States committed, and those who opposed redressing past wrongs with monetary payments.

A fourth factor was that the Japanese American community faced a catch-22 over how the general American society perceived them. Many Americans often failed to differentiate between Japanese Americans and Japanese from Japan. Although Japan was an ally in 1988, many also viewed it as an economic competitor, and "Japan bashing" was popular. This sentiment carried over to the general American public's attitude toward Japanese Americans. When Japanese Americans were distinguished from Japanese, however, they had to overcome being perceived as a "model minority" who had surmounted their "victimization."

A fifth factor was that Japanese Americans were a small minority group with limited experience in mobilizing and organizing a communitywide, much less a national, political effort. The few favorable pieces of legislation or judicial decisions affecting the Japanese American community resulted from the efforts of a few well-placed and involved Japanese Americans. The Japanese American community, as a whole, was unaccustomed to influencing federal policy.

The final factor was the difficulty of passing any legislation through Congress where there are numerous points at which bills can be killed, especially special legislation like redress. The congressional structure was designed to limit the passage of excessive legislation. For example, in the One-hundredth Congress (1987–88), 6,263 bills were introduced in the House and 3,325 bills in the Senate. Of these, 713 were enacted into law. Most of the rest died in committee.[2]

Faced with these difficulties, most Japanese Americans initially viewed the possibility of obtaining redress as highly unlikely. Very few of the over sixty individuals interviewed for this case study thought that Japanese Americans would ever be compensated for their imprisonment. Almost all agreed that in the beginning they viewed redress as "an impossible dream." Ironically, if the question had been asked prior to 1941 whether the United States would soon be at war with Japan and all Japanese in the United States, both citizens and legal residents, would be forcibly removed from their homes and placed behind barbed wire, many Japanese Americans would have answered, "Impossible." In one lifetime Japanese in the United States have seen two "impossible" actions become reality.

The idea of obtaining redress for Japanese Americans was conceived in the community, nurtured and facilitated by concerned individuals and community groups, and ultimately effected by the three branches of the U.S. government. Many individuals played roles that varied in length, focus, and scope; all were crucial to the process. Throughout the process, political strategy, personal commitment, framing of the issue, timing, and, at times, luck emerged as influential factors in the movement. The purpose of this case study is to analyze how redress was obtained. The critical variables are identified, and a model is presented that demonstrates how this "impossible dream" became reality.

The Use of Language to Define Reality

Language is a very powerful tool that serves to frame and define reality. The concentration camp experience is full of attempts by the federal government to have the Japanese American experience described with euphemistic terms belying the truth. Such terms as *evacuation, relocation camps,* and *non-aliens* were used by the federal government in 1942. Individuals of Japanese ancestry were being "evacuated," as if to imply that for their own welfare they needed to be "remove[d] from a dangerous place."[3] The places where Japanese Americans were confined were described as "assembly centers" and "relocation centers," not "concentration camps."[4]

The most blatant euphemism was the term *non-aliens,* which was used to describe native-born U.S. citizens. The posted exclusion notices stated that "all Japanese persons, both alien and non-alien will be evacuated."[5] To post notices that "citizens" were to be "evacuated" would have revealed more clearly the federal government's violation of the constitutional rights of U.S. citizens.

The most common semantic error found in describing the concentration camp experience is the use of the term *internment.* The terms *interned* and *internment* are often used by the general public and members of the Japanese American community when referring to the concentration camps. This usage, however, fails to accentuate appropriately the legal injustice. As Roger Daniels commented, "Internment is a long-sanctioned legal process common to the usages of nations in which, during time of war, selected nationals of enemy nations, usually adult males, are placed in confinement or otherwise restrained. While there are often individual injustices involved, internment itself has the color of law. What happened to the bulk of the Japanese-American people was, in and of itself, a lawless outrage. . . . Most of the Japanese living in America were incarcerated, not interned."[6] In this book we call things by their right names.

An Overview

The Japanese American experience started late in the nineteenth century with the immigration of the first generation of Japanese, the Issei,[7] to the United States. The Issei, like most other immigrants, came in search of a better life but soon became targets of prejudice and discrimination. Like other Asians, they were aliens ineligible for citizenship and thus not allowed to vote, own land, or become naturalized. However, since the Fourteenth Amendment made "all persons born . . . in the United States" citizens, their American-born children, the second generation known as the Nisei, were Americans by birth. Despite being U.S. citizens, the Nisei also faced prejudice and discrimination. What happened after the attack on Pearl Harbor on December 7, 1941, made a mockery of the Nisei's U.S. citizenship. They, along with their Issei parents, were kept in American concentration camps. There was no trial, no determination of guilt, and no evidence of sabotage. All Japanese Americans were viewed as members of an enemy race. Years of anti-Japanese propaganda had conditioned the public to accept the negative images.

During the incarceration and in the years immediately following World War II, there was some discussion about redress. It was an idea, however, whose time had not yet come. The Japanese American community, the mass media, and the political community provided little support for the idea. When the camps closed in 1944–46, redress was simply not a priority for the Japanese American community. Deciding where to resettle, making a living, and reestablishing their lives were their major concerns. The idea that the federal government and the public would be sympathetic to anything that would be favorable to Japanese Americans was unrealistic. Sending all Japanese Americans "back" to a defeated Japan would have been a more popular policy.

In the decades to follow there were some positive changes in the treatment of Japanese Americans. In the late 1940s legislation favoring Japanese Americans was enacted. Congress passed the Japanese-American Evacuation Claims Act of 1948, which provided compensation for some of the property lost during the wartime exclusion and incarceration. The compensation provided, however, was a minor fraction of actual losses.

In 1952 the McCarran-Walter Act assigned a quota to immigrants from Japan and made Asians, including Issei, eligible for citizenship. In the 1950s and 1960s the civil rights movement of African Americans heightened awareness of the injustices suffered by all ethnic minorities. The addition of Hawai'i as the fiftieth state of the union in 1959 resulted in the election of Chinese and Japanese Americans to the U.S. Congress. Most important for redress, there was also a growing awareness in the Japanese American community of the injustice of the wartime treatment and a developing mood that something should be done.

In 1967, twenty-five years after the creation of the camps, Harry H. L. Kitano and Roger Daniels organized an academic conference at UCLA focusing on the exclusion and incarceration. It was the first such conference held at any university. Kitano remembers getting a number of phone calls about the conference asking, "Why dredge up repressed memories? Let sleeping dogs lie, why stir up trouble?"[8] The conference received wide coverage by the Los Angeles media and contributed to a momentum for future gatherings of a similar nature. Although there were many presentations and numerous workshops, there was not a single word about reparations, redress, or an apology from the U.S. government. As the awareness of the American public changed, however, the Japanese American community also experienced changes. In 1970 Edison Uno, a community activist from northern California, made the first formal proposal for redress at the national Japanese American Citizens League meeting.

During the 1970s redress was still a long way from becoming a reality. It was uncertain whether the hostile, "anti-Jap" feelings of World War II had changed enough to allow for redress legislation. An equally important uncertainty was whether the Japanese American community would unite around this issue. Would the community speak with a loud and unified voice or as a disparate group of competing voices?

By 1980 Japanese Americans had made tremendous educational, professional, social, and economic strides. As their status and acceptance into the American society increased, the question was whether Japanese Americans wanted to remember the camps. Had the desire for redress dwindled in those decades, or had its need been intensified?

During the 1970s and the 1980s the Japanese American community began to answer these questions by changing its stance from not wanting to relive the past to articulating the past injustices and demanding restitution. The changes in the attitudes of the American public and changes in the Japanese American community propelled the redress movement into the formal policy domain of the federal government. In the federal branches of government the "impossible dream" eventually became a reality. It was the convergence of these elements (history, the community, and actions by the legislative, judicial, and executive branches of the government) that created the context in which redress was obtained.

The Case Study

The case study is divided into several sections. The first section, covered in chapter 1, presents four theoretical models to highlight the key elements and dynamics that influence policy-making. Included in these models is the Kitano-Maki proper alignment model for public policy, a framework for understanding the dynamics of the successful movement to obtain redress.

The second section of the book covers the exclusion and incarceration experiences during World War II through the beginning of the modern redress movement in 1970. Chapter 2 presents the historical background of the Japanese in the United States. Specifically, the experiences of the Issei and the Nisei and the historical backdrop for the decision to exclude and incarcerate individuals of Japanese ancestry are discussed. Chapter 3 describes life for Japanese Americans in the concentration camps and in the military. This chapter also includes a brief description of the experiences of the Aleutian Pribilof Islanders, a community that became unanticipated partners in the fight for redress. Chapter 4 discusses the period from 1945 to 1969 and how the different streams of influence slowly began to align themselves in a manner more favorable to the Japanese American community in general and to the idea of redress in particular.

The third section of the case study covers the modern redress movement. Chapter 5 discusses the period from 1970 to 1978, when the movement toward redress became a priority in the Japanese American community. Chapter 6 focuses on the period from 1979 to 1982, during which the Commission on Wartime Relocation and Internment of Civilians (CWRIC) was created and functioned. Chapter 7 describes the lawsuits and parallel redress efforts. Chapter 8 examines the movement from 1983 to 1986, when redress legislation was introduced in the Ninety-eighth Congress and the Ninety-ninth Congress.

The fourth section of the case study focuses on the passage of the redress legislation, the Civil Liberties Act of 1988. Chapter 9 describes the events and strategies that led to the passage of H.R. 442 in the One-hundredth Congress. Chapter 10 presents the strategies involved in obtaining President Ronald Reagan's support and the subsequent fight to fund the redress legislation. The implementation of the redress legislation that made the dream a reality is discussed in chapter 11. This chapter also includes a description of the categories of individuals who were not covered by the redress legislation and their efforts to be recognized. Chapter 12 summarizes the lessons learned from the redress movement and their potential application to other issues.

Throughout the book there is discussion of the contributions of community groups, political figures, and individuals. Different elements facilitated the aligning of all the necessary streams of influence that came together to make redress a reality.

The story of the Civil Liberties Act of 1988 may be viewed as the passage of one more federal statute. The redress story, however, is much more. It is the story of a community coming together, finding its voice to demand recognition, and beginning its own healing process. It is the story of a great nation, unused to acknowledging its mistakes, admitting a past injustice and attempting to make amends. This case study tells that story. It also draws the parallels between the events of the redress movement and different theoretical perspectives of public policy-making.

1   Theoretical Perspectives

Once legislation is passed, there are many explanations of how it happened. Among the factors in passing legislation are its merits, political strategy and power, personal commitment, community support, and possibly luck. An additional factor often cited is timing. John Kingdon writes that policy development can sometimes occur because "it was an idea whose time has come."[1]

Several questions about the passage of the Civil Liberties Act of 1988 come to mind. Why did it take nearly fifty years? What initiated and maintained community support? What were the characteristics of the specific legislation and the sociopolitical context that facilitated its passage?

Various theoretical models might explain the passage of legislation. This chapter presents four models (the Campbell model, the garbage can model, resource mobilization theory, and collective behavior theory) relevant to understanding public policy-making in general and the redress movement in particular. In addition the Kitano-Maki proper alignment model provides an explanation for the successful passage of the Civil Liberties Act of 1988.

Campbell Model

The Campbell model is based on John C. Campbell's case study of Japanese government policy toward the elderly. The model proposes that ideas and energy are influential in decision making. Ideas, which may be more or less institutionalized, are "goals, preferences, norms, beliefs about cause-and-effect relationships, [and] conceptions of social problems that deserve attention."[2] Ideas represent a "repertoire of policy solutions" available to policy-makers.[3] Sources of energy include money, time, and other resources.

Campbell defines four possible modes of decision making: *political, arti-*

factual, cognitive, and *inertial.* New ideas are important in the political and cognitive modes, but they are less important in the artifactual and inertial modes. New energy is a determining factor in the political and artifactual modes, but it is less important in the cognitive and inertial ones.

Political Mode

In the political mode of decision making, policy change is viewed as conflictual. Both energy and ideas are important and inextricably linked. Participants have a variety of goals and preferences. The decision-making process encourages fighting and bargaining, and the results are determined by such variables as the relative power of the participants, the amount of time and energy spent on the issue, and the skillful use of resources.

The major element in the political mode is the need for information. Participants require constant and valid answers to the following questions: Who are the various players? What do they want? How much time and energy is each willing to spend to get the desired outcome? In the struggle for the Civil Liberties Act of 1988 the Japanese American community's belief in and commitment to the principle of redress provided the initial ideas and energy. The community struggled with the concept of redress for many years, and throughout the process different proposals created internal community conflicts.

The Japanese American community leaders had to communicate their knowledge of the exclusion and incarceration to the members of Congress. Political power and leadership came largely from Japanese American legislators in the House and Senate. The creation of a presidential commission to investigate the exclusion and incarceration was an important political step that provided vital information.[4] The interaction between these elements facilitated the passage of redress.

Artifactual Mode

In the artifactual mode Campbell sees policy change as occurring by coincidence. A choice opportunity opens, and there is enough energy to overcome inertia so that something new becomes possible. From this perspective unrelated ideas and issues are thrown together. Problems receive attention without regard to priorities or problem-solving strategies.

The creation of policy depends on the presence of opportunity. What policy is developed is largely accidental and heavily dependent on happenstance. Whether an important and influential individual with high energy shows up at a crucial meeting, whether a particular problem emerges when decision makers are occupied with other business, or whether the general public mood is supportive of some sort of change is pivotal in the creation of policy.

The artifactual mode addresses the importance of timing, which was critical in the redress movement. The changes in the Japanese American community, the presence of Japanese American legislators in the Congress, the changes in key subcommittee chairs, and Democratic majorities in both the chambers of Congress were all elements in the timing that affected redress.

Cognitive Mode

In the cognitive mode Campbell views policy-making as a problem-solving process. The process is technocratic and based on logic. Problems are addressed, and the "best" ideas and solutions are selected according to rational criteria. By using the best knowledge available to them, policymakers select the alternative that maximizes achievement at the least cost. It makes little difference who comes up with the solution since the power of the participants is subordinate to the logic of the decision. The cognitive mode is often used by foreign affairs journalists and writers to explain policy change as a reasonable response to some shift in the international environment relative to national interest. Domestically, the cognitive mode is used by policy analysts to explain why certain problems are more important and why certain solutions are better than others.

Rationality is often relative and culturally bound. It is necessary to analyze how participants actually think and feel. What meanings do they attribute to cultural ideas and symbols, and what are their normative reference groups? There is seldom an objective "rationality," nor is there usually adequate time, information, viable alternatives, or wisdom to obtain consensus on what is a rational policy.

Despite these imperfect conditions the achievement of redress had its cognitive elements. The issue was constructed and presented in such a way that the recommended policy of redress was viewed as a rational course of action. The various branches of the federal government eventually concurred, and the result was the passage of the Civil Liberties Act of 1988. The cognitive mode, however, downplays the struggles, the use of power, the negotiations, and the accidental, artifactual occurrences that made the redress movement anything but a smooth, rational process.

Inertial Mode

In the inertial mode Campbell views policy change as routine, involving neither energy nor new ideas. The other three modes addressed policy change as a result of something new happening in the decision-making process. The inertial mode views changes as being processed in a routine and predictable way. For example, the amount of spending on unemployment compensation is a mechanistic decision based on actuarial data that occurs without the introduction of much new energy or ideas.

Although the inertial mode offers explanations for institutionalized and routine decisions, it does not contribute to an understanding of how a policy is initiated, maintained, and completed. If the Japanese American community had ignored redress and had not provided the energy for it, it is clear that the federal government would never have considered the issue. The inertial mode thus has no relevance for this study. The Campbell model does, however, provide a framework for analyzing and appreciating the contributions of new ideas, energy, valid information, political power (political mode), timing (artifactual mode), and the presentation of rationality (cognitive mode).

Three Additional Theories

Policy-making is addressed by three additional theories: the garbage can model, resource mobilization theory, and collective behavior theory. The policy-making process of the federal government is conceptualized by Michael D. Cohen, James G. March, and Johan P. Olsen in their "garbage can model" of policy development,[5] while the community can be understood by resource mobilization theory, as described by Aldon D. Morris,[6] and collective behavior theory, as described by Ralph H. Turner and Lewis M. Killian.[7] The federal government was the realm in which formal policy was introduced, sanctioned, and implemented. The community, including both the general public and Japanese Americans, was the source from which both positive and negative ideas and energy emanated, helping to shape the formal policy-making process. Both arenas were equally important in obtaining redress.

The Garbage Can Model

Cohen, March, and Olsen formulated the garbage can model of policy development by examining academia. They describe universities as organized anarchies with three general properties: problematic preferences, unclear technology, and fluid participation. Kingdon asserts that these properties are common to both universities and the federal government.[8] The amount of time, effort, and involvement given to issues can vary. Who gets invited to critical meetings, who shows up, and their degree of involvement make a critical difference in the policy outcome.

Kingdon stresses the absence of a comprehensive understanding of the organizational process and the inherent fluidity of organizational membership as factors influencing policy development: "People also don't necessarily understand the organization of which they are a part: The left hand doesn't know what the right hand is doing. Participation is definitely fluid. . . . [It] changes from one decision to another and one time to the next. Turnover of personnel adds to the fluidity."[9]

The garbage can model identifies four separate streams that influence policy development: problems, solutions, participants, and choice opportunities. *Problems* arise from a variety of sources and are defined in different ways. Crisis conditions or disasters are brought to the attention of government officials. However, members of Congress or of the executive branch may define a problem differently than do interested individuals, organizations, and pressure groups that are also attempting to influence the federal agenda. Issues that obtain significant consensus generate policy proposals.

Solutions are proposed responses primarily generated by self-interest. Possible solutions to problems meet several criteria, such as their "technical feasibility, their fit with dominant values and the current national mood, their budgetary workability, and the political support or opposition they might experience."[10]

Participants are the players affecting the development of policy. Kingdon notes that participants often drift in and out of the decision-making process and may vary in status. Generally, the most important players in setting government policy are the elected officials and their appointees.[11] Career bureaucrats, however, can have a significant effect on policy. For example, Major Karl R. Bendetsen, a career army officer, was a major player in establishing the exclusion and incarceration policy of World War II.

Choice opportunities arise when proposals for action are coupled with favorable political forces, resulting in the likelihood that policy windows will open. Windows may open because of a change in administration, a shift in the national mood, or influential congressional legislators' awareness of a particular problem. Windows of opportunity for policy making are often present only for short periods.

Once a legislative proposal is submitted, it is thrown together with a number of diverse ideas, often unrelated to the primary issue. These additional ideas range from complementary, to oppositional, to indifferent. They create a "garbage can" process from which policy emerges.[12] Modifications, amendments, new directions, and extraneous items lead to such descriptions as "opening Pandora's box." While windows of opportunity are often sought, there may be occasions when participants choose to avoid such a window because the outcomes might be worse than the status quo.

The garbage can model identifies the separate streams in the system and how the coupling of such streams results in policy outcomes. One criticism of the garbage can model is there can be different interpretations of how a policy was developed since policy-making is so complicated. The data used in making decisions are often fragmented and subject to the interpretations of individual actors and organizations. As a result, various individuals and groups can take undue credit for a policy decision. Nonetheless, the garbage can model, with its emphasis on identifying different streams, can reveal possible explanations that otherwise might be overlooked.

Important in obtaining redress was the way in which the problem was defined, the manner in which the solutions were presented, the activities of key participants, and the creation of a unique window of opportunity for the legislation. The redress legislation emerged from the "garbage can" of policy-making in a form that achieved its original objectives and managed to minimize any negative effects of "opening Pandora's box."

Resource Mobilization Theory

Another theory that helps to explain how public policy is made is resource mobilization theory. A central element in the redress movement was the mobilization of the Japanese American community and its sustaining influence on the formal policy-making efforts. In explaining how communities participate in social movements, Morris presents the resource mobilization theory. This theory emphasizes the organization, mobilization, and management of key resources that influence policy change, including pre-existing formal and informal organizational networks, charismatic leaders, appropriate levels of funding, and effective communication networks. Of equal importance is the climate of the broader political environment and the degree to which it will facilitate or inhibit the development of collective action by a community.

Morris sees social movements as deliberate, conscious efforts to effect social change. Creativity and innovation are central to efforts seeking to establish a new social order. An example is the civil rights movement, which demonstrated the important roles of community organizing and planning. Although emotions ran high and excitement was important, they were not the determining characteristics. Morris argues that the crucial element was the ability of the African American community to spread the movement through preexisting formal and informal communication networks. The resource mobilization theory predicts that social actors who have access to resources and are well integrated in the institutions of a community are more likely to be effective than individuals who are marginal and unconnected.

Collective Behavior Theory

Turner and Killian propose using collective behavior theory to explain how communities evolve into mobilizing networks. The theory rests on the principle that collective behavior differs from everyday organizational behavior since it is a response to unusual situations. As Morris points out, collective behavior arises "during periods of rapid social change or crises."[13] Collective behavior, Morris continues, therefore does not adhere to "traditional norms, customs, communication systems, and institutions."[14] While collective behavior may not adhere to traditional norms, Turner and Killian indicate that it may interact with preexisting social structures. The question is, what transforms existing communities and their structures into agents for social change?

Turner and Killian identify five major elements: the development of an emergent norm, feasibility, timeliness, the utilization of preexisting groups, and the presence of extraordinary event solidarity. The *development of an emergent norm* within a group occurs when the group perceives that what it is doing is justified and right. The group redefines what previously was seen as a misfortune into an injustice. This redefinition, or emergent norm, provides a sense of mission and conviction and facilitates the coordination of collective action to fight against the perceived injustice.

Feasibility involves both objective and subjective resources. Objective resources include such items as financial backing, donated services, legal assistance, and access to the mass media and to those in powerful decision-making positions. Subjective resources include the perception of resource availability, which in turn influences how amenable individuals are to take action on behalf of the issues that concern them. Vision, hope, belief, and self-confidence are crucial subjective resources. Objective and subjective resources often interact. For example, self-confidence can be enhanced by the building up of resources or by small but successful confrontations with the authorities, while the confidence, hope, and fervor of activists can be dealt a blow by unsuccessful confrontations with those in power.

There are two elements that determine the *timeliness* of an issue: a sense of urgency that promotes the present moment as the "last chance" to push for an issue and the "cultural appropriateness" or historical timing of an action. Promoting a social action during a particular season, on a specific anniversary, or at the same time as a cultural celebration is a way of enhancing the "timeliness" of an issue.

The importance of *preexisting groups* is their established communication networks and the ability to utilize the mass media. Both are essential to sustaining collective behavior. Preexisting groups can also provide individuals who do the tedious and often unheralded day-to-day tasks that keep movements on track.

Finally, an *extraordinary event* or condition (most often of a distressful nature) tends to facilitate solidarity as people look to one another for help in their struggle to make sense of and respond to these situations. Natural disasters that inspire a united community response are common examples of such extraordinary events. Another more political example is the assassination of President John F. Kennedy, which promoted solidarity that benefited the agenda of his successor, President Lyndon B. Johnson.[15]

There is also a need for strategic and expressive considerations in a social movement. Turner emphasizes that social movements must constantly maintain a course based on the careful reflection of the consequences for both.[16]

Strategic actions contribute directly to the acquisition of the movement's goals through the use of such tactics as persuasion, direct negotiation, discussion, and compromise. Strategic considerations provide for the calculated mobilization and utilization of resources to attain stated goals.[17] Expressive considerations include the exercise of power and symbolic displays, such as sit-ins and marches. These dramatic gestures of support give participants a sense of involvement.[18]

Both types of considerations are crucial to the success of a movement. There is, however, an inherent conflict between the strategic and expressive considerations. The strategic group can provide the movement with meaningful access to the policy-making circle but must endure the outspoken tactics of the expressive group, which can be viewed as disruptive to the negotiation process. The actions of the expressive group help ensure that the strategic group will not compromise away the stated goals. Sometimes, however, this conflict is too destabilizing and can destroy a movement.

Each of these elements played a central role in transforming a once victimized community into one that successfully gained redress. By the late 1980s the Japanese American community had arrived at a consensus that redress was a goal worth pursuing. The community had the necessary resources and believed in its ability to succeed. Japanese Americans knew that the Issei were dying quickly. The community had a preexisting group that had a national network and relationships with national groups from other communities. There were individuals and organizations that performed many expressive considerations. Finally, the redress movement was viewed as an extraordinary opportunity to stand up for the rights of Japanese Americans. The community blended its strategic and expressive considerations in the process of standing up for these rights.

Kitano-Maki Proper Alignment Model

The Kitano-Maki proper alignment model recognizes the importance of a number of elements considered by the various other models. It emphasizes that specific streams of influence need to be properly aligned for certain types of federal laws to be passed. These include the historical context and the legislative, judicial, and executive branches of the federal government. The initial idea for the alignment model came from an interview with Congressman Norman Y. Mineta. In response to the question of how redress passed, he humorously responded that it might have been "the lineup of the stars, the moon, and the sun" and that such a lineup was rare.[19] The analogy of lining up different celestial bodies also reflects the notion that while these bodies are independent, they have gravitational influence on each other. The streams of influence in the Kitano-Maki model are independent of one another but also exert influence on each other.

The Kitano-Maki proper alignment model is pictured in figure 1. The columns identify the significant streams that make up the proper alignment. The columns include the following: (a) history: community; (b) history: U.S. society; (c) legislative branch: Senate; (d) legislative branch: House; (e) judicial branch; and (f) executive branch.

History involves the events, experiences, and treatment of a particular group during different time periods. Such events, experiences, and treatment create a context that may serve to either prevent or facilitate policy change. The *community* refers to the particular group's mood, attitude, and organization concerning a particular proposed policy. The *general U.S. society* refers to the mood, attitude, and organization of the mainstream society concerning a proposed policy. The two streams are interdependent and are heavily influenced by the general U.S. society's view of the particular group and the particular group's reaction to that view.

The *legislative branch* (represented by the Senate and House) reflects the mood and general predisposition of the U.S. Congress regarding a policy issue. Since many public policy decisions are made by Congress, this stream is essential. The *judicial branch* reflects important legal cases and decisions that define the legal context of policy development. For federal policy this stream involves decisions by federal courts and the Supreme Court. The judicial context determines whether a particular public policy is lawful and the degree to which it can be implemented. The *executive branch* reflects the importance of the presidents who have the influence and power to initiate and sustain new policy or to block new policy through the veto.

The rows identify specific time periods: (a) pre-1945: prior to World War II and the wartime exclusion and detention; (b) 1945–69: the immediate postwar years (1945–52) and the years of adjustment (1952–69); (c) 1970–78: the genesis of the modern redress movement; (d) 1979–82: the Commission on Wartime Relocation and Internment of Civilians; (e) 1983–86: Ninety-

Years	History		Legislative Branch		Judicial Branch	Executive Branch
	Community	U.S. Society	Senate	House		
1987–88						
1983–86						
1979–82						
1970–78						
1945–69						
Pre-WWII/Exclusion/ Incarceration						

Figure 1. Kitano-Maki Proper Alignment Model

eighth Congress and Ninety-ninth Congress; (f) 1987–88: the passage and signing of the Civil Liberties Act of 1988.

For each time period in the different streams, there is a rating reflecting the degree of support and advocacy that a particular policy issue has garnered. A rating of "positive" (+) reflects a high degree of support and advocacy for the proposed policy issue. A rating of "neutral/positive" (N+) reflects more support than opposition or the absence of any significant resistance. A "neutral" (N) reflects either an equal amount of support and opposition or a general ambivalence. "Neutral/negative" (N-) reflects greater opposition than support. "Negative" (-) reflects a high degree of opposition or general apathy.

The proper alignment for the creation of new public policy occurs when each of the columns has a "positive" or a "neutral/positive" rating. In this particular context a window of opportunity has been created that could facilitate new public policy. When all the columns are rated "negative" (-) or "neutral/negative" (N-), not only is the passage of the identified public policy highly unlikely, but also there is a likelihood that a converse policy toward a particular group will be enacted. The model indicates that no one stream of influence is inherently more important than the other. Any stream out of alignment negates the proper alignment and reduces the opportunity for policy to be enacted.

Movement within each of the streams is determined by new ideas and energy, information, political power, timing, and rationality. Each stream at times resembles a "garbage can" of competing and unrelated issues. The general U.S. society and community streams are directly affected by the dynamics of resource mobilization and collective behavior. In turn, the general U.S. society and community streams influence the other streams of the federal government by exerting pressure and affecting the context in which the federal government operates. The status of a particular community within the general U.S. society is closely tied to the chances for passage of specific types of legislation. As the Japanese American community grew in resources and became more positively viewed by the general U.S. society, the federal branches of government became more sympathetic to the issue of redress. Each of the different streams experienced a progression from negative ratings prior to World War II to neutral ratings in the 1960s to positive or neutral/positive ratings in 1988. The process involved in this progression is discussed in the following chapters.

There are almost no single-factor explanations for how an issue rises in importance, becomes a part of a policy agenda, and ultimately becomes adopted as policy. Kingdon indicates that a policy item's place on the political agenda is "due to the joint effect of several factors coming together at a given point in time, not to the effect of one or another of them singly."[20] Similarly, it is the proper alignment of the different streams that creates the context within which policy can be passed. The notion of a proper alignment is reflected in the common phrases "lining up the ducks" or in Japanese "ne ma washi." These sayings refer to working behind the scenes with key people to facilitate an issue's rise in importance and support.

The Kitano-Maki proper alignment model was developed specifically to address the issue of Japanese American redress. It can, however, be applied to the examination of other policy issues. The following chapters present each time period and the movement, interaction, and management of the major streams within each.

2   Historical Factors prior to World War II

Prior to World War II a number of events reflected the country's attitude toward Japanese Americans. The years before and during World War II were not a time for passing proposals that were sympathetic to Japanese in America. From their initial significant immigration in the 1890s to the World War II exclusion and incarceration, governmental and societal policies excluded Japanese Americans from meaningful participation in American society. The only place for them was at the bottom of the stratification system. This partial segregation turned into mass incarceration during World War II.

Early Immigration

The first Asian immigrants to the United States were Chinese laborers, who began to arrive in significant numbers during the gold rush that began in 1849. Chinese immigrants were viewed as unassimilable and belonging to an inferior race. They were "aliens ineligible to citizenship," which prohibited them from becoming naturalized citizens. They were segregated, limited occupationally and socially, and hemmed in by discriminatory laws (e.g., until 1870 they could not testify in court against whites). The phrase "A Chinaman's Chance," commonly used at the time,[1] reflected the fact that Chinese immigrants had no chance at all in dealing with the injustices heaped on them. Japanese immigrants entered this context and were also considered "aliens ineligible to citizenship" and subjected to discriminatory laws.

The majority of the early Japanese immigrants were young males from agricultural backgrounds. They began to arrive in the United States during the 1890s. The need for laborers in the independent monarchy of Hawai'i led to the first Japanese immigration. Some 150 Japanese males from the streets of Tokyo and Yokohama were recruited as contract laborers in 1868, but they were ill-suited to work in Hawai'i's sugar plantations. Initially, Japanese, Chinese, Pilipino, and Portuguese immigrants were segregated on Hawaiian plantations. For the Issei this isolation led to a partial reproduction of Japanese village life. They organized and developed a cohesive community, which in time led to their prominent sociopolitical presence in Hawai'i.

Between 1890 and 1924, the year when all Japanese and other Asians were legally excluded from immigration, a total of 295,820 Japanese entered the United States. Not everyone stayed. The U.S. Census reported 111,010 Japanese Americans in the continental United States in 1920 and 138,834 in 1930.[2] How this small number, constituting less than 2 percent of California's population, could be viewed as a threat remains a source of wonderment. Self-proclaimed nativists,[3] however, continued to be alarmed about being overrun by "yellow hordes."[4]

In 1907–8 the "Gentlemen's Agreement" was reached between the United States and Japan. This agreement was in response to heightening racism toward Japanese on the West Coast and Japan's indignation that Japanese were racially segregated in the American public school systems. The agreement was worked out through diplomatic correspondence in late 1907 and early 1908. Japan agreed not to issue any further passports for laborers wanting to emigrate to the United States. The United States promised not to prohibit immigration of Japanese and pledged to integrate most Japanese students into the public school systems. It also agreed that laborers who had been in the United States could return and that family members could join laborers already here. The general population's sentiment on the West Coast, however, was summarized in a *San Francisco Chronicle* article in 1910: "Had the Japanese laborer throttled his ambition to progress along the lines of American citizenship and industrial development, he probably would have attracted small attention of the public mind. Japanese ambition is to progress beyond mere servility to the plane of the better class of American workman and to own a home with him. The moment that this position is exercised, the Japanese ceases to be an ideal laborer."[5]

One unanticipated result of the Gentlemen's Agreement was that women began to dominate Japanese immigration to the United States. Tens of thousands of female immigrants provided the opportunity for Issei men to marry and together create Japanese American families. Marriage was often arranged through an exchange of pictures, a practice that was not significantly different from some of the local practices in Japan. These women, called "picture brides," often met their husbands for the first time upon arriving in the United States. This influx of Japanese women led many West Coast residents to believe that there was a conspiracy between Washington, D.C., and Japan to inundate the Pacific Coast states with Japanese.[6]

By 1909 Issei farmers controlled about 1 percent of California's agricultural land, which produced approximately 10 percent of the value of California's annual harvest.[7] In 1913 and 1920 the California legislature passed the Alien Land Acts, which made aliens who were "ineligible to citizenship" (e.g., any Asian) also ineligible to own agricultural land. In 1914 Attorney General Ulysses S. Webb candidly stated the motives behind the measures: "The fundamental basis of all legislation . . . has been, and is, race undesirability. . . . It [the law] *seeks to limit* [the Japanese] *presence by curtailing their privileges which they may enjoy here; for they will not come in large numbers and long abide with us if they may not acquire land.*"[8] The Issei circumvented these restrictions either by registering their holdings in the names of their citizen children or by setting up corporations to hold title to the land. These strategies, while effective, also served to heighten the general public's antagonistic feelings toward and suspicion of Japanese in the United States.

The U.S. Immigration Act of 1924, which was chiefly a measure to reduce all immigration, also ended Japanese immigration by outlawing immigration of "aliens ineligible to citizenship." This, of course, abrogated the Gentlemen's Agreement. Eastern and southern European immigration was also negatively affected, while immigrants from northern and western Europe were favored because of the nativist belief that the "Nordic and Aryan" branches of the white race were superior. The prohibition of Japanese immigration remained in effect until 1952.

This period, from their immigration up to the World War II exclusion, formed the Issei period. Like other immigrant groups who were denied access to the mainstream, the Issei developed their own ethnic enclaves, such as "Little Tokyo" in Los Angeles and "Little Osaka" in San Francisco. Health and legal services, employment, recreation, and other resources were available in these communities. In urban settings many Japanese were employed in domestic service, producing the image of the Japanese "houseboy," or ran small businesses, such as laundries, dry cleaners, rooming houses, grocery stores, and barbershops.[9] Through these vocations they developed an interdependent ethnic network. Agricultural communities developed similar ethnic networks. Community organizations and friendship patterns among Japanese Americans were essential to their survival in small farming communities.[10] Friendships with influential white people also assisted in their adaptation.

The strength of the ethnic community was its inner cohesiveness. The Issei realized that individual complaints could be easily ignored but that concerted action by civic organizations could attract attention. They started their own local protective, educational, religious, and banking (the tanomoshi) organizations. The leadership was male, and its activities included sponsoring picnics, providing interpreters, participating in Fourth of July parades, and developing cemetery space. A basic purpose of the community organizations was to uphold the reputation of the Japanese in the United States. Although they were excluded, they wished to be recognized as good and loyal citizens.

The Issei brought with them the values, beliefs, and lifestyles of the Meiji period (1868–1912) in Japan. These included a vertical, male-dominated family and community structure; the values of hard work, loyalty, and obedience; and prescriptions on how to interact with the "superior" dominant community. As "outsiders" wanting in, however, the Issei in American society were very weak.

Such scholars as Roger Daniels and Yuji Ichioka,[11] however, indicate that the Issei were neither as passive nor as docile as portrayed by some early stereotypes. The Issei constantly organized, demonstrated, held meetings, made speeches, and published books and pamphlets against limiting Japanese immigration. However, they had minimal access in their political dealings with the dominant community, a problem that was to plague them well into the future.

One consequence of this discrimination was that some Issei returned to Japan, while others turned inward to their own community. Many of the latter placed their hopes for their family's future on their American-born Nisei children. By the standards of the 1990s the Issei community was conservative and encapsulated, and it had limited interaction with and access to the larger political system. When they had problems outside the Japanese American community, the Issei (who were not allowed to be attorneys because they were aliens ineligible for citizenship) were dependent on hiring non–Japanese Americans to represent them and help resolve these problems.

By the 1920s it was clear that the Issei had to adjust to American life without the protection and the benefits of naturalization and citizenship. They expected the Japanese government to provide some protection, but Japanese officials were more concerned about Japan's economic and political relations with the United States than about the well-being of the Issei. Nevertheless, the Japanese government provided symbolic strength through their military exploits. Japan was the first modern Asian nation to defeat a European power during the Russo-Japanese conflict in 1905, and it was rapidly challenging the United States and European powers over the colonization of Asia.

The Nisei

An important characteristic of the Issei immigration was that although a majority came as young, single males, after the Gentlemen's Agreement many established family life in the United States. One important result of this family life was the birth of the next generation, the Nisei. The Japanese population now included an American-born generation that held citizenship as a birthright. The expression *kodomo no tame ni* (for the sake of the children) reflected the common parental value of making sacrifices for the children. These sacrifices were made to ensure that the Nisei would have a better life than their parents had.

Most Nisei were born between 1910 and the 1940s. Although U.S. citizens by birth, they, too, encountered discrimination in the larger society and often clashed with their parents. The Issei wanted them to become involved in the mainstream yet also to retain their ethnic roots. Nisei children were expected to attend both American schools and Japanese language schools, but very few became fluent in the Japanese language.

Many Issei felt that the Nisei were becoming too Americanized and were rejecting their Japanese heritage. The Great Depression of the 1930s, coupled with high expectations, racism, and discrimination, meant a future full of obstacles for the Nisei. Even academics viewed them as a "problem generation." Edward Strong Jr., a psychologist, received a $40,000 grant from the Carnegie Corporation of New York in 1929 to study the "problem" Nisei. His findings, subsequently published in his book *The Second-Generation Japanese Problem,* showed that some Nisei were beginning to question the values of working hard and obtaining a good education. One Nisei reported, "So, many of my friends are giving up the fight. 'Why get an education?' they say. 'Why try to do anything at all? Probably we were meant to be just a servile class. We can't help it, so let's make the best of a bad bargain.'"[12] According to the Japanese author Kazuo Kawai, this attitude reflected "the new shiftless, pleasure-seeking second-generation element in the heretofore industrious, thrifty Japanese community."[13]

Another Nisei commented, "Ever since I was able to lick the pink water off my rattle, it has been made known to me that I am a 'Jap,' was a 'Jap,' and always will be a 'Jap'! . . . My first tragedy was when our first grade dancing class was practicing in the music room. Every boy was paired off with a girl. . . . [when the yellow haired girl] learned that I was to hold her hand . . . she stamped her foot and shrieked, 'I won't be his partner—he's a "Jap"!'"[14]

A Nisei's 1934 essay described a person partaking in both cultures: "I sat down to American breakfasts and Japanese lunches. My palate developed a fondness for rice along with corned beef and cabbage. I became equally adept with knife and fork and with chopsticks. I said grace at mealtimes in Japanese, and recited the Lord's Prayer at night in English. I hung my stocking over the fireplace at Christmas and toasted 'mochi' at Japanese New Year. . . . I was spoken to by both parents in Japanese and English. I answered in whichever was convenient or in a curious mixture of both."[15]

The Nisei faced difficult questions. Should they identify as Japanese or as American? Should they remain in the United States or go to Japan? Should they marry as their parents wished, or should they make their own choices? Should they choose a Buddhist church or a Christian one? Should they attend college or go to work? Should they try to work in the ethnic community or in the larger society? The average white American was confused enough about life choices during the depression, but the Nisei had many additional causes for bewilderment.

Strong wrote that the major problem for the Nisei was occupational discrimination. One of his recommendations was to remove all discriminatory legislation against them. He argued, "They [Japanese immigrants] were admitted by 'our' laws and have a legal right to remain [in the United States]."[16] As is often the case, the contemporary climate of opinion would not accept Strong's logical recommendations. College educated Nisei could find only limited employment outside their community and were forced into low-paying jobs in the ethnic economy. The American society regarded them as too Japanese, and their parents' generation criticized them as being too American.

Few Nisei had any interest in politics and the political process. Ernest Iiyama, a Kibei from Oakland, California, recalled a group of approximately forty Nisei who formed the Young Democrats of the East Bay (Berkeley and Oakland, California) in the mid-1930s.[17] This group discussed discrimination, political participation, and civic issues. They were ignored by the vast majority of their Nisei peers, who were more interested in dating, athletics, and social activities. Iiyama recalled being accused of being sympathetic to communism while in the temporary Assembly Center in Tanforan in 1942. The Young Democrats were considered too radical by the majority of Japanese Americans. Even more "radical" were the Japanese American Communists, such as Karl Yoneda.

An important event in the early years of the Japanese American community was the organization of the Japanese American Citizens League (JACL). The JACL was begun in the late 1920s to increase Nisei involvement in politics.[18] The JACL, which extended membership only to U.S. citizens, was organized in partial response to the Issei-run Japanese Associations (Nihonjinkai). The JACL held its first convention in Seattle on August 29, 1930, with 102 registered delegates.

As had occurred with other immigrant groups, the Americanization of the second generation created tension and dissonance between the generations. The Issei and Nisei were on a generational collision course. The bombing of Pearl Harbor and subsequent actions of the United States changed the context of their generational differences.

World War II and the Decision to Incarcerate

For Japanese Americans the wartime exclusion and incarceration stand out as a defining experience. This period was the high point of anti-Japanese segregation and isolation. There was a consensus of the U.S. public in support of the exclusion. The Congress, executive branch, mass media, and influential community leaders all voiced their concerns about the loyalty of the Japanese in the United States, whether citizens or aliens.

Japan's military expansion was viewed with alarm long before World War II. In the 1930s fear of Japanese aggression in Asia led the State and Justice departments, as well as the U.S. Navy and Army Intelligence (G-2), to monitor the Japanese American community. Intelligence gathering included documenting the daily activities of selected Japanese Americans. Surveillance of the community was complicated by the government's inability to differentiate between Japanese Americans and Japanese from Japan. A State Department report in 1934 warned that the Japanese government had agents in every large city and that "when war breaks out, the entire Japanese population on the West Coast will rise and commit sabotage."[19]

The idea of a concentration camp for Japanese in Hawai'i, whether citizens or aliens, was considered well before the attack on Pearl Harbor.[20] President Roosevelt was so concerned about Japan that he sent a one-page memo to the chief of naval operations on August 10, 1936, regarding visiting Japanese ships. The memo reflected the mind-set of the president: "every Japanese citizen or non-citizen on the island of Oahu who meets these Japanese ships or has any connection with their officers or men should be secretly but definitely identified and his or her name placed on a special list of those who would be the first to be placed in a concentration camp in the event of trouble."[21]

Ironically, for most Japanese Americans in Hawai'i and on the West Coast, visiting the Japanese naval training ships was simply an exciting social event. It was a time for community picnics and a chance to meet some distant relatives from Japan. Harry Kitano, who was twelve years old during one of these visits, remembers:

> We didn't have the slightest idea of why the sailors came, but my parents inquired as to whether there were any from their home province. Somehow, someone put us in touch with a sailor who was from Oita-ken; I still remember that they served a soda pop with a marble inside the bottle. I found out much later that many of the sailors were more interested in visiting the burlesque theaters along Kearny Street, than in meeting Japanese American families from their home province.
>
> On another visit, father got in touch with a Japanese naval officer who was a distant relative. I remember having dinner at the Officers' Mess on the battleship and how proud my father was of this connection. But now I wonder if this innocuous trip was one of the reasons why father was picked up by the FBI and suspected of being an agent of the Japanese government.[22]

An "ABC" list of aliens was developed before World War II, which targeted individuals for arrest if there was war.[23] The "A" list of potential enemy aliens included the most "dangerous" Japanese, defined as those with influential positions in the community or with demonstrable ties to the Japanese government. Those on the "B" list were deemed potentially dangerous, while the "C" list contained individuals who were watched because of possible pro-Japanese inclinations. Sources for "ABC" identification included names that appeared in the ethnic press, such as the *Rafu Shimpo,* and those involved in community activities.[24]

In March 1941, nine months before Pearl Harbor, the Office of Naval Intelligence surreptitiously and illegally entered the Japanese Consulate in Los Angeles. It turned up names that were allegedly part of the Japanese espionage network and made the U.S. government aware of the identities of those involved. Ultimately, the Office of Naval Intelligence felt that the Japanese espionage rings had been broken well before President Roosevelt signed Executive Order 9066.[25]

The Japanese attack on Pearl Harbor on December 7, 1941, set off the chain of events leading to the incarceration of Japanese in the United States living along the Pacific Coast. Immediately after the attack the FBI arrested selected "enemy aliens," including 2,192 individuals of Japanese ancestry. Curfew regulations and other restrictions were soon instituted. Japanese Americans were confronted by rumors about what would happen to them. Some anticipated incarceration; others expected the Nisei to be treated like "regular American citizens." There was talk about Japanese Americans being made hostages as part of an exchange for white Americans stranded in Japan. Organizations attacking the Japanese in the United States and setting the stage for the exclusion were very diverse. As Kitano has pointed out, they included "the American Legion, the State Federation of Labor, the Native Sons of the Golden West . . . and individuals like then California Attorney General Earl Warren and 'liberal' columnist Walter Lippmann, as well as the usual racists."[26]

Newspapers across the country, especially on the West Coast, ran numerous articles that contributed to the anti-Japanese hysteria. In the *Los Angeles Times* such headlines as "Japan Pictured as Nation of Spies,"[27] "Eviction of Jap Aliens Sought,"[28] and "Lincoln Would Intern Japs"[29] were commonplace. Such statements as "A viper is nonetheless a viper wherever the egg is hatched" in the newspapers were directed at Japanese.[30] Japanese were labeled as spies, and their removal from the West Coast was seen as a common-sense remedy. Mayor Fletcher Bowron of Los Angeles went so far as to indicate that if President Lincoln were alive, he would round up the Japanese and put them where they could do no harm.[31] The *San Francisco Examiner* printed Henry McLemore's opinion: "Herd 'em up, pack 'em off and give them the inside room of the badlands. Let 'em be pinched, hurt, hungry and dead up against it."[32] The anti-Japanese sentiment was the result of not only xenophobic sentiment but also economic competition. The farmlands of Japanese Americans were among the most productive on the West Coast.

Only a few religious groups, such as the Quakers, and individuals, such as the Socialist leader Norman Thomas and a few members of the American Civil Liberties Union (ACLU), provided visible support to the Japanese American community. The national body of the ACLU, however, did not initially protest the exclusion and incarceration. Many months later it did participate in challenging the curfew and exclusion orders in the Supreme Court.

The first formal military proposal for mass incarceration came from Lieutenant General John L. DeWitt, head of the Western Defense Command, on December 19, 1941. This proposal recommended the removal of all "alien subjects" fourteen years of age and over to the interior of the United States, where they would be restrained. The proposal included Italian and German nationals and was forwarded to Major General Allen W. Gullion, the army's provost marshal general. Subsequent proposals by the War Department and the provost marshal general included having zones around key installations from which Japanese and other enemy aliens would be prohibited. At this point, however, the control of enemy civilian aliens was the responsibility of the Department of Justice, not the War Department, and neither Secretary of War Henry L. Stimson nor Attorney General Francis B. Biddle supported the idea of a mass removal.

Gullion sought Stimson's support in transferring this responsibility to the War Department. When Stimson showed no interest, Gullion contacted DeWitt and attempted to persuade him to recommend a mass removal of Japanese aliens and citizens alike. DeWitt initially was reluctant to support the idea and stated, "An American citizen, after all, is an American citizen."[33] DeWitt, in keeping with his inconsistent nature, eventually changed his mind.

Gullion continued to pressure the Justice Department to support a mass removal of Japanese from the Pacific Coast, and the Justice Department began conducting warrantless raids on homes of Japanese aliens. Communication about a mass removal was established between the Justice Department and the War Department. James Rowe Jr., an assistant attorney general, and Edward J. Ennis, head of the Justice Department's Alien Enemy Control Unit, represented the Department of Justice, while Major Karl R. Bendetsen, chief of the Aliens Division, Provost Marshal General's Office, represented the War Department. Bendetsen displayed his bias in favor of incarceration through his statements about the threat of sabotage. Two months after the bombing of Pearl Harbor, there had been no evidence of any sabotage or espionage on the part of Japanese in the United States. In response to this Bendetsen proclaimed, "The very fact that no sabotage has taken place to date is a disturbing and confirming indication that such action will be taken."[34] Chief Justice Earl Warren, then attorney general of California, later echoed these same sentiments.[35]

Bendetsen eventually prepared the "final recommendation" on the exclusion for DeWitt. Although sometimes ambivalent and unable to make decisions, DeWitt actively supported the exclusion policy. There was constant pressure from politicians, newspaper columnists (such as Walter Lippmann and Westbrook Pegler), patriotic groups, and California farmers, who advocated a quick solution to the "Japanese problem."

On February 1, 1942, John J. McCloy, the assistant secretary of the War Department, Gullion, and Bendetsen met with Biddle, Rowe, Ennis, and J. Edgar Hoover, the head of the FBI, in an attempt to coordinate the efforts of the War and Justice departments. The Department of Justice was still unwilling to support a mass removal policy. This stance prompted a retort by McCloy, who declared, "You are putting a Wall Street lawyer in a helluva box, but if it is a question of the safety of the country [and] the Constitution. . . . Why the Constitution is just a scrap of paper to me."[36] Despite this comment McCloy remained unconvinced about supporting a mass removal. Two days later Stimson, McCloy, Gullion, and Bendetsen met again. After the meeting Gullion reported that "the two Secretaries [Stimson and McCloy] are against any mass movement."[37] Meanwhile, congressional members from the Pacific Coast states, California's Governor Culbert Olson, and other West Coast officials increased political pressure for mass removal.

By February 10 Gullion and Bendetsen convinced McCloy that mass action was necessary. Stimson, however, still supported the idea of restricted zones around strategic areas. At the urging of his subordinates the secretary changed his mind by the next day. On February 11 Stimson telephoned President Roosevelt and recommended the mass removal of individuals of Japanese ancestry from the West Coast. President Roosevelt told Stimson that he was to go ahead with whatever he thought necessary and to "be as reasonable as you can."[38]

Biddle continued to oppose any mass removal program until February 17. On this day he sent a memorandum to President Roosevelt outlining his objections but also noting, "If complete confusion and lowering of morale is to be avoided, so large a job must be done after careful planning."[39] Biddle spoke to President Roosevelt later that day and at an evening meeting in his living room indicated to others he would endorse the "final recommendation."[40] McCloy, Bendetsen, and Gullion represented the War Department, while Biddle, Rowe, and Ennis represented the Justice Department. Rowe and Ennis presented constitutional arguments against the exclusion and were shocked to learn that Biddle was now ready to support the War Department's position.

Biddle, the last cabinet member to endorse the mass removal, was unable to withstand Stimson's pressure. In his memoirs he recalled that if "I had urged [Stimson] to resist the pressure of his subordinates, the result might have been different. But I was new to the Cabinet, and disinclined to insist on my view to an elder statesman whose wisdom and integrity I greatly respected."[41] Gullion's and Bendetsen's persistent support of a mass removal came to fruition. All that remained was the president's signature on an executive order.

President Roosevelt's willingness to authorize the removal of U.S. citizens and residents of Japanese ancestry from restricted areas was not surprising. The president had limited awareness of the plight of racial minorities, he had to win a war that was going badly, he was politically dependent on southern racists who dominated Congress, and the idea was generally supported by the American public (especially on the West Coast).[42] These influences superseded any commitment that he had to the notion of equal protection under the law. On February 19, 1942, President Roosevelt issued Executive Order 9066.

Executive Order 9066 authorized the secretary of war and his military commanders to designate "military areas" from which "any or all persons may be excluded" and to control the rights of individuals to "enter, remain in, or leave" such areas. Executive Order 9066 also authorized the secretary of war to provide "transportation, food, shelter, and other accommodations" to the affected individuals.[43] Executive Order 9066 did not specify any particular group of individuals or any particular geographic areas, but it was the foundation upon which more than 110,000 Japanese in the United States—both citizens and legal residents residing along the Pacific Coast—and selected individuals and their families from Hawai'i were forced into concentration camps.

Congress Aligns Itself with the Exclusion

With the issuance of Executive Order 9066 attention shifted to its implementation and enforcement. Congress had the power to enforce the executive order with criminal sanctions. The issue was how to deal with Japanese Americans who refused to obey the exclusion orders. Initially, Bendetsen drafted a bill proposing penalties of a $5,000 fine and a prison term of five years. McCloy subsequently modified the bill, making refusal a misdemeanor with a maximum penalty of one year in jail. The bill moved quickly to the floors of the House and Senate. Senator Robert Taft, a conservative Ohio Republican, raised the sole objection to the bill. After indicating that it was one of the "sloppiest criminal" law bills that was ever drafted, Senator Taft acknowledged that the bill could be enforced in wartime. He continued to have constitutional qualms about the bill, however: "I have no doubt that in peacetime no man could ever be convicted under it, because the court would find that it was so indefinite and so uncertain that it could not be enforced under the Constitution."[44] Despite his objections to the bill Senator Taft voted for it.

On March 21, 1942, the Congress unanimously enacted section 1383 of Title 18 of the U.S. Code (Public Law 503) as a wartime measure. Public Law 503 gave legal authority to Executive Order 9066 and provided penalties for anyone who failed to obey related proclamations. Although the executive order did not specifically identify the Japanese, it was the grounds upon which all Japanese in the United States, whether citizens or aliens, were labeled the "enemy."

Implementation of the Forced Exclusion

Following Executive Order 9066 Lieutenant General DeWitt issued several other public proclamations and exclusion orders. Public Proclamation No. 1 and No. 2 created military areas, which had "prohibited" and "restricted" zones targeted for "Japanese, German and Italian" aliens and "any person of Japanese ancestry."[45] Public Proclamation No. 3 instituted a curfew on March 27, 1942, and subsequent exclusion orders (Civilian Exclusion Order No. 57) removed all persons of Japanese ancestry from the western parts of California, Arizona, Oregon, and Washington.

The first visible sign that the exclusion was a reality were the notices posted on telephone poles and storefronts.[46] The notices opened with a message to those of Japanese ancestry ordering them to follow a number of orders and typically provided individuals with little time to prepare. Individuals were instructed to gather those belongings they could carry and were told where to report for mass transport to the temporary assembly centers. Personal property and belongings were often hastily sold to "human vultures in the guise of used-furniture dealers,"[47] given away to friends and neighbors, or simply left behind. For many in the Japanese American community the fruits of their labor disappeared in a matter of days.

Japanese Americans in these regions were instructed to report to places in their own neighborhood and then were taken by the U.S. Army to detention centers, euphemistically referred to as "assembly centers." These centers were usually converted fairgrounds, livestock exhibition centers, or racetracks. In some cases, such as the Santa Anita and Tanforan racetracks, some people were housed in quarters that had been used only weeks earlier to shelter livestock.

Executive Order 9066 and the ensuing military proclamations marked the beginning of a nightmare for Japanese Americans. They were forced to give up their independent living, leave their homes, and abandon their careers. They became wards of the government, were forced to adjust to life behind barbed wire, and endured the humiliation of being "prisoners" of their own country. To add to the problem, there was no timetable for their release except the vague notion of remaining incarcerated for the duration of the war.

Summary

The decision to exclude the Japanese in America had the "proper alignment" of the different streams of influence (see table 1). In 1942 the general American society's mood was against both the Japanese in the United States and the Japanese nation. The Japanese American community was disorganized, divided, and in a state of confusion. The legislative and executive branches both pursued the policy of exclusion and incarceration, while the judicial branch remained silent. The alignment of these streams facilitated the relatively unchallenged creation and implementation of a policy that violated the constitutional rights of Americans.

Table 1.

Years	History		Legislative Branch		Judicial Branch	Executive Branch
	Community	U.S. Society	Senate	House		
Pre-WWII/Exclusion/ Incarceration	–	–	–	–	–	–

3   World War II (1941–45)

The U.S. Army completed placing the Japanese Americans and resident aliens in temporary "assembly centers" by August 1942, later moving them into more permanent camps under the War Relocation Authority (WRA).[1] The ten camps were located in Manzanar and Tule Lake, California; Poston and Gila River, Arizona; Heart Mountain, Wyoming; Granada (Amache), Colorado; Topaz, Utah; Minidoka, Idaho; and Rohwer and Jerome, Arkansas. There were also two other types of camps: Department of Justice/Immigration and Naturalization Service internment camps and citizen isolation camps.[2]

In addition to Japanese Americans 2,260 individuals of Japanese ancestry were taken by the U.S. government from more than a dozen Latin American countries and incarcerated. Approximately 80 percent of them were from Peru. In an agreement reached in January 1942 at the Conference of Foreign Ministers of the American Republics held in Brazil, the United States offered to pay for the deportation, transportation, and detention of Axis nationals. It also volunteered to include these individuals in any exchange programs it made with the Axis countries. These Japanese Latin Americans were incarcerated in the Justice Department's camps, and approximately 500 were eventually sent to Japan in exchange for U.S. citizens. After the war the United States deported over 1,100 of these individuals because of their status as "illegal aliens."

The Japanese American Citizens League's Response

As the leading Japanese American national organization, the JACL was in a pivotal position. The JACL leadership initially voiced opposition to any plans for exclusion or incarceration. Ultimately, however, they chose to cooperate with the federal government. Mike Masaoka, the longtime JACL lobbyist and primary liaison between the JACL and the Washington, D.C., establishment during World War II, reflected in 1987 on the anguish involved in the decision to cooperate:

> Our government was asking us to cooperate in the violation of what we [the JACL] considered to be our fundamental rights. The first impulse was to refuse, to stand up for what we knew to be right.
>
> But on the other hand there were persuasive reasons for working with the government.
>
> First of all was the matter of loyalty. In a time of great national crisis the government, rightly or wrongly, fairly or unfairly, had demanded a sacrifice. . . . to defy our government's orders was to confirm its doubts about our loyalty. . . .
>
> We had been led to believe that if we cooperated with the Army . . . the government would make every effort to be as helpful and humane as possible. . . . Moreover, we feared the consequences if Japanese Americans resisted evacuation orders and the Army moved in with bayonets to eject the people forcibly. . . . At a time when Japan was still on the offensive, the American people could well consider us saboteurs if we forced the Army to take drastic action against us. . . . I was determined that JACL must not give a doubting nation further cause to confuse the identity of Americans of Japanese origin with the Japanese enemy.[3]

In early March 1942 the national JACL board voted without dissent to urge all JACL members to cooperate with the exclusion, assist Japanese Americans during this transition, maintain communications with the federal authorities, and carry on a public relations campaign to demonstrate the loyalty of Japanese Americans. The JACL hoped that if the Japanese American community demonstrated its loyalty, the government would respond positively and benevolently. Throughout the incarceration the JACL assumed a patriotic, pro-American stance and urged Japanese Americans to answer yes to the loyalty questions on the WRA's Application for Leave Clearance.[4] It also approved of the segregation policy of sending the "no-nos" to Tule Lake.[5]

The actions of the JACL angered many Japanese Americans who felt that it had forsaken its responsibility to advocate for and protect the Japanese American community. Some chapter leaders of the JACL not only submitted to the incarceration process but also contributed to its implementation. For example, a telegram sent to U.S. Attorney General Biddle on February 16, 1942, from the Los Angeles JACL and other local Japanese American organizations implored Biddle to safeguard the "citizenship rights" of Japanese Americans, but it also stated, "We have cooperated with all federal agencies in apprehending subversives and have actually become informants for the F.B.I."[6] These Japanese American organizations viewed informing on fellow

Japanese Americans as a way of demonstrating their loyalty to the United States. It was a strategy that proved to be of little value and one that caused much bitterness in the Japanese American community for decades to come.

Individual Voices of Protest

The curfew, exclusion, and incarceration orders were legally challenged by four individuals during the World War II period: Minoru Yasui, Gordon K. Hirabayashi, Fred T. Korematsu, and Mitsuye Endo. All four cases eventually were heard before the U.S. Supreme Court. The Yasui, Hirabayashi, and Korematsu cases addressed the constitutionality of the curfew and exclusion order, while the Endo case focused on the incarceration.

Minoru Yasui was not only a JACL leader but also a lawyer and an army officer by training.[7] He anticipated that the exclusion and incarceration of Japanese Americans was imminent and was particularly incensed about Public Proclamation No. 3, which issued the curfew orders for all individuals of Japanese ancestry in the designated geographical areas regardless of citizenship. Japanese Americans were to remain indoors between the hours of 8:00 P.M. and 6:00 A.M. Yasui reflected on the unconstitutionality of the proclamation, later stating, "because it makes distinctions between citizens on the basis of ancestry."[8] On March 28, 1942, the day the curfew order went into effect, Yasui walked the streets of Portland, Oregon, unsuccessfully trying to get arrested. Finally, he went to a police station at 11:00 P.M. and insisted on being arrested for violating the curfew.

Yasui's case was heard before the U.S. district court in Oregon. Judge James Alger Fee ruled that the curfew order was unconstitutional as applied to U.S. citizens but that Yasui had renounced his citizenship by working for the Japanese Consulate. Yasui was convicted and sentenced to one year in prison and fined $5,000. The conviction was immediately appealed.

Nearly two months later, on May 16, 1942, Gordon Hirabayashi violated Civilian Exclusion Order No. 57, which required Japanese Americans to register for exclusion by May 12, 1942. Hirabayashi, a twenty-four-year-old senior at the University of Washington and a Quaker, objected to the exclusion orders on moral grounds, stating, "If I were to register and cooperate . . . I would be giving helpless consent to the denial of practically all of the things which give me incentive to live. I must maintain my Christian principles. I consider it my duty to maintain the democratic standards for which this nation lives. Therefore, I must refuse this order for evacuation."[9] Hirabayashi turned himself into the FBI and was charged with curfew and exclusion violations. He served five months in jail before the U.S. district court in Seattle heard his case. At this one-day trial on October 20, 1942, Judge Lloyd D. Black ordered the jury to convict Hirabayashi on both counts: violation of curfew and failure to register for exclusion under Public Law 503. He was sentenced to ninety days for each count to be served concurrently,[10] a sentencing convenience that eventually affected the Supreme Court's ruling. As it had in Yasui's case, the American Civil Liberties Union agreed to appeal Hirabayashi's conviction and make his situation a legal test case.

The third individual whose case was heard by the Supreme Court was Fred Korematsu. Korematsu was not motivated to violate the curfew and exclusion orders by constitutional or moral principles. His reasons were more pragmatic. Korematsu was employed as a shipyard welder in San Francisco in 1941. After Pearl Harbor was attacked, Korematsu volunteered for the military but was rejected for medical reasons by both the U.S. Navy and the Coast Guard. Korematsu's family reported to the Tanforan Assembly Center in northern California on May 9, 1942, but Korematsu did not report for exclusion because he wanted to stay behind with his girlfriend, Ida Boitano, an Italian American.

Korematsu had undergone plastic surgery a month before the exclusion orders to alter his facial features. He and his girlfriend planned to move to Arizona and marry without having his Japanese American background revealed. Three weeks after the exclusion order deadline Korematsu was arrested as he was waiting for his fiancée on a street corner.

The American Civil Liberties Union approached Korematsu and suggested that his situation be made a legal test case. Although motivated by personal and pragmatic reasons, Korematsu felt it very important to challenge the violations of his personal and constitutional rights. On September 8, 1942, the U.S. district court in San Francisco heard Korematsu's case. Korematsu was convicted of violating the exclusion order and sentenced to five years probation. Represented by an ACLU attorney, Wayne Collins, Korematsu also filed an appeal.

All three cases were heard before the U.S. Supreme Court. In June of 1943 the Court upheld the convictions in the Hirabayashi and Yasui cases. In the Hirabayashi case the Court unanimously upheld the constitutionality of the conviction based on the claimed military necessity for the curfew at the time. Chief Justice Harlan F. Stone stated that the curfew and exclusion orders were designed for "the protection of our war resources against espionage and sabotage."[11] The Court further asserted that the orders were the result of appropriate judgment on the part of the military commander: "those facts, and the inferences which could be rationally drawn from them, support the judgment of the military commander, that the danger of espionage and sabotage to our military resources was imminent, and that the curfew order was an appropriate measure to meet it."[12] On a legal technicality the Court ruled only on the curfew violation and avoided discussing the constitutionality of the exclusion orders. Since the sentences for both convictions were to be served concurrently, sustaining one conviction negated the need to review the other conviction.

On June 21, 1943, the same day that the opinion on the Hirabayashi was rendered, the Court also rendered its opinion on the Yasui case. In a technical maneuver the Court reversed Judge Fee's decisions, ruling that the curfew orders were constitutional and that Yasui had not renounced his citizenship. Despite these reversals the Court upheld Yasui's conviction and found him guilty of violating a constitutional curfew order. Justice Harlan Stone, in delivering the opinion of the Court, stated, "The conviction will be sustained but the judgment will be vacated and the cause remanded to the district court for resentence of appellant, and to afford that court opportunity to strike its findings as to appellant's loss of United States citizenship."[13] With this decision the Court remanded the case back to the district court for resentencing. Yasui served nine months in solitary confinement for not cooperating with his jailers and for deliberately resisting what was in his view an unconstitutional and discriminatory order.

In December 1944 the Supreme Court handed down a decision that was consistent with the previous two decisions. In *Korematsu v. United States* the Court determined that the identification and exclusion of a single racial group was allowable through the war powers of Congress and the president. The Court reiterated the importance of military necessity and the appropriateness of military judgment for the exclusion order. The Court ruled only on the constitutionality of the exclusion orders and remained silent on the incarceration directives.

The Court's decision, however, was not unanimous. Three of the justices, Justices Owen J. Roberts, Frank Murphy, and Robert H. Jackson, issued dissenting opinions. Justice Roberts stated, "I think the indisputable facts exhibit a clear violation of Constitutional rights. . . . it is the case of convicting a citizen as a punishment for not submitting to imprisonment in a concentration camp, based on his ancestry, and solely because of his ancestry, without evidence or inquiry concerning his loyalty and good disposition towards the United States. . . . I need hardly labor the conclusion that Constitutional rights have been violated."[14]

Justice Murphy described the exclusion as an act that goes over "'the very brink of constitutional power' and falls into the ugly abyss of racism."[15] He went on to contend that the main reasons for the exclusion appeared to be "misinformation, half-truths and insinuations that for years have been directed against Japanese Americans by people with racial and economic prejudices."[16] He concluded by dissenting from this "legalization of racism" and stated, "Racial discrimination in any form and in any degree has no justifiable part whatever in our democratic way of life. It is unattractive in any setting but it is utterly revolting among a free people who have embraced the principles set forth in the Constitution of the United States."[17]

In an equally forceful dissenting opinion Justice Jackson stated, "Korematsu was born on our soil . . . Korematsu, however, has been convicted of an act not commonly a crime. It consists merely of being present in the state whereof he is a citizen, near the place where he was born, and where all his life he has lived. . . . Now, if any fundamental assumption underlies our system, it is that guilt is personal and not inheritable."[18] Despite the dissenting opinions Korematsu's conviction was upheld. As a result, the Supreme Court opinions in the Hirabayashi, Yasui, and Korematsu cases upheld the constitutionality of the wartime curfew and exclusion orders but did not address the constitutionality of the incarceration of U.S. citizens and legal residents.

A fourth Japanese American case was heard in October 1944. Mitsuye Endo, a Nisei woman, filed a writ of habeas corpus petition. The federal district court in San Francisco initially denied the petition, and the decision was subsequently appealed to the U.S. Supreme Court. The Court's decision in this case coincided with the policy decision to reopen the West Coast to Japanese Americans (this case is further discussed later in the chapter).

The Community's Response

A poem composed by Miyuki Aoyama described the mood of the Japanese American community during this period:

> Snow upon the rooftop,
> Snow upon the coal;
> Winter in Wyoming—
> Winter in my soul.[19]

The words of an older Nisei reflected the sentiment of many in the community: "You hurt. You give up everything that you worked for that far, and I think everybody was at the point of just having gotten out of the Depression and was just getting on his feet. And then all that happens! You have to throw everything away. You feel you were betrayed."[20]

Others who shared their wartime experiences used the analogy of feeling raped. They acknowledged having nightmares and feelings of helplessness. One Nisei said, "I am bitter. There's a constant reminder of what I missed or lost out on because of the war, and then how they treated us."[21]

The camps were located in desolate areas, and the housing and food were often substandard. In many of the camps the dust penetrated the walls and floors of the crudely constructed wooden barracks. Numerous families would share a barrack, sometimes with only hanging blankets dividing their living quarters. The winters were freezing, the summers unbearably hot.

Harry Kitano, who spent his adolescent years in Topaz, remembered boredom, isolation, camp food labeled "slop suey," the attitude of "waste time," and inmates' attempts to construct a meaningful existence.[22] His high school experience was mixed. There were some well-trained, credentialed white teachers from outside the camp but also inmates who taught with little or no experience. There was a campus yearbook, a football and a basketball team that played against surrounding Utah high school teams, and even a cap-and-gown graduation ceremony. All this existed in an isolated barbed wire enclosure in the middle of a desert.

Joseph Y. Kurihara, a World War I veteran who renounced his U.S. citizenship while incarcerated in Tule Lake, reflected in an interview:

> The desert was bad enough. . . . The constant cyclonic storms [in Manzanar] loaded with sand and dust made it worst. After living in well furnished homes with every modern convenience and suddenly forced to live the life of a dog is something which one can not so readily forget. Down in our hearts we cried and cursed this government every time when we were showered with sand. . . . The government could have easily declared Martial Law to protect us. It was not the question of protection. It was because we were Japs! Yes, Japs![23]

"I thought," another Nisei remembered, "that the Nisei had no chance anyway they turned. Japan really don't want us and this country don't want us either. I don't give a damn who wins the war just so they don't bother me. But we are getting a raw deal. . . . As long as I look like a Jap, they make me act like one. Even if I want to be a good American . . . they don't want to give me a chance. They think I am inferior. That's why I want Japan to win the war in a way. Then in other ways, I want America to win. I don't know."[24]

Early Sources of Protest

During the war a few Japanese Americans asked for some form of compensation or recognition of the constitutional violations. James Omura (1912–94), a Nisei living in San Francisco, was a publisher of *Current Life*, a literary magazine. When the public proclamations were issued, Omura left the West Coast and resettled in Denver, Colorado. He established the Pacific Coast Evacuee Placement Bureau, which assisted Japanese Americans with job placement and housing. Omura focused on restoring the constitutional rights and compensating the economic losses of the Japanese American community through legal action.[25] The timing was not right, however, and Omura's cause remained unpopular. Another Japanese American demanding compensation was Joseph Y. Kurihara, who was arrested after the December riot in

Manzanar in 1942 and sent to an isolation camp. Kurihara demanded payment of $5,000 for each evacuee.[26]

A third early source of protest came from the Heart Mountain concentration camp. Shortly after Pearl Harbor the military draft for Japanese Americans was suspended. After its reinstatement on January 14, 1944, 315 Japanese Americans incarcerated in the concentration camps resisted the draft. Sixty-three inmates from Heart Mountain, led by Kiyoshi R. Okamoto, Isamu Sam Horino, Frank Seishi Emi, Minoru Tamesa, Tsutomu Ben Wakaye, Guntaro Kubota, and Paul T. Nakadate, resisted the draft and were arrested, convicted, and sentenced to three years in federal penitentiaries at McNeill Island and Leavenworth. The Heart Mountain resistance referred to itself as the Fair Play Committee, whose motto was "Free us before you draft us." The committee declared its loyalty to the United States but demanded the restoration of their rights as guaranteed by the Constitution. Although a small movement, the significance of the Fair Play Committee was its organized attempt to demand the restitution of constitutional rights. Following the example of the Fair Play Committee, a small number of young Japanese American men in other camps resisted the draft.

The JACL actively opposed and denounced the draft resistance movement. JACL officials personally attempted to persuade members of the Heart Mountain Fair Play Committee to change their positions.[27] Such actions by the JACL served to exacerbate further the division in the Japanese American community between those who supported the opportunity to prove the community's loyalty to the United States and those who viewed the draft as another unconscionable demand on an oppressed group.

Japanese Americans in the Military

From the oppressive environment of the camps emerged a dramatic story of loyalty and patriotism. Despite the racism, discrimination, and wholesale violation of constitutional rights, Japanese Americans participated in segregated combat units in the European theater and in military intelligence in the Pacific. These units included the Military Intelligence Service, the 100th Battalion, and the 442d Regimental Combat Team (R.C.T.).[28]

The Military Intelligence Service

Prior to 1940 the students at the Military Intelligence Service Language School (MISLS) were all white, while many of the instructors were Japanese nationals. During the summer of 1942 Nisei recruits were asked to volunteer from camp because the school needed language interpreters and translators. MISLS graduates served in the Military Intelligence Service and played an extremely important but unpublicized role in the war against Japan. Their linguistic skills were used to translate captured enemy documents and determine the enemy's battle plans. The Military Intelligence Service took part in every landing in the island-hopping campaign from New Guinea to Okinawa and played a valuable role in the postwar occupation of Japan.

An often repeated story is that of Kenny Yasui, a Nisei in the Military Intelligence Service, who impersonated a Japanese officer and convinced a Japanese unit to surrender.[29] A less publicized aspect of the Military Intelligence Service was its inclusion of over forty Nisei women who served in the Women's Army Corps in the United States and in postwar Japan.[30]

The 100th Battalion

The 100th Battalion was originally part of the Hawai'i National Guard. Although there were plans to release Japanese Americans from the unit, Lieutenant General Delos Emmons, impressed by the desire of the Nisei to demonstrate their loyalty, recommended the formation of a special Nisei battalion to be sent to the European theater. In June 1942 the 100th Battalion was sent to Camp McCoy, Wisconsin, and subsequently to Camp Shelby, Mississippi, for training. Unlike other recruits, however, the Nisei of the 100th Battalion were not allowed to travel with their weapons from Hawai'i to Camp McCoy.

The 100th Battalion compiled an impressive war record in North Africa and Italy, where they suffered heavy casualties. By the time they were finally pulled from battle, they had earned nine hundred Purple Hearts and were appropriately nicknamed the Purple Heart Battalion. After a brief rest, they were sent to the Anzio beachhead in Italy, where they joined and became the first battalion of the other Nisei unit, the 442d R.C.T.

The 442d Regimental Combat Team

In November 1942 JACL representatives met in Salt Lake City and passed a resolution calling for the restoration of Selective Service responsibilities for the Nisei. Many believed that without a military record Japanese Americans would face insurmountable obstacles in attempting to regain their full share of civil liberties. The U.S. Army had been discussing how to utilize Japanese American personnel and the possibilities of an all-Nisei combat unit since the spring of 1942. A committee recommendation for an all–Japanese American unit, supported by Lieutenant General Emmons, Elmer Davis (director of the Office of War Information), and John J. McCloy (assistant secretary of War), was officially announced by Secretary of War Henry L. Stimson on January 28, 1943.

The decision to create an all-Nisei fighting unit was met with mixed reactions from the Japanese American community. Mike Masaoka expressed many Japanese Americans' initial disappointment: "We Japanese Americans were demanding equal rights, not special status."[31] Masaoka and the JACL, however, were eventually convinced by the army's argument that to disperse the few thousand Japanese American soldiers among the millions of Americans already in uniform would make their contribution virtually invisible. Furthermore, a unit of Japanese American soldiers the size of a regiment would attract attention and possibly admiration if it fought heroically.[32]

Japanese Americans were divided on this issue. On one side many welcomed the chance to demonstrate their loyalty to the United States in either segregated or integrated units. On the other side many were repulsed and disgusted with the notion of sending young men to fight and die for freedom, liberty, and justice while their own country imprisoned their families.

One rumor that circulated in the camps was that the Nisei volunteers would be cannon fodder and that most would not return. There was strong sentiment against any Nisei's volunteering. Kitano recalled a block meeting to discuss it: "My older sister got up and indicated that volunteering was an individual decision and that the block should respect the choice. Evidently, the mess hall cooks disagreed. My family was not served at mealtime for several days and my mother had to apologize for my outspoken sister. It was clear that at least in our block, there was a definite risk for the individual and his family who volunteered."[33] Tom Kawaguchi, a volunteer from Topaz, said that "people asked, 'Why do you want to volunteer?'. . . They looked at me and said, 'You must have holes in your head.'"[34]

After the announcement by the secretary of war to create an all-Nisei unit, General Emmons in Hawai'i publicly issued a call for volunteers. Nearly 10,000 Nisei from Hawai'i volunteered almost immediately. Of these men, 2,686 were accepted for induction. The Japanese Americans in Hawai'i were not living behind barbed wire and were eager to contribute to the war effort.

The mainland response was quite different, which reflected the effects of the camps. Of the over 23,000 draft-age Nisei, many of whom had spent the last eight months behind barbed wire, only 1,256 Nisei volunteered. Of these, approximately 800 passed their physicals and were inducted.[35] Many of these mainland volunteers came directly from the concentration camps.

The reasons many of the soldiers in the 442d R.C.T. fought ranged from demonstrating the loyalty of Japanese Americans, to restoring and preserving their rights as Americans, to avoiding bringing dishonor to their families. Many believed they were fighting for their own future and that of their families. One Nisei soldier wrote, "I know that this will be the only way that my family can resettle in Berkeley without prejudice and persecution."[36]

The 442d R.C.T. trained in Camp Shelby, Mississippi, and joined the 100th Battalion in 1944 to begin heavy fighting in Italy. Members of this unit went on to wear proudly the regimental patch of an upheld torch on a blue background with red and white borders. The 442d R.C.T. enthusiastically adopted the motto "Go for Broke," a Hawaiian pidgin gambling phrase that meant to go all out and "shoot the works." It entered into battle and became the most decorated unit of its size and length of service in U.S. military history.[37] Many of the decorations were for the more than 600 men killed. A total of almost 10,000 were wounded, over three times the operating size of the regiment.[38]

The 442d's most famous battle was the rescue of the 141st Regiment's 1st Battalion, commonly known as the Lost Battalion. The 442d R.C.T. was ordered to find and bring back this Texas battalion, which was trapped in the Vosges Mountains of France behind enemy lines. The 442d R.C.T. suffered over 800 casualties in this action alone. At one point the combat team was cut to less than half of its original strength. In the end they succeeded in saving the Lost Battalion and its 211 soldiers.

The extent of the casualties inflicted on the 442d was reported by Senator Daniel K. Inouye (Democrat from Hawai'i) in his autobiography:

> When General Dahlquist called the regiment out for a retreat parade to commend us personally, he is reported to have said to the C.O., "Colonel, I asked that the entire regiment be present for this occasion. Where are the rest of your men?" And Colonel Charles W. Pence . . . replied, "Sir, you are looking at the entire regiment. Except for two men on guard duty at each company, this is all that is left of the 442nd Combat Team." And there we were, cooks, medics, band and a handful of riflemen, a ragged lot at rigid attention, without a single company at even half its normal strength. . . . My outfit, E Company, with a normal complement of 197 men, had exactly 40 soldiers able to march to the parade ground.[39]

A question often asked about the 442d R.C.T. was, "What made them fight so hard?" For many the answer lay in the belief in the long-term benefits of their action. A few days before being killed in action, Sergeant Kazuo Masuda told Mike Masaoka that he was convinced that if the men of the 442d could prove their worthiness on the battlefield, it would create a better place for his family in the United States.[40] Masuda's belief was prophetic because his death eventually played a significant role in securing redress.

Despite their contributions Nisei veterans still faced harassment and discrimination upon their return to the United States. A barber in San Francisco refused to give Captain Daniel Inouye a haircut, even though the future senator had lost his arm fighting for freedom. Racial slurs, such as "Jap," were still directed at these men, and problems in housing and occupation were common.

Effects of the Camps

The concentration camp experience had a long-lasting effect on the Japanese American community. Many Japanese American families were ruined economically. The loss of most of their material possessions was hardly offset by the relocation allowance ($25 for individuals and $50 for families) that all inmates received when leaving the camps. The structure of the community and the family had been unalterably changed as well.

The influence of mess-hall conditions led to the deterioration of the family structure. Meals were no longer a family affair. Mothers and small children usually ate together, while the fathers ate at separate tables with the other men. Older children joined peers of their own age group for meals. Many husbands lost prestige, while many wives and some children gained more independence. The men were no longer seen as the financial heads of the household. Providing the family with food, shelter, and minimum clothing was no longer their responsibility. In addition all jobs paid essentially the same ($16 to $19 a month) regardless of their nature.

Riots, assaults, and other forms of violence, which were not typical of the prewar Japanese American community, became a part of camp life. In December 1942 a protest in the Manzanar camp escalated and became known as the "Manzanar Riot." Initially, it involved conflict over those who were deemed collaborators and informers and given the derogatory name of *inu* (dog). This tension was followed by a rumor that the administrators were "skimming" food that was supposed to go to the camp residents and selling it for private profit. Residents began to feel a shortage of food, especially sugar, a main ingredient in making liquor. Camp administrators subsequently admitted that in October alone 6,100 pounds of sugar was missing. The tension in Manzanar reached a boiling point, and the military was called to intervene. Togo Tanaka, a well-known journalist, described the event:

> The soldiers . . . now lined up, armed with submachine guns, shotguns and rifles. Evacuees jeered and made insulting gestures. The soldiers thereupon donned gas masks and threw a number of tear gas bombs into the crowd. The evacuees fled blindly in every direction and some were piled up against a telephone pole, covering it with blood. The crowd re-formed and the soldiers fired, without orders. . . . One evacuee died almost immediately. . . . A second evacuee, nineteen years old, died on December 11 from complications resulting from his wounds.[41]

Despite these and other horrors of the camp experience, there were *some* positive aspects. Opportunities became available for Nisei that might not have been possible in the outside world. Students became student body leaders and athletic, political, and social heroes, roles usually reserved for whites. Other community positions became available for the first time to Nisei adults. They became block leaders, firefighters, police officers, work group leaders, and supervisors.[42] For Japanese Americans, however, the price of a forced existence behind barbed wire far outweighed any of these benefits.

The camp policies of using U.S. citizens (Nisei) in positions of responsibility facilitated the shift of power and influence from the Issei to the Nisei. This shift in power profoundly affected the structure of the Japanese American family and lessened the amount of influence the Issei had over the Nisei. Many Nisei came out of the camps with cynicism about the role of government and mixed feelings about Japan and the United States. Age, gender, education, occupation, length of time in camp, geographic area of settlement, amount of personal losses, and innumerable other variables combine in different ways to make simple generalizations inappropriate. Nonetheless, many Japanese Americans felt betrayed about how the government, from President Roosevelt on down, engaged in a conspiracy to malign and scapegoat persons of Japanese ancestry.

Mental health professionals have analyzed the psychological price of the incarceration. Amy Mass, a clinical social worker, wrote, "The truth was that the government we trusted had betrayed us. . . . We used psychological defense mechanisms such as repression, denial, rationalization, and identification with the aggressor to defend ourselves against the devastating reality of what was being done to us. . . . Acceptance by submission, however, exacts a high price at the expense of the individual's sense of true self-worth."[43] Harry Kitano and Roger Daniels, summarizing the impact on the community, observed that "for thousands of Japanese Americans . . . lives had been ruined, their property lost or badly damaged by neglect, vandalism, and theft, their self-esteem shattered. Some 5,000 persons of both generations, hopelessly embittered by the treachery of American democracy that had promised so much and delivered so little, chose to emigrate or repatriate to Japan after the war. Others, particularly older people, were never able to resume their shattered lives."[44]

The exclusion and incarceration were blatant violations of human rights, civil rights, and the spirit of the Constitution. Japanese Americans were stigmatized as disloyal, put at the mercy of administrative agencies, and intimidated by pressure groups in the camps. They experienced disruption of family roles, they were separated from family members, they were forced to adapt to concentration camp norms, and they were left unprepared to face the outside world. They lost most of their possessions and were afraid of returning to a hostile society. Most, however, still felt that their futures were in the United States.

Closing the Camps

On July 12, 1942, Mitsuye Endo, who had been a resident of Sacramento and a California state employee, filed a habeas corpus petition through her attorney, James Purcell, asking the federal district court in San Francisco to release her from incarceration. The petition was based on the 1866 decision in *Ex Parte Milligan,* which stated that only an act of Congress could suspend the writ of habeas corpus. Judge Michael J. Roche heard the petition on July 20, 1942. Nearly a year later, on July 3, 1943, he issued an order to dismiss Endo's petition.

During the year-long waiting period for Judge Roche's decision Endo was granted a permit to leave the Tule Lake detention camp. Although she was not allowed to leave immediately because of "resettlement problems," the granting of her leave application was an indication that the WRA found her to be "a loyal and law-abiding citizen."[45] After her petition was dismissed by the federal district court, an appeal was filed. The Supreme Court heard the case in October 1944 and on December 18, 1944, issued an unanimous ruling granting Endo her petition.[46] The Court ruled that the WRA did not have the authority to subject loyal citizens to its regulations. One day earlier, however, on December 17, 1944, the War Department announced the issuance of Proclamation No. 21, which removed the general exclusion orders prohibiting Japanese Americans from the West Coast. On January 2, 1945, restrictions preventing the resettlement of Japanese Americans on the West Coast were removed. By the end of March 1946 all the WRA camps were closed.[47]

Although the Court's decision upheld the rights of Japanese Americans, the Court's actions in delivering the opinion were questionable. The opinion was written and approved by the Court in early November 1944, but Chief Justice Harlan Stone did not release the opinion for over a month. He held up the decision until, as Howard Ball put it, "two days after he received final word from the War and Justice departments about the major policy change."[48] This major policy change was the rescinding of the exclusion of loyal Japanese Americans citizens from the West Coast. The Court's delay effectively prevented the release of loyal citizens during that time. The decision to withhold the release of the Court's opinion was apparently the result of "informal and secret discussions between [Justice] Stone and officials at the War Department."[49] Such discussions violated the division between the judicial and executive branches of the federal government. Chief Justice Stone was not the only Supreme Court justice guilty of ethical violations. Ball noted that "at least four of the justices had some contact with government officials involved in the development and implementation of the Japanese exclusion policy and should have recused themselves. Frankfurter had frequent contacts with John J. McCloy of Secretary of War Henry Stimson's staff. Stone acted in concert with War Department officials. Justices Douglas and Black evidently were acquaintances of General DeWitt."[50] These justices neither removed themselves nor cited any potential conflicts of interest.

Understanding Why the Concentration Camp Policy Occurred

An analysis of the events leading up to Executive Order 9066 and Public Law 503 indicates that there was a proper alignment for public policy actions against Japanese Americans. Historical events were unsupportive of the Japanese in the United States. The Japanese American community was powerless. The mass media and the dominant community were against them. Both chambers of Congress supported the exclusion. Later the Supreme Court upheld the curfew and exclusion orders through the convictions of Hirabayashi, Korematsu, and Yasui. The executive branch, from President Roosevelt down, supported the policy.

The end of World War II and the closing of the camps in 1944–46 signified the end of one traumatic era for Japanese Americans, but racism, discrimination, prejudice, segregation, and ignorance took their toll. The exclusion and incarceration fractured the structure of the Japanese American family and community. Traditional family roles were lost and generational changes became evident. Some Japanese Americans, in an effort to demonstrate loyalty, turned in other community members suspected of disloyalty. Individuals argued over whether to fight in the armed services. The American dream of working hard, owning property, and enjoying the rights of citizenship was replaced by a nightmare of forced removal and imprisonment.

The World War II period saw the peak of anti-Japanese sentiment with the exclusion of the Japanese. Ironically, it also saw the beginning of the end of racial restrictions on immigration and naturalization for Asians. One of the most significant changes in this period was the repeal of the 1882 Chinese Exclusion Act by the U.S. Congress and President Roosevelt at the end of 1943. This repeal not only gave Chinese an immigration quota but also allowed Chinese aliens (but not other Asians) to become naturalized. It is now clear that this seemingly minor act was actually the hinge on which American immigration policy turned, since in less than a decade all ethnic and racial bars to immigration and naturalization were dropped.

The Aleut Experience

Although the government improved opportunities for Chinese aliens through its immigration policies, it continued to mistreat other minority groups during World War II. Japanese Americans were not the only ones forcibly moved in the United States during the war. The Aleut people from the Aleutian and Pribilof Islands in Alaska were treated similarly. The remote Aleutian Islands were a chain of islands spanning nearly nine hundred miles, from the Alaska Peninsula to Attu Island. Migrants from Asia settled the Aleutian Islands approximately ten thousand years ago and became known as the Aleuts.[51] The Russians colonized the islands in the eighteenth century and converted the Aleuts to the Russian Orthodox religion. In 1867 the United States purchased Alaska, including the Aleutian Islands, from Russia.

During World War II both the United States and Japan considered the Aleutian Islands strategically critical. The military value of the islands intensified as Japan's naval strength increased in the Pacific. Attu Island was only six hundred miles from Japan's Kurile Islands and a mere eight-hour flight for U.S. bomber planes from Seattle. Either power could use the Aleutian Islands to launch attacks on its enemy.

Three months after Pearl Harbor U.S. military intelligence predicted an imminent Japanese invasion of the Aleutian Islands. Initially, the military and civilian authorities could not reach a consensus as to whether the Aleuts should be evacuated. Brigadier General Simon B. Buckner of the Alaska Defense Command was against evacuating the Aleuts. He informed Alaska's Governor Ernest Gruening with prophetic accuracy that to evacuate the Aleuts would be, in essence, to destroy them.[52]

On June 3, 1942, the Japanese bombed U.S. naval installations at Dutch Harbor near Unalaska.[53] On June 8 Japanese troops invaded and occupied Attu Island and subsequently Kiska Island. On June 12 the United States began evacuating the Aleuts from their homelands.[54] In total, 881 Aleuts and 30 non-Aleuts from the Pribilof Islands and Aleutian villages west of Unimak Island were evacuated.

The evacuation process was hasty, and villagers lost most of their personal possessions. Usually villagers were given less than twenty-four-hours notice to prepare. Those living in Atka were given only twenty minutes to pack, and their village was purposely burnt to the ground by the U.S. Navy to prevent the Japanese military from using it.[55] Aleuts were ordered aboard the army's U.S.A.T. *Delarof* and shipped to Dutch Harbor on route to their final destinations. Health conditions were poor, and the *Delarof*'s doctor refused to go into the ship's hold, leaving the sick Aleuts untreated.[56] The first Aleut to die during the evacuation was a newborn baby, who died from pneumonia and was thrown overboard.[57]

Aleuts were sent to five "relocation" camps in Alaska.[58] They were forced to live in broken-down fish cannery buildings and abandoned gold miners' shacks and had virtually no medical care. They lacked adequate living quarters, safe food, and water facilities. Initially, people slept in shifts at the Funter Bay sites because of overcrowding.

Measles, influenza, pneumonia, and tuberculosis were widespread at the different camps. At Funter Bay one toilet placed above the low-water mark on the beach served over two hundred Aleuts, and human waste flowed into the bay. Many Aleuts became ill. Some of the Aleut men who secured construction jobs and were unaccustomed to big cities soon contracted venereal disease and succumbed to alcoholism at a high rate. Most were never adequately treated for these conditions.[59]

Approximately 10 percent of all Aleuts who were evacuated died during the two or three years they were kept in the camps.[60] The elderly and young children suffered the highest mortality rates. These deaths threatened the longevity of the Aleut culture. For many children the official death records listed the cause of death simply as "pain."[61] The government's ineffective management and neglect prevented meaningful interventions to address the poor living conditions for over a year and a half.[62]

The U.S. government intentionally exploited the Aleut people to prosper from their lucrative fur seal trade, a valuable source of revenue. The Aleuts were necessary in the harvest of the fur because of an international treaty stipulating that fur seal could be harvested only by Pribilovian Aleuts. In January 1943 the U.S. government therefore decided to return Pribilovian men and older boys to the Pribilof Islands to harvest the fur.

The U.S. government, concerned that the men would stay behind to be with their families, declared that any man who refused to participate in the 1943 seal harvest would be permanently banned from ever returning to his homeland.[63] On May 6, 1943, 151 Pribilovian men and boys were shipped to the Pribilof Islands for the sealing season. The summer sealing operations harvested over 117,000 seals, producing $1,580,000 in sales for the U.S. government.[64]

By the end of 1943 the U.S. military recognized that the Japanese no longer posed any threat to Alaska and the Western Hemisphere.[65] However, it was not until May 1944, nine months after the United States drove the Japanese troops off the Aleutian Islands, that the Pribilovians saw their homeland again. The Pribilovians' return was expedited because the sealing operations were a high priority in the Pribilofs.[66] The remaining Aleuts were not returned to their islands until June 1945, a full year and a half after their return was authorized.

The Aleut people faced a devastating situation upon their return home. Their Orthodox churches had been desecrated or destroyed. Cultural and community items, such as religious icons (some dating back from the Czarist Russia period), musical instruments, cultural craft work, and hunting and fishing equipment, had been stolen by U.S. military personnel and civilians stationed on the islands.[67] The islands were permanently damaged by oil spills, dumped excess ammunition, and other war debris. A substantial portion of the breeding and fishing habitat was ruined, and the Aleuts forever lost the use of some of their most productive seal harvesting areas. Those from Attu were deprived of their homelands by government order. The subsistence economy of the Aleutian and Pribilof islanders was permanently changed.

The federal budget for 1946–47 indicated that Aleut and white evacuees received $31,441 for "refunds, award and indemnities."[68] Supplies and equipment were provided to the Aleuts to rebuild their communities. The Aleuts, however, claimed that they never received some of the shipped goods and that what they did receive was of poor quality.

The evacuation of the Aleuts was a governmental action designed to protect them. Paradoxically, it nearly destroyed them. Philemon M. Tutiakoff, chairman of the Board of the Aleutian/Pribilof Islands Association, described the situation: "We were the first and only people in Alaska to be assaulted by our own government and an enemy foreign power in W.W.II simultaneously. We were the first Alaskans to be stripped of our constitutional rights."[69] John C. Kirtland and David F. Coffin Jr., legal counsel for the Aleutian/Pribilof Islands Association, Inc., further stated, "There is no doubt that the Aleut people suffered unacceptable casualties, under intolerable conditions, at the hands of their government 'protectors' during the war years."[70]

Although it remained an untold story for many years, the unjust treatment of the Aleuts eventually propelled them to link their cause with that of the Japanese Americans. The joining of these two communities was an unanticipated union since they were so different in size and cultural heritage. But they shared the experience of being denied liberty and justice by their own government.

Children being hauled by truck from Redondo Beach, California, to the Santa Anita Detention Center (note shipping tag on the little girl in the truck), April 5, 1942. (Photo by Clem Alberts; courtesy of the National Japanese American Historical Society)

Train from San Pedro, California, arrives at the Santa Anita Detention Center, April 5, 1942. (Photo by Clem Alberts; courtesy of the National Japanese American Historical Society)

Manzanar Concentration Camp, July 3, 1942. (Photo by Dorothea Lange, WPA; courtesy of the National Archives)

Members of the 442d Regimental Combat Team after the Vosges Mountains campaign. (U.S. Army photo; courtesy of *Pacific Citizen*)

Members of the National Committee for Redress (standing) meet with the Japanese American members of Congress in Washington, D.C., in January 1979. Seated (*left to right*): Sen. Spark Matsunaga, Sen. Daniel Inouye, Rep. Robert Matsui, and Rep. Norman Mineta; standing: Karl Nobuyuki, Ron Mamiya, Clifford Uyeda, Ron Ikejiri, and John Tateishi. (Courtesy of *Pacific Citizen*)

President Jimmy Carter signs the act creating the Commission on Wartime Relocation and Internment of Civilians. Directly behind President Carter (*left to right*): Sen. Ted Stevens, Sen. Daniel Inouye, Rep. Norman Mineta, and Sen. Spark Matsunaga; back row (*far left*): Clifford Uyeda and John Tateishi. (Courtesy of *Pacific Citizen*)

CWRIC hearing in Washington, D.C., on November 2, 1981. Seated at the table (*left to right*): Hon. Arthur Goldberg, Father Robert Drinan, Hon. Hugh Mitchell, Hon. Edward Brooke, Rep. Daniel Lungren, Joan Bernstein, Angus Macbeth, Arthur Flemming, Hon. William Marutani, and Father Ishmael Gromoff. (Courtesy of *Pacific Citizen*)

CWRIC hearing in Los Angeles, August 1981. (Photo by Roy Nakano; courtesy of Visual Communications)

Coram nobis attorneys and their clients. Seated (*left to right*): attorneys Dale Minami, Don Tamaki, and Peter Irons; standing: plaintiffs Fred Korematsu, Gordon Hirabayashi, and Min Yasui. (Photo by Chris K. D. Huie)

Supporters of the NCJAR class action lawsuit on the steps of the U.S. Supreme Court, April 20, 1987. (*Left to right*): Fred Korematsu, Gordon Hirabayashi, Michi Weglyn, William Hohri, Aiko Herzig-Yoshinaga, and Harry Ueno. (Photo by Doris Sato)

Participants in the NCRR lobbying trip to Washington, D.C., gather in front of the Capitol, July 1987. (Photo by Glen Kitayama)

President Ronald Reagan signing the Civil Liberties Act of 1988 on August 10, 1988. Standing in the row behind President Reagan (*left to right*): Sen. Spark Masunaga, Rep. Norman Mineta, Rep. Patricia Saiki, Sen. Peter Wilson, Rep. Don Young, Rep. Robert Matsui, Rep. Bill Lowery, and Harry Kajihara; partially pictured in the back row: Sen. Daniel Inouye, Rep. Jim Wright, and Sen. Ted Stevens. (Courtesy of the Ronald Reagan Library)

NCRR "No More Broken Promises Rally" in Los Angeles, California, August 2, 1989. (Photo by Janice Harumi Yen; courtesy of the NCRR)

U.S. Attorney General Dick Thornburgh presents national apology and redress payment to Hisano Fujimoto, 101. Senkichi Yuge (*far left*), 101, and Kisa Iseri (*right*), 102, look on during the Washington, D.C., ceremony, October 9, 1990. (Photo by Mike Theiler; courtesy of Reuters Archive Photos)

Redress supporters witness the first presentations of the apology and monetary redress payments, Washington, D.C., October 9, 1990. Second row (*left to right*): Sen. Daniel Inouye, Daniel Akaka, Rep. Mervyn Dymally, Rep. Norman Mineta, and Rep. Robert Matsui; seated behind them: Sen. Spark Matsunaga and K. Patrick Okura. (Courtesy of *Pacific Citizen*)

4   The Postwar Decades (1945–69)

The alignment of the various policy streams in favor of redress began to take place in the period after World War II. The Japanese American community (N-), the mainstream society (N-), and the different branches of government moved slightly in a positive direction for Japanese Americans. Overall, however, the policy streams were in a state of "inertia." There was little "energy" to identify the problem and no compelling reason for the legislative (N-), the judicial (-), and the executive (N-) branches to bring up the issue (see table 2).

The Years Following the Camps, 1945–49

Between 1942 and 1945 a "leave" policy had existed that encouraged inmates to apply for government clearance to move to such areas as the Midwest and the East Coast. The primary beneficiaries of the leave policy were college students and young adults. The movement of these individuals, as well as those who served in the armed forces, resulted in their greater exposure to white Americans. In turn white Americans were also increasingly exposed to Japanese Americans. After the war the majority of Japanese Americans moved back to the West Coast. There was, however, a significant number who moved to locations in the Midwest and East, such as Chicago, Minneapolis, Seabrook

Table 2.

Years	History		Legislative Branch		Judicial Branch	Executive Branch
	Community	U.S. Society	Senate	House		
1945–49	N-	N-	N-	N-	–	N-
Pre-WWII/Exclusion/ Incarceration	–	–	–	–	–	–

Farms, New York City, Cleveland, Cincinnati, and St. Louis. The percentage of Japanese Americans on the West Coast was never again as high as it had been before the war.

In 1945 most in the Japanese American community were busy rebuilding their lives. Some, however, were discussing reparations. The members of the Heart Mountain Fair Play Committee renamed their group and were incorporated as the Fair Rights Committee, whose stated purpose was to pursue redress. In February 1945 Japanese Americans organized the All Center Conference, which was held in Salt Lake City, Utah.[1] Japanese American representatives from seven of the ten War Relocation Authority camps attended and addressed such issues as more tangible forms of assistance for former inmates and the need for the federal government to make amends. The tone of the conference's discussions reflected the representatives' anger toward the U.S. government. One of the main issues was the closing of the camps. There was disagreement over whether and when the camps should be mandatorily closed. Although the immediate effect of the conference was negligible, there was consensus that the inmates deserved some form of reparations.

For the vast majority of Japanese Americans, however, everyday concerns, such as making a living, finding decent housing, and getting an education, were higher priorities than redress. The mood of Japanese Americans toward a redress movement was at best "less than neutral," and there was no active organizing on the part of the community for redress.

During this postwar period the general society's view of Japanese Americans improved slightly. In the years following the incarceration, other groups (e.g., African Americans, immigrant Mexicans, and Mexican Americans) took the place of Japanese Americans as the primary scapegoats for societal ills.[2] For example the "zoot suit riots" in 1943 involved both Mexicans and blacks and cast them in a negative light. Moreover, the postwar rehabilitation of Japan tended to evoke more favorable attitudes among mainstream Americans toward the former enemy and, in turn, toward Japanese Americans.

In June of 1946 Congress passed Public Law 79-471, the G.I. Fiancées Act, which allowed alien fiancées of American soldiers in World War II to enter the United States and remain in the country as permanent resident aliens. Under this law some 40,000 war brides were allowed entry into the United States. Later that year, in November, California voters rejected Proposition 15, which would have incorporated the Alien Land Laws into the California Constitution. This was the first time in the state's history that an anti–Asian American measure was defeated.

The Japanese-American Evacuation Claims Act of 1948

A significant event for Japanese Americans was the passage of legislation recognizing their documented property losses resulting from the forced exclusion. In 1946 two evacuation claims bills (S.R. 2127 and H.R. 6780) were introduced in the Senate and House, respectively. These bills proposed an evacuation claims commission supervised by the secretary of the interior to pay for property losses of Japanese Americans who had been excluded. President Harry S. Truman sent letters to the chairmen of both the Senate and House judiciary committees supporting the bills.

President Truman's acknowledgment of the Japanese American experience also extended to the accomplishments of the 442d Regimental Combat Team. On July 15, 1946, the 442d R.C.T. was received by the president on the White House lawn. At this ceremony the president stated, "You fought not only the enemy, but you fought prejudice—and you have won."[3] The presidential reception demonstrated that the 442d's contributions extended well beyond World War II and were noticed by the White House. The honoring of the 442d helped generate congressional interest in the evacuee claims bill.[4]

Despite presidential support opposition to the evacuation claims legislation developed in the Seventy-ninth Congress. In the House opponents were concerned that renunciants and those who initially intended to repatriate to Japan would also receive benefits under the proposed legislation. Objections in the Senate included concerns that Japanese Americans were being singled out for special treatment, while Italian Americans and German Americans would be excluded from receiving benefits. The bill died in the House, but it passed the Senate with minor amendments on July 29, 1946.

In the Eightieth Congress a revised version of the bill, H.R. 3999 (the Evacuation Claims Commission bill), was introduced in the House. In sharp contrast to the bill presented in the Seventy-ninth Congress, it passed unanimously on July 23, 1947, after only twenty minutes of debate. No members spoke in opposition to the bill. Representative Angier L. Goodwin (Republican from Maine) stated, "This will show to the world that when our Government by voluntary action of its own affecting a special racial group brings about a situation where these individuals suffer loss of their property, even though the act of the Government is caused by military necessity, we are ready, willing, and anxious to go forward with remedial legislation and attempt to redress those wrongs and do the right thing in the interests of simple justice."[5]

The Japanese American Citizens League viewed the House action positively. Mike Masaoka commented, "We are very much encouraged by the unanimity of opinion among both Republican and Democratic congressmen from all parts of the country. . . . The fact that there was not a single dissenting voice raised against the bill is indicative of the healthy attitude which Congress seems to be adopting toward persons of Japanese ancestry."[6]

In early 1948 President Truman gave a special civil rights message to Congress in which he urged the passage of ten civil rights measures. Included in these measures were evacuation claims and the removal of racial or national barriers to U.S. citizenship. It was the first time that a U.S. president had recommended legislation that specifically benefited Japanese in the United States.

The Senate held subcommittee hearings in May 1948. Most notable among those testifying was John J. McCloy, the former assistant secretary of war.[7] While maintaining that exclusion had been a military necessity, McCloy praised the cooperation of persons of Japanese ancestry, paid tribute to the 442d R.C.T., and urged passage of the bill. The bill had the unanimous approval of all relevant governmental departments and every member of the West Coast congressional delegation. On June 18, 1948, the Senate unanimously passed H.R. 3999 with only minor amendments.[8] The next day the House approved the amendments, and the bill was sent on for President Truman's signature.

On July 2, 1948, President Truman signed the Japanese-American Evacuations Claims Act of 1948.[9] Of President Truman's ten civil rights items, the Japanese-American evacuation claims bill was the only one to be signed into law that year. Approximately $38 million was paid out in claims under this act. The act, however, required documented proof of property losses, such as receipts, something most Japanese Americans did not have. Holding onto receipts had not been a high priority for many Japanese Americans, who were given only a few days to pack up one bag of belongings. As a result, most of the property losses were not compensated.

The last evacuations claims case was not settled until 1965. Although Keisaburo Koda died a few months before the settlement, his family was awarded $362,500 in October 1965 as compensation for its forced exclusion. This award did not come close to matching the claimed $1 million property loss and $1.4 million in lost profits the Koda family sustained.[10] Although the Japanese-American Evacuation Claims Act was a victory for the Japanese American community, it was limited in scope. The act addressed only documented property loss, not the loss of freedom and human dignity.

During this period, however, the federal and state judiciary branches of government began to issue decisions promoting equality across racial lines. In 1947 two significant federal district court decisions were rendered. The first decision was in response to a suit brought by the attorney Wayne Collins on behalf of individuals who had renounced their citizenship during World War II and were interested in having it restored. On June 30, 1947, a U.S. district court stated that American-born citizens could not be imprisoned or repatriated because they had renounced their U.S. citizenship while incarcerated behind barbed wire. As a result, over three hundred people were released from incarceration. The second court decision involved Yuichi Inouye, Miye Mai Murakami, Tsutako Sumi, and Mutsu Shimizu, who had renounced their U.S.

citizenship while they were at the Tule Lake concentration camp. The decision restored their citizenship, and the Ninth Circuit Court of Appeals upheld the decision on August 26, 1949.

In the late 1940s different courts began to rule that the Alien Land Laws, which were enacted by various states, were unconstitutional. In 1948 the U.S. Supreme Court ruled in *Oyama v. California* that the Alien Land Laws violated the equal protection clause of the Fourteenth Amendment of the U.S. Constitution. In 1952 the California Supreme Court in *Fujii Sei v. California* ruled similarly that the Alien Land Laws violated the equal protection clauses of the constitutions of both California and the United States. These decisions negated key aspects of the Alien Land Laws. Various western states, however, kept the laws on the books for many more years.[11]

The 1950s: A Time for Change

In May 1952 Representative George P. Miller (Democrat from California) introduced legislation (H.R. 7641) that restored seniority rights[12] to all Nisei civil service workers (including those in Hawai'i) who, on the basis of their race, were discriminated against by federal government policy during World War II.[13] The JACL Anti-Discrimination Committee and its national legislative director, Mike Masaoka, lobbied for the bill as it passed the House in June and the Senate in July 1952. President Truman signed the bill, known as the Nisei civil service workers bill, into law (Public Law 82-545) on July 15, 1952. This law, in conjunction with the Japanese-American Evacuation Claims Act of 1948, indicated that Japanese Americans were beginning to be disassociated from the acts of wartime Japan.

During the 1950s Joseph McCarthy introduced the Communists as the new target for attack. Japan was an ally in the American anti-Communist crusade, whose importance was reinforced by the Korean War. As a result, Japan improved in the eyes of most mainstream Americans. Since the image of Japanese Americans was still closely tied to the image of the Japanese in Japan, the Japanese American community also experienced a slightly better reception from the general American public.

McCarran-Walter Act of 1952

In the decade following the close of World War II the Congress passed legislation that was less discriminatory toward all immigrants from Asia. In the early 1950s Congress overrode President Truman's veto and passed the Immigration and Nationality Act of 1952, which became known as the McCarran-Walter Act. This act was the first general immigration act since 1924, and it had a mixed effect on the Japanese American community. On the positive side the act allowed individuals of all races to become eligible for naturalization. For the first time the Issei, classified as "aliens ineligible to citizenship," were given the opportunity to become U.S. citizens. The bill also provided family reunification as a legitimate reason for immigration. Spouses and children of U.S. citizens were allowed to immigrate on a nonquota basis. The bill, however, restricted immigration based on race and included a national-origins quota system. Japan was given a yearly quota of 185 immigrants. Between 1952 and 1964 nearly 63,000 Japanese, more than 5,000 per year, immigrated to the United States.[14]

The Supreme Court rendered decisions that were also favorable to ethnic and racial minorities. On May 17, 1954, the U.S. Supreme Court handed down a landmark decision in the case of *Brown v. the Board of Education*. This ruling struck down the doctrine of "separate but equal," which served as the underpinning for legal segregation. This decision was one of the foundations for the social movement toward full equality for all Americans. There was no mention of redress by the Congress during this period, however, and the judicial stream was still less than neutral for redress.

The First Japanese American Congressman

The most significant event in the Congress for the redress movement during this period occurred in 1959, when the Territory of Hawai'i became the fiftieth state. This addition to the Union resulted in the election of Daniel K. Inouye, a representative in the Territory of Hawai'i, to the U.S. Congress. Representative Inouye was a decorated World War II veteran of the 442d R.C.T. who lost his right arm in combat. He would be subsequently elected to the U.S. Senate in 1962. Senator Inouye was soon followed by other Japanese Americans, each of whom would eventually play an important role in the passage of redress.

An Amendment to the Nisei Civil Service Workers Act

President Dwight D. Eisenhower (1953–61) demonstrated mixed support for the Japanese American community. He addressed Japanese American issues on three separate occasions. On July 8, 1959, he vetoed legislation extending the filing deadline for the Japanese-American Evacuation Claims Act of 1948 for a certain Japanese American individual.[15] In 1960 at the Honolulu International Airport President Eisenhower made favorable remarks about the 100th Battalion and the 442d R.C.T. On September 14, 1960, President Eisenhower signed a law (Public Law 86-782) that expanded the Nisei Civil Service Workers Act. The new law provided Nisei civil service workers with retirement and sick-leave credit for the time they were incarcerated or otherwise denied employment opportunity. As with the original law, the JACL was active in initiating this legislation.

Generational Differences in the Japanese American Community

During the 1950s and 1960s differences existed in how the Japanese American community remembered the camps. A significant portion of the Japanese American community knew little about the camps. Sansei children, the third generation, had little understanding of the personal and group impact of the exclusion and incarceration experience. The Issei and Nisei rarely discussed the experience of being abruptly removed from homes and incarcerated in desolate locales. Details surrounding the decisions of volunteering for military service, seeking repatriation to Japan, or openly resisting the draft were also left unspoken. The racial hatred and wartime hysteria that prevailed were often a part of what many families wanted to leave in the past.

It was not uncommon for Sansei children who grew up during the postwar decades to have acquired only the most basic facts about their elders' incarceration experiences. Names and locations of the concentration camps were often the extent of the Sansei's knowledge. Roger Daniels reflected on a teaching experience in the mid-1960s at UCLA, when two Sansei students emphatically told him that they were born in Los Angeles in 1943. Knowing that this was impossible, he carefully directed them to discuss this with their parents. What resulted was the disclosing of a "family secret" from which the parents had attempted to "protect" their children.[16] The Sansei's growing awareness of the past helped move the community from seeing the exclusion and incarceration as a misfortune to recognizing it as a social injustice.

The 1960s: A Time of Empowerment

During the late 1950s and the 1960s social and political empowerment in response to unyielding oppression occurred. Ethnic minorities, especially blacks and Chicanos, participated in protest marches, demonstrations, and sit-ins. Urban riots in Harlem (1964), Watts (1965), and many other urban ethnic minority ghettos throughout the nation occurred. These dramatic events put the spotlight on race relations in the United States and created the civil rights movement, which sought to overthrow the system of racial discrimination and oppression of blacks by the dominant power structure.

The civil rights movement relied on a spectrum of organizations ranging in organizational structure from the highly bureaucratic National Association for the Advancement of Colored People (NAACP) to such grass-roots groups as the Montgomery Improvement Association (MIA), the Southern Christian Leadership Conference (SCLC), and the Student Nonviolent Coordinating Committee (SNCC). While at times in conflict with one another's strategies, the different structures complemented one another. The effectiveness of bureaucratic organizations lay in their preexisting formal networks, stability, and perceived legitimacy. The grass-roots organizations' effectiveness stemmed from their ability to mobilize and involve the masses in the cause.

The black churches were a powerful source of organizational power in the South. These churches were indigenous institutions that provided a mass base of support, existing fund-raising mechanisms, and relative autonomy from the white power structure.[17] The black congregations had a culture rich with freedom and protest songs, oratory by charismatic ministers, and prayers that helped create and sustain a sense of mission and enthusiasm to fight for social change.[18] Black ministers were effective in drawing political, moral, and financial support for the civil rights movement. The people rallied behind them and continued to demonstrate and be imprisoned because of their belief in the justice and morality of what they were being called to do. Along with generating a moral conviction about the movement, civil rights organizers recognized the need to educate the black community to assume responsibility for righting an injustice rather than waiting for the oppressor to initiate change.

Both the expressive and strategic considerations described by Ralph Turner and Lewis Killian were evident in the civil rights movement. Churches, ministers, and grass-roots organizations used their mass base of people as effective vehicles for the expressive considerations. Organizations such as the NAACP were better suited to strategic considerations and primarily utilized a judicial and educational approach.[19] The success of the civil rights movement also left a legacy for other groups. Many activists who later worked in the women's, farm workers', and student movements received their training in the civil rights movement and antiwar movement.

The Japanese American community was not united in its response to the civil rights movement. For many Issei and older Nisei, who worked diligently to rebuild their lives financially and psychologically, the goals of the civil rights movement were not a priority. Stability and maintenance of the social gains they had made since the camps were their main concerns. The confrontation between ethnic minorities (especially blacks) and the established system was threatening and distressful to many Japanese Americans. During this time a "yellow flight" occurred as many Japanese American families moved out of urban communities that had growing black populations.

There were, however, younger Nisei who saw a clear relationship between the concentration camp experience and the oppression and assault on civil rights of all ethnic minorities. In 1948 the JACL, represented by Mike Masaoka, was one of the founding organizations of the Leadership Conference on Civil Rights (LCCR), which represented ethnic minority groups, labor unions, churches, and human rights advocates.[20] The JACL continued to be active in civil rights issues throughout the 1950s. Japanese Americans participated in the 1963 March on Washington. As representatives of the JACL, Mike Masaoka and K. Patrick Okura, president of the JACL, had reserved seats on the platform of the Lincoln Memorial where Dr. Martin Luther King Jr. delivered his famous "I have a dream" speech.[21]

Other Japanese Americans supported the more militant ideology of Malcolm X. Yuri Kochiyama, a Nisei political activist who had been incarcerated in Jerome, established a close and on-going relationship with Malcolm X and supported his internationalist concept of human rights. She was by Malcolm X's side when he was assassinated, and after his death she continued to promote the vision of self-determination and self-reliance for minorities.

Japanese Americans' participation in the civil rights movement, while not widespread or highly publicized, was instrumental in gaining the community a legitimate place among civil rights supporters. The efforts by key individuals and the JACL, as the main Japanese American organization, produced dividends for the redress movement in the decades to come. The civil rights movement supplied concrete models of organizational structure and tactics and illustrated how both expressive and strategic considerations were important in a movement. Most important, it provided an example that social and moral change could be obtained.

The 1960s was also the era of anti–Vietnam War protests. Cities and college campuses were the sites of antiwar rallies and demonstrations. A few Japanese Americans, such as Ray Okamura, Kathy Reyes, and Edison Uno, participated in the San Francisco Peace March of November 15, 1969, which drew well over 100,000 marchers. In 1970, during a demonstration at Kent State University in Ohio, four white students were killed. In the same year the Chicano Moratorium Committee organized an antiwar demonstration that drew over 20,000 protesters in Los Angeles. Black and white students in the SNCC were vocal in their protest of the Vietnam War and in drawing the connection between the use of nonviolence in the civil rights movement and in foreign affairs. The civil rights movement and antiwar movement provided important lessons that the redress movement would incorporate.

Presidential and Congressional Actions of the 1960s

The presidents to follow President Eisenhower, John F. Kennedy (1961–63) and Lyndon B. Johnson (1963–69), remained silent on any notion of redress or reparations to the Japanese American community. However, they did address some significant civil rights issues. President Kennedy made proposals supporting the civil rights movement and President Johnson signed legislation promoting the civil rights of all Americans. While not specifically targeted at the Japanese American community, significant pieces of legislation were enacted in the 1960s. Two of the most notable were the Civil Rights Act of 1964 and the Voting Rights Act of 1965. The Civil Rights Act of 1964 made racial segregation illegal, while the Voting Rights Act of 1965 ensured the rights of all individuals to vote, regardless of their race. Both of these acts demonstrated the federal government's willingness to address the issues of racism and inequality. Another piece of legislation, the 1965 Immigration Act, abolished the national-origins system and substituted hemispheric quotas. The act gave high priority to family reunification, and the most visible beneficiaries were Asians, especially Chinese, Koreans, Pilipinos, and eventually Vietnamese and other Southeast Asian ethnic groups.

By the mid-1960s the American media's portrayal of Japanese Americans was becoming more positive. In 1965 Walter Cronkite hosted a CBS documentary entitled "The Nisei: The Pride and the Shame," which took a sympathetic look at the Japanese American experience during World War II. In 1966 the *New York Times* published an article by William Petersen entitled "Success Story: Japanese American Style," which looked at the Japanese American as a model minority.[22]

By the late 1960s Japanese Americans were beginning to assume more responsible and visible positions in society. They were also becoming more politically active. Such groups as the Asian American Political Alliance, the Council of Oriental Organizations, the Yellow Brotherhood, the Third World Liberation Front, and the Red Guards were emerging in Asian American communities. Many of these groups were pan-Asian, represented the younger generations, and questioned the assimilationist-integration model of the older Asian American leadership.[23]

A Favorable Supreme Court Ruling

On April 10, 1967, the U.S. Supreme Court issued a ruling in *Honda v. Clark* that permitted approximately 4,100 Japanese Americans to recover bank deposits from the Yokohama Specie Bank, Ltd. These assets were seized by the U.S. government at the outset of World War II. At the conclusion of the war the Congress amended the Trading with the Enemy Act and set aside $10 million dollars with which to return the deposits. In 1957, however, the Office of Alien Property ruled that the deposits would be returned at the postwar yen-dollar conversion rate. This rate was approximately 360 yen to the dollar, as opposed to the prewar rate (which was in effect when the assets were seized) of approximately 4 yen to the dollar.

Approximately 7,500 Japanese Americans held certificates of deposits, and they were instructed to submit these certificates for redemption. Only 1,817 did so. Another 1,600 Japanese Americans sought to redeem the certificates in Japan. Approximately 4,100 individuals did not submit their certificates because they did not understand the legal technicalities, they did not want to part with their only evidence of deposits, or they were unwilling to accept such a paltry reimbursement rate.

Harry Kitano remembered that his father had put a small amount of money in the Yokohama Specie Bank before World War II. When the bank accounts were settled, he recounted, "I remember getting an official government letter . . . and a government check. It was for the magnificent sum of one cent. I threw it away in disgust."[24]

The federal government eventually changed its reimbursement rate and agreed to pay the prewar rate. However, the decision was not applied to the 4,100 Japanese Americans who had not originally submitted their certificates. The case was appealed to the U.S. Supreme Court, which unanimously ruled that the 4,100 Japanese Americans were entitled to the same terms of settlement. A statement by A. L. Wirin, the plaintiffs' attorney, proclaimed that the ruling "brings to an end the last injustice visited by the U.S. Government on Americans of Japanese descent during the war."[25] While the ruling was favorable to Japanese Americans, the media challenged this self-congratulatory statement. *Time Magazine* retorted, "Not quite. In last week's decision—as in all previous ones—the court sidestepped the prickly problem of the legality of the government's 1942 action in interning U.S. citizens without benefit of charges or trial. That precedent thus remains intact."[26] Not only did the Japanese American community receive a favorable ruling, but also it was apparent that some in the media were now sensitive to the injustices of the exclusion and incarceration.

Manzanar Pilgrimages

In the late 1960s some in the Japanese American community began to remember and commemorate their past experiences publicly. In 1969 the Organization of Southland Asian American Organizations, a coalition of activists—including Warren Furutani, Jim Matsuoka, Mori Nishida, Amy Ishii, Sue K. Embrey, and Edison Uno—who worked on civil rights and educational issues, organized a pilgrimage to the former concentration camp at Manzanar, California. On December 28 and 29, 1969, former inmates and others returned to clean and restore Manzanar's cemetery and to draw attention to the community's campaign to repeal Title II of the Internal Security Act.

The organizing of the pilgrimage displayed not only the community's desire to remember but also the gaps in its knowledge. Warren Furutani, a Sansei/Yonsei, remembers making a preliminary visit with Victor Shibata to the Manzanar site. As they were surveying the site and imagining what the event would look like, a local white resident approached them and inquired about what they were doing. Donning his best militant attitude, Furutani confidently explained the event that was being planned. Much to Furutani's displeasure, the local resident began to laugh. Before Furutani could confront this perceived disrespect, the local man declared, "Well then, you boys are in the wrong place. The Manzanar camp was on the other side of the highway."[27] Knowing the exact locations of the camps was just the beginning. The Japanese American community still had a long way to go before it could begin to fully know and argue its reasons for redress.

The Manzanar pilgrimage became an annual event organized by the Manzanar Committee, which was led by cochairs Embrey and Furutani. Pilgrimages to other concentration camps soon followed. These pilgrimages contributed to the overall redefinition of the Japanese American experience that was later to become important in building support for redress.

Activism among Asian Americans began to rise as Asian American studies programs at various West Coast universities began in 1969. Courses, seminars, speaker forums, and conferences were created and implemented. Younger generations were exposed to the historical treatment of Japanese Americans. Students became active in challenging the Eurocentric bias of traditional history, including the accounts of the wartime exclusion and detention. There was a progressive change in the Japanese American community. In the pre–World War II era the leaders were Issei. During the concentration camp period the Nisei, even those with little experience and training, were thrust into leadership positions. During the late 1960s younger Nisei and Sansei assumed leadership in questioning the status quo and the role of government.

Summary

By the end of the 1960s there were changes in all of the policy streams. Japanese Americans were better off; they had greater mobility in occupation, education, and housing. The newer generations of Japanese Americans, as well as the Nisei, had a growing sense of ethnic pride and an interest in assessing the wartime exclusion. Many of the Issei and older Nisei, however, did not want to remember the camp years (N). The mainstream U.S. society, in reaction to pressure from ethnic minority groups, began to grapple with issues of inclusion and equal opportunity (N). The federal legislative, judicial, and executive branches of government reflected the changing mood by passing legislation and issuing decisions that were more favorable to ethnic minorities. However, the notion of the country's apologizing and providing monetary redress to the Japanese American community for past injustices was not even remotely considered (N) (see table 3).

The influence of the civil rights movement was critical in aligning the policy streams. The civil rights movement taught the lessons, provided the energy, and instilled the inspiration through which the modern redress

Table 3.

Years	History		Legislative Branch		Judicial Branch	Executive Branch
	Community	U.S. Society	Senate	House		
1945–69	N	N	N	N	N	N
Pre-WWII/Exclusion/ Incarceration	–	–	–	–	–	–

struggle emerged. Both the civil rights and redress movements had an over-all aim of fighting injustice. Both sought to ensure that the "legalization of racism" would never again be sanctioned. The specific goals of each movement, however, differed considerably. The civil rights movement pursued constitutional guarantees of human and civil rights and endeavored to change the country's social order on a massive scale. The redress movement sought compensation for violations of such constitutional rights and safeguards that these rights would not be violated again in the future. The immediate objective of the redress movement, however, was narrower in scope: it sought to make redress a law. While the policy streams were still a long way from being properly aligned for a redress policy, they were moving toward such an alignment going into the 1970s.

5   The Genesis of the Modern Redress Movement (1970–78)

As the 1970s unfolded, Japanese American community leaders faced two fundamental questions: should they seek some sort of redress from the federal government; if so, what form should redress take? As Japanese Americans heatedly debated and contested these two questions, the shape of the redress movement evolved. During the 1970s the Japanese American community engaged in several campaigns that were implemented by the legislative and executive branches of the federal government. These included the repeal of Title II, the revocation of Executive Order 9066, and the pardoning of Iva Ikuko Toguri d'Aquino (also known as Tokyo Rose). Such campaigns contributed to the development of the modern redress movement. Judicial rulings in this period were neutral toward redress.

Published works by Japanese Americans about the camp experiences also began to appear. The ethnic community began shedding the role of victim and demanding redress of past injustices. However, not all of the U.S. society supported redress. Many individuals and particularly veterans groups, such as the Veterans of Foreign Wars and the American Legion, initially resisted the idea of redress.[1]

The modern redress movement began in 1970, when Edison Uno (1929–76) introduced a redress resolution at the biennial JACL convention.[2] Uno's resolution called for federal legislation to provide tax-free monetary "reparations" to Japanese Americans (or their heirs) who were excluded and incarcerated during World War II and a $400 million fund for community projects.[3] The national council of the JACL adopted Uno's resolution in principle, but it took no further action. Few in the community took redress seriously, and many had a "strong sense of reluctance" about pursuing the issue.[4]

Generational Differences

In the 1970s many Sansei were beginning to participate in community affairs. They grew up during the civil rights movement and the anti–Vietnam War protests and thus looked at exclusion and incarceration through the sociopolitical lenses of community empowerment and resistance. Initially, they viewed their parents' and grandparents' failure to resist the incarceration as cowardice. What they overlooked was that the Issei were not citizens and had no political power and that the Nisei were mostly teenagers and young adults. This rift between the generations was further exacerbated by the reluctance of many Nisei to talk about their wartime experiences. The redress movement had many obstacles to overcome, one of which was the community's generational differences.

The Nisei writer Yoshiko Uchida expressed this generational difference in her memoir, *Desert Exile:*

> Sansei children, who experienced the Vietnam War, with its violent confrontations and protest marches, have asked questions about those early World War II years.
>
> Why did you let it happen? they ask of the evacuation. Why didn't you fight for your civil rights? Why did you go without protest to the concentration camps? . . . It is my generation, however, who lived through the evacuation of 1942. . . . As they listen to our voices from the past, however, I ask that they remember they are listening in a totally different time; in a totally changed world.[5]

The Repeal of Title II

In 1971 the struggle to repeal Title II of the Internal Security Act of 1950 came to fruition, which was a significant civil rights victory. The internal security bill had been introduced shortly after the outbreak of the Korean War and during the McCarthy era of communist witch-hunts. The bill consisted of two parts: Title I, the Subversive Activities Control Act; and Title II, the Emergency Detention Act. Title I required the registration of Communists,[6] and it placed restrictions on organizations and individuals labeled "Communist" by the Subversive Activities Control Board. Title II gave the federal government the power to seize and hold persons expected to attempt acts of espionage or sabotage in the event of invasion, war, or insurrection. Title II used the incarceration of Japanese Americans as a model and the Supreme Court decisions in the Korematsu, Yasui, and Hirabayashi cases as the legal justification.

President Truman vetoed the legislation, more out of concern about the effectiveness of Title I to control communists than about the creation of concentration camps.[7] Congress overrode the veto, however, and the Internal Security Act became law on September 23, 1950. In 1952, under the provision of Title II, the Department of Justice designated six sites as detention camps, one of which was located at Tule Lake, California. Title II did not resurface as an issue until mid-1967, when black community leaders, including Dr. Martin Luther King Jr., Stokely Carmichael, and H. Rap Brown, expressed concerns and fears about the potential use of the concentration camps. Adding to their concerns, U.S. Attorney General Ramsey Clark appeared on national television and denied the past and present existence of concentration camps in the United States.[8] Shortly thereafter, on May 6, 1968, the House Committee on Un-American Activities (HUAC) issued a report that stated that "communist and black nationalist elements" should be imprisoned in detention camps. Mainstream activists initiated efforts to repeal Title II in the late 1960s, and Japanese American activists joined in the movement.

In 1968 seven JACL members from the Berkeley, Contra Costa, and Oakland chapters urged the national JACL to become involved in the repeal effort. This small group appreciated the unique position that Japanese Americans as past victims of American concentration camps held in the quest for the repeal of Title II. The national JACL was not quick to endorse the movement to repeal Title II, however. Arguments against such a movement included the cost, the inappropriate timing, the lack of widespread support, and the possibility of a greater backlash against dissenters and activists. Despite these concerns the JACL established the National Ad Hoc Committee for Repeal of the Emergency Detention Act at its 1968 national convention.

In the Ninety-first Congress Senator Daniel Inouye (Democrat from Hawai'i) introduced a bill to repeal the Emergency Detention Act of 1950. On the House side Representatives Abner Mikva (Democrat from Illinois), Masayuki ("Spark") Matsunaga (Democrat from Hawai'i), and Chet Holifield (Democrat from California) introduced similar bills. During the next two years the bills were guided through the legislative process in both houses of Congress. On September 25, 1971, President Richard M. Nixon signed the bill into law (Public Law 92-128), thus repealing Title II of the Internal Security Act of 1950. The impact of the repeal of Title II was largely symbolic, but it provided the Japanese American community with political experience in obtaining federal legislation.

The 1972 JACL National Convention

At the 1972 JACL National Convention the delegates affirmed the 1970 redress resolution. The resolution demanded that evacuees be paid $5 per day in camp (an amount equal to that paid to American prisoners of war), but it limited total reparations payments to the $400 million property loss estimated by the Federal Reserve Bank of San Francisco.[9] Along with passing resolutions, the JACL actively lobbied representatives and senators to introduce legislation sympathetic to the Japanese American community.

In 1972 the Congress passed a bill permitting Japanese Americans to file claims for reimbursement of funds deposited in the Yokohama Specie Bank, Ltd.[10] This bill was necessary because of the way in which the Department of Justice had interpreted the 1967 Supreme Court rulings allowing 4,100 Japanese Americans to be paid for their certificates of deposit. The Department of Justice used an obscure provision of the Trading with the Enemy Act that prohibited repaying "enemy aliens." During World War II Issei were "enemy aliens," and the Department of Justice interpreted the provision to mean that Issei, even those who had subsequently become naturalized citizens, were barred forever.

President Richard M. Nixon signed the legislation into law on October 4, 1972. His remarks reflected the growing status of the Japanese American community:

> The signing of this act . . . symbolized how far we have finally come in our human relationships in this country since World War II. . . . Japanese-Americans were recruited for the United States Armed Forces, and their 442d Regimental Combat Team became famous as the "Go For Broke" outfit that was one of the most highly decorated units in the United States Army in World War II. . . . and I now take this opportunity to express my gratitude for the contributions Japanese-Americans have made, and make today, to our country.[11]

Twenty-six days later President Nixon approved the social security amendments of 1972 (Public Law 92-603), which provided social security retirement credit for Japanese Americans incarcerated in War Relocation Authority or Department of Justice camps during World War II. JACL leaders had actively lobbied for these two acts, which reflected growing understanding about the Japanese American experience.

The 1974 JACL National Convention

The 1974 national JACL convention took no action about "reparations," but JACL district councils and chapters conducted surveys and held panel discussions on redress. The results of the surveys indicated that redress was becoming a topic of greater importance. More education about redress was needed in the JACL, however. In addition to gaining consensus in the JACL, redress supporters faced the challenge of educating members of Congress. It was unclear what individual legislators knew of or remembered from the World War II years. In 1974 there were only ten senators and eleven representatives who had been in office during World War II. Of these, only six senators and eight representatives had been in office on December 8, 1941, when the United States declared war on Japan.[12]

The First Redress Bill

The first redress legislation was introduced by Representative George E. Danielson (Democrat from California) on June 28, 1974. Danielson, whose suburban Los Angeles district was home to many Japanese Americans, proposed establishing a relocation benefits commission to provide assistance in securing grants, loans, or other types of aid through existing governmental programs to those incarcerated under Executive Order 9066. The bill died in committee, but represented growing congressional attention to the issue of redress.

Redress Surveys

In May 1975 the JACL Political Education Committee recommended creating a separate committee to push for legislation providing a lump sum "reparation" award to be placed in trust. There was disagreement about how the money would be used: whether it should be paid to the Issei first or be spent on community centers, scholarships, Nikkei service groups, and other special projects that would benefit evacuees and their heirs.[13] Uno thought the reparation fund should be used to construct multipurpose community centers, regional offices, and a national headquarters for the JACL.[14]

Surveys of JACL chapters indicated a strong interest in pursuing redress legislation and a preference for individual payments. For example, the results of surveys in Chicago, Cincinnati, Milwaukee, and Minneapolis–St. Paul indicated that 80 percent favored reparations, 15 percent opposed them, and 5 percent were undecided.[15] Of reparations supporters, 42 percent favored individual payments, 16 percent preferred creating a trust fund, and 42 percent wanted a combination of the two.[16] Comments reflecting support for redress included "This should have happened 20 years ago . . . [as the Issei and Nisei have put up] with a lot of grief" and "This step is long overdue. . . . People today, both young and old, do not realize this can happen or has happened in the U.S."[17]

Not all members of the Japanese American community were initially supportive of redress. Negative comments included "I am highly insulted by your mercenary demands. I have not heard any Issei or Nisei who had been victims complain (or) ask for reparations. It seems to me that the Sansei, Yonsei and others who had never experienced life in camp are demanding reparations more for themselves."[18] Another remarked that reparations "won't make a wrong right nor will it endear the Japanese Americans to the general public in these troubled economic times . . . shaking our fists and demanding cash reparations for a 30-plus year-old injustice somehow cheapens the strength of Japanese spirit and pride (Yamato Damashii)."[19] Another remarked that other Asians might view the redress campaign "as a self-serving gesture on the part of JACL. There are so many other worthy causes to which we should turn our energies."[20] Tension existed during the early days of the redress struggle between the Issei and the older Nisei on one side, and the younger Nisei and Sansei on the other.

During the remainder of the decade many other surveys of Japanese Americans were conducted. All indicated that a majority desired to pursue some form of redress. Although there was no consensus, most reflected a preference for individual payments.[21]

In September 1975 Kaz Oshiki, chairman pro tem of the JACL National Political Education Committee and administrative assistant for Representative Robert Kastenmeier (Democrat from Wisconsin), cautioned JACLers to keep in mind the realities of the era. The weak national economy meant that neither the Ford White House nor the Congress would be inclined to support any costly new program. Moreover, the American public had the impression that Japanese Americans were a minority group "that has it made." Oshiki, who supported reparations, warned, "You have to remember that a just cause does not mean automatic legislative approval. . . . It depends upon the amount of enthusiasm and community support it has generated."[22]

Although he had not always favored the idea of redress, Mike Masaoka came out for individual reparations in the 1975 holiday issue of the *Pacific Citizen*. According to Masaoka, "JACL is . . . duty-bound to its members, supporters, friends, and evacuees, and all who believe in justice, equity, and civil rights, to seek . . . 'reparations.'"[23] He urged individual lump sum payments and argued that the JACL was uniquely situated to provide leadership. Masaoka saw reparations as a sorely needed cause to unify the JACL and argued that the bicentennial year of 1976 would be an appropriate time to launch the campaign.

Leadership of the Redress Effort in the House

Early in 1976 the redress movement received the support of the first U.S. congressman to have been held prisoner in an American concentration camp. In 1974 Norman Y. Mineta, mayor of San Jose, California, was elected as a Democrat to the House of Representatives. In January 1976 Representative Mineta, the first Nikkei congressman elected from the continental United States, signaled his willingness to support the redress effort.

Representative Mineta had clear memories of the camp experience. He had just celebrated his tenth birthday a few weeks before the attack on Pearl

Harbor. Shortly after the attack his family's insurance company was closed down, and the family's savings were confiscated. Representative Mineta, recalling the exclusion, noted that "we even had to give away our dog, Skippy . . . to a stranger. We were told that we could take to the camp only what we could carry. People would just come and knock on your door and say, 'I'll give you five bucks for your refrigerator.'"[24]

Representative Mineta, whose family was sent to Heart Mountain, described the camp experience: "We were treated as prisoners of war, really—not Americans. You have to imagine how we felt looking up at the guard towers, knowing that their guns were pointed not outward but in, at us. And I think that the stigma of being accused of disloyalty was even worse than being sent to camp."[25]

Although Representative Mineta represented a district with a Republican voting record and less than 10 percent Asian American population,[26] he became a major player in the struggle for reparations. Representative Mineta wrote to JACL's President Shig Sugiyama on January 30, 1976:

> . . . unless we agree upon one, reasonable, and manageable approach [to reparations], we are doomed to fail. . . . I believe that the Japanese American Citizens League is the logical organization to spearhead the drive for reparations. While the efforts of other groups should be encouraged, the JACL is the only organization with the national base and credibility to coordinate the lobbying campaign which must take place. . . . we would be less than realistic if we attempted to enact legislation without wide public support of our grievances.[27]

Later that year, he remarked at a JACL function that he would take the lead in the House of Representatives to obtain redress.[28] He asked for the JACL's help in determining the form of reparations, gaining the support of a wide variety of groups, and unifying Japanese American efforts to gain redress.

Revocation of Executive Order 9066

During the initial discussions of how best to secure redress, community members were cognizant that Executive Order 9066 was still in existence. In early 1975 Henry Miyatake, Ken Nakano, and Tom Koizumi, members of the Seattle JACL Evacuation Redress Committee (SERC), led an effort to get it revoked.[29]

In response to community and inside the beltway lobbying President Gerald R. Ford revoked Executive Order 9066 on February 19, 1976, and pronounced, "We now know what we should have known then—not only was that evacuation wrong but Japanese-Americans were and are loyal Americans. . . . I call upon the American people to affirm with me the unhyphenated American Promise that we have learned from the tragedy of that long ago experience—forever to treasure liberty and justice for each individual American and resolve that this kind of error shall never be made again."[30]

There followed the repeal of Public Law 77-503, which attached criminal penalties to Executive Order 9066.[31] The successful effort to repeal Executive Order 9066 and Public Law 503 enhanced the Japanese American community's belief in its capacity to obtain some form of redress.

Other Social Justice Efforts

Another nonprofit reparations group, E.O. 9066, Inc. had formed in Los Angeles on April 26, 1975, to educate the public and fight for redress. The group was an outcome of a reparations panel sponsored by the San Fernando Valley chapter and the Pacific Southwest district of the JACL. The members of E.O. 9066, Inc. were mainly Nikkei living in the San Fernando Valley of southern California.[32] Paul Tsuneishi, a board member of E.O. 9066, Inc., recalled:

> The primary reason for starting a grass-roots movement for redress was two-fold: the belief that JACL would not move beyond resolutions unless public pressure from within the Japanese American community was brought to bear upon JACL . . . . . and the second reason was the obvious fact that JACL could not, and did not speak for many within the Japanese American community because of JACL's track record of cooperating with the government to the extent of informing on persons they thought held loyalty to Japan or perhaps could not be trusted as loyal Americans.[33]

Much of the work of E.O. 9066, Inc. focused on educational campaigns. E.O. 9066, Inc. typically asked churches to pass resolutions in support of the concept of reparations without any specific provisions (such as individual payments and block grants).[34] In the summer of 1979 E.O. 9066 merged its program with the JACL and dissolved as a separate entity.

Other ethnic minority groups during the late 1960s and 1970s were also seeking social justice in the form of reparations. The black militant leader James Forman advocated for reparations from white churches for the wrongs done to blacks over the years.[35] The NAACP, a centrist organization similar to the JACL, however, strongly opposed any such reparations. The NAACP instead urged the churches to work to open up equality of opportunity for all blacks, lest the advances made between 1958 and 1968 be nullified. In the 1970s American Indian peoples sought redress for the injustices in their own history, including the 1890 massacre of Sioux people by the U.S. Army at Wounded Knee, South Dakota.[36] In December of 1975 the results of a historical study of Wounded Knee conducted by the U.S. Army were announced. The study found that "the Wounded Knee massacre of 1890 was not really a massacre at all but an 'episode,' in which the Army showed 'great restraint and compassion.'"[37] Many historians denounced the study.

Senator James Abourezk (Democrat from South Dakota) introduced a bill in 1976 to provide reparations of $3,000 to each of the descendants of the Sioux people killed at Wounded Knee (for a total of $600,000). The main argument against the bill was the fear of setting a precedent of reparations for other oppressed groups, and the bill died in committee. This bill's death was a reminder of the necessity of demonstrating not only that a wrong was committed but also that the United States had an obligation and responsibility to redress such a wrong monetarily.

Japanese American Published Works

In the late 1960s and 1970s publications about Japanese Americans and their incarceration experiences emerged and served to educate the public. After eight years of research Michi Weglyn, a Gila River inmate, published *Years of Infamy: The Untold Story of America's Concentration Camps* in 1976, the first piece on the incarceration to be written by a Japanese American. She used primary documents to reconstruct and describe the exclusion and incarceration experience. She described the experience of the Japanese from Peru and the ordeal of Japanese Americans who renounced their U.S. citizenship. Weglyn presented documentation demonstrating that the federal government knew in 1942 that the incarceration of Japanese Americans was not necessary for national security.

Other influential books written in the late 1960s and 1970s included Harry H. L. Kitano's *Japanese Americans: The Evolution of a Subculture* (1969), Bill Hosokawa's *Nisei: The Quiet Americans* (1969), Roger Daniels's *Concentration Camps USA: Japanese Americans and World War II* (1971), Frank Chuman's *Bamboo People: The Law and Japanese Americans* (1976), and Dennis Ogawa's *Kodomo No Tame Ni: For the Sake of the Children* (1978). The work of Stetson Conn, the chief military historian of the United States, was also instrumental in presenting an accurate record of the Japanese Americans during World War II. In addition to published books there was an increase in published articles, student papers, and literary works describing the Japanese American experience.

The Seattle and Columbia Basin Plans

Not all members and chapters of the JACL were in agreement during the initial years of the redress movement. The Seattle Evacuation Redress Committee pushed for different and innovative ideas. Henry Miyatake, a systems engineer at Boeing who was incarcerated as a youth at Minidoka, began seriously thinking about redress in 1970. In 1973 Miyatake wrote a paper on redress that served as the underpinning of what was to become known as the Seattle Plan. This plan proposed that Japanese Americans could designate their federal tax dollars to a special fund. This special fund, which became known as the bootstrap concept, would be used to amass revenue for individual redress payments over the following ten years. In this way it would not be necessary to obtain direct congressional appropriation of funds.

The Seattle Plan was formally described in written form on November 19, 1975, by Shosuke Sasaki, Henry Miyatake, and Mike Nakata of the SERC. The document was entitled "An Appeal for Action to Obtain Redress for the World War II Evacuation and Imprisonment of Japanese Americans." The Seattle chapter distributed an audiotaped appeal for the Seattle Plan, which focused on the need for legal action to "disprove the false accusations in the minds of most white Americans."[38] The plan's proponents argued:

> By custom and tradition, any American who has been injured as a result of false accusations is expected to bring those responsible into court and obtain a judgment clearing his name and awarding him monetary damages from the offending parties. Failure by the slandered or libeled person to take legal action against his accusers is often regarded by the public as an indication that the charges are true. . . . If Japanese Americans are as American as the JACL has often claimed, then they should act like Americans and make every effort to seek redress.[39]

The Seattle Plan called for a payment of $5,000 per individual excluded or incarcerated and $10 for each day of incarceration. The figures were derived from what was felt to be meaningful to most recipients and comparable to compensation awarded to other victims of unjustified imprisonment.

An alternative, the Columbia Basin Plan, was formulated by other JACL members. This plan proposed that all of the reparations funds (estimated at $1 billion) go into a Nikkei-directed trust rather than to individuals. Half the principal and interest generated from the trust would go to support human service activities in the community and half to promote "Japanese American understanding."[40] The Columbia Basin plan reflected a continuing opposition to individual payments.

National Committee Redress Plans

In March 1976 the JACL finally created a national committee to focus specifically on the redress issue. Edward M. Yamamoto, chairman of the JACL Reparations Campaign Committee,[41] held a meeting to prepare a reparations proposal for consideration at the June 1976 JACL convention. Both the Seattle and Columbia Basin plans were considered. At the meeting Miyatake, on behalf of supporters of the Seattle Plan, compromised and agreed to add a provision to set up a trust fund with any reparations monies that were left unclaimed.[42] The Seattle group cited the results of their "appeal for action," in which 70 percent of the respondents supported the Seattle proposal over a bill requiring congressional appropriations and 89 percent favored individual reparations.[43]

Eventually Yamamoto's committee presented three redress plans to the 1976 convention. The first was the National Committee Redress Plan No. 1: The Basic Plan. A variant of the Seattle Plan, it called for $5,000 individual payments and $10 per day of incarceration. All unclaimed funds would be used for Japanese American educational and cultural purposes and for a legal defense fund for Japanese Americans. Plans 2 and 3 incorporated those denied due process but not actually incarcerated, including Japanese Americans stranded in Japan. Plan 3 also included Latin American Japanese incarcerated in the United States.

Redress supporters became aware of the need to enlist the support of all Japanese Americans. Paul Tsuneishi, in a letter to Yamamoto, argued that it was important as a practical matter to include former Japanese American inmates from Hawai'i as recipients of redress, since the Hawai'i congressional legislators would be asked to cosponsor reparations legislation.[44] Tsuneishi had received the signatures of fifty-seven Japanese American former inmates from Hawai'i on a petition for redress,[45] and he insisted that it was imperative to build the broadest possible coalition of support.

In late June 1976 Wayne Horiuchi, the JACL's Washington representative, made a confidential report on prospects for reparations legislation. Horiuchi's interviews with key congressional staffers indicated that the prospects were not good for redress legislation. The staffers felt that there might be educational value in conducting a redress campaign but that there was little chance of monetary redress.[46] Horiuchi argued that it was essential for the JACL to reach consensus on an approach to redress and to achieve consensus in the larger Japanese American community as well. Otherwise, prominent Japanese Americans could testify against the bill and doom its chances. While none of the staffers said that redress was impossible, that was clearly the subtext of Horiuchi's report.

JACL representatives met with Arthur J. Goldberg, former Supreme Court justice and ambassador to the United Nations, in San Francisco on June 11, 1976, to discuss reparations.[47] Goldberg had previously stated that the incarceration of Japanese Americans was "an horrendous violation of constitutional rights sanctioned by the Supreme Court,"[48] and he had later asserted, "I know of no way to overturn the Court's ruling in this case except by joint resolution of Congress expressing the sense of Congress that the action taken was completely outrageous."[49]

By the June meeting, however, Goldberg believed that such a congressional resolution would be of little worth. He suggested seeking legislation for monetary reparations. He thought that an apology by itself would not be adequate compensation for the wrongs done and that Germany's monetary payment to Jews set a precedent for reparations to Japanese Americans.[50] Goldberg suggested that an action could be brought in the Court of Claims to have the United States waive its sovereign immunity.[51] Goldberg spoke of how Chief Justice Earl Warren admitted that his role in the exclusion was one of his two greatest mistakes.[52] Goldberg put it bluntly to the JACLers: "Money is the demonstration of the injustice done. It is better than a paper resolution."[53]

The 1976 JACL Convention

The 1976 JACL convention unanimously adopted a resolution calling for monetary reparations: "The basic principle involved is one of equity, justice, dignity, and freedom. While conceding that the probabilities of success in persuading the Congress to provide substantial and meaningful token reparations are slim, JACL intends to campaign vigorously for the enactment of this corrective and remedial legislation."[54] The details, however, were left for later. The JACL leadership thought that there might be important collateral benefits from a reparations campaign, including the development of the legislative capability of the JACL and Japanese Americans at all levels of politics, the opportunity to educate and inform Americans about the unconstitutional treatment of Japanese Americans during World War II, and a warning to Americans to be vigilant in order to avoid future injustices. It also hoped redress could be a common cause that would unite the Japanese American community.[55] The 1976 convention produced a mandate for the organization to make federal legislation providing reparations its highest priority.

Support from Outside the Japanese American Community

As the momentum for redress grew within the JACL, support was also expanding outside the Japanese American community. Members of E.O. 9066, Inc. obtained the support of Representative Yvonne Braithwaite Burke (Democrat from California) in late 1975. This was especially significant since Representative Burke was the head of the Congressional Black Caucus. A June 4, 1976, survey of six hundred randomly selected registered voters in Alameda County found that 73.9 percent disagreed with the policy of incarceration, and 64.0 percent supported providing reparations to Japanese Americans who had been incarcerated.[56] The support for reparations continued to build. At its annual session in 1976 the Western Baptist State Convention, an association of one hundred black churches in California, adopted a resolution supporting Japanese American redress and commended President Ford for rescinding Executive Order 9066.[57]

The redress movement received its first support from a non-Nikkei national organization in August 1976. At its national convention the Veterans of Foreign Wars (VFW) passed a resolution urging reparations. The resolution was initiated by Alex Yoriguchi and Everette Sprague of the VFW post in Okinawa, Japan. Non-Nikkei members of the Okinawa post stated, "We should not whitewash the Evacuation."[58] This resolution passed largely because of the efforts of Nisei veterans groups.

Redress as a campaign issue for non–Japanese Americans in California began to surface in the late 1970s. David Harris, who was running for Congress in the Twelfth Congressional District in northern California, announced his support of the VFW redress resolution.[59] The redress movement also gained the support of many church groups, including the California-Arizona Conference, United Methodist Church; Lutheran Churches of America Commission on Social Concern; Asian American Baptist Caucus, American Baptist Convention; and the Japanese Free Methodist Church Executive Board, Los Angeles.[60]

The 1976 Elections

In 1976 two more Nikkei were elected to the U.S. Senate: Masayuki Matsunaga (1916–90) from Hawai'i and Samuel Ichiye Hayakawa (1906–92) from California. The senators brought differing views and experiences from the World War II era. Senator Matsunaga, fondly called "Spark" by those who knew him, had served in the U.S. House of Representatives since 1962 and in Hawai'i's territorial house prior to that. He was born and reared in Kauai, Hawai'i, and graduated from Harvard Law School in 1951. Senator Matsunaga was a decorated member of the 100th Battalion and was wounded twice in combat. Although he had not been excluded or incarcerated, Senator Matsunaga felt the importance of redress and eventually made a great contribution to the pursuit of redress legislation.

In contrast, Senator Hayakawa became a significant obstacle to the redress movement. Senator Hayakawa, born and reared in Canada, had obtained a doctorate from the University of Wisconsin. He spent the World War II years in Chicago and was not subjected to the camp experience. Prior to his election he was an internationally known semanticist and president of San Francisco State College. As a senator, he was vocal in his opposition to redress. He labeled the notion of redress a "radical-chic fad" and stated, "Japanese-Americans did indeed undergo suffering and injustice during the war. War is no picnic. But thanks, kids, most Japanese-Americans will not join your little game. As Japanese, we find it beneath our dignity. As Americans, we know a racket when we see one."[61] Senator Hayakawa criticized the Seattle JACL chapter's "Appeal for Action" redress campaign.[62] He claimed that the exclusion and incarceration were justified, and he argued that the Sansei (whom he mistakenly claimed authored the appeal) showed contempt toward older Japanese Americans and ignorance about their experiences, culture, and motivation. Such rhetoric, coming from a fellow Japanese American who had not been incarcerated, angered many in the Japanese American community.[63] Despite many attempts by members of the Japanese American community to negate or distance the community from Senator Hayakawa's opinions, his highly publicized views were used by redress foes to support the arguments against reparations.

The Pardoning of Iva Ikuko Toguri d'Aquino

In 1977 the movement for redress received a boost from the campaign to obtain a presidential pardon of Iva Ikuko Toguri d'Aquino (also known as Tokyo Rose). Born and reared in Los Angeles, California, Iva Toguri had traveled to Japan in July of 1941 to care for her critically ill aunt. Sensing the approaching conflict between the United States and Japan, Toguri attempted to gain passage back to the United States on December 1, 1941. Denied passage twice because of inconsistent bureaucratic procedures, Toguri found herself trapped in Japan when the war broke out. Shortly thereafter the Japanese secret military police demanded that Toguri renounce her U.S. citizenship. She refused to do so throughout the war. She eventually found a job as a typist at Radio Tokyo and was later assigned to be a radio announcer for *Zero Hour,* a program aimed at Allied troops. Toguri assumed the name Orphan Ann and broadcast a music program.

In April 1945 Toguri married Filipe J. d'Aquino. After the war she returned to the United States. In the summer of 1949 Toguri d'Aquino was charged with treason in a federal district court in San Francisco for allegedly broadcasting propaganda for Japan.

Toguri d'Aquino was represented by a team of dedicated attorneys: Wayne Collins, Theodore Tamba, and George Olshausen. The three worked without a fee and often contributed from their own pockets to cover court fees. The national JACL was noticeably absent from this effort. During the trial, which lasted for nearly three months, American and Allied prisoners of war who had been at the same radio station as Toguri d'Aquino refuted the treason accusation. Other American veterans who heard Toguri d'Aquino's broadcasts also testified that there was simply music and chatter on her show and no propaganda. The Department of Justice, however, produced two witnesses, George Nakamoto Mitsushio and Kenkichi Oki, who testified that they were present at the radio station and saw Toguri d'Aquino broadcast propagandistic statements. Both Mitsushio and Oki were Nisei who had repatriated to Japan in 1940.

The all-white jury deliberated for nearly four days. At one point jury members informed the judge that they were "hopelessly deadlocked,"[64] but they were instructed to continue to deliberate and return a verdict. Despite the absence of evidence indicating Toguri d'Aquino's intent to betray the United States, she was found guilty. She was convicted of only one of an original eight alleged acts of treason. Her conviction was for allegedly asking in a 1944 broadcast, "Now you have lost all your ships. You really are orphans of the Pacific. How do you think you will ever get home?"[65] She was sentenced to ten years in the Alderson Federal Reformatory for Women in West Virginia, where she served six years and two months. Ironically, it was Toguri d'Aquino's act of patriotism that qualified her to be tried for treason. Had she renounced her citizenship during the war, there would have been no foundation for her conviction.

Several decades after her release from prison, efforts were made to obtain a presidential pardon for Toguri d'Aquino. Such attempts with the Eisenhower, Johnson, and Nixon administrations proved futile. However, evidence was discovered indicating that the Department of Justice did not believe her to be guilty but nevertheless pursued her conviction. Key witnesses who testified against her stated that they had been forced by U.S. prosecutors to lie. Veterans groups, many of whom had fought in the Pacific theater, came forth in support of Toguri d'Aquino by claiming that her program had not spread propagandistic messages. Wayne Collins Jr. maintained the legal counsel that his father had provided three decades earlier. Senator Matsunaga worked the halls of the U.S. Senate and generated support for Toguri d'Aquino. Senator Hayakawa personally spoke to President Ford in December 1976, which prompted the president to direct the FBI to complete the investigation by the end of the year. Dr. Clifford I. Uyeda, chair of the JACL committee for Iva Toguri, rallied JACL members to maintain community support for Toguri d'Aquino. On his last day in office, January 19, 1977, President Gerald Ford granted Iva Toguri d'Aquino an unconditional pardon.[66]

The Toguri d'Aquino case was an opportunity for the JACL to support an issue it had previously avoided. It also provided an important lesson to the Japanese American community: through political maneuvering and community involvement, past wrongs could be addressed.

Preparing for the 1978 Convention

On September 12, 1976, the executive committee of the national JACL replaced Ed Yamamoto with Edison Uno as chair of the National Reparations Committee and appointed Dave Ushio as cochair.[67] On December 24, 1976, Uno died of a heart attack. Shortly thereafter Mike Honda was appointed as co-chair of the committee to fill the vacancy.

In shaping its "reparations" efforts, the JACL sponsored a number of "community input" meetings and continued to conduct surveys of the Japanese American community.[68] Results of the studies consistently demonstrated support for the idea of reparations in general and individual reparations in particular.[69] In March 1977 the Seattle Evacuation Redress Committee produced a paper entitled "Case for Individual Reparations Payments" that argued against block grant payments to the Japanese American community. Its basic argument was that since individuals had suffered from incarceration, the remedy should be provided to individuals.

In October 1977 Clifford Uyeda was appointed as the chair of the National JACL Reparations Committee, and Ken Hayashi and Peggy N. Iwasaki were named members. Ray Okamura joined them the following year. The original members represented different perspectives on the incarceration experience. Uyeda lived outside of the exclusion zone as an adult, Hayashi was incarcerated as a young adult, and Iwasaki was a Sansei born after the war. The committee quickly began publishing weekly articles about redress in the *Pacific Citizen*. The committee generated much publicity for redress, including a booklet entitled *The Japanese American Incarceration: A Case for Redress*.[70] By the end of 1977 the majority of the JACL was clearly in favor of redress, but there was still much debate over what form redress should take. Six major plans were submitted to the JACL for consideration. Three advocated individual payments,[71] and three favored a trust fund.[72] In the 1978 New Year special issue of the *Pacific Citizen*, the Reparations Committee's article insisted that there was no irreconcilable division between individual payments and payment to a trust fund. The committee argued that there could be a third method that combined the best of both by having a Nikkei-administered trust fund to process both individual and organizational claims.[73] Responding to previous criticism, the article argued that the purpose of compensation would be to deter future violations of freedom and human rights, not to put a "price tag" on such rights.

In April of 1978 Uyeda brought together representatives from all the JACL districts. They worked at the JACL headquarters in San Francisco for two days and developed redress guidelines, including a $25,000 compensation figure. Uyeda stated, "We all agreed that no amount of money would ever compensate for the material losses, the humiliations, the sufferings and the loss of Constitutional rights due to eviction and incarceration. Our judicial system does, however, entail redress for damages incurred. It is a concrete expression of an attempt at restitution. We felt that $25,000 was a starting figure for discussion, knowing that Congress will determine the final amount."[74]

Until then there had been some debate over the use of the terms *reparations* and *redress* to define the movement.[75] In May 1978 the committee changed its name to the JACL National Committee for Redress since it felt that there were "strong emotional reactions attached to the term 'reparation,'" that distracted "public attention from the main issue of the campaign."[76] The term *reparations* was usually applied in the context of compensation paid to the victor by those defeated in war. *Redress* carried the connotation of putting right or making amends for past injustices.

Increased Civil Service Retirement Credit

While the broader redress movement was gaining support, additional pieces of legislation that addressed specific groups of Nikkei were being introduced. In the Ninety-fourth Congress (1975–76) Representative Mineta acted on his pledge to lead the redress effort. He introduced legislation that would grant civil service retirement credit to Japanese Americans who were over the age of eighteen when incarcerated and joined the civil service system after their incarceration.[77] The bill died in the Ninety-fourth Congress but was reintroduced in the Ninety-fifth Congress as H.R. 9471 with more than seventy-five cosponsors.[78] The bill passed the House on January 23, 1978.

A companion bill, S.R. 224, was introduced in the Senate by Senators Inouye and Matsunaga. The JACL and the Committee for Internment Credit, headed by Bill Kyono and Toshi Yoshida, provided community support as the bills worked their way through Congress. The final bill was passed by the Senate on August 18, 1978, and was accepted by the House on September 11, 1978. In arguing for the passage of the bill, Representative George Danielson (Democrat from California) made a prophetic statement: "We have been attacking the problem of repairing the damage of the World War II Japanese internment piecemeal. This particular bill is an important step. There may be one or two other bills still to come."[79]

On September 22, 1978, President Jimmy Carter signed the bill entitled Civil Service Retirement Credit for Japanese Americans Interned during World War II (Public Law 95-382). In signing the bill President Carter stated, "This bill represents years of unceasing effort by many Members of Congress who wished to redress the injustices suffered by this unique group of American citizens. I am pleased to have the opportunity to share in that effort today."[80]

The 1978 JACL Convention: A Time for Action

Eight years after Uno's initial redress proposal the JACL committed itself to a detailed redress agenda. At the July 1978 convention the JACL national council unanimously adopted a resolution calling for $25,000 in individual monetary restitution. Payments would go to excluded or incarcerated individuals or to their heirs. Individuals of Japanese ancestry who had been deported from Central and South America, sent to the United States, and incarcerated by the U.S. government were also included. The resolution stressed that both a trust fund and individual payments were necessary.

The national council urged that a redress bill be submitted to Congress and that it be as inclusive as possible.[81] John Tateishi, a Nisei who had been incarcerated at Manzanar, was appointed chair of the JACL National Committee for Redress (NCR). As chair, Tateishi was given a mandate to implement the resolution. Despite the delegates' unanimous vote of approval, there was still not a consensus by all JACL members to pursue redress. An awareness of this reluctance prompted Clifford Uyeda, the newly elected president of the JACL, to write, "The success of the redress campaign is predicated on a unified effort of the JACL."[82]

Ironically, the convention closed with an address by Senator Hayakawa at the traditional Sayonara Banquet. The selection of Senator Hayakawa as the main speaker was the result of miscommunication between the national JACL and the local host chapter. Upon learning that Senator Hayakawa had already been invited to speak, Uyeda wanted to ensure that Hayakawa would address the issue of redress. Uyeda asked to meet with Senator Hayakawa several times to discuss recent redress developments, but Senator Hayakawa failed to do so.[83] Senator Hayakawa's twenty-minute address made no mention of redress. Instead, he urged the JACL not to look back on the war years and to be wary of the possible repercussions of a trade imbalance between the United States and Japan.

The next morning JACL delegates and members were shocked and angered when they read about Senator Hayakawa's opposition to redress printed in the *Salt Lake City Tribune*. Senator Hayakawa asserted that the JACL had no right to ask for reparations and characterized the JACL's redress resolution as "ridiculous."[84] He declared, "For the JACL to ask for the restitution is merely the rekindling of resentment and racism that no longer exists."[85]

While many in the Japanese American community were dismayed by Senator Hayakawa's remarks, the article provided immediate national attention and exposure for redress.[86] Uyeda immediately fired off an angry rebuttal, which he hand delivered to the *Salt Lake City Tribune* that same morning. He attempted to discount Senator Hayakawa's remarks and stated, "Sen. Hayakawa's views on Japanese Americans have little or no understanding of our history, thoughts or feelings."[87] Despite this immediate rebuttal the supporters of the redress movement were painfully reminded that this would not be an effortless fight.

Representative Robert T. Matsui

Congressional elections at the end of 1978 resulted in a valuable addition to the redress movement. Robert Takeo Matsui, a Sansei, was elected to the House of Representatives. Representative Matsui had been born and reared in the Sacramento, California, area and, as a six-month-old baby, had been incarcerated with his family in the Tule Lake camp. Upon graduating with a law degree from the University of California, Hastings College of the Law, he practiced law and served on the Sacramento City Council before being elected. With the arrival of Representative Matsui, redress proponents now had two Nikkei (both of whom had been incarcerated) in the House of Representative and two Nikkei decorated war veterans in the Senate. These legislators, however, were initially very cautious about the redress issue. The Japanese American community's challenge was now to inspire them to assume leadership roles in the legislative pursuit for redress.

Day of Remembrance

The struggle for redress required more than the presence of Nikkei legislators in Congress and more than the organizing efforts of community leaders. The membership of the JACL was only a small fraction of the overall Japanese American community and tended to include the more activist-minded Nikkei. The energy and strength of the community was needed for redress to become a reality. The support of the "average" Japanese American, the many Issei and Nisei who lived the camp experience and their children who heard about the experience, was essential if redress were to have a chance.

The effort to get the community to remember and commemorate the camp experience began in the late 1970s. The first Day of Remembrance was held on Thanksgiving weekend 1978 at the Puyallup Fairgrounds, known as Camp Harmony in the state of Washington. The idea for the event originated with the playwright Frank Chin's response to a request from ABC-TV's 20/20 news show for a story.[88] Chin and the Seattle chapter of the JACL went on to organize and promote the event.

A caravan, several miles long, traveled from Seattle to the fairgrounds. The event consisted of speakers and entertainment designed to educate and remind people about the concentration camps. Upon arriving at the fairgrounds, everyone was "issued" buff-colored name tags similar to the ones inmates were forced to wear thirty-six years earlier. Thousands of people participated and demonstrated that the Japanese American community had not forgotten how its members were treated during World War II. The Washington State Commission on Asian American Affairs, having announced its unanimous support for the Japanese American redress campaign on November 13, 1978, also actively participated in this first Day of Remembrance. Miyatake recalled, "It was the first time that Japanese Americans faced up to the issue and were able to relate to the evacuation process and to the redress movement."[89] Tateishi recalled his reaction to the huge turnout, "It was surprising how many Japanese Americans were there . . . willing to go through this. To relive something, we knew they didn't want to relive."[90]

The essence of the redress movement was taking shape. Redress was not about monetary payment. Redress was the healing of the wounds through confronting the injustice. Monica Sone, a former inmate at Minidoka and author of *Nisei Daughter* stated, "The buried anger over Evacuation has been corruptive of the Nisei, but now our feelings are open and that's healthy. It's only right to show our anger openly over the injustice."[91] In the years to come, the Day of Remembrance (held on or close to February 19 to commemorate Executive Order 9066) was held annually in other cities, including Los Angeles and San Francisco. Redress proponents used this commitment to remember to involve more people in the struggle for redress.

Summary

The modern redress movement began in the 1970s. Initiated by a small group of activists, it facilitated the shifting of the different streams of influence toward redress. The general U.S. society began to view Japanese Americans much more positively. Historical sentiment that was anti-Japanese (and anti–Japanese American) during and after World War II was changing. The stereotypes of Japanese Americans as sly, tricky, and treacherous were replaced by stereotypes of being industrious, hard working, and successful. Japanese Americans were even called the "model minority." Influential segments (e.g., veterans groups) still opposed the concept of redress (N), however.

Individuals and groups in the Japanese American community were beginning to develop a strong inclination toward redress. They were much more knowledgeable about the past and willing to affirm their present rights as U.S. citizens. Scholarship about Japanese American history and courses in Asian American studies helped produce an educated cadre of community activists who rallied the Japanese American community around the notion of redress (N+).

The executive and legislative branches produced minor legislation sympathetic to the Japanese American experience in World War II. The various civil service and social security amendments, the repeal of Title II, the revocation of Executive Order 9066, and the pardon of Iva Toguri d'Aquino were all indications that the executive and legislative branches were moving toward the proper alignment. In addition the Congress had four Democratic

Nikkei legislators who, while initially cautious about redress, were becoming more sympathetic to the idea (N+). While the Supreme Court handed down rulings that were supportive of civil rights for minorities in general and for Japanese Americans in particular, it did not render any decisions that directly affected redress (N). Overall, the events of the 1970s indicated that the quest for redress was becoming a not-so-impossible dream, but one that was still far from fruition (see table 4).

Table 4.

Years	History		Legislative Branch		Judicial Branch	Executive Branch
	Community	U.S. Society	Senate	House		
1970–78	N+	N	N+	N+	N	N+
1945–69	N	N	N	N	N	N
Pre-WWII/Exclusion/ Incarceration	–	–	–	–	–	–

6 The Commission on Wartime Relocation and Internment of Civilians (1979–82)

Mr. Commissioner . . .
So when you tell me my time is
up I tell you this.
Pride has kept my lips
pinned by nails,
my rage coffined.
But I exhume my past
to claim this time.
My youth is buried in Rohwer,
Obachan's ghost visits Amache Gate,
my niece haunts Tule Lake.
Words are better than tears,
so I spill them.
I kill this, the silence . . .

—Janice Mirikitani, "Breaking Silences"

As the Ninety-sixth Congress met in 1979, many redress supporters felt the time was right to pursue federal legislation. Despite the JACL resolution to pursue redress legislation directly, several working in the civil rights field advised John Tateishi that it would be beneficial to have a presidential commission to educate the public about the facts of the incarceration.[1] This was difficult for Tateishi to accept: "In my heart of hearts . . . I didn't want to go for a Commission."[2] He preferred to pursue immediately redress legislation that would provide direct monetary payments to surviving inmates.

It was apparent, however, that the JACL would need to work closely with the Nikkei legislators, whose support was critical. At the end of January five JACL officials (Clifford Uyeda, JACL president [1978–80]; John Tateishi, chair of the JACL National Committee for Redress; Karl Nobuyuki, executive director of the JACL; Ron Mamiya, Seattle JACL member; and Ron Ikejiri, the JACL's Washington representative) met with Senators Inouye and Matsunaga and Representatives Mineta and Matsui. Senator Hayakawa was not invited because of his outspoken opposition to redress. Tateishi characterized the JACL NCR's request for a meeting with the Nikkei legislators as "extraordinary . . . because Inouye, Matsunaga, and Mineta had never met together . . . as a group in one room ever before."[3]

The JACL team was prepared to discuss a variety of redress strategies, including legislation for direct monetary payments and the Seattle Plan.[4] Senator Inouye, however, recommended establishing a commission to explore the different methods of payment. Representative Mineta initially expressed concern that a congressional committee could address these issues, but he eventually agreed that having a government document from an impartial body would be "absolutely critical" for advocating future redress legislation.[5] Even though the JACL convention had mandated pursuing monetary compensation directly, the JACLers felt that they had to accept the approach suggested by the Nikkei legislators. Tateishi recalled:

> Japanese Americans really didn't know much about [the redress movement], and certainly members of the Congress didn't know and weren't convinced that the internment was wrong . . . before we could do anything we needed to educate the public. My feeling then was that [Inouye] is a ranking member of the United States Senate, one of the most powerful men in the United States government . . . . He just said, "Think about it [a commission]." . . . [when we left] I turned to Clifford [Uyeda] and I said, "I think we got our walking orders."[6]

Senator Inouye remembered:

> I recall a pitch being made for the immediate consideration by Congress. When I was called upon I said I think it is premature, I don't think it will fly. I suggested first an educational program, not only to educate the non-Japanese of the United States but the Nikkei members also of the United States. . . . Needless to say, the JACL officials were very much disturbed and disappointed. They were hoping that all of us would come in flags waving and say let's make the charge up the hill. I think for a moment they were ready to take away my membership card.[7]

The Japanese American legislators' reluctance to "charge up the hill" was not surprising. During the late 1970s not one of the Nikkei legislators was convinced that redress was a viable legislative issue; instead, they viewed it as a political liability. Representative Mineta recalled that Senator Matsunaga initially responded to the idea of a redress bill by jokingly uttering "Ko mata ne" (meaning "big trouble" in Japanese), reflecting the potential conflict he anticipated for the careers of the Japanese American legislators.[8] Glenn Roberts, Representative Mineta's legislative director, noted, "These are people . . . who spent their whole lives trying to be seen not as Japanese Americans, but as just plain old Americans."[9] Mineta's support on redress was not without risk since the demographics of his district did not guarantee future reelection. Moreover, Representative Matsui had just been elected to Congress and was the most vulnerable of the four.

The idea for a commission was essentially a "hedged bet" for the legislators. If the commission was created and found that a wrong had occurred and redress payments were in order, the pursuit of redress would be strengthened. If the commission idea was voted down by Congress or if its findings were not favorable to redress, the Nikkei legislators could not be accused of weakly supporting the redress effort.

The idea of a commission generated significant controversy in 1979. Many redress advocates felt that a favorable recommendation on behalf of Japanese Americans was a critical step toward obtaining redress. Without the presidential commission, monetary redress legislation might be seen as special-interest legislation and result in a political backlash against the Nikkei community.

Opponents of the commission argued that commission hearings would be risky because of the potential for unfavorable recommendations. The hearings would also delay the process, while many of the older Issei died. Opening old wounds would be necessary because Issei and Nisei would be called upon to give painful testimony about their personal experiences in the camps. Some opponents of the commission route preferred an immediate all-out effort to obtain redress and felt that if they failed, their conscience would at least be clear.

The JACL NCR met in San Francisco on March 3–4, 1979, to make a recommendation on which redress strategy to follow. Along with the commission approach, direct payment legislation and the Seattle Plan were considered. The committee membership included Ron Mamiya, William Marutani, Henry Miyatake, Ray Okamura, Phil Shigekuni, John Tateishi, and Min Yasui. Mamiya and Miyatake, both of whom were from the Seattle JACL, were not expected to support a commission approach. The positions of the other members were less certain.

Present at this meeting were several other JACL members, who were not eligible to vote: Frank Abe, Ron Ikejiri, Debra Nakatomi, Patrick Okura, Kaz Oshiki, and Clifford Uyeda. Oshiki, the administrative assistant for Representative Robert Kastenmeier (Democrat from Wisconsin), recommended that the commission's mission be fact-finding in nature. He argued that the commission should not operate on the premise that wrongs had been done but should concentrate on the historical facts. Oshiki indicated that both he and Mike Masaoka were convinced that such a commission would alleviate Representative Mineta's apprehensions and present an opportunity for Senator Hayakawa to support this more neutral fact-finding approach.[10] Because he was a Washington, D.C., insider, Oshiki was directly questioned by Yasui about what course to pursue. Oshiki, who supported the commission route, maintained that "the less you ask for the easier it is to get it approved. . . . If you were to ask for twenty-five thousand dollars to be paid to each individual person you would lose the Japanese American members of Congress." Oshiki also described the Seattle IRS plan as being an "unrealistic plan that will go nowhere."[11]

After a morning and afternoon of discussion Yasui declared, "The committee's going to have to bite the bullet right here." He went on to summarize the quandary the committee was facing by humorously remarking, "We've got several bad alternatives, which one is the least one to pick. . . . We are going to have to decide or we could talk forever." A few moments later Yasui moved that the JACL NCR support the idea of proposing a commission. The members of the committee took a roll-call vote in alphabetical order. Tateishi asked members to make short statements explaining their vote, because he believed that the action of the committee would be a historic decision.

Mamiya voted first and stated he was "adamantly opposed" on the grounds that there had not been an adequate discussion of alternative options and that a commission was not within the mandate of the JACL National Convention. Marutani voted second and was in favor of the commission approach. He argued that while he wanted to proceed with a plan that would make the "membership happy," to pursue a direct appropriations bill would be "disastrous." Marutani stated that he saw no other alternatives and that the commission approach might help garner Senator Inouye's support. As anticipated, Miyatake voted against the commission approach because it did not fulfill the resolution passed at the JACL National Convention. Okamura voted for the commission "with reluctance." He stated his opposition to the commission "in principle," but he agreed to support the commission approach "due to the political realities." Shigekuni also voted for the commission approach. Shigekuni commented that the commission approach would be the best way to educate the American public about the exclusion and incarceration. He also argued that it was important not to go against the advice of the Nikkei congressmen. The final vote was cast by Yasui. He "reluctantly" voted for the commission and stated his "firm conviction" that the commission approach did not violate the mandate of the JACL National Convention.[12]

The final JACL NCR recommendation for a commission, on a 4 to 2 vote, was submitted to the national JACL board. The plan included two steps. The first was to advocate for a federal commission to study the exclusion and incarceration. The second was to use the findings of the commission as the foundation from which to draft a redress bill.

Some members of the Japanese American community reacted angrily to this plan. Tateishi reported, "I started getting threats from Japanese Americans . . . they said that we were backsliding and that we'd really sold everyone out . . . better to go directly after monetary compensation on an honest fight and lose it."[13]

The national JACL board approved the committee recommendation by a 13 to 1 vote (two members abstained) on June 2, 1979. Given the sensitivity of the issue, the JACL conducted a survey of its chapters. Of the 107 JACL chapters, 57 voted for the commission route, 10 voted against a commission, 3 abstained, and 37 did not report.[14]

Clifford Uyeda supported the commission approach, but he recalled the difficulty of the decision: "We decided . . . to push forward . . . to educate the American public . . . but that meant delaying redress for another 2 or 3 years. We also knew that the Issei were dying off . . . it was a very hard decision to make."[15]

New Advocates for Redress

National Council for Japanese American Redress

In response to the JACL's decision to pursue the commission, members of the Seattle Nikkei community founded the National Council for Japanese American Redress (NCJAR) in May 1979. Initially, the members of the NCJAR came primarily from Seattle and Chicago, and the NCJAR board included a number of members of the JACL. William Hohri, a Nisei who had been incarcerated at Manzanar, was chosen as chairperson. Hohri had been a member of the JACL and was active in the National Liberation Caucus, which was involved in civil rights issues. Hohri and the NCJAR were vocal in their opposition to the JACL strategy. Hohri felt strongly that Japanese Americans should take their case directly to Congress, and the NCJAR eventually sought redress through a class action suit. Their presence presented an alternative to the JACL approach to redress.

National Coalition for Redress/Reparations

The JACL's decision to pursue the formation of a commission also resulted in the creation of a grass-roots group in the redress movement. In Los Angeles during the late 1960s and throughout the 1970s Japanese American community activists addressed concerns that the Japanese American urban center of Los Angeles (Little Tokyo or "J-Town") was being exploited and demolished by corporate interests. Such organizations as the Japanese American Community Services Asian Involvement, the Little Tokyo Anti-Eviction Task Force, and the Little Tokyo Peoples Rights Organization (LTPRO) promoted low-income housing and tenants' rights.

By 1979 LTPRO began to address redress but considered it a relatively "low priority."[16] The JACL's decision to pursue the commission route, however, led the LTPRO to focus on redress. In the spring of 1979 the Los Angeles

Community Coalition on Redress/Reparations (LACCRR) was formed to increase grass-roots involvement with redress. LACCRR members, such as Alan Nishio, questioned the JACL's commitment to redress: "When the resolution was passed, they (the JACL) just thought that that would be it. . . . If it was left up to the JACL, it would have died because they didn't have any plans to do anything with that resolution."[17]

In 1980 the LACCRR pulled together a network of related groups, including the Japanese Community Progressive Alliance of San Francisco, the Nihonmachi Outreach Committee of San Jose, Asian Pacific Student Unions, and the Concerned Japanese Americans of New York. On July 12, 1980, this network of grass-roots groups and activists became the National Coalition of Redress/Reparations (NCRR). The NCRR focused on educating and uniting the Japanese American and Asian American communities. This emphasis linked the NCRR with the civil rights struggles of other ethnic minorities in the United States.

A leading voice of the NCRR was Bert Nakano. When Nakano was a fourteen-year-old in Hawai'i, his father was identified as a Japanese community leader. He and his family were sent to Jerome, Arkansas, and later to Tule Lake. After the war the Nakanos and other former camp inmates went home to Hawai'i on the same ship as the returning Japanese American soldiers, who received a hero's welcome. The former camp inmates, however, were kept in the ship's hold so that they would not dampen the festivities.[18] Nearly thirty-five years after the war Nakano and his wife, Lillian Nakano, were convinced by their son, Erich, to become active in the redress movement. Because of his commitment and willingness to speak his mind, Nakano quickly became the national spokesperson for the organization.

The NCRR identified five principles of unity, which provided direction for the organization: (1) monetary compensation to individuals incarcerated or their heirs; (2) restitution to the Japanese American community (the exact form to be determined by the needs of each community); (3) the overturning of the legal basis that justified the evacuation and the camps; (4) support for others suffering from unjust actions taken by the U.S. government; and (5) education of the American public so that future generations might learn from the mistakes of the past and not allow them to happen again.[19]

The NCRR provided a grass-roots approach that reached Japanese Americans who were either disillusioned by or uninvolved in the actions of the JACL. The NCRR held open community meetings, sponsored educational workshops, promoted community rallies (including demonstrations and candlelight marches), and organized community lobbying efforts. The NCRR began to function as the expressive voice of the redress movement.[20]

The NCRR was a volunteer organization, and although it engaged in fundraising activities, it operated on a minimal budget and depended on community members' time and energy. Lillian Nakano stressed that the NCRR helped build the redress movement with an "underlying faith in the people's desire to fight against the odds, to fight for justice . . . and the people came through."[21] Despite their disappointment with the JACL, the NCRR supported the creation and implementation of the commission.

Unanticipated Partners in Redress: The Aleuts

As most redress supporters turned their attention to obtaining a commission, they found themselves paired with unanticipated partners: the Aleutian and Pribilof Islanders. Until the commission hearings in the early 1980s the situation of the Aleuts was largely an untold story.[22] The similarities in the two experiences prompted Senator Ted Stevens (Republican from Alaska) to urge including an investigation of the U.S. government's treatment of the Aleut people as part of the presidential commission's charge.

Coupling the Aleut experience with the Japanese American experience expanded the focus of the redress movement. It was argued that in the case of the Aleuts the federal government had not taken appropriate measures to ensure they were safely evacuated and had adequate living conditions in the relocation camps.

By joining forces with the Aleuts, the redress movement gained the backing of Senator Ted Stevens, the ranking minority member of the Governmental Affairs Subcommittee on Federal Services, Post Office, and Civil Service, which had jurisdiction over redress legislation. Alaska's other senator, Frank H. Murkowski, and its representative, Don Young, both Republicans, were also supportive. With the inclusion of the Aleuts, opponents were less able to argue that redress was special-interest legislation that would benefit only Japanese Americans.

The Passage of the Commission Bill

Two bills were introduced in the Ninety-sixth Congress, one in the Senate and one in the House, which would establish a presidential commission. Senate Bill 1647, the Commission on Wartime Relocation and Internment of Civilians (CWRIC) Act, was introduced on August 2, 1979, by a bipartisan group of senators, led by Senators Inouye and Matsunaga.[23] An amendment for the inclusion of the Aleuts and commission hearings in Anchorage, Unalaska, and St. Paul was eventually added to the bill.[24]

Senator Hayakawa was one of the original cosponsors of the commission bill since he was in favor of a study to clarify the facts of the incarceration period. Although his opposition to monetary redress was well known, the lack of trust the other Nikkei senators had in him was less recognized. According to Clifford Uyeda, Senator Inouye suggested the two of them meet with Senators Matsunaga and Hayakawa. Inouye felt that Hayakawa might be apprehensive about meeting alone with the two Democratic Nikkei senators. Uyeda recalled:

> Sen. Inouye said to make it easier for [Hayakawa] to accept our invitation . . . let's meet in Hayakawa's office . . . but under only one condition. No one is to know that the meeting is taking place. So I called up Hayakawa's office and they made the arrangements according to that one stipulation. . . . On the 1st of August, 1979, we all filed into the room. Not more than 2 or 3 minutes after we were there the front door of his office opens and there were three television cameras . . . and I remember that Dan Inouye's face just dropped.

In front of the cameras, Uyeda and the senators talked about everything except redress. Uyeda stated that upon leaving, "I asked the reporter who told you [about the meeting]. He said that Hayakawa's office called them."[25]

Senators Inouye and Matsunaga were concerned that if Senator Hayakawa opposed the bill, he would influence other legislators to do likewise. In private conversations Senator Inouye told Uyeda that it was important to recruit Hayakawa's support or neutralize him. Bringing him on board as a cosponsor was a way to do so.

The House companion bill, H.R. 5499, was introduced on September 28, 1979, by 9 Democrats and an additional 105 cosponsors.[26] The House version, unlike that in the Senate, did not include the Aleuts. Another difference was that the House bill was not introduced by Japanese American legislators. Representative Mineta realized that if he authored the commission bill, it could be perceived as being self-serving since he had been incarcerated. As he considered who would be the best author for the bill, Representative Mineta recalled a conversation he had had with Majority Leader Jim Wright (Democrat from Texas): "When I had first got to Congress, Congressman Jim Wright had told me that he had come back on leave from the South Pacific in 1944 and he said to me, 'You know I picked up the newspaper, and I saw this thing in the paper about the Supreme Court confirming that [the] Yasui, Korematsu and Hirabayashi [decisions] were okay. And I thought to myself, I'm not fighting over there for this. This is a total injustice.' "[27]

Representative Mineta and his legislative director, Glenn Roberts, met with Majority Leader Wright and reminded him of the conversation that they had had in the mid-1970s. Wright readily agreed to be the lead sponsor.[28] His support of the bill was clearly based on principle since Texas had few Japanese American voters. By the time the bill was introduced, it had 114 cosponsors.

Despite the support the commission bill was gaining, the Seattle chapter of the JACL declared that the JACL NCR had sold out the community and that the Nikkei members of Congress had taken the politically cautious route.

Moreover, a number of Japanese Americans in the community found it insulting that the proposed commission would call on them to prove that their rights had been violated and that they had been wronged.

The Seattle chapter wanted to pursue legislative redress immediately and get its bill to the House as quickly as possible. Members of the chapter approached Representative Michael E. Lowry, a newly elected Democrat from Seattle. Representative Lowry, who had a Sansei legislative aide, Ruthann Kurose, readily agreed to introduce a redress bill that asked for direct monetary compensation. Lowry grew up in a farming community in eastern Washington and was convinced that the incarceration was wrong. He stated, "I recall at my earliest age, my parents talking about what a terrible thing the internment was . . . when [the request to introduce the bill] was raised, it was frankly the most natural thing for me to say, 'Of course, I'll do it,' because it seemed so much the right thing to do."[29] Along with the Seattle JACL chapter, the NCJAR also supported the Lowry bill and continued to oppose the commission bill.

Representative Lowry introduced his bill (H.R. 5977), known as the Japanese American Human Rights Violation Redress Act, in the Ninety-sixth Congress on November 28, 1979.[30] H.R. 5977, the first monetary redress bill, called for a formal apology to each inmate and compensation of $15,000 plus $15 for each day spent in camp. It eventually died in the House Judiciary Subcommittee on Administrative Law and Governmental Relations. The bill received no support from the Japanese American legislators. Moreover, the timing of the bill was poor, since it was introduced several months after the better-orchestrated commission bill.

Representative Matsui later said that Representative Lowry was at a disadvantage when he introduced H.R. 5977.[31] Representative Lowry was a freshman member of Congress, did not serve on the committee that would hear the bill, and had not built up a track record in the House. These factors lessened the perceived credibility of the bill. Representatives Mineta and Matsui realized that the Lowry bill, while a sincere attempt to address the problem, had little chance of passing. Representative Matsui described the situation at the time: "My greatest fear all along was that we might be misleading the Japanese American community. . . . And I felt that we couldn't let these people down. I would go home and my mother would ask me is this really going to happen, and I needed to keep telling her, 'Well Mom, it's still a long ways off.' . . . It would have been such a disservice to mislead them. . . . We could have just cosponsored Lowry's bill and then let it die. But we were more honest than that."[32]

The commission bill was the choice of the Nikkei legislators. Redress advocates from the community focused their lobbying for the commission bill on the House side. Tateishi recalled that the JACL NCR did not lobby any of the U.S. senators because Senator Inouye told him that he would handle the Senate.[33]

Senate hearings for S.R. 1647 were held on March 18, 1980, by the Senate Committee on Governmental Affairs.[34] Nearly all of the testimony was supportive of the commission. Representatives from various Asian American community groups, Clarence M. Mitchell of the Leadership Conference on Civil Rights, and Representatives Wright, Mineta, and Matsui testified in favor of the commission. In his testimony Roger Daniels framed the establishment of a commission as meeting the needs not only of Japanese Americans but of all Americans. He quoted Morton Grodzins: "Japanese Americans were the immediate victims of the evacuation . . . [its] larger consequences are carried by the American people as a whole. Their legacy is a lasting one of precedent and constitutional sanctity for a policy of mass incarceration under military auspices. This is the most important result of the process by which the evacuation decision was made. That decision betrayed all Americans."[35] Mike Masaoka also testified that the commission was to benefit more than just the Japanese American community: "I have faith in America and this is why I ask this Congress and this commission to look into the wrongs inflicted upon us, to determine what the best remedy ought to be, not just in interest of the evacuees, but in the national interest of the United States."[36]

The voice of the Japanese American community was not unanimous at these hearings, however. William Hohri, speaking for the NCJAR, presented the analogy of Germany's creating a commission to investigate whether wrongs had been committed against Jews before providing redress.[37] Hohri voiced the only opposition to establishing a commission: "The people are not asking for a study commission. We know it was wrong. We do not need Congress . . . to undertake a study to determine whether a wrong was committed. . . . Dismiss this sorry excuse for justice. Let us, instead, resolve to redress the victims and repair the Constitution."[38] Despite Hohri's argument S.R. 1647 was passed out of committee and onto the floor of the Senate. On May 22, 1980, the Senate passed S.R. 1647 by voice vote.

The House Judiciary Subcommittee on Administrative Law and Governmental Relations heard testimony on three related bills (the commission bills, S.R. 1647 and H.R. 5499, and the Lowry bill, H.R. 5977) on June 2, 1980.[39] The testimony at these hearings was in support of a commission. Mike Masaoka presented testimony regarding the Nisei Lobby's opposition to H.R. 5977 (the Lowry bill) and support for the establishment of a commission. Through the bipartisan efforts of Representatives George Danielson (Democrat from California), the chair of the subcommittee, and Robert McClory (Republican from Illinois), the ranking minority member of the subcommittee, H.R. 5499, the House commission bill, emerged from this "markup" session.[40] This bill was amended to incorporate the Senate provision to investigate the Aleuts' wartime experiences. Similar bipartisan support by the Judiciary Committee chair, Peter W. Rodino (Democrat from New Jersey), and the ranking minority member, Carlos J. Moorhead (Republican from California), moved the bill out of committee and onto the House floor.

H.R. 5499 was debated by the full House on July 21, 1980. During the debate Majority Leader Wright recalled his personal commitment to this legislation:

> With still remembered pain, I recall reading from the Southwest Reporter in 1944 the digest of the Supreme Court's ruling in this case. I had just returned from a tour of military duty in the Pacific where I had participated in combat missions against the armed forces of Japan. But I could not agree with that ruling. Ingloriously and to our everlasting shame, the Court upheld as constitutional the act of our Government in rounding up the Japanese-American citizens, almost as though they were cattle, and herding them into corrals. . . . I swore then that whenever I had a chance to do so, I would speak out against it. For it was an unconstitutional and unconscionable undertaking, totally inconsistent with our most fundamental precepts. It deserves to be condemned today, just as it deserved to be condemned even then.[41]

Representatives Mineta and Matsui told of their personal involvement with the incarceration, and several other Democratic and Republican representatives spoke in favor of the bill. Representative McClory told the House membership of his personal experience with the incarceration; his family had taken into its home a young Japanese American named Tyler Tanaka. Arguing in favor of the bill, Representative McClory pointed out that "the consideration of this legislation recalls events in American history that do not inspire pride. During World War II, some 120,000 Japanese-Americans and other persons of Japanese ancestry suffered what can only be characterized as an egregious denial of their basic civil rights."[42]

The only representative to speak in opposition was Representative Robert E. Bauman (Republican from Maryland). While conceding the injustice of the incarceration, Representative Bauman cited the inappropriateness of creating a federal commission "to go back and look at history with the only apparent purpose . . . of allowing Americans to know what might have happened, the true facts, so that it might not happen again." He also argued that the Evacuation Claims Act of 1948 was the proper vehicle to address the incarceration. Representative Bauman concluded his argument by stating that "these commissions and the end toward which they proceed inexorably . . . are improper. They are not the proper course to follow. It certainly does nothing to wipe out the wrong that was done. It could do a great deal to set a precedent that will do wrong in the future."[43] Despite Representative Bauman's opposition, H.R. 5499 had bipartisan support and passed by a vote of 279 to 109.[44]

With the passage of the commission bills in the House and Senate, all that remained was to obtain President Jimmy Carter's signature. In a talk with

John Tateishi, Senator Inouye reported that President Carter, more than any other president, "really felt a responsibility to rectify what a fellow Democrat had done."[45] On July 31, 1980, the Commission on Wartime Relocation and Internment of Civilians Act (Public Law 96-317) was signed into law by President Carter, who acknowledged the unjust treatment of Japanese Americans during World War II: "I don't believe anyone would doubt that injustices were done. . . . we want to make sure that [the commission's] recommendations will prevent any recurrence of this abuse of the basic human rights of American citizens and also resident aliens, who enjoy the privileges of the protection not only of American law but of American principles and ideals."[46]

Public Law 96-317 created the CWRIC and directed it to pursue three goals:

1. To review the facts and circumstances surrounding Executive Order Numbered 9066 . . . and the impact of such Executive Order on American citizens and permanent resident aliens;
2. To review directives of United States military forces requiring the relocation and, in some cases, detention in internment camps of American citizens, including Aleut civilians, and permanent resident aliens of the Aleutian and Pribilof Islands; and
3. To recommend appropriate remedies.[47]

With the signing of the commission bill, the excitement in the community grew. On November 15 and 16, 1980, approximately 350 Japanese Americans gathered at a conference sponsored by the NCRR at California State University, Los Angeles, to develop a strategy for the coming redress campaign. Members of the JACL, NCJAR, and NCRR presented their views and discussed the various approaches. Although the three groups had deep-rooted differences, they formed a tentative alliance.[48]

In November of 1980 Ronald W. Reagan, the former governor of California, defeated President Carter in the presidential election. A large number of Republican representatives and senators were also elected. The Republicans, for the first time in twenty years, held a majority of the seats in the Senate (53–47). The general public appeared to be sending a conservative message, which was not favorable for the redress movement.

Creating the Commission

Members of the Japanese American community and the JACL advocated that the majority of the commissioners be Japanese American. Senator Inouye disagreed and insisted on having just one Japanese American on the commission. Senator Inouye understood that this commission "would have to sell the Congress on the idea" of redress and that the message would be best heard if it came from non-Japanese Americans.[49]

Initially, seven individuals were appointed to the commission. President Carter selected three commissioners, while the Speaker of the House and the President Pro Tempore of the Senate appointed two each. Carter appointed Dr. Arthur S. Flemming, chairman of the U.S. Commission on Civil Rights and Secretary of Health, Education, and Welfare under President Eisenhower; Joan Z. Bernstein, former general counsel of the Department of Health and Human Services; and Judge William Marutani, the only Japanese American to sit on the commission.[50] The House appointed Arthur J. Goldberg, former ambassador to the United Nations and former U.S. Supreme Court justice; and Representative Daniel Lungren, a Republican from Long Beach, California.[51] Representative Lungren was the only commissioner who was a current member of Congress and had asked to be appointed to the commission. Those appointed by the Senate were Edward W. Brooke, an African American Republican and former U.S. senator from Massachusetts, and Hugh B. Mitchell, a former U.S. Democratic senator and representative from Seattle, Washington.[52] Bernstein was selected as chair and Lungren as vice-chair.

On February 10, 1981, President Reagan signed Public Law 97-3, which expanded the commission to nine members. This law allowed the Speaker of the House and the President Pro Tempore of the Senate to select one additional commissioner each. The Reverend Robert F. Drinan, a Jesuit priest, president of Americans for Democratic Action, and a former Democratic congressman from Massachusetts, was selected by the House. The Senate chose Father Ishmael Vincent Gromoff, an Aleutian Russian Orthodox priest, to sit on the commission.[53]

Commissioner Marutani reflected on his appointment to the commission: "I thought when they asked me to go on the commission that you have to be a fool to go on it. The Japanese American community here in the United States is going to jump on you whether you win, lose, or draw. . . . Perversely, it was precisely for that very reason I took on the challenge."[54] The commission had a number of staff members, consultants, and volunteers.[55] The first executive director was Paul Bannai, a retired California state assemblyman. Eventually, Bannai resigned, and Angus Macbeth, a partner in the Washington, D.C., law firm of Bergson, Borkland, Margolis and Adler and a former deputy assistant attorney general in the Department of Justice, was hired as special counsel to the commission.

While the work of the commission was to be very public, much of the work supporting the commission's eventual findings and recommendations was done behind the scenes by such dedicated researchers as Aiko Herzig-Yoshinaga and Jack Herzig. Despite having no formal training as a researcher or archivist, Herzig-Yoshinaga, a former community activist from New York, joined the CWRIC staff as a researcher several months after the commission started its work. Herzig-Yoshinaga and her husband, John (Jack) A. Herzig, former army counterintelligence officer and combat paratrooper, had already been conducting their own personal research in the National Archives and provided the commission with 9,000 pages of documents, which helped form the basic information used in the CWRIC findings. Working for the commission allowed Herzig-Yoshinaga to have access to documents that she could not have had as a private citizen. She could make requests from government agencies to provide their records (e.g., the WRA, the War Department, the State Department, and the Western Defense Command). With the exception of the FBI records these records were not edited or blacked out.[56]

Preparing the Community

With the commission bill signed into law, it was necessary to plan for the commission hearings. Members of the Japanese American community would need to testify. While some looked forward to this opportunity, others felt it distasteful. Japanese Americans were to be asked to retell and relive the pain, anger, and humiliation that they had been trying to forget. Many of these individuals, some of whom did not speak English, were uncomfortable speaking in front of small groups, let alone the U.S. government.

Tateishi remembered, "I could see the reluctance was really housed in a sense of fear of dealing with the past and dealing with the pain. . . . Over and over again I heard Nisei say to me, 'We can't do it. Don't force us.' It was almost a pleading, but there was anger behind it."[57]

In February of 1981 Tateishi resigned as chairman of the JACL NCR and shortly thereafter assumed the role of staff coordinator and eventually director of the committee. Jim Tsujimura, the JACL national president (1981–82), appointed Min Yasui the new chair of the JACL NCR. The change in chairs also resulted in a change in the membership of the national committee.[58]

The national JACL and its chapters, the JACL NCR, the Washington Coalition on Redress,[59] and the NCRR and its affiliates all helped in the preparations for the hearings. Tension existed among the different community groups at the national level and between some of the local JACL chapters and the national JACL. The national JACL did not openly welcome the participation of the NCRR in the hearings, partly because of NCRR's more "radical" involvement with other causes. The relationship between the NCRR and local JACL chapters, however, was often cooperative and productive. Community members, especially in California, supported both groups.

The JACL and the NCRR worked at preparing individuals to testify. In mock hearings they advised people on how to present their testimony effectively, conveying their true emotions and maintaining eye contact with the commissioners instead of merely reading prepared statements. Preparing witnesses was not an easy task. Ron Wakabayashi, executive director of the national JACL (1981–88), remembered feeling overwhelmed by the emotional reactions of the participants in the mock hearings:

We worked with JACL chapter presidents . . . for about three months getting them ready. I asked some Superior Court judges, members of the board of supervisors in San Francisco, people who were authority figures to sit in and play the commission, so that you got a real sense of authority figures sitting there.

The first guy who practiced his testimony couldn't finish. He broke down and started crying. He was a chapter president and somewhat used to talking in public. The second guy couldn't finish, the third, the fourth, nobody could finish . . . none of the fifteen people could finish. I got scared. I had never seen anything like that. We weren't sure what we were stepping into.[60]

Once the commission was established, the NCRR lobbied the commission to provide hearings in the evening, community sessions, additional hearing sites, transportation services, simultaneous Japanese translations, and adequate overflow space for those who wished to attend. It was particularly successful in obtaining these accommodations in California. The NCRR's two basic goals were to support the passage of the redress bill and to facilitate the healing process within the community. The NCRR's active work with the commission hearings and its commitment to $25,000 monetary redress payments elevated its status as an organization representing the Japanese American community's pursuit of redress.

During this preparation period the Japanese American community was advised to temper its expectations. At a JACL installation dinner in Berkeley in March of 1981 Representative Matsui urged Japanese Americans not to have unrealistic expectations about the commission. He stressed that the Ninety-seventh Congress, elected with Ronald Reagan in 1980, was likely to be the most conservative Congress in recent years and unlikely to support monetary redress.[61]

The Commission Hearings

From July to December 1981 the CWRIC held eleven hearings (twenty days of testimony) in ten cities throughout the United States: Washington, D.C.; Los Angeles and San Francisco; Seattle; Anchorage, Unalaska, and St. Paul, Alaska; Chicago; New York; and Boston.[62] More than 750 witnesses testified before packed audiences. At each hearing the auditoriums and halls were filled with hundreds of people. At the Los Angeles hearings additional rooms were needed to handle the overflow of audience members.[63]

Mitchell and Marutani were the only commissioners who attended every hearing. As Marutani explained, "I was [at every commission hearing], I had to be . . . I had an obligation. If you are a Nikkei and you're dealing with Nikkei problems [you had to be there]."[64]

The hearings were covered by the local news media, Japanese press, and Japanese American publications. Local news stations and the national networks also aired interviews with some who testified at the hearings. This media coverage generated publicity and helped educate the general American public about the facts of the incarceration of Japanese Americans during World War II.

The Legislators

The first hearings were held in Washington, D.C., on July 14 and 16, 1981. Commission chair Bernstein opened the hearings by reviewing the purpose of the commission and explained that the witnesses before the CWRIC did not testify under oath.[65] Following Bernstein's opening statements, Representative Lungren, the vice-chair, warned redress advocates that they should not set their sights on monetary compensation. He suggested that the cost of such compensation would be billions of dollars, that the Japanese American community had not reached consensus over the issue, and that Congress did not create the commission with the intention of automatically recommending monetary restitution.[66]

The four Democratic Nikkei legislators who pushed for the creation of the commission were restrained in their support of monetary redress at the first hearing (the remaining Nikkei legislator, Senator Hayakawa, eventually opposed monetary redress at the Los Angeles hearings). Senator Inouye's statement did not advocate monetary redress and even suggested that such a measure would likely be defeated in Congress: "If nothing else results from this inquiry other than a reasoned, thorough and accurate record of what took place and why it took place, you will have done your job well. It may come to pass that a budget-conscious Congress will find itself unable to provide any significant form of monetary redress or reparations. . . . Make your report one that will awaken this experience enough to haunt the conscience of this nation, haunt it so that we will never forget that we are capable of such an act."[67]

Senator Matsunaga stressed that while Japanese American victims of the incarceration could never be fully compensated, "a formal recognition of the wrong committed against the internees, and an offer of token compensation to every former internee . . . would once again prove that this great nation of ours is so strong and so steeped in righteousness that it is unafraid to admit its mistakes of the past."[68] Representatives Mineta and Matsui did not appear at the hearings but issued a joint statement that was read by Commissioner Bernstein. Their statement did not mention redress but urged a thorough review of the wartime experience of Japanese Americans.[69]

The Community Groups Leaders

The representatives of the three main Japanese American organizations advocating redress (the NCRR, JACL, and NCJAR) presented forceful testimony in favor of redress at the hearings. Although the NCJAR was not in favor of the commission hearings, it was supportive of redress.[70] William Hohri announced, "We want reparations for the deprivation of our civil and constitutional rights; for wrongful evacuation, detention, and imprisonment and the suspension of due process; for our loss of income, property, and education; for the degradation of internment and evacuation and for the psychological, social, and cultural damage inflicted by our government. . . . We believe that the further study of this matter would serve only to delay justice long overdue. . . . We have been exploited enough."[71]

The national spokesperson for the NCRR, Bert Nakano, demanded a minimum of $25,000 for each Japanese American who was excluded or incarcerated, which would be at least $3 billion in monetary compensation. Nakano declared, "As the victims, we indict the U.S. Government for violations of human and constitutional rights, for dispersing our Japanese American communities, for destroying countless lives and homes, and for contributing to economic exploitation, greed and racism."[72]

Min Yasui, chairman of the JACL NCR, stressed that while monetary payments were needed, they could not make up for what Japanese Americans endured: "Who is going to give me back nine months of solitary confinement? . . . There is no way that a dollar amount will ever satisfy. But if it is a significant amount . . . at least that will be a valid indication whereby this country makes some degree of restitution."[73]

The Architects of the Incarceration

Roger Daniels presented documentation to the commission that six figures who played a prominent role in the exclusion, removal, and incarceration of Japanese Americans during World War II eventually acknowledged that they had been wrong. Included was a statement by Chief Justice Earl Warren: "I have since deeply regretted the removal order and my own testimony advocating it, because it was not in keeping with our American concept of freedom and the rights of citizens."[74] A personal letter by Milton S. Eisenhower, the first director of the War Relocation Authority, written not long after the start of the relocation of Japanese Americans stated, "I feel most deeply that when the war is over and we consider calmly this unprecented [sic] migration of 120,000 people, we as Americans are going to regret the avoidable injustices that may have been done."[75] In memoirs and statements Henry L. Stimson, Francis Biddle, Justice William O. Douglas (who had ruled on the original *Korematsu* case), and Justice Tom C. Clark all expressed regrets about their actions concerning the wartime incarceration.[76] Such acknowledgments were included in and strengthened the foundation of the findings of the commission.

There were other architects of the incarceration, however, for whom time and hindsight had not changed their perspectives. Karl R. Bendetsen and John

J. McCloy testified at the second round of hearings held in Washington, D.C., and maintained their view that the incarceration was the proper course of action. Karl R. Bendetsen, retired colonel and self-described "chief architect" of the program to exclude and incarcerate Japanese Americans during World War II,[77] provided lengthy testimony in which he adamantly defended his wartime actions.[78] He claimed that the atrocities committed by the Japanese troops in the Philippines, as well as the climate of public hostility and racism toward Japanese (Bendetsen referred to Japanese Americans as "Japanese" throughout his testimony), justified the exclusion and detention of persons of Japanese ancestry. According to Bendetsen, those in command had not been racist, nor had they used the word *Japs*. He minimized the experience of Japanese Americans in his written statement: "I did not recommend [mass exclusion and detention]. . . . We harvested *all* crops, we sold them, we deposited the money to their respective accounts. . . . [Japanese Americans] were not to be restricted so long as they did not seek to remain or seek to return to the war 'frontier' of the West Coast."[79]

John J. McCloy was an institution in American political circles. He personally had known every American president since Herbert C. Hoover (1929–33), sat on many powerful boards and councils, and served as U.S. high commissioner of occupied Germany. Because of his instrumental role in the formation of the 442d R.C.T., McCloy was also an honorary member of the 442d. McCloy characterized the camps as benign and humane, and he objected when Commissioner Marutani referred to the Japanese Americans as having been "incarcerated." Commissioner Marutani recalled the feelings that he had about McCloy. "I had no doubts whatsoever that McCloy was a racist. He may not have even been aware that he is a racist, but he's a racist."[80]

McCloy opposed monetary compensation or even an apology to Japanese Americans who were in the camps. He justified the military need for the camps and minimized the hardships. McCloy's portrayal of the experience infuriated Commissioner Marutani. Marutani recalled, "At that hearing when John J. McCloy was testifying. . . . He was sort of pooh-poohing the entire thing. I didn't want to hear that kind of stuff and let it get away."[81] Marutani asked McCloy whether he could identify any other American group whose young men went off to fight in battle while their parents were incarcerated by their own country. McCloy's response reflected his core perspective: "I don't think the Japanese population was unduly subjected, considering all the exigencies . . . they did share in the way of retribution for the attack that was made on Pearl Harbor."[82]

McCloy's use of the word *retribution* exemplified his inability to differentiate between Japanese from Japan and Japanese Americans in the United States.[83] It reflected McCloy's sentiments that the incarceration camps were a payback for the bombing of Pearl Harbor. Commissioner Marutani immediately interrupted McCloy. What followed was a dramatic moment in the day's proceedings. The room was very quiet as Commissioner Marutani called for McCloy's statement to be read back by the stenotypist. The stenotypist, caught off guard by this rare request, fumbled with the equipment and played back McCloy's own voice from an audiorecording, repeating the word *retribution*. McCloy immediately responded that he wanted to replace the word *retribution* with *consequences*. The impression, however, had already been made.

Commissioner Marutani recalled, "The cat was out of the bag as far as I was concerned. I was sitting at the very end . . . and a piece of notepaper comes down and I open it up, McCloy is still on the witness stand, and it says, 'You are harassing the witness.' I don't know who wrote that, but I would have [questioned McCloy] the same way anyway. You cannot let a man, no matter how powerful he is or how big he is, get away with stuff like that."[84]

McCloy continued to insist that the mass exclusion and incarceration of Japanese Americans was an appropriate military decision. His deeply held suspicions of the disloyalty of Japanese Americans persisted nearly forty years after the war. Even when complimenting the 442d R.C.T., McCloy testified that he "created [the 442d R.C.T.], because so many Japanese wanted to prove their loyalty. If Midway had been lost, there might have been some who would have re-pledged allegiance to the Emperor's side."[85]

Later that day during a break in the hearings, Commissioner Marutani approached John J. McCloy. Marutani recalled:

> I chatted with him a little bit . . . I said Mr. McCloy, you have to understand that when the War broke out . . . my parents told us that, "This [the United States] is your country. You must serve this country." I told him that my brother was already in the Air Corps. And you know what his response was, "On which side?"
>
> Here was a man so steeped in the poison of racism that he could not even hold a decent conversation without striking back. Now it is true, I have to admit, that I wounded him and I intended to wound him. Because he deserved to be wounded. There's no way this man should walk out of that hearing room without anybody challenging [him with] the fact that we paid a heavy price. The Nikkei paid a heavy price. We fought for this country, our country. The same country which inflicted a grievous injury upon our parents and our family members. I could not let that man walk out of there [without challenging him].[86]

Other Voices of Opposition

Not all the witnesses agreed on the facts of the exclusion and incarceration. Along with the architects of the exclusion and incarceration, other individuals testified that there was a military necessity, that camp conditions were not harsh, and that other Americans also suffered during the war. It was not surprising that the mood of the hearings was at times tense and volatile.

A leading voice of opposition was Lillian Baker, who testified at the first hearings in Washington, D.C. She represented her organization, Americans for Historical Accuracy. In her testimony Baker argued that the use of the term *concentration camps* was unjustified, that the movement of Japanese Americans into "relocation centers" was largely voluntary, and that the Supreme Court ruled that the curfew was constitutional.[87] Her testimony was repeatedly challenged and corrected by Commissioner Goldberg, a former Supreme Court justice. Baker stated, "Now surely the lawyers that are assembled here know that this Commission has no power to overturn a Supreme Court edict. Because only the Supreme Court can do that." Commissioner Goldberg immediately responded that "Congress cannot pass laws which take away fundamental rights protected by the Bill of Rights. . . . But the courts and Congress have the right to enlarge the scope of protection for people, and of course Congress has clean authority to say someone was abused . . . and . . . give them an award. Even when the Supreme Court decides that the award wasn't justified."[88]

On August 4, 1981, Commissioner Lungren had to warn the audience to refrain from jeering and booing Senator Hayakawa's testimony. The audience reacted explosively to Hayakawa, who argued that the "relocation centers" were not "concentration camps" and that Japanese Americans had experienced a good time in the camps. He stressed that for "many older Japanese . . . [the internment] turned out to be a three-year vacation from long years of unremitting work on farms, in fishing boats, and in little shops, and they used their leisure . . . to recover and to relive the glories of their traditional culture."[89] Senator Hayakawa callously stated that his "flesh crawls with shame and embarrassment" at the former inmates' demands for redress.[90] Commissioner Goldberg responded immediately to Senator Hayakawa's assertion that the camps were not "concentration camps" by affirming that the American camps were "concentration camps"[91] and that the Nazi camps were "death camps."[92]

The next day the *Los Angeles Times* ran an article entitled "Hayakawa Jeered at Hearing on Internment."[93] The following day the *Los Angeles Times* ran a political cartoon that depicted Senator Hayakawa playing a piano, with Adolf Hitler leaning up against it. The caption simply read, "Play it again, Sam."[94] Some redress supporters argued that the audience's booing Senator Hayakawa degraded the Japanese American community more than it did the senator. Frank Chin called the Los Angeles hearings a "circus of freaks" and admonished the Los Angeles audience: "They booed and jeered S. I. Hayakawa. They made Hayakawa look good. . . . No matter how they felt as individuals, the members of the audience joining in one big boo, with hate on their faces are wrong to mob Hayakawa."[95] Lillian Nakano disagreed: "Would these people have preferred a controlled and passive audience? That we should have bowed our heads when Commissioner Lundgren [sic] said that Congress is in no mood for reparations; or remained silent when Hayakawa called the camps a 3-year vacation for the issei? Should we have turned the other cheek when Lillian Baker physically assaulted a nisei testifier? Yes, the audience cheered in support and approval and angrily booed when appropriate because our very pride and dignity were on the line!"[96]

The mood of the Japanese American community was defiant. At the Los Angeles hearings several Issei, who could speak only Japanese, were prepared to testify before the commission. They had only one written copy of their testimony in English, and Commissioner Lungren requested that their testimony be summarized in English. For a moment the Issei were uncertain about the nature of the request. Bert Nakano immediately rose and stated, "These Japanese speaking individuals [have been] told to shut up most of their life, so I think it's about time that they be able to speak and no time limit [be placed] on them."[97] The crowd cheered, and the Issei were given the time to present their full testimonies in their primary language.

The Veterans and the Draft Resisters

One of the casualties of World War II was the rift between those who served in the army and those who resisted the draft. While the groups differed on how to uphold American principles, one area of agreement was the rightness of redress. Thomas Kinaga, who volunteered for the 442d while he was incarcerated at Heart Mountain, said, "I would like to state that in spite of the many different ways in which we internees responded to the evacuation this Commission should not jump to the conclusion that any of us approved of the evacuation. . . . Let me assure you that the evacuation was universally condemned by all of its victims—even those of us who volunteered for the Army, from the relocation centers."[98]

Another veteran at the New York hearings, William Kochiyama of the 442d, refuted McCloy's insinuations about the loyalty of the Nisei: "I heard John J. McCloy, the former Assistant Secretary of War, allege that if the Battle of Midway had been lost, some of us Nisei might have pledged our allegiance to the other side. McCloy's opposition tore through me like a dum-dum bullet. For the record, I bitterly resent his assumption and categorically deny that some of us would have become turncoats."[99]

Jim Kawaminami, president of the 100th/442nd Veterans Association of Southern California, had his testimony abruptly interrupted in Los Angeles. As he was testifying, Lillian Baker approached him and tried to rip his testimony out of his hands. Baker had to be forcibly removed from the proceedings by two security police, as the audience applauded and yelled, "'Sit down!'

Then, 'Out! Out! Out!' and 'Nazi!'"[100] Kawaminami remarked to Commissioner Lungren, "Now you can all see what kind of people we have to put up with."[101]

At the New York hearings Jack Tono, one of the Heart Mountain draft resisters, expressed the view of those who had resisted the draft: "All we wanted was our natural-born rights returned . . . simply the restoration of our livelihood . . . and our families leading the normal lives they once had. Then and only then will we bear arms for our country to preserve democracy."[102]

Silent No More: The Community Testifies

Having waited over four decades to have their stories heard, the Issei and Nisei who spoke in front of the commission frequently delivered impassioned testimony, oftentimes accompanied by tears and painful emotions. The silence of forty years was broken as audience members applauded, jeered and booed, and expressed their anger.

The voices of the community reminded the commissioners, as well as the general U.S. public, that redress was about more than lofty principles, historical revision, and constitutional issues. Redress was about real people who had endured real suffering. Redress was a human issue.

The testimony of Mas Fukai, a city councilman from Gardena, California, reflected the essence of the community's testimony. He stated to the panel of commissioners in Los Angeles, "You will hear today hurt, hate, fear, love and probably even tears in the testimony. . . . But most important, they will speak the truth . . . . It happened to us; it could happen to anyone."[103]

Richard Katsuda, an educator and longtime NCRR member, recalled the difficult process of convincing the Issei to participate in the hearings. Many of the Issei had never spoken publicly about the incarceration. Umeno Fujino, an eighty-year-old woman, was the first to be swayed by Katsuda. Katsuda convinced Fujino to testify by saying, "If not for yourself, *kodomo no tame ni* [for the sake of the children], for your grandchildren."[104] This appeal to the Issei's sense of obligation to their children and grandchildren convinced many to participate.

Katsuda also recounted the experience of Mas Hirata, who drove a van load of Issei from San Jose to San Francisco to testify at the commission hearings in 1981. On the way to the hearings, Katsuda stated, "There was dead silence. You could see how nervous they were."[105] For the Issei, going before the U.S. government to demand an apology was a daunting task. Nonetheless, the Issei testified at the hearing, demonstrating their courage and determination to appear before the U.S. government and demand their story be heard. By doing so, the Issei replaced their long held silence with words of anger and vindication. On the way back to San Jose the once quiet bus was filled with Issei voices laughing and singing. The healing process was occurring.

People in the concentration camps were separated from loved ones, they endured terrible conditions that produced physical and mental problems, and some died or were killed. The testimony of Kima Konatsu, incarcerated at Poston and Gila River, Arizona, provided one example: "[We] were told that my husband could not be allowed to go with us. . . . During that four years we were separated, my children and I were allowed to see him only once. . . . my husband became ill and was hospitalized. He was left alone, naked, by a nurse after having given him a sponge bath. It was a cold winter and he caught pneumonia. After two days and two nights, he passed away. Later on, the head nurse at the hospital told us that this nurse had lost her two children in the war and that she hated Japanese."[106]

Others shared their stories of outrage and personal sagas. Emi Somekawa, a nurse at Tule Lake and Minidoka camps, described the lack of adequate medical care: "The Government by its policy of imprisonment and traumatizing us by not providing adequate medical accommodations to care for all the needs of the patients brought death to many patients. . . . no thought or care was provided for the handicapped and the mentally retarded patient. . . . No allowances were made in the latrines, laundry room, mess hall or any place where a handicapped person could go."[107]

Amy Iwasaki Mass, a clinical social worker who had been incarcerated at Heart Mountain as a child, in a tearful testimony tried to make sense out of the experience:

> I also loved America. I get goose bumps when I sing the Star Spangled Banner. I believed what our teachers taught regarding what a great country America is. . . . We were told that we were being put away for our own safety. . . . that this was a patriotic sacrifice. . . . The pain, trauma, and stress of the incarceration experience was so overwhelming we used the psychological defense mechanism of repression, denial, and rationalization to keep us from facing the truth. The truth was that the government we trusted, the country we loved, the nation to which we had pledged loyalty had betrayed us, had turned against us.[108]

Dr. James Tsujimura, president of the JACL, dispelled the notion that the armed sentries were to protect the inmates and that the inmates were free to leave any time they wished. He presented a list of eight inmates and the circumstances surrounding their being shot and killed by armed sentries and guards at six different camps.[109]

The camp experience victimized members of the Japanese American community. Individuals testified that the victimization continued in the hearings. At the Chicago hearings the Reverend Jitsuo Morikawa decried the fact that "witnesses are allowed five minutes to tell their story of months and years of internment, of confinement, of deprived civil rights. Even in the course of a Commission hearing, we appear to be under orders to minimize and restrict our testimony. . . . How can we voice our pain in five minutes? . . . We have

suffered enough without the added burden of begging or demanding reparations and offering the luxury to those ultimately responsible, of simply
saying yes, or no, to our painful demands."[110] His testimony drew a round
of applause from the audience.

The testimony of non–Japanese Americans revealed that Japanese Americans were not the only ones affected. In Seattle Louise Crowley, a white
American, testified about her feelings regarding what happened to her Japanese American friends: "I felt then and I still feel a passionate sense of outrage, helplessness and betrayal. . . . Suddenly, with ten days notice, half of my
friends and their whole families were imprisoned behind barbed wire, cy-
clone-topped fences around the fairgrounds at Puyallup, bound for who
knew where. . . . I must have been a pretty naive kid; I hadn't known such
despotism was legally possible in the United States. Well, I learned, and I
haven't forgotten."[111]

The commission hearings provided a forum through which the true meaning of redress was proclaimed. Yuji Ichioka, a child of six when he was incarcerated, described what redress and reparations meant to him: "To me,
[the CWRIC hearings are] a collective catharsis. . . . we're saying we're tired
of deferring to white people, basically. We've shown too much respect, too
much deference for too long. . . . We will not *gaman* no more."[112]

At the San Francisco hearings Karen Umemoto, a Sansei, spoke about the
coming together of the community and the generational healing process: "For
Sansei here today, we feel pride and dedication to our Issei grandparents and
Nisei parents for voicing their experiences and opinions over these three days
in a step towards justice. A step that is only the beginning of a longer road
towards full equality."[113]

Commission Staff Contributions

The commissioners did not hold regular meetings and had very little interaction with the commission staff. Aiko Herzig-Yoshinaga had been told by
Paul Bannai not to talk directly with the commissioners. As a result, she was
not able to brief them personally on important facts she had uncovered in
her research that would have helped them question the witnesses.[114]

The research staff, however, provided invaluable documentation that revealed the questionable motivations behind the incarceration. While the
majority of the research involved gathering and presenting already published
or previously located documents, there was one particularly important new
discovery. Herzig-Yoshinaga conducted a painstaking search for a copy of the
original version of General DeWitt's report, *Final Report: Japanese Evacuation from the West Coast 1942.* The original version of this report reflected
the racist underpinnings and falsehoods that "justified" the exclusion and
incarceration. It failed to include findings from the Federal Bureau of Inves-

tigation and the Office of Naval Intelligence that asserted there was no evidence of espionage, fifth column activity, or the military necessity of removing persons of Japanese ancestry from the West Coast.[115] DeWitt originally prepared ten bound copies of this report.

McCloy was not pleased with the original report and directed the incorporation of fifty-five changes, which toned down the racist nature of the arguments.[116] The undocumented falsehoods of Japanese American espionage remained in the document, however, while the governmental department reports denying military necessity continued to be intentionally omitted. McCloy ordered the existing ten copies of the original DeWitt report to be destroyed. All ten copies were thought to have been burned,[117] until Herzig-Yoshinaga discovered the remaining copy.

The discovery of this remaining copy was fortuitous. Herzig-Yoshinaga was sitting at an archivist's desk while waiting to meet with another National Archives staff member on an unrelated issue. She began to look through a document (which happened to be on the archivist's desk) that she thought was a copy of DeWitt's revised edition. Much to her surprise, she noticed that the document was dated April 1942, not June 1942, which was the date of the revised edition. After further analysis, she and the archivist realized that this document was substantially different from the revised version and deduced that it was a copy of the original DeWitt report. This original copy would serve as a major piece of evidence in establishing the federal government's deliberate manufacturing of the military necessity rationale.

An example of the research staff's contribution of previously published documents came in response to a request by Commissioner Brooke for any evidence that the camps were kept operating longer than necessary for political reasons. Herzig-Yoshinaga and Donna Komure, the commission's legal counsel, obtained a memo from Chief of Staff George C. Marshall to John J. McCloy dated May 13, 1944, which documented the existence of political rather than military reasons for not returning Japanese Americans to the West Coast:

> I have gone over your memorandum of May 8th concerning the return of persons of Japanese ancestry to the West Coast and the related papers. In my opinion the only valid military objection to this move is the one presented by G-1 that the return of these people to the West Coast will result in actions of violence that will react to the disadvantage of American prisoners in the hands of the Japanese. There are, of course, strong political reasons why the Japanese should not be returned to the West Coast before next November, but these do not concern the Army except to the degree that consequent reactions might cause embarrassing incidents.[118]

The "strong political reasons" referred to the upcoming presidential election in November of 1944. The closing of the camps was thought to be an unpopular decision that could only hurt President Roosevelt's reelection bid.

Press Coverage

Many of the newspapers covering the hearings provided sympathetic cover-age. After the San Francisco hearings the *San Francisco Chronicle* ran a sup-portive story that highlighted the contributions of the Japanese American veterans.[119] The national press and media were generally supportive of Japa-nese Americans. *Time Magazine* printed a sympathetic article in August of 1981, entitled "The Burden of Shame." The article stated that at the Los An-geles hearings, "the audience listened with hushed respect to stories almost too painful to remember, but too important to forget."[120]

Not all publications, however, were supportive of Japanese Americans. The *Wall Street Journal* on July 27, 1981, ran an editorial entitled "Keep Internment Interred." The editorial suggested that there was no need for a commission investigation, that the 1948 Evacuation Claims Act had "reflected a genuine effort to make amends," and the Japanese Americans had been "far safer and healthier than GIs in the jungles of New Guinea or on the beach at Iwo Jima."[121]

The commission held its last community hearing on November 23, 1981, in New York. After the close of these formal hearings the commission held two additional meetings to discuss the legal and sociopsychological impli-cations of the exclusion and incarceration. Meanwhile, the CWRIC contin-ued to prepare its official findings and recommendations.[122]

Congressman Dymally Introduces a Bill

On December 8, 1982, even before the CWRIC had released its findings, Rep-resentative Mervyn Dymally (Democrat from California) introduced two bills related to the exclusion and incarceration. The NCRR assisted Dymally in their preparation. The first bill, H.R. 7383, called for the restoration of the economic, social, and cultural well-being for those of Japanese ancestry who had been excluded and suffered at the hands of the U.S. government during World War II. The second bill, H.R. 7384, called for individual monetary repa-rations for the wrongs committed by the U.S. government against Japanese Americans and Aleut Americans and others relocated during World War II. Both bills were assigned to committee, where they died.[123]

The Dymally bills did not win support from other legislators in Congress, including the Nikkei legislators. Representative Matsui noted at the time, "It's my feeling that the Dymally bills have absolutely no chance of passage now, or in the immediate future, or maybe even forever. That is not to say that I favor or oppose it. That's just a realistic assessment of what 435 representa-tives would do at this time."[124]

The Commission's Findings and Recommendations

The commission released its unanimous findings in February 1983 in a 467-page report entitled *Personal Justice Denied*. The major finding of this report concerned the nature of the incarceration:

> The promulgation of Executive Order 9066 was not justified by military necessity. . . . The broad historical causes which shaped these decisions were race prejudice, war hysteria and a failure of political leadership. Widespread ignorance of Japanese Americans contributed to a policy conceived in haste and executed in an atmosphere of fear and anger at Japan. A grave injustice was done to American citizens and resident aliens of Japanese ancestry who, without individual review or any probative evidence against them, were excluded, removed and detained by the United States during World War II.[125]

The CWRIC documented the extensive economic and intangible losses Japanese Americans suffered. The commission estimated that the total losses of income and property incurred by Japanese Americans came to between $810 million and $2 billion in 1983 dollars.[126] The commission also recognized the "physical illnesses and injuries," "psychological pain," and "unjustified stigma" resulting from the camp experience.[127]

The CWRIC also documented many injustices the U.S. government perpetrated on the Aleuts and Pribilof Islanders. Although the CWRIC accepted the reason for the evacuation of the Aleuts, the commission could not find any justification for the treatment of the Aleuts in the camps or for the inadequate compensation they received for the material losses they incurred as a result of the evacuation.[128]

The Nikkei Democratic legislators and the general Japanese American community reacted positively to the commission's findings. Senators Inouye and Matsunaga and Representatives Mineta and Matsui released supportive statements. Representative Matsui acknowledged the wisdom in the strategy of releasing the findings first: "It's appropriate that the commission did not deal with the issue of redress (at this time), because I think the attention of the American public should be on what happened, and the individual tragedies that occurred during (the war)."[129] The JACL was equally supportive of the findings. However, in a public statement JACL leaders issued a thinly veiled challenge to the commission: "The Commission's official recognition of the basic injustices is an important first step toward rectifying one of the gravest and darkest blemishes in the constitutional history of our nation and preventing a repetition against other citizens in times of hatred and hysteria. . . . The Commission's recommendations will be a test of courage and integrity."[130]

The commission released its recommendations on June 16, 1983, four months after it released its findings. The CWRIC recommended that the United States provide redress to the former inmates because the federal government had violated the constitutional principles and laws governing the nation. The CWRIC asserted, "Nations that forget or ignore injustices are more likely to repeat them."[131] The CWRIC made five recommendations regarding the former Japanese American inmates:

1. Congress should pass a joint resolution apologizing for the injustice done, and the president should sign this resolution;
2. A presidential pardon should be given to those convicted of curfew or exclusion order violations;
3. Congress should direct executive agencies to review with liberality Japanese Americans' applications for "restitution of positions, status, or entitlements lost" during the war;[132]
4. Congress should appropriate money for an educational and humanitarian foundation that would sponsor research and public educational activities; and
5. Congress should appropriate $1.5 billion to provide $20,000 in individual compensation to every surviving evacuee and internee.[133]

The CWRIC figures were based on the estimate that 60,000 individuals were still alive and therefore eligible.[134] Unlike the findings the CWRIC recommendations were not backed by all of the members of the commission. While all agreed on the first four recommendations, Representative Dan Lungren did not accept the final recommendation of individual payments.

The CWRIC made five recommendations concerning the Aleuts and Pribilof Islanders, including a suggested $5,000 for each Aleut:

1. The establishment of a $5 million trust fund to compensate both the Aleut community and individuals for losses and injuries they suffered because of their evacuation;
2. Direct individual payments of $5,000 to those surviving Aleuts who were evacuated from the Aleutian or Pribilof Islands by the federal government during World War II;
3. The government restoration of Aleut village churches that were damaged or destroyed during World War II;
4. The removal of military debris remaining on the Aleutian Islands; and
5. A declaration by Congress that Attu Island is native land and the transfer of Attu Island to the Aleuts' Native Corporation.[135]

Commissioner Lungren also dissented from the other commissioners when he opposed the $5 million trust fund for Aleuts and the individual payments of $5,000 to each Aleut survivor. Despite his dissent the commission stated that Congress should enact its recommendations because of "compelling reasons of preserving a truthful sense of our own history and the lessons we can learn from it."[136] The CWRIC findings captured the essence of redress by stating that "though history cannot be unmade, it is well within our power to offer help, and to acknowledge error."[137]

Reaction by the Nikkei legislators to the recommendations was mixed. Senator Inouye was en route to Hawai'i when the recommendations were released and did not immediately issue a statement. Senator Matsunaga, however, not only praised the recommendations but also pledged his commitment: "I will do all within my authority and influence to move Congress into approving appropriate legislation to carry out the recommendations of the commission."[138] Representatives Mineta and Matsui also both praised the recommendations. Mineta stated his intention to work with other members "to develop a plan to implement these long overdue recommendations."[139] Matsui, however, expressed concern that the commission's recommendations might create "false and misleading expectations" among Japanese Americans and cautioned that he did not "see in the foreseeable future" the passage of any redress bill.[140]

Senator Hayakawa was clear about his reaction to the recommendations: "I do not agree with the decision for monetary redress. . . . An official national apology for the old injustice, such as is recommended by the commission, is in order, however, even at this late date. . . . the successes Japanese Americans have enjoyed in business, education, the professions and in politics have amply demonstrated the esteem in which they are held by their fellow Americans. All this is redress enough."[141]

The community groups also expressed differing perspectives. The JACL issued a statement indicating that it was "extremely pleased" with the recommendations for individual monetary compensation and the establishment of a public education fund.[142] The NCRR was not so congratulatory of the commission's work. At a press conference in Los Angeles Bert Nakano described the recommendations as "a victory for the Japanese American community" and as "a first step in a continuing struggle for a congressional bill for reparations." However, he went on to say that the membership of NCRR felt that "the commission's recommendation does not go far enough." He cited the ineligibility of (the heirs of) already deceased inmates, the absence of a means for Japanese Americans to file claims for losses in excess of the $20,000 figure, and the recommendations for pardons (which implied a crime was committed) rather than the striking of the convictions from the books.[143] William Hohri reflected the NCJAR's perspective by stating, "I don't think it has any chance of ever becoming a reality. . . . the way to tell is to watch the reaction and action, or lack thereof, of the Japanese American members of Congress."[144]

Among the most vehement denouncements of the recommendations were the comments of John J. McCloy. McCloy telephoned reporters to say that the commission ought to be investigated and that "it is utterly unconscionable and unfair to all those who suffered from the attack on Pearl Harbor that Sunday morning, none of whom were adequately compensated. . . . [it is an] effrontery to suggest that the president and Congress should apologize—just to think of it makes me stagger—apologize for the attack on Pearl Harbor."[145] McCloy, like many other Americans, still could not differentiate between the wartime acts of Japan and American's own citizens of Japanese ancestry.

Others, however, understood very well the impact of the findings and recommendations. As Mas Fukai stated, "It is not what it means so much to me, but it is what it will mean to my grandchildren. The history books will show what happened. And my grandchildren will now grow up in the mainstream of America without being stereotyped as enemies during time of war."[146]

Commissioner Marutani explained why the recommendations were released four months after the findings: "We deliberately cut [the report] in two parts. If we had issued the report in one piece, all the newspapers would focus upon the twenty thousand dollars per person rather than the injustice inflicted. So we issued the report in two parts. We had unanimity on the first part."[147]

Commissioner Marutani was a strong supporter of monetary compensation.[148] To avoid allegations of a conflict of interest, however, he formally relinquished all personal claims to monetary redress payments. He later described his perspective on the need for monetary payments: "My view had always been that in our society, an apology doesn't mean much. If you think it does, the next time you get a moving violation you go down to the traffic court and try to apologize. The only thing we understand is money, you have to pay a fine. And this government has got to pay a fine. Not to be venal about it, but so they won't forget."[149]

Roger Daniels acknowledged an arbitrary nature to the process of deciding the redress figure: "The JACL had set the top figure [$25,000]. . . . The commission needed to strike a balance between an adequate monetary amount and not appearing to be overly influenced by the community. The twenty thousand dollar figure met both criteria."[150]

The Significance of the CWRIC Hearings

By the end of the CWRIC hearings the Japanese American community had become much more focused on pursuing redress (N+). The general American public was also more sympathetic to the redress movement (N+). The legislative and judicial branches had remained quiet during this period (N).

Only the executive branch, with the election of Republican Ronald W. Reagan, was less than neutral (N-) (see table 5).

The CWRIC helped educate the general public and members of Congress about the actual experience of Japanese Americans during World War II. *Personal Justice Denied* clearly documented the injustice perpetrated on the Japanese American community. It dispelled the myth of military necessity and indicated that the exclusion and incarceration were the result of failed political leadership. While the vast majority of the American public would never read *Personal Justice Denied,* redress proponents would refer to it countless times throughout the redress struggle. The CWRIC's recommendations, particularly the individual monetary payment provision, were a slightly scaled-down version of what the JACL, the NCRR, and other supporters of redress advocated. The CWRIC findings and recommendations and the status of its members provided credibility for the redress bills eventually introduced in Congress. As many had expected, it made it easier for the Democratic Japanese American legislators to provide full support for redress.

The CWRIC's findings and recommendations became the foundation on which the subsequent redress bills were built. The commission hearings, along with the media coverage of the hearings and the commission's report, changed the nature of the debate. The issue was no longer whether a wrong had occurred but what should be done about that wrong. Redress supporters could now focus their efforts on convincing members of the Congress that money should be given for redressing those wrongs.

The commission hearings also helped solidify the community around the issue of redress and gave voice to those who had remained silent for nearly forty years about the injustices they had suffered. The hearings served to expand the base of support for the redress movement. Redress was no longer simply a strictly JACL, NCRR, or NCJAR issue. Instead, it was a Japanese American issue.

The hearings were a cathartic experience for many Japanese Americans on a personal, generational, and community level. Many who testified related stories and expressed emotions they had not previously shared. The commis-

Table 5.

Years	History		Legislative Branch		Judicial Branch	Executive Branch
	Community	U.S. Society	Senate	House		
1979–82	N+	N+	N	N	N	N-
1970–78	N+	N	N+	N+	N	N+
1945–69	N	N	N	N	N	N
Pre-WWII/Exclusion/ Incarceration	–	–	–	–	–	–

sion hearings were a dramatic theater through which America could come to know the Japanese American experience and through which Japanese Americans would come to know themselves in a new way.

This process could be seen in the testimony of Dr. Kiyoshi Sonoda, a dentist in the Poston camp. Dr. Sonoda described his attempt to care for a dehydrated infant in camp. Under routine circumstances the baby's life could have easily been saved. With no supplies in camp, however, Dr. Sonoda could do nothing. Through his tears, Dr. Sonoda described how he held the young baby and felt the last twitch of his fragile body as he died. As Ron Wakabayashi sat in the audience listening to this painful testimony, he overheard Dr. Sonoda's wife say, "I've never seen Kiyoshi cry before. Kiyoshi didn't even cry at his father's funeral. Kiyoshi doesn't cry."[151] Japanese Americans began to see new sides of themselves and the sources of their pain.

Generationally, the Sansei began to understand the Nisei. The Sansei began to put aside their view of the Nisei's cowardice and accommodation and began to appreciate and feel the struggle of their Nisei parents. The Nisei, in turn, drew strength from and were empowered by the Sansei's willingness to challenge those in authority. As moving as the testimonies were at the hearings, Japanese American families began to share even more significant testimonies around their dinner tables and living rooms. Japanese Americans began talking about their camp experiences with friends and family. As the stories were shared and validated, a collective memory emerged, and individual stories became community stories.

On the community level the hearings instilled a sense of hope and focus in the community. Prior to the commission hearings redress was not a priority in the Japanese American community because it had been a long time since the incarceration, the remaining former inmates were aging, and their energies lay elsewhere. The commission hearings helped draw a connection between redress and their own present lives. Redress was no longer about abstract racist policies and constitutional wrongs that happened a long time ago. Redress was now about the real pain and humiliation that family members (mothers and fathers, sisters and brothers, grandparents) and friends still felt. It was about the misery and suffering that Japanese Americans currently carried in their hearts and in their memories. For individuals, the community, and the different generations a great healing process had begun.

7   Other Efforts at Redress

In the early 1980s three parallel movements contributed to the overall redress movement: California redress for state employees; the judicial battle of the National Council for Japanese American Redress (NCJAR); and the *coram nobis* legal cases. The California redress effort for state employees involved legislation addressing the loss of constitutional and civil rights during World War II as a result of actions of the state of California. The NCJAR's case articulated the specific constitutional rights violated by the federal government, and it eventually was heard before the Supreme Court. The *coram nobis* cases addressed the fundamental wrong that the federal government knowingly committed during World War II. Each of these efforts brought attention and clarity to the argument for redress.

Redress for Japanese American California State Employees

In 1942, shortly after the bombing of Pearl Harbor, the state of California presented its Japanese American employees with a multipage questionnaire focusing on issues not related to their jobs (e.g., whether they could speak Japanese, their citizenship status, their membership in Japanese or Japanese American organizations). On the basis of their Japanese ancestry, three hundred and fourteen individuals were indefinitely "suspended" without pay from their jobs regardless of position, performance, or citizenship.

One of these employees was Janet Nishio Masuda, who was fired from her job at the California Department of Motor Vehicles in Sacramento on April 7, 1942. "It was my first real job," Masuda recalled, "and I was planning on taking my first vacation the second week in December [the week right after Pearl Harbor was attacked]."[1] A resolution of the state legislature inspired by E. Vayne Miller, secretary to the State Personnel Board, was the instrument of dismissal. The resolution cited possible "fifth column" activity and espionage on the part of Japanese Americans that allegedly promoted dissension, dissatisfaction, and low morale throughout the work force. Masuda did not recall any dissension or low morale. "My supervisor had tears in her eyes, and co-workers hid Sally Taketa under her desk," Masuda recalled, when the state officials came to serve dismissal papers.[2]

Between December 1941 and May 1942 Japanese American employees were dismissed from their jobs without any further paychecks or severance pay.[3] In 1946 the State Personnel Board reinstated all of the employees who could report to work within ten days of the reinstatement notice.

Assembly Bill 2710

The experience of California civil service employees during World War II was well known to Priscilla Ouchida, a Sansei whose parents were incarcerated at Tule Lake, Topaz, and Amache. Ouchida's aunt repeatedly told her about the incarceration and her personal experiences as a state civil service employee. In 1978 Ouchida, then a legislative assistant to California's Assemblyman Floyd Mori, and Eugene Itogawa embarked on a project to record the state employee story. Ouchida made use of the subpoena power she had as a staff member of the Joint Legislative Audit Committee to obtain a number of the necessary documents to create a legal foundation for a wrongful-termination suit.

In 1978 the efforts of Ouchida and Itogawa to document this injustice were independent of the JACL's pursuit of a commission. The two efforts, however, were linked in their strategies. Ouchida described the early significance of the state redress effort: "We were two separate things, but now what we had was a test case for legislation. Just like the federal legislation, we had to go back forty years and the statutes of limitations had run out."[4]

Ouchida and Itogawa put together a clearly documented case of unconstitutional governmental action. Many of the victims also provided original documentation. Numerous fired state employees had kept their original dismissal papers, which showed that the dismissal action was based on a charge of treason.

State Redress Finds an Author

In 1981, after a close recount, Patrick Johnston won the California state assembly seat from the San Joaquin district by twenty-six votes. The recount delayed his arrival to Sacramento by a month, and the freshman assemblyman scrambled to hire his legislative staff, including Ouchida.[5] As a freshman legislator, Johnston needed to develop a legislative agenda. Ouchida approached him with the idea of introducing legislation that would address this particular injustice. Johnston knew about the plight of the Japanese

Americans during World War II. His parents had differing views on the incarceration. His father, a veteran who had fought in the Pacific theater, was inclined to believe the camps were justified; his mother did not. Johnston had also participated in mock commission hearings at the request of the JACL. He immediately agreed to author the bill.

Ouchida approached John Tateishi to obtain the national JACL's support. She asserted the redress movement's need to establish a precedent at the state level first. The national JACL was initially focused on establishing the commission, but it eventually supported the bill. The NCRR and the local Sacramento JACL were very supportive. Such individuals as Henry Taketa, Shizu Yoshino Ueda, and Diane Tomoda were very active in lobbying, letter writing, and attending the hearings.

The California redress bill originally addressed all those Japanese American individuals who were identified and terminated from their state jobs solely on the basis of race. The bill initially called for monetary redress in the amount of $5,000, the minimum documented losses suffered by a state employee, to be paid over five years.

Assemblyman Johnston introduced Assembly Bill 2710 on February 19, 1982 (the fortieth anniversary of the signing of Executive Order 9066).[6] Throughout its legislative journey, Ouchida carefully chose state employees, such as Janet Nishio Masuda and Sumio Miyamoto, to testify at each hearing.[7]

The bill framed the issue as an employee wrongful-termination issue. The victims were fired not on the basis of individual performance but on the basis of their ethnicity. Ouchida recalled how the issue was presented: "We have a state employment system where if someone is wrongfully terminated, they automatically get back-pay. In some situations they get punitive damages, and normally they would get interest payments. This was the norm by 1982. Therefore, these employees should have gotten that, but they hadn't. The only thing that was different was that this was a forty-year-old case."[8]

The appropriations mechanism in the bill was removed to avoid requiring a two-thirds vote by each chamber. The per annum expenditure was drastically reduced by spreading the payments over five years. This maneuver avoided the likelihood that someone would argue the bill would be too costly for any given year.

With the introduction of A.B. 2710 the stage was set for a mini dress rehearsal for the federal redress movement. Assemblyman Johnston received over five hundred angry opposition letters from individual citizens (e.g., "Those Japs bombed Pearl Harbor," "It was for their own protection").[9] Nonetheless, the bill passed through the Committee on Public Employees and Retirement on March 24, 1982.[10] Next it passed the Ways and Means Committee, where Assemblyman Johnston put the bill "on call" until he attained majority support.[11] On June 7, 1982, the full assembly passed the bill by a vote of 53 to 12.[12]

In the California state senate the bill was crafted so that it went to the Committee on Governmental Organizations chaired by Senator Ralph Dills (Democrat from Torrance),[13] a longtime friend of the Japanese American community. Under his watchful eye the committee approved the bill,[14] and it went on to be passed out of the Committee on Finance.[15] On August 12 the bill was passed by the California senate by a vote of 24 to 4.[16]

On August 17, 1982, Governor Edmund G. Brown Jr. signed A.B. 2710 into law. With this signing came the first direct monetary redress payment from a governmental body for the constitutional losses suffered by Japanese Americans. Unlike the 1948 Evacuation Claims Act, which compensated only property losses, A.B. 2710 addressed legal injustices, specifically the wrongful termination of employees on the basis of ethnicity. Of the originally identified 314 California state workers, 280 initially received state redress payments. The majority of the others received later payments through subsequent legislation. In the next year several other governmental jurisdictions would follow California's example and pass monetary redress legislation (e.g., the city of Los Angeles, the county of Los Angeles, the city and county of San Francisco, the county of Sacramento, the county of Santa Clara, and the state of Washington).

Implementation of the Redress Bill

The implementation of the California redress bill provided valuable experience that eventually influenced how the federal redress bill was carried out. Ouchida, with the help of others, worked to get broad interpretations of the law in order to include many different categories of state employees and to have the state accept alternative means of establishing eligibility (e.g., signed affidavits) for people who did not have original documentation. Ouchida and Assemblyman Johnston contemplated drafting subsequent legislation that would formally exempt the payments from state and federal taxes.[17] Both venues proved to be very problematic, and the payments remained taxable. Ouchida then pursued legislation to establish state tax-exempt status for the federal redress payments. This bill (Assembly Bill 4087) became law on August 24, 1988, and provided state income tax exemption for the national redress payments and the right of surviving spouses to receive the state redress payments if the original state employee was deceased. Although the federal redress payments had not begun, Ouchida was intent on "stretching the state bill to stay ahead of the federal bill."[18] Through these efforts California became the first state to exempt the anticipated federal redress payments from state taxes.

Contribution of the California Redress Bill

The California redress bill passed largely because of Ouchida's perseverance and Assemblyman Johnston's political courage. Its passage changed the institutional political perspective on redress. Ouchida, a self-described "optimist and doer," admitted there were times she was not sure whether the bill would pass. Her persistence and dedication made the bill a reality. Ouchida reflected on the bill's political importance: "Patrick Johnston went out there with no constituent base, fought this battle and won. The Japanese American community supported him . . . and he didn't get hurt by this bill. . . . He made other legislators realize that it was not a political liability to go out on this issue. Patrick made this issue a winner."[19]

In 1991 Assemblyman Johnston was elected to the state senate. Senator Johnston later recalled the personal significance of redress: "I've been in the legislature for fifteen years, and my proudest achievement is this legislation. And it happened in my first year. I knew it was an important thing, and I was real pleased when it passed. But I didn't know that over time it would stand the test of time in my memory of what I felt best about."[20]

The successful passage of the California redress bill exemplified the contributions of certain key elements: community support, the framing of the issue, good political maneuvering, and personal dedication. The element of good timing was also important; the state government's economy was healthy enough in the early 1980s to support such a bill.

The elements of luck and irony also played a role. It was fortuitous that Assemblyman Johnston's initial election was close enough to delay him in hiring staff, because otherwise he might not have been in a position to hire Ouchida. The irony of this case lies in the State Personnel Board's haste to enact a racist policy. If the board had waited a month, the state employees would have been excluded, and there would have been no need to fire them. Forty years later this hasty action provided a catalyst for a national redress movement.

The California bill demonstrated that at least in California redress was not a political liability. It set a precedent for a governmental body to pay redress for a constitutional wrong. In the years immediately following the passage of the California bill several other local municipalities passed monetary redress legislation for their Japanese American employees. Because of the success of the California bill, Japanese Americans in the state of Washington pursued similar legislation in 1982. The legislation passed in 1986 and granted redress payments to forty state employees, four Seattle city employees, and twenty-seven Seattle school district employees.[21] The California and Washington redress bills both provided valuable experience that would enhance and facilitate the redress work to be done on the federal level.

The NCJAR's Pursuit of Redress in the Courts

While the commission hearings were underway, the NCJAR worked on a different approach to redress. In September and November of 1980 William

Hohri, Yuriko Hohri, Jack Herzig, and Aiko Herzig-Yoshinaga met with Mike
Rauh and Benjamin Zelenko, attorneys from the law firm of Landis, Cohen,
Singman, and Rauh in Washington, D.C. The attorneys advised the NCJAR
that it would face two major obstacles: the *statute of limitations*[22] and *sovereign immunity.*[23] Many legal scholars and practicing attorneys believed that
these two obstacles would be insurmountable. Members of the NCJAR decided to pursue a lawsuit despite the legal advice that it would be a risky case.

The NCJAR chose to pursue redress in the courts for several reasons. First,
a judicial decision would be based on the merits of the case. Unlike the passage of congressional legislation, judicial success did not require a popular
issue or huge constituency support. In reflecting on this choice, Hohri stated,
"The Courts require only the logic of the law and evidence to undergird the
logic, and the money to pay those who provide this. The Congress requires
lots of public pressure on lots of members . . . Congressional action also takes
lots of money."[24]

Second, the NCJAR believed the judicial route was an appropriate avenue
for expressing the grievances of the victims. The injuries suffered by Japanese Americans were of a constitutional and legal nature and were most
fittingly addressed by the court system.

Finally, the judicial route allowed the NCJAR to operate with autonomy.
This reason cannot be overstated. Beyond the merits and pitfalls of a judicial approach, the NCJAR and William Hohri in particular were motivated
by an intense dislike of the national JACL. Hohri disdained the JACL for its
compliance with the exclusion orders during World War II and for its decision to pursue a commission rather than direct redress legislation. In 1979
he wrote:

> It's deja vu to '42. The JACL has taken a turn on redress which reminds me of
> March, 1942. . . . The [JACL] National Council voted for redress. The Committee, its creature, overrode that vote by moving for a Study Commission. . . . That
> is plainly unparliamentary. A committee may not act against the direction given
> to it by the main body. . . . I do not believe the actions of the JACL national
> leaders reflect the wishes of their rank-and-file member . . . If the JACL has
> stumbled irretrievably, if the JACL leadership will not turn themselves around,
> then it is time to think of alternatives. There are plenty of people who will not
> let '42 happen again.[25]

An approach to redress different from the JACL's was extremely attractive
to Hohri. Throughout the judicial and legislative redress campaigns, antagonistic feelings existed between the NCJAR and the other redress groups.

The fee to cover the initial cost of legal research and preparation of the
case was $75,000. The NCJAR organized as a "non-membership" organization so it would not threaten other established organizations in the Japanese
American community. The NCJAR's fund-raising campaign featured two

noteworthy aspects. First, it openly described its lawsuit as being risky. Hohri thought that this, along with asking for money only when it really needed to, helped establish the NCJAR's credibility and build a solid basis of support.[26] Second, the NCJAR did not solicit foundations or attempt to retain a pro bono law firm. Hohri was convinced that the members of the Japanese American community who were affected had to be the ones to finance the effort. If he could not raise the money from them, then the lawsuit would be dropped.[27]

The NCJAR bestowed the title of *ronin,* masterless samurai, on anyone who donated $1,000.[28] The idea came from the Japanese story "Forty-Seven Ronin." In this famous story forty-seven samurai avenged the wrongful death of their master. The NCJAR's contributors were "masterless" citizens seeking to right a past wrong. At the height of its existence the NCJAR had over thirty-five hundred names on its mailing list, including sixty five ronin, and raised over $400,000.[29]

Ellen Godbey Carson was hired by the law firm of Landis, Cohen, Singman, and Rauh on November 2, 1981, to work full-time preparing the lawsuit. She was a young attorney who had recently graduated with honors from Harvard Law School and specialized in constitutional and civil rights law. Carson played a critical role in preparing the lawsuit. Another vital player in the NCJAR effort was Aiko Herzig-Yoshinaga. Herzig-Yoshinaga not only conducted primary archival research to support the NCJAR's judicial claims but also lobbied in Washington, D.C., making important congressional contacts for the organization. Despite the NCJAR's initial resistance to the CWRIC, Herzig-Yoshinaga urged it to advocate for the appointment of supportive commissioners to the CWRIC.

Herzig-Yoshinaga and Jack Herzig exhibited tremendous commitment and creativity in their archival work, the result of which aided the commission hearings, the NCJAR lawsuit, and the *coram nobis* cases. An example of their thoroughness and tenacity was their involvement with Peter Irons, an attorney and academician, in securing copies of an important document. Over the course of several years Irons unsuccessfully searched for a copy of Solicitor General Charles Fahy's oral arguments in the original *Korematsu* case. Knowing that such a copy would be vital to the *coram nobis* cases, Irons searched numerous times through Department of Justice files at the National Archives. Finally an archivist directed Irons to the "enclosures" file, a file of documents that people did not know where to put. To Irons's astonishment and delight, the index listed Fahy's oral argument. The particular box containing the oral argument was not, however, in the archives but in Maryland at the Washington Records Center, which was not open to the public.

Irons asked the Herzigs for help in securing a copy of the document. Herzig-Yoshinaga was told she had to get permission from Victor Stone, the

Department of Justice attorney fighting against *coram nobis*, before she could see the document. After a call from Herzig-Yoshinaga, Stone agreed to go to the Records Center to search for the document. Stone was not eager to find the document because it would weaken the Justice Department's arguments that military necessity was not the reason for the camps. Not leaving anything to chance, the Herzigs went to the Records Center early the next morning. Herzig-Yoshinaga recalled, "Bright and early we went out and seated ourselves in a position where we could see every car come in. . . . We saw him [Stone] come strutting down about eleven o'clock. . . . We said, 'Oh, how are you? We're here to help you look for that stuff.' His face fell flat. . . . When they found the box, we were right behind [Stone]. His heart must have sunk. I'm sure he didn't want to find it. I counted the pages to make sure he wasn't going to take anything out."[30]

The document confirmed what Irons suspected it would. Fahy's oral argument attempted to convince the Supreme Court that the DeWitt report was truthful and that military necessity was the reason for the military exclusion program, even though he knew this was not true. This evidence was crucial on two counts. First, it reflected the fundamental wrong that was crucial to the *coram nobis* effort. Second, it served as a rebuttal to an argument by the Department of Justice in the NCJAR case that the exclusion and incarceration were the result of racism.

By 1983 the leadership of the NCJAR was prepared to press ahead forcefully for a Supreme Court reversal of the exclusion and curfew decisions and a monetary settlement. The NCJAR decided, however, to wait to file its lawsuit until the CWRIC published its report, because it planned to use some of the commission's findings and conclusions. The NCJAR also hoped the report would recommend that Congress enact enabling legislation for the NCJAR complaint. If enacted by the Congress, such enabling legislation would, in effect, grant jurisdiction to the courts to hear the case. The NCJAR's attorney Ben Zelenko explained: "This enabling statue would wipe out all of these obstacles [to hearing the case]. . . . It would waive sovereign immunity. It would waive statute of limitations. It would waive laches. It would waive all objections, procedural objections, to hearing the claim of constitutional deprivation."[31] Unfortunately for the NCJAR the commission's report did not recommend such enabling legislation.

The NCJAR filed its lawsuit in the U.S. District Court for the District of Columbia on March 16, 1983, more than two years after its initial legal consultation. The case was assigned to Judge Louis F. Oberdorfer, who had a reputation for being fair. The NCJAR complaint replaced such euphemisms as "evacuation" and "relocation centers" with more accurate descriptions, such as "forced exclusion" and "prison camps."[32]

The NCJAR lawsuit chose twenty-five people as plaintiffs to represent all the excluded and incarcerated Japanese Americans.[33] Those listed as plaintiffs included some who had been interned in the Justice Department camps; Issei, Nisei, and Sansei who were excluded and held in the WRA camps; a Buddhist priest; veterans of the 442d; a draft resister; several individuals from the District of Columbia (this was essential because the case was filed in the D.C. federal district court); and a cross section of others. The list of plaintiffs was very broad and even included some individuals who were already deceased.

Securing the agreement of individuals to be listed as a plaintiff was not always easy. Herzig-Yoshinaga recalled that some Japanese Americans were still uneasy about standing up to the federal government. Herzig-Yoshinaga recounted, "When I asked one Nisei lady if she would agree to be named as a plaintiff, she said, 'No, I just retired not too long ago from the federal service and I'm getting my pension now and if I get named the government might do something to me.' There was still that deep-seated fear."[34]

The NCJAR complaint eventually articulated twenty-two causes of action that laid out the constitutional and legal rights that the defendant, the U.S. government, had violated.[35] The NCJAR demanded $10,000 for each of the causes of action. As a result, the lawsuit sought roughly $27.5 billion, or $220,000 for each of the roughly 120,000 individuals affected.

On May 16, 1983, the Justice Department attorney, Jeffrey Axelrad, filed a motion to dismiss the NCJAR lawsuit based on three basic contentions: the statute of limitations had expired; the Japanese-American Evacuation Claims Act of 1948 was the sole remedy for the injustices cited; and the federal government was protected by sovereign immunity.

The NCJAR's response was filed on July 15, 1983, and answered each contention. The NCJAR argued three main points. First, it argued that the statute of limitations should be *tolled* while the government was engaged in acts of concealment, fraud, misrepresentation, and suppression of evidence.[36] The federal government should also be *estopped* from revising the reasons for the exclusion and incarceration in order to raise the issue of statute of limitations.[37] If approved, the statute of limitations would be tolled to the time of the commission hearings because the government's withholding of evidence was not sufficiently disclosed until then.

The NCJAR's second argument was that the "unjust takings clause" circumvented sovereign immunity. The Fifth Amendment includes the unjust takings clause, which prohibits private property from being taken for public use without just compensation. The NCJAR argued that the interpretation of the Fifth Amendment included constitutional rights. Finally, the NCJAR asserted that the Japanese-American Evacuation Claims Act of 1948 did not address all types of losses.[38] The claims act was therefore not the exclusive remedy for the losses suffered during the exclusion and incarceration.[39]

Nearly a year later, on May 17, 1984, Judge Oberdorfer issued several rulings:

1. The protection of sovereign immunity prevailed because the plaintiffs had not obtained the government's consent to be sued on fourteen of the fifteen constitutional issues.
2. The unjust takings clause was the only cause of action that was not affected by sovereign immunity. The NCJAR's attempt to extend this clause to include constitutional rights was denied, however.
3. The Japanese-American Evacuation Claims Act of 1948 was not the sole remedy for all the injuries sustained by the plaintiffs during the exclusion and incarceration.
4. The U.S. government concealed evidence during World War II. However, since the reports of the FCC, FBI, and Naval Intelligence were published in the late 1940s, the statute of limitations would be tolled from that point, thus voiding the NCJAR's suit.[40]
5. The government's motion to dismiss was granted because the alleged acts of the federal government did not violate the plaintiff's statutory, civil, and constitutional rights.

The NCJAR's appeal of the decision was heard by the U.S. Court of Appeals for the District of Columbia Circuit sixteen months later, on September 24, 1985. A panel of three justices, Ruth Bader Ginsburg, James Skelly Wright, and Howard Thomas Markey, heard the case. During the arguments Judge Ginsburg hinted at her perspective on the case. She asked the Justice Department attorney when the Japanese American community could have realistically refuted the assertion of military necessity established by the Supreme Court. Her question supported the NCJAR's position that such a lawsuit could be filed only after learning about the government's misconduct, which was not widely revealed until the commission hearings.

The appeals court granted the NCJAR's appeal. In a 2-1 decision on January 21, 1986, it reversed Judge Oberdorfer's decision regarding the statute of limitations and remanded the lawsuit to trial. Judges Wright and Ginsburg agreed that the CWRIC's investigation marked the point at which the government's concealing of evidence was sufficiently disclosed. The appeals court tolled the statute of limitations to the creation of the CWRIC in 1980, thus clearing the way for the suit to be heard in court.

In response to the NCJAR's successful appeal Ron Wakabayashi, the national director of JACL, stated, "We are pleased that the court has recognized the concealment of information by the U.S. Government. . . . This decision expands the vehicles for Japanese Americans to seek redress on the issue of internment through both the legislative and judicial processes."[41]

Not all JACL members were optimistic about the possible impact of the now truncated NCJAR lawsuit. Min Yasui, chair of the JACL NCR, asserted that the decision would affect only those individuals who could prove that they had property taken by the government during the exclusion yet had not been awarded compensation under the Japanese-American Evacuation Claims Act of 1948.[42] Yasui was correct. Of the original twenty-two causes of action only the unjust takings clause (Fifth Amendment) was left intact, and those who had already been compensated by the Evacuation Claims Act were prohibited from asserting the takings clause in this lawsuit.

Neither the NCJAR nor the Department of Justice was satisfied with the ruling. The Department of Justice requested a rehearing of the three-judge panel by the entire U.S. Court of Appeals. This request was denied in a 6-5 vote on May 30, 1986, and the Justice Department appealed to the Supreme Court. In response the NCJAR, joined by a number of organizations as friends of the court,[43] also formally petitioned the Supreme Court on August 26, 1986, to review its case. The Supreme Court granted the Justice Department's petition on November 17, 1986, while the NCJAR's petition was left pending.

Solicitor General Charles Fried represented the government and argued that the case should be dismissed based on two technicalities: wrong court jurisdiction and statute of limitations. Fried claimed that the case had been heard in the wrong court of appeals. He argued that it should have been tried in the U.S. Court of Appeals for the Federal Circuit rather than the U.S. Court of Appeals for the District of Columbia Circuit because it was actually a mixed case that involved both national and regional issues.[44]

In addressing the statue of limitations issue, Fried argued that it was not military necessity but racism that propelled the government to exclude and incarcerate the plaintiffs. Since it was widely understood by the Japanese American community during World War II that the exclusion and incarceration were based on racism, the statute of limitations should be tolled from that point. Fried's claim directly contradicted what Charles Fahy, solicitor general during World War II, presented to the court in *Korematsu v. United States*. Fahy had claimed that military necessity was the sole basis for the government's wartime actions.

The Supreme Court heard *United States v. Hohri et al.* on April 20, 1987. Of the two arguments presented in his brief, the solicitor general highlighted the jurisdictional issue while downplaying the statute of limitations. Justice Thurgood Marshall showed his displeasure with the government's arguments when he challenged Fried to describe the difference between "exclusion and killing" and between "banishment and hanging." Hohri described the exchange as having "brought tears to some eyes. Marshall's anger was anger we victims still suppress. The Court became human."[45]

Benjamin Zelenko, arguing for the NCJAR, also was subjected to difficult questioning. Justice Rehnquist challenged Zelenko on the issue of military necessity and the statute of limitations.

The Supreme Court issued its unanimous decision on June 1, 1987.[46] The Court ruled in favor of the jurisdictional argument presented by the Department of Justice and addressed neither the statute of limitations issue nor the merits of the case. The Court remanded the case to the U.S. Court of Appeals for the Federal Circuit. While this was a major disappointment for the NCJAR, its board members voted to continue the lawsuit.

The U.S. Court of Appeals for the Federal Circuit issued its decision on May 11, 1988. The case was dismissed by a 2-1 vote that affirmed Judge Oberdorfer's 1984 ruling.[47] By this time the legislative redress effort had produced a bill in the One-hundredth Congress that was quickly coming to fruition.

Significance of the NCJAR Case

The NCJAR lawsuit faced an uphill battle from the beginning and, in the minds of many legal experts, had little chance of succeeding. Nonetheless, the lawsuit contributed to the overall redress effort. The extensive archival research conducted for the NCJAR lawsuit resulted in the articulation and documentation of the constitutional and civil rights injustices the Japanese American community had suffered during World War II. The NCJAR's research helped educate public officials and the society at large that the violation of constitutional rights was the central issue in the exclusion and incarceration of Japanese Americans during World War II. Most important, the high settlement figure of their case made the monetary demands in the legislative effort appear moderate in comparison. As a result, the advocates of the congressional route were able to claim the more moderate middle ground.

Coram Nobis

Between 1983 and 1988 a series of legal cases addressed a fundamental error in the U.S. Supreme Court's rulings on the historic *Korematsu, Hirabayashi,* and *Yasui* cases. Fred T. Korematsu, Gordon K. Hirabayashi, and Minoru Yasui, represented by a team of attorneys initially organized by Peter Irons and Dale Minami, filed petitions to have their cases reopened. The basis of their petitions was the rarely used legal mechanism of writ of *coram nobis,* which is used when a decision is believed to be fundamentally unjust and the defendant has been convicted and already served a sentence.

In 1981 Peter Irons decided to write a historical account about the first ten years of the FBI. He visited the National Archives in Washington, D.C., only to be told that the archives had over a thousand rolls of microfilm that were unexpurgated. The simple indexing of this volume of data would take years. Irons decided to think of some other project on which to work. While reviewing Supreme Court decisions, the *Korematsu, Hirabayashi,* and *Yasui* cases caught his eye and imagination. He wondered how the Supreme Court made such terrible decisions in these cases. Irons reflected, "I had only met one Japanese American before this. All I knew about the internment was what I had learned about this case in law school."[48] Despite his lack of personal knowledge or experience with the issue, Irons was inspired to research the topic further.

Irons initiated his research at the War Relocation Authority Solicitor's Office. He quickly found that the materials he wanted were missing. Someone else had beaten him to it. As it turned out, that someone else was Aiko Herzig-Yoshinaga, who was perusing the materials in her official capacity as researcher for the CWRIC. Irons and Herzig-Yoshinaga struck a deal to share information each discovered.

This newly developed partnership produced dividends almost immediately. Irons came across the Justice Department's files on the Supreme Court cases, which were misfiled in the Commerce Department's Freedom of Information Office. The first two or three documents that Irons looked at were smoking guns. They verified that the federal government not only was aware of the lack of military necessity but also intentionally suppressed this awareness and presented statements to the Supreme Court that it knew to be false. The evidence was statements by the Federal Communications Commission, the Federal Bureau of Investigation, and the Office of Naval Intelligence to the effect that there was no evidence of espionage, disloyalty, or fifth column activity on the part of Japanese Americans. General DeWitt intentionally omitted this information in his official army report.

At the time of the Supreme Court cases, two Justice Department attorneys, Edward J. Ennis and John L. Burling, attempted to convince the solicitor general, Charles Fahy, to give the Supreme Court the perspectives not included in DeWitt's report. Fundamental to the case was a memo by Ennis dated April 30, 1943, which questioned whether the Department of Justice had an obligation to advise the Supreme Court of a January 26, 1942, memo from Lieutenant Commander Kenneth D. Ringle. Ringle's memo reflected the Office of Naval Intelligence's assessment that there was no military threat or evidence of disloyalty on the part of the vast majority of Japanese Americans.[49] Fahy did not include this information in the government's brief. In fact during the trial he defended Korematsu's conviction and clearly stated that he agreed with every "line, word, and syllable" of DeWitt's disputed report.[50] The government's action was a deliberate and intentional withholding of information from the Supreme Court. This deliberate withholding of information was the basis of the writ of *coram nobis*. Had the government honestly believed the military necessity theory in 1943 and 1944, there would have been no grounds for the writ.

As luck would have it, on the day that Irons came across the files, the person who was to screen the records was out sick. No one had screened these boxes of documents, and Irons was not allowed to duplicate any records. Irons called Herzig-Yoshinaga to inform her of his discovery and his dilemma. She indicated that she had the authorization to examine any government document related to the exclusion and incarceration. Herzig-Yoshinaga promptly copied all the documents, which proved to be invaluable to the commission hearings as well as to the *coram nobis* cases in establishing the "suppression of evidence" that had occurred in the original *Hirabayashi, Yasui,* and *Korematsu* cases.

Irons decided to explore the possibility of a *coram nobis* case. The writ of *coram nobis* is not familiar to most practicing attorneys. Irons learned about it earlier in his career when he filed a successful *coram nobis* petition to overturn his own conviction for violating the draft law. Reflecting on the importance of his personal experience with the *coram nobis* writ, Irons stated that without it "there wouldn't ever have been *coram nobis* cases [related to redress]."[51]

By January 1982 Irons had approached Min Yasui, Gordon Hirabayashi, and Fred Korematsu individually and had presented the discovered records and his basic strategy of pursuing the *coram nobis* writ. Yasui and Hirabayashi were enthusiastic about Irons's strategy. This was the first legal strategy presented to them that provided an opportunity to reopen their cases and clear their names. Fred Korematsu was initially hesitant, but after hearing Irons's strategy and reviewing the copies of the documents, he declared, "They did me a great wrong."[52] Like Hirabayashi and Yasui, Korematsu agreed to pursue the case.

Although precedent and the law did not make it clear whether *coram nobis* cases needed to go back to the original court, this was the general practice. Irons needed to find attorneys to spearhead the cases in each of the original trial sites: San Francisco, Portland, and Seattle. Yasui sent him a list of ten Japanese American lawyers. Only one attorney, however, was from any of the original sites: Dale Minami. Minami specialized in discrimination law and was an active member of the Bay Area Attorneys for Redress (BAAR). He enthusiastically responded to Irons's request to participate and identified two lawyers in the Portland and Seattle areas. Peggy Nagae, a member of a small Portland firm, agreed to join the effort. Kathryn Bannai, an activist in the Seattle redress movement, assumed leadership for that particular court's case.

Initial preparation for the legal strategy began at two all-day meetings in Minami's home in Oakland. These sessions were attended by over a dozen volunteer lawyers and law students. Included in this group were Bob Rusky and Karen Kai, who assisted as primary petition drafters. The attorneys' familiarity with and trust in each other from working together in the past strengthened their effectiveness in waging this judicial effort.

One of the first dilemmas was whether to file one single petition with the

Supreme Court or to file three separate petitions in the original trial courts. The advantage of filing with the Supreme Court would be the immediate publicity that would be created. The disadvantage was that there was no guarantee that the Court would hear the case. If the Court dismissed it, there might not be grounds for an appeal. The group decided to go the safer route and file petitions in each original court. Irons recalled, "We had long debates about which court to petition, and we decided that we would rather have three bites at the apple than just one."[53]

With the general strategy in place Minami assumed the role of lead counsel. Irons and Lorraine Bannai, an attorney in Minami's law firm, took the lead in factual research and were aided by Aiko Herzig-Yoshinaga. Bob Rusky, Karen Kai, and Dennis Hayashi headed the legal research effort. Donald Tamaki directed the public education effort as well as the legal strategy. The services of all the *corum nobis* team were provided on a *pro bono* basis, with the estimated value nearly $1.5 million dollars.[54]

Each of the petitions, while individually tailored, argued that the government's intentional suppression of evidence at both the trial court and Supreme Court level resulted in fundamentally unjust convictions. The petitions sought the vacating of the convictions at the trial court level on the basis of five claims. First, War Department officials altered and destroyed evidence and withheld this evidence from the Department of Justice and the Supreme Court. Second, War Department officials and the Department of Justice suppressed evidence related to the loyalty of Japanese Americans. Third, government officials failed to advise the Supreme Court of the false allegations in the General DeWitt's final report. Fourth, the government's abuse of the doctrine of judicial notice and the manipulation of amicus briefs constituted a fraud upon the courts. Finally, the petitioners were entitled to relief because their convictions were based on governmental orders that violated current constitutional standards.[55]

After a series of logistical obstacles and unfavorable published sentiments (including a letter from the former Supreme Court justice Arthur J. Goldberg), the Korematsu petition was filed on January 19, 1983, in San Francisco. The decision was made to file in San Francisco first because it had the most liberal court.

When petitions are filed in the federal district court in San Francisco, the cases are randomly assigned by computer to one of fifteen different justices. Realizing the role that luck would play, Irons and Minami, doubting their own personal good fortune, deferred to Lorraine Bannai to file the case. Initially, the clerk in San Francisco did not understand what a writ of *coram nobis* was and called in the chief clerk for clarification.[56] The clerk entered the case, waited for a moment, and then announced with a smile, "Congratulations. You got Judge Patel."[57] Judge Marilyn Hall Patel was the most liberal of the justices and the preferred choice.

Peggy Nagae filed the Yasui petition in Portland in late January 1983. The case was assigned to Judge Robert C. Belloni, whose record on civil rights was not distinguished. He was, however, typical of the judges in Portland. The *Hirabayashi* case was assigned in Seattle to Judge Donald S. Voorhees, whose record on civil rights was strong. The *coram nobis* team was very pleased that Judges Patel and Voorhees would hear their cases. They were uncertain of what to expect from Judge Belloni.

The Korematsu Case

Judge Patel's court moved first. On March 14, 1983, she laid out her timetable for the court proceedings. A month earlier the findings of the CWRIC had been published in *Personal Justice Denied*. This report stated that the incarceration was the result of "race prejudice, war hysteria and a failure of political leadership" and condemned the Supreme Court's *Korematsu* decision.[58] In response to these findings the Justice Department lawyer, Victor Stone, asked that the government be allowed to wait until after the CWRIC had announced its recommendations before filing its response to the Korematsu petition. Stone insisted that he did not want to interfere with the commission's work and that the recommendations might serve to end any controversy in the case. Judge Patel granted the federal government up to sixty days after the release of the CWRIC's recommendations.

The CWRIC recommendations, released in June, demonstrated the difference between the objectives of the *coram nobis* team and those of the Department of Justice. The commission recommended a presidential pardon for those convicted of violating the curfew and exclusion orders. The *coram nobis* attorneys were not happy with this recommendation. A presidential pardon would erase only the civil disabilities that resulted from the petitioners' previous convictions on criminal charges (e.g., loss of voting rights, professional licenses). It would not acknowledge the "suppression of evidence" and the constitutional violation of the camps. The original conviction and finding of guilt of the petitioners would remain on the record. Such a pardon would allow the federal government to avoid responding to the merits of the petitions unless forced to do so by one of the three presiding judges. Stone explored whether the petitioners would accept a presidential pardon. Korematsu, Yasui, and Hirabayashi flatly refused.

Stone then suggested that a different kind of presidential pardon, a *pardon for innocence*, might be arranged. This pardon would include a statement that the president found them innocent of the charges of which they were convicted. Neither pardon would indicate that the laws and military orders under which the three petitioners were convicted were unlawful or unconstitutional, although Stone indicated to Peter Irons that such a statement could be included in the pardon.

Stone and Irons informally discussed the possibility of pardons, but they were never officially offered. Furthermore, in consultation with Korematsu, Yasui, and Hirabayashi, the lead attorneys decided that they would reject any offer of a presidential pardon. They wanted their petitions heard by the court, while the Department of Justice was eager to avoid a hearing. Minami recounted Fred Korematsu's reaction when told of Stone's suggestion of a pardon: "We should be the ones pardoning the government."[59]

After several extensions the government filed its response to the writ of error *coram nobis* petition in the *Korematsu* case on October 4, 1983. Stone asked that Korematsu's conviction be vacated and his petition dismissed without holding any hearings. The Department of Justice was willing to give up the convictions but was unwilling to explore the alleged wrongdoing on the part of the government.

At the subsequent November 10, 1983, hearing on the matter, Dale Minami argued, for the first time in American history, that a conviction that was upheld by the U.S. Supreme Court was so tarnished that it should be vacated. He stated, "The allegations we put forth are perhaps unique in legal history, charging that high government officials suppressed, altered and destroyed information and evidence in order to influence the outcome of a Supreme Court decision."[60] Judge Patel reasoned that the Justice Department's response to the petition was analogous to admitting its error. She went on to state:

> Those records show the facts upon which the military necessity justification for the executive order, namely Executive Order 9066, the legislative act that was enacted thereafter attaching criminal penalties to a violation of an exclusion order, and the exclusion orders that were promulgated thereafter were based upon and relied upon by the government in its arguments to the court and to the Supreme Court on unsubstantiated facts, distortions and representations of at least one military commander, whose views were seriously infected by racism. . . . the substance of the statements contained in the documents and the fact that the statements were made demonstrate that the government knowingly withheld information from the courts when they were considering the critical question of military necessity in this case.[61]

Judge Patel granted Korematsu's writ of error *coram nobis*. The announcement of the decision was a jubilant moment for the *coram nobis* team, the Japanese American community, and mostly, Fred Korematsu. While the granting of the petition did not reverse the 1944 Supreme Court decision, it did acknowledge the fundamental error in the decision.

Yasui's Coram Nobis *Case*

Of the two remaining petitions, Yasui's was heard next by Judge Belloni on January 16, 1984, in Portland. Stone, who represented the Department of

Justice in all three of the *coram nobis* cases, made essentially the same arguments in the Yasui case that he had made in the *Korematsu* case. Judge Belloni rendered his decision on January 26, 1984. He sided with the government's position to vacate the conviction but not grant the petition. Judge Belloni did not want to engage in making findings on an event forty years post facto that he thought had no legal consequences.

Yasui appealed Judge Belloni's ruling to the Ninth Circuit Court of Appeals, but he died in November 1986, before a decision on his appeal was reached. After his death Yasui's family petitioned the Supreme Court to review Yasui's case, but this was denied because his cause of action perished with him.

Hirabayashi's Coram Nobis *Case*

The government pulled out all its trump cards for the *Hirabayashi* case. This reflected the strong sentiment within the Department of Justice and the Reagan administration for assuming a "hard line" rather than a conciliatory stance toward the petitioner. Judge Voorhees scheduled a hearing for May 18, 1984, on the *Hirabayashi* case. Before the hearing Judge Patel's written opinion on *Korematsu* was issued. Patel wrote that "there is substantial support in the record that the government deliberately omitted relevant information and provided misleading information in papers before the court [in the 1940s]. The information was critical to the court's determination."[62]

Stone, bolstered by his victory in Portland, articulated three jurisdictional bars to the Hirabayashi petition. The first bar was that the petitioner suffered no lingering legal disabilities from the conviction (e.g., no loss of civil rights). Second, there was no continuing case or controversy remaining since the government was willing to vacate the conviction and ensure that in the future they would not prosecute others for a similar offense. Third, the statute of limitations had run out because all the crucial government documents needed to make their claim had been available since the end of the 1940s. Stone argued that Hirabayashi's petition should be denied without an evidentiary hearing.

Judge Voorhees was not persuaded and denied the government's motion, stating, "We can only admire his [Hirabayashi] courage for standing up for his rights. What he really is seeking now is vindication of his honor, and I feel that he has that right."[63] Hirabayashi had his case argued by Rodney Kawakami on June 17, 1985.

Unlike the previous two *coram nobis* petitions, Stone drew heavily on the Magic cables for his defense of the government's actions in the Hirabayashi case. The Magic cables were a series of secret Japanese diplomatic codes decoded by U.S. intelligence in late 1940 that allegedly indicated espionage activities by Japanese Americans. The Magic cables also indicated African

Americans, whites, foreign company employees, movie industry Americans, communists, socialists, and anti-Semites had been recruited. Only a limited circle of top military and administration officials, including President Roosevelt, had had access to the decoded Magic cables because the information was considered highly sensitive. The sources of these intelligence messages, however, were never discovered, and their relevance remained disputed. No evidence was ever produced indicating that any Japanese Americans were involved in espionage activities.

Edward Ennis, who volunteered to testify on behalf of Hirabayashi, challenged the claims that the Magic cables were an important factor in deciding to exclude Japanese Americans. He asserted that at the time of the initial Supreme Court case McCloy had intentionally withheld from the Justice Department DeWitt's original report on the exclusion. The original report indicated that the lack of time to conduct loyalty hearings of individual Japanese Americans was not the reason they were excluded en mass. The report contended that it was impossible to determine which Japanese Americans were loyal and which were disloyal.

On February 2, 1986, Judge Voorhees issued his written ruling, which held that the withholding of evidence in the original case seriously undermined the ability of Hirabayashi's attorneys to counteract the government's claims of military necessity in excluding Japanese Americans. Judge Voorhees granted the writ of *coram nobis* for the exclusion charge but not for the curfew charge. He ruled that the burden of the curfew had been "relatively mild when contrasted with the harshness of the exclusion order."[64] His decision was appealed in Seattle's federal appellate court on March 2, 1987.

In September 1987 the three judges on the federal appellate court, Alfred Goodwin, Mary Schroeder, and Joseph Farris, unanimously reversed Voorhees's decision not to vacate the curfew conviction. They based their ruling on the grounds that both charges were based on simultaneous indictments and were tried, briefed, and decided together by the Supreme Court. As a result, they ruled it was proper to vacate both the exclusion and curfew charges together. The *Hirabayashi* case was remanded back to Judge Voorhees, who heeded the orders of the appellate judges on January 12, 1988, and reversed his decision on the curfew charge.

Significance of the Coram Nobis Cases

In the *coram nobis* cases the government was very willing to vacate the original decisions but did not want to address the military necessity issue. The crux of the *coram nobis* cases, however, was the government's misconduct in suppressing evidence about the lack of military necessity in excluding Japanese Americans. The three cases, particularly the Hirabayashi and Korematsu victories, were invaluable in publicly discrediting the "military necessity" defense of the exclusion and incarceration. Furthermore, they clearly demonstrated that the federal government attempted to mislead the Supreme Court by suppressing evidence. The *coram nobis* cases were not without risk, but their victory provided additional credibility to the redress movement.[65]

Minami reflected on how the *coram nobis* cases and the redress movement complemented each other:

> The activism of organizations in the community such as the Japanese American Citizens League and the National Coalition for Redress and Reparations also contributed to the more sympathetic environment in which we filed the petitions. Their efforts continued and expanded the educational focus to expose the unfairness of the exclusion and imprisonment and explain the enormous toll in human suffering and other losses. Thus, the disclosure of evidence attacking the underlying legal bases which upheld the exclusion and detention coincided perfectly with the redress efforts seeking to persuade the public and Congress that no legal, moral, or factual basis existed for the mass imprisonment. The direct relationship between the *coram nobis* petitions and redress became clear as the attorneys began to appreciate the strength of their cases. By challenging these convictions, the petitioners were actually attacking the underlying legality of the exclusion and imprisonment.[66]

Summary

While the California redress effort, the class action suit of the NCJAR, and the *coram nobis* legal cases did not directly affect legislation in the U.S. Congress, they contributed greatly to the energy, momentum, and overall support for the redress movement. A.B. 2710 demonstrated that redress was not a political liability but an issue that would generate community and legislative support. The court cases advanced the general public's and the Congress's understanding of the reasons for redress. There was judicial acknowledgment of the federal government's intentional withholding of key information. While the general public's opinion of redress was still often negative, the public's awareness of the issues addressed by the redress efforts was increasing. As legislative redress bills were about to be introduced into the Ninety-eighth Congress, these parallel movements had a synergistic effect on bringing into alignment the Congress, the judiciary, and the Japanese American community.

8   The Continuing Legislative Battle (1983–86)

As the Ninety-eighth Congress convened in 1983, the published findings and recommendations of the CWRIC, the *coram nobis* cases, and the NCJAR lawsuit provided direction and enthusiasm for the movement. The Japanese American community was becoming united behind the idea of monetary redress and had a variety of efforts they could join or support. This variety of choices was the source of some internal conflict between Japanese American groups and at times within particular groups, such as the JACL. These different efforts, however, had a positive synergistic effect in the Japanese American community (+). The general U.S. society was less hostile to Japanese Americans and more receptive to examining the redress issue (N+). Similarly, the judicial branch was willing to review aspects of the incarceration decisions, resulting in judicial decisions that supported the redress movement (N+).

It was unclear, however, whether the Congress and the president would support redress. While the Democrats were the majority in the House, the Senate had a majority of Republicans (N). For those pushing for legislative redress the battle switched from the commission's hearings in the community to the congressional committee structure. It was possible that a two-thirds majority in the Congress would be necessary to override a presidential veto. Under President Ronald Reagan, the Department of Justice consistently opposed the judicial redress cases. Decreased governmental spending on social programs, tax cuts, and increased defense spending characterized the Reagan agenda. In addition the country was in a deep recession, and the budget deficit was at a record high (-) (see table 6).

Table 6.

Years	History		Legislative Branch		Judicial Branch	Executive Branch
	Community	U.S. Society	Senate	House		
1983–86	+	N+	N	N	N+	–
1979–82	N+	N+	N	N	N	N-
1970–78	N+	N	N+	N+	N	N+
1945–69	N	N	N	N	N	N
Pre-WWII/Exclusion/ Incarceration	–	–	–	–	–	–

The Ninety-eighth Congress

By the Ninety-eighth Congress all the Democratic Nikkei legislators supported redress, and Senator Hayakawa was no longer in office. The Nikkei
legislators and their staffers knew that passing redress legislation would require more than political maneuvering and intellectual arguments. It would
require personal commitment and conviction. Glenn Roberts, Representative Norman Mineta's legislative director from 1983 to 1987, recalled that

> those of us who were moving the bill had to . . . make an act of faith. We had
> to choose to believe that the bill was going to pass. Not pretend to believe . . .
> if we did not have the force of that conviction . . . the bill was never going to
> go anywhere . . . there was a group of three people who made that choice [early
> on]: Norm [Mineta], myself, and the AA in our office (Susie Elfving). . . . We
> had a bunch of conversations with Norm late at night where he started to tell
> us his stories . . . he had not told those stories to anybody in forty years. . . . He
> had tears telling us this stuff . . . and then the circle [of supporters] expanded.[1]

Legislative staffers played a critical role in drafting the redress legislation
and advocating the bill's passage. Representative Mineta asked Roberts to
draft the redress bill for the House. The bill needed to be written so that it
would be assigned to only one committee. Roberts understood that the more
committees it went before, the greater the chances were that the bill would
die before ever making it to the floor of the House. Roberts knew that the
bill would need to go before the Judiciary Committee so he included ample
references to judicial issues in the preamble to the bill. In order to bypass the
Ways and Means Committee, the tax benefits provision was not included in
the final draft of the legislation as introduced. The way in which Roberts
crafted the bill proved successful in the end.

In the early drafts the legislation was titled the "Japanese American Redress Internment Bill." Roberts and John Tateishi concluded that the most
persuasive argument for redress was to link it to the loss of civil rights. They
were not able to use the title "The Civil Rights Act" since that name was al-

ready being used by another bill. After much thought Roberts and his colleague, Paul Schoellhamer, came up with the name "The Civil Liberties Act."[2]

Roberts secured the support of over thirty members through his routine contact with other staffers. He recalled, "There are some bills that can proceed with virtually no member involvement. This was not one of them." Roberts recounted how Representative Mineta "spent two days on the telephone and got [the number of cosponsors] up to about seventy-five, which is very impressive for a bill like this [the first time it's introduced] . . . and that was just Norm spending a day and a half on the phone. There's no way staff could have done that."[3]

The efforts of Representative Mineta and Roberts to gain the support of fellow legislators were not always easy or successful. Before the bill was introduced in the Ninety-eighth Congress Representative Mineta and Roberts went to see Representative Thomas Kindness (Republican from Ohio) to solicit his support. Representative Mineta quickly learned that obtaining Representative Kindness's support was a lost cause. According to Roberts Representative Kindness told them, "'Well, I actually know about this [the internment] because I've worked with somebody who was involved in it, and I'll certainly look to him for guidance on that.' Norm said, 'Oh really, who?' And [Kindness] said, 'Karl Bendetsen.' And Norm just said, 'Oh,' and he finished the conversation and left. I said to Norm in the hallway, 'What was that all about?' Norm said, 'Don't you know Bendetsen? He . . . put us in the camps.'"[4]

Significant Changes in the Senate

The political makeup of the Senate changed dramatically in the early 1980s. When the commission was created in 1980, the Democrats controlled both chambers in Congress and Democratic President Jimmy Carter was supportive of the effort. Conservative Republican Ronald Reagan won the presidential election in late 1980, and with his victory many new Republican representatives and senators came into office. In the Ninety-seventh Congress (1981–82), there were 53 Republican senators and 47 Democratic senators. The number of Republican senators increased to 55 in 1983 during the Ninety-eighth Congress, leaving only 45 Democratic senators. The Republican majority in the Senate was significant since Republicans in general are less supportive of civil rights issues.

Redress Bills Introduced in the Senate

The first redress bill in the Ninety-eighth Congress, S.R. 1520, was introduced by Senator Alan Cranston (Democrat from California) on June 22, 1983, on behalf of himself and Senator Ted Kennedy (Democrat from Massachusetts). The bill sought redress payments for Japanese Americans and Aleuts and was referred to the Senate Judiciary Subcommittee on Administrative Practice and Procedure, chaired by Senator Charles E. Grassley, a conservative Republican from Iowa. The first congressional hearings following the CWRIC's published findings and recommendations were held on July 27, 1983. The list of witnesses included Commissioner Joan Bernstein, accompanied by Angus Macbeth, the commission's special counsel; Representative Daniel Lungren; Senator Alan Cranston; John Tateishi; Ken Masugi, resident fellow and director of the Bicentennial of the Constitution Project, Claremont Institute, California; and Lillian Baker. The themes of the testimony given at this hearing would be repeated countless times in the years to come by redress supporters and opponents.

In his questions to witnesses Senator Grassley focused on several issues. He asked how many individuals were actually detained, whether any U.S. citizens were actually "interned," who would be eligible for the monetary payments, and whether those who repatriated to Japan would be included. In addition he questioned whether the Japanese-American Evacuation Claims Act of 1948 had not satisfactorily redressed losses and whether the U.S. government had "military reason for believing a military danger existed."[5] Finally, Senator Grassley commented that many Americans had "suffered just as much if not more due to Government action during the war. Yet, they are not requesting compensation."[6]

In response to Senator Grassley Angus Macbeth asserted that all individuals of Japanese ancestry, citizen or alien, were to be covered by the bill. Macbeth explained the rationale by pointing out that "the Commissioners came to the conclusion that one really could not effectively draw distinctions in terms of what happened further down in the course of time as, for instance, the segregation program at Tule Lake, without realizing that a very large part of that sprang from the initial order [Executive Order 9066]."[7] In response to Senator Grassley's question regarding the Japanese-American Evacuation Claims Act of 1948 Commissioner Bernstein stated that the proposed payment was "at best symbolic of the overall loss"[8] that individuals experienced. This symbolic nature of the bill would be referred to innumerable times in the years to come.

Macbeth rebutted the military necessity argument by stating that "when you look at [the reasons] hard, [the reasons] are really not military reasons. They are put in terms of ethnicity determining loyalty, and that simply isn't a military judgment."[9]

Commissioner Bernstein reacted to the question that implied everyone suffered during the war by reminding Senator Grassley of the contributions Japanese American veterans made. She described the plight of the Japanese American community by pointing out that "these people were American citizens who were loyal, who were ready to serve their country, and who were denied the very basis of our civilization, the very basis of our constitutional rights."[10]

Representative Lungren presented his arguments against monetary redress:

> I hope we haven't reached a situation in this country that sincere actions taken by the Congress and the President of the United States on behalf of all the American people have no value unless they have a monetary amount connected to them. . . . Second, and I have heard from members of the Japanese American community. . . that they would consider it an insult to be offered this money, as if a price tag could be placed on their loss of liberty . . . Third . . . If you establish a precedent that we go back 40 years . . . why not go back 100 years? I don't know how to answer that question in a logical manner unless you say that you have to treat all these groups the same.[11]

Lillian Baker presented the subcommittee with a voluminous amount of documentation of weakly supported assertions and extraneous issues. She insisted that all Japanese Americans had dual citizenship, that the term *concentration camp* was as offensive as the term *Jap,* and that Japanese Americans who were pro-Japan had posed a threat to the West Coast.[12] Ken Masugi testified against the bill because he thought that the CWRIC's report and recommendations were based on "intellectual dishonesty, moral posturing, and political opportunism."[13]

John Tateishi maintained that the bill reflected a fundamental American right: "This is not, Mr. Chairman, a special interest group issue . . . but an issue that has relevance for all Americans." He added, "The Japanese Americans today are looking to the Congress for recognition of a wrong that was committed against us as Americans. . . . We are talking about . . . the loss of our constitutional rights."[14]

Senator Cranston provided his personal account of visiting friends in the camps and working to dissuade President Roosevelt from implementing the exclusion and incarceration policy.[15] Despite the bulk of favorable testimony S.R. 1520 was not voted on and thus never made it out of Senator Grassley's subcommittee.

Subsequent to the introduction of S.R. 1520 Senator Spark Matsunaga introduced S.R. 2116 (the Senate companion bill to H.R. 4110) on November 17, 1983, with thirteen additional cosponsors. S.R. 2116 called for the Senate to accept the findings and implement the recommendations of the CWRIC. S.R. 2116 was assigned to the Governmental Affairs Subcommittee on Civil Service, Post Office, and General Services, chaired by Senator Ted Stevens. Subcommittee hearings were held on August 16, 1984, in Los Angeles, California, and on August 29, 1984, in Anchorage, Alaska. In Los Angeles Senator Stevens opened the hearings by stating his personal support for the bill but noting that "our subcommittee has not reached a conclusion as to whether the reparation recommendation is appropriate."[16] Testimony was heard from twenty-seven individuals, including Representative Mervyn Dymally; former Senator S. I. Hayakawa; Representative Norman Mineta; Commissioner Arthur Flemming; Senator Alan Cranston; Retired Lieutenant Colonel John (Jack) A. Herzig; representatives from the JACL, the NCRR, the Washington Coalition on Redress, and the Asian Law Caucus; community members; and opponents of redress, such as Baker and Rachel Kawasaki, a white woman married to a Japanese American. At the hearings held in Anchorage, Alaska, thirty-five people testified, including many Aleutian community members. Despite the supportive testimony from both sites and Senator Stevens's strong support of redress, the bill was not voted on and died in subcommittee.

Action in the House

Three redress bills were introduced in the House during the first session of the Ninety-eighth Congress. Representative Mike Lowry (Democrat from Washington) introduced the first bill, H.R. 3387, with twenty-four additional cosponsors on June 22, 1983, which called for trust funds and individual payments of $20,000 to Japanese Americans and Alaskan Aleuts. Representative Jim Wright (Democrat from Texas) introduced H.R. 4110 on October 6, 1983, with seventy-four additional cosponsors. The bill called for the House to accept and implement the findings and recommendations of the CWRIC.[17] Representative Don Young (Republican from Alaska) introduced H.R. 4322, which called for redress for the Aleuts, in the House on November 4, 1983.[18]

As the various redress bills were introduced, the Nikkei legislators and community activists heightened their activities. On January 17, 1984, Senator Matsunaga hosted a briefing in Washington on redress for representatives of forty-five civil rights, labor, veterans, and religious organizations. In February Representatives Mineta and Matsui arranged for three showings of Loni Ding's award winning documentary, *Nisei Soldier,* on the House's closed-circuit television system.

In June, as a result of lobbying efforts by community members and Washington, D.C., insiders, members of the black and Hispanic caucuses in the House announced their support of H.R. 4110.[19] The JACL through its Washington, D.C., representative and its National Committee for Redress continued its efforts to gain legislative support for redress. The NCRR conducted its first lobbying trip to Washington, D.C., during the subcommittee hearings in June 1984. Ten NCRR members met with congressional members to discuss redress.[20] Representative Dymally (Democrat from California) assisted the effort by making office space and logistical help available.

The three House bills were assigned to the House Judiciary Subcommittee on Administrative Law and Governmental Relations, chaired by Representative Sam B. Hall Jr. Representative Hall, a very conservative Democrat, represented a rural area in Texas and had a poor voting record on civil rights issues. Redress was not a priority for him, and the atmosphere of the hearings reflected this.

Hearings for the three bills were held on several days in June and September of 1984.[21] On the first day, June 20, 1984, only two members of the subcommittee were present (Chairman Hall and Representative E. Clay Shaw Jr., a Republican from Florida). After opening remarks by Chairman Hall, a statement by Representative Wright was read, which noted the contrast between the heroic events at D-Day and the U.S. government's shameful treatment of those of Japanese ancestry during the war.

Some Americans were outraged that these bills would receive a congressional hearing. Representative Matsui acknowledged that the hearings took place in a less than supportive atmosphere: "I know that you are probably receiving a lot of hate type mail. But the mere fact that you have decided to hold these hearings indicates to me that our system does work and that there are opportunities for all Americans, irrespective of our race, our color, creed, or religious background."[22]

Over the course of four days of hearings thirty-three individuals testified: twenty four in support of the bills, two in partial support, and seven against. Like many others, Representative Samuel S. Stratton (Democrat from New York) demonstrated his inability to distinguish between Japanese from Japan and those of Japanese ancestry living in the United States: "I am perhaps the most supportive Caucasian in the Congress as far as Japan is concerned, and am one of the few members of the House who has at least some knowledge of the Japanese language and who has regularly attended a number of Japanese-American parliamentary exchange programs during my years in the House. However, . . . I am opposed to this legislation."[23] While Stratton admitted that the imprisonment of "Japanese" was unjust, he held that "it was in a higher cause—the effort . . . to keep America free and alive."[24]

The centerpiece of the hearings was the examination of the Magic cables, which detracted from the injustices of the exclusion. The questions from subcommittee members reflected their belief that these cables legitimately influenced the decision to exclude Japanese Americans from the West Coast. David Lowman, a former official with the National Security Agency, described the cables as presenting "to the U.S. Government the frightening specter of massive espionage nets."[25] He submitted a series of Magic cables, including a cable from Los Angeles to Tokyo: "We have already established contacts with absolutely reliable Japanese in the San Pedro and San Diego area, who will keep a close watch on all shipments of airplanes and other war materials, and report the amounts and destinations of such shipments. . . . We shall maintain connection with our second generations who are at present in the U.S. Army, to keep us informed of various developments in the Army.

We also have connections with our second generations working in airplane plants for intelligence purposes."[26] Lowman argued that the Magic cables were central to the intelligence reports President Roosevelt received and that these intelligence reports provided a "compelling reason" for the president to sign Executive Order 9066.[27]

Pro-redress witnesses, including Retired Lieutenant Colonel Jack Herzig, argued that the Magic cables at best indicated the Japanese government's intention to recruit Japanese Americans to engage in espionage. The cables did not provide any concrete evidence that Japanese Americans were actually conducting any acts of espionage or sabotage.

Chairman Hall sided with those opposed to redress and suggested that testimony indicated there was a military necessity for excluding and incarcerating those of Japanese ancestry. He cited a Supreme Court's ruling that the military's behavior was justifiable if a danger was deemed urgent or sufficiently threatening, even if it was later discovered that the facts about the level of danger were not accurate.[28]

Beyond the issue of the Magic cables, individuals testified about a wide range of other themes. Subcommittee member Representative Kindness, along with Retired Colonel Frederick Bernays Wiener, David Lowman, and several others, attacked the commission's credibility. David F. Trask, chief military historian for the army, questioned the historical accuracy of the CWRIC findings, including the conclusion that the exclusion and incarceration were not based on military necessity. John J. McCloy insisted that the exclusion and incarceration were the result of fear and military necessity rather than racial prejudice. McCloy demonstrated his selective memory of the historical facts: "We didn't intern them. We let them go any place they wanted to go. I think this was benign and proper."[29] Karl Bendetsen emphasized the camps were needed to "protect the evacuees" and claimed that except for Tule Lake there were no guards or barbed wire.[30]

A response by Representative Kindness to one witness reflected his and some other subcommittee members' perception of the need for redress. Kiku Hori Funabiki, a Heart Mountain camp inmate, described the economic, personal, and psychological losses her family endured. After her testimony Representative Kindness revealed his feelings about the camps by rhetorically asking Funabiki, "And to the extent that the evacuation might have, under ideal circumstances, have provided you, and your mother, and your brothers with protection from the elements and from physical needs—hunger, and the need for shelter, and so on—to that extent, it might have operated to your benefit if it had operated well; would that be correct to state?"[31]

Some Japanese Americans who testified before the committee were not supportive of the commission's recommendations. Harry Kubo, president of the Nisei Farmers League, spoke in opposition to monetary payments and in favor of a trust fund for educational and humanitarian purposes. Ken Masugi characterized H.R. 4110 as ethically flawed, special-interest legislation.

In contrast redress supporters spoke of the need to right a grievous wrong and the importance of protecting individual rights. Among those who testified in support were Representatives Matsui and Mineta, who shared their personal stories. Representative Dymally, who was accompanied by Bert Nakano and Bill Kochiyama of the NCRR, also testified on behalf of the bill. The findings and recommendations of the CWRIC were presented by the commission's chair, Bernstein; Commissioner Flemming; and Angus Macbeth. Commissioner Bernstein stated that similar measures had been enacted, such as the Indian Claims Act of 1946.[32] Many stressed that Japanese Americans had nothing to do with what happened in the Pacific and highlighted the contributions of the 442d R.C.T. Redress supporters argued that even if there was reason to distrust a few Japanese Americans, there was no reason to incarcerate 120,000 Japanese Americans without a trial.

Redress supporters were frustrated by the amount of attention given to the Magic cables. The damage, however, was done. The chorus of voices in support of redress was not enough to overcome the still present suspicion of Japanese American disloyalty. An unsupportive chair and influential opposing witnesses created a stifling context for redress, which hastened the death of H.R. 3387, H.R. 4110, and H.R. 4322.

Summary of the Ninety-eighth Congress

Although the redress bills died, the Ninety-eighth Congress was important for redress. The increasing number of cosponsors in both chambers and the subcommittee hearings reflected growing congressional support. Redress was a legitimate legislative issue, complete with written language, political supporters, and political foes.

Support from the general American society grew as the efforts of community activists across the nation produced some monetary redress policies and scores of supportive proclamations and resolutions from a broad array of groups. Japanese Americans actively solicited support from national church groups.[33] Nikkei veterans were crucial in recruiting endorsements from veterans groups, including the American Legion; the Veterans of Foreign Wars, Department of California; and the Jewish War Veterans.[34] Labor groups, such as the International Longshoremen's and Warehousemen's Union (ILWU) and the executive council of the American Federation of Labor and Congress of Industrial Organizations (AFL-CIO), endorsed redress legislation, as did civil rights groups, such as the Anti-Defamation League of B'nai B'rith (ADL), the American Civil Liberties Union (ACLU), the National Association for the Advancement of Colored People (NAACP), the National Council of La Raza, and the Leadership Conference of Civil Rights (LCCR). Professional groups, such as the American Bar Association (ABA), the National Association of Social Workers (NASW), the National Education Association (NEA), and the American Psychiatric Association (APA), also passed resolutions. These diverse groups provided the foundation for a broad coalition of support.

State governments also passed resolutions in favor of redress (e.g., Hawai'i, Minnesota, Wisconsin, Oregon, and New Jersey). Large cities, such as Philadelphia, New York, Sacramento, and Chicago, and numerous small cities passed redress resolutions as well. The U.S. Conference of Mayors and the National League of Cities passed favorable resolutions. Several cities, counties, states, and other elected boards also passed measures that provided monetary restitution for their Nikkei employees who had been wronged in World War II (e.g., California, Los Angeles City Council, Alameda County, Seattle City Council, Seattle School Board, Santa Clara County, San Joaquin County, and Placer County).

The national election in 1984 helped propel redress into the national political conscience. The Democratic party platform and the three Democratic candidates endorsed the concept of redress,[35] while the Republican party platform declared the incarceration an injustice. The movement for redress was gaining strength.

Changes in the JACL

The national JACL board met on May 17–19, 1985, and officially activated the JACL Legislative Education Committee (JACL LEC) and appointed Min Yasui as chair. The idea for the JACL LEC originated in 1982, when the JACL recognized the need to have an independent lobbying committee. The JACL LEC was created because of growing internal tensions between different factions within the JACL and the concern that the JACL might lose its nonprofit status if it engaged in significant lobbying. The JACL LEC was given the responsibility of raising funds for the redress campaign.[36] The nonprofit side of the JACL, in particular the NCR, remained responsible for the education function of the redress campaign and for the overall direction of the campaign.

The May meeting was heated and tense as the national JACL board wrestled with the relative priority to be given to the issues of redress and U.S.-Japan relations. Denny Yasuhara, the governor from the Pacific Northwest district, openly questioned whether redress or U.S.-Japan relations was the priority of the JACL.[37] Arguments about the JACL's role in U.S.-Japan relations centered on various JACL "delegations" to Japan sponsored by Japan's Liberal Democratic party (LDP). The issue that would be argued for months to come was whether the JACL's involvement with Japan would ultimately hurt the redress movement.

Grant Ujifusa, the eventual JACL LEC legislative strategy chair, believed in having as little involvement as possible with Japan. Ujifusa argued that any such relationship weakened the argument that Japanese Americans were purely and completely American. Ujifusa recalled arguing that "we can't look like we're in bed with the Japanese now, because we're doing redress. [If we do so] . . . the first question that will be asked will be if you are in bed with these guys now what were you doing in 1942?"[38] Yasuhara and Hid Hasagawa agreed with this perspective. Over the coming years they led the fight for keeping redress as the JACL's top priority.

John Tateishi, Frank Sato (the national president from 1984 to 1986), and Ron Wakabayashi disagreed. They argued that to make the JACL a "single issue" organization was a major error. U.S.-Japan relations affected the Japanese American community, and the JACL had a responsibility as a civil rights organization to be involved with such an issue.

Wakabayashi recalled that the issue was debated in the context of an economically developing Japan: "Trade across the Pacific, trade with Japan, exceeds trade across the Atlantic for the first time in 1981. . . . As the Japanese economy is growing, the issues of free trade and Japan bashing begin to come up. . . . The growth of the Japanese economy and its presence was such that we couldn't ignore its impact on perceptions that transferred onto us."[39] Wakabayashi and others thought that the JACL could either attempt to distance itself from Japan or become an active player in helping the media report events accurately concerning Japan or Japanese Americans. Wakabayashi recalled that the difference in strategy "tended to split generationally." He described the strategy to distance the JACL from Japan as being "the Nisei voice, and it was consistent with the postwar Nisei strategy. The strategy was that being identified with Japan got us in trouble, so that we should adopt basically an accommodationalist strategy that does not call attention to ourselves being Japanese."[40]

The national JACL board voted in September for a moratorium on LDP-sponsored trips because it created the impression that Japanese Americans were spokespersons for Japan. This issue would serve as a defining issue in the upcoming 1986 JACL elections.

Despite such internal conflicts in the JACL, the different community groups continued to work together or at least not against one another. On July 13, 1985, members from the JACL LEC, NCRR, NCJAR, and Washington Coalition for Redress (WCR) met at the JACL headquarters in San Francisco. The outcome was an agreement to support each others' efforts.

In the fall of 1985 the JACL LEC was given the responsibility to lobby for redress. Tateishi recognized the tension between the JACL NCR and the JACL LEC and thought the educational emphasis of the JACL National Committee for Redress would be eliminated.[41] On September 20, 1985, Grayce Uyehara was appointed as the acting director of the JACL LEC.[42] Uyehara was a Nisei from West Chester, Pennsylvania, who served as the eastern district's redress chairperson. Uyehara, a social worker by training, was a well-known and active JACL member and had many contacts with social service, civil rights, labor, and religious organizations.

Uyehara commuted regularly from her residence in Pennsylvania to Washington, D.C., to coordinate the grass-roots effort. She recalled, "All of the chapters had been working on getting various national organizations, city councils, mayors, unions, and professional organizations to pass resolutions in support of redress."[43] She informed the Nikkei legislators about which representatives or senators might be wavering in their support for redress. She kept the Japanese American community informed by disseminating weekly "Action Alerts," which provided current information about legislative developments and lobbying directives. Uyehara was effective in motivating and organizing JACL members across the nation to speak at churches, schools, civic groups, and media events.

A formidable challenge in lobbying legislators was that many states did not have a large number of Japanese American constituents. Uyehara sought "proxy" Japanese American constituents in states with few Japanese Americans and motivated them to advocate on behalf of redress. She conducted exhaustive searches for non–Japanese Americans who had ties (e.g., religious, professional, and social) with Japanese Americans and were sympathetic to redress. She urged Japanese American members of churches to convince non-Nikkei church members and ministers in other states to lobby their legislators. Sometimes Uyehara located prominent non-Nikkei individuals who favored redress and personally knew legislators. Nikkei veterans contacted their fellow non-Nikkei veterans to lobby their support. Such personal contacts and letters from well-connected supporters helped obtain the support of many legislators. In the absence of well-organized opposition this strategy was often very effective.

Despite Uyehara's connections and personal drive she lacked access to many of the key players in the legislative process. In 1985, at the suggestion of Min Yasui and Mike Masaoka, the JACL recruited Grant Ujifusa to be the legislative strategy chair of the JACL LEC. Ujifusa was a Sansei born and reared in Worland, Wyoming, where his family farmed. Most important, he was the coauthor of the *Almanac of American Politics,* a comprehensive review of the president, the members of Congress, and the state governors that served as an important source of information. As the coauthor, Ujifusa possessed a very precious commodity in Washington, D.C.: access to legislators. Few people in the capitol would refuse to see Ujifusa; even fewer people would fail to return his phone calls.

Although he had not been incarcerated, Ujifusa had a firsthand view of the Heart Mountain camp. Ujifusa recalled that his grandfather told him that the camps should teach him a lesson:

Grandpa said, "Be careful in life, Masashi. You come from a dumb family."

"Why do you say that, grandpa?" I replied.

"Because we voluntarily chose to settle a part of the world to which 11,000 people were involuntarily removed."[44]

The kid from the "dumb family" proved his worth and commitment to the redress movement. Ujifusa stressed that the bill needed to be framed so that "Ronald Reagan and Barney Frank could agree on it."[45] He described the rationale for this strategy: "We needed to make redress something conservative Republicans could buy into as consistent with their values and principles. . . . The thing not to do was to define our bill as a piece of traditional civil rights, ethnic, special-interest legislation. Instead, we defined it as a piece of general-interest legislation consistent with the most conservative, even original-intent reading of the Constitution."[46]

Ujifusa firmly believed that the bill needed to be presented as being about equal opportunity: "Democrats believe in equality of opportunity and the use of some government to ensure some equality of outcome. Republicans, meanwhile, believe in equality of opportunity, but are wary of government intervention. . . . What they both agree on is the equality of opportunity. . . . That is precisely what Japanese Americans in camps were denied. . . . In 1942, what we really wanted was something contemporary conservatives extol— to be left alone by the government."[47]

Framing the issue as a matter of equal opportunity is what made redress "an apple pie and motherhood issue."[48] Along with developing this strategy Ujifusa was able to deliver this message to conservative Republicans. Representative Matsui recalled, "Grant Ujifusa talked about this strategy at my house. We needed the conservatives. The liberals we knew we would ultimately get. . . . but that's at most only about one hundred and twenty or so members. And not all might vote for the bill. . . . We didn't know how to break through and get two hundred and eighteen votes. Then it hit me that I was sitting with the editor of the *Almanac.* . . . He could get access to every right winger and we needed access to the conservatives."[49] Beginning in the Ninety-eighth Congress, Ujifusa went office to office and got better acquainted with many key conservatives, including Newt Gingrich and Vin Weber. By framing the issue as an equal opportunity violation by big government he obtained key Republican support.

Lobbying Efforts from the Community and inside the Beltway

Community activists and redress supporters in the Congress worked to convince more legislators to support the bill. Framing redress as a matter of constitutional rights paid dividends as the Nikkei members lobbied their fellow legislators. Representative Matsui recalled his interaction with Representative Henry J. Hyde (Republican from Illinois), a noted conservative:

> I was on the floor of the House and I walked over to the Republican side and I handed Henry Hyde this little booklet (*The Japanese American Incarceration: A Case for Redress*).[50] I said 'Henry, can you look at this and could you get back to me. I'd like you to cosponsor H.R. 442.' He looked at me and said, 'Oh, put me on that.' I said 'Don't you want to look at it.' He said, 'You know, we minorities always get picked on and this is just outrageous.' I said 'What do you mean?' He said, 'Well, Catholics, Asians, Japanese Americans. . . .'"[51]

On September 20, 1985, Representative Hyde announced his support for the bill.

Lobbying efforts were also important in the community. The grass-roots efforts of the JACL Central California District Council chapters, especially the JACL Fresno chapter, produced significant support from Republican legislators in California. Senator Pete Wilson, an opponent of the monetary provision of redress, was approached by Harry Kubo of the Nisei Farmers League.[52] Kubo, members of the Fresno JACL, and members of the Central California District Council met with the senator's aide, Otto Bos, on several occasions. At the annual Nisei Farmers League banquet Fred Y. Hirasuna and several other JACL members spoke to Senator Wilson about redress and pressed him for his support.[53] In late February 1985 Senator Wilson announced his support and cosponsorship of the redress bill.

The redress movement got a significant boost in the latter half of 1985, when Representative Charles "Chip" Pashayan (Republican from California) also became a cosponsor. Representative Pashayan had indicated his support for an apology, presidential pardons, restitution of lost positions or status, and a community trust fund. He had, however, steadfastly opposed any individual payments. Tom Shimasaki, a Republican from Visalia, California, who was a JACL member, spearheaded the local lobbying efforts directed at Representative Pashayan.

Shimasaki met with Representative Pashayan on several occasions. He arranged a dinner meeting between the congressman and local JACLers on April 12, 1985. At this meeting Representative Pashayan reiterated his stance on the bill. Fred Hirasuna reported in a memo to Min Yasui, "After an extended question and answer period, he [Representative Pashayan] claimed that he was surprised at the insistence on individual compensation. (I think that his thinking was influenced by the stand of persons like Harry Kubo, Yori Wada and others who opposed individual compensation.)"[54] During the discussion Representative Pashayan was reminded of the Armenian effort to get a national day of remembrance for the Armenians who had been massacred in 1915 by the Turks and of President Reagan's reluctance to support this effort because he feared the Turkish government would be offended. Six months later, on October 5, 1985, Representative Pashayan announced his support in a letter to Representative Matsui: "While it is true that the nation was at war, it was an unfair and a wrong policy to single out a whole group of people. . . . That is a policy of discrimination, which has no place in America. I now feel that it is Congress that should act to remedy the wrong."[55] Representative Pashayan's support was especially significant since he was the first Republican representative from California to become a cosponsor.

One particular congressman was persuaded by a constituent who was known in the Japanese American community as the "little girl with the apple." As a three-year-old girl, Yukiko Okinaga Llewellyn appeared in a War Relocation Authority photograph. She was sitting on a leather suitcase, surrounded by duffel bags; on her face was the look of fear and bewilderment; her hands were clutching a small purse and a half-eaten apple. This picture was used thousands of times by redress supporters because it vividly portrayed the essence of the exclusion process. In the fall of 1986 Okinaga Llewellyn wrote to her congressman, Representative Terry Bruce (Democrat from Illinois), and spoke with his staff. Through her persistence the "little girl with the apple," now an adult with a cause, helped win the support of her representative for the redress movement.

Not all community efforts during this period supported redress. For example, in the Seattle area Mary Lou Winchell, Bob Auchter, and Bill Kubick personally delivered two hundred pounds of anti-redress material to federal and state officials. These individuals were young adults during World War II, and their arguments centered on wartime military necessity, the generosity of the United States in rebuilding postwar Japan, the Japanese American Evacuation Claims Act of 1948, and the harsh treatment that captured American G.I.s received at the hands of the Imperial Japanese Army. Similar to other redress opponents, they failed to differentiate between Japanese Americans and the Imperial Japanese Army.

Relationships among the Redress Groups

Despite the working alliance arranged in the 1980 meeting at Cal State Los Angeles and solidified at the 1985 JACL headquarters "summit," the relationships among the various redress groups were tenuous and, at times, hostile. Differences in strategies and the personalities of leaders often led to intergroup competition and the desire for autonomous functioning. The NCJAR, for the most part, worked autonomously in pursuing its lawsuit. The JACL and the NCRR collaborated at times but mostly worked independently. Despite their independent operations, the NCRR used the strategy of maintaining the image of a "united front." Bert Nakano stressed the importance of being perceived as a working coalition of different groups pushing for redress.[56] The NCRR knew that it was important to keep the community's focus on the issue of redress rather than on interorganizational conflicts. At every Day of Remembrance organized by the NCRR, speakers from the NCRR, JACL, NCJAR, *coram nobis* effort, and 442d R.C.T. were included in an effort to bring the community together and present an image of unity.

The JACL tended to reflect a more bureaucratic and formal approach to redress, while the NCRR was more grass-roots and to the political left of the JACL. Those who were members of both organizations oftentimes played crucial behind-the-scenes roles in keeping the two organizations pushing in the same direction, especially on the local level. There are many stories, however, of various individuals from the different community groups openly arguing with, sniping at, or degrading the efforts of other individuals and organizations. Informal agreements were made not to publicly denounce the efforts of the other groups. Such agreements often were violated, resulting in both parties feeling angry with and betrayed by individuals from the other organizations. Peoples' egos and passionate commitment to their own strategy presented the potential for fragmentation in the redress effort.

The NCRR was criticized for its strategy of grass-roots organizing and involvement with movements of other oppressed minority groups. Critics claimed that the NCRR's actions jeopardized the mission of redress because of their association with other controversial or unpopular movements.[57] Despite this criticism the NCRR strove to remain consistent with the principles it had established. Bert Nakano recalled saying that "we have our principles . . . we can't be hypocrites, we can't ask [people] to help us and when they ask us to help them we say no 'we can't touch it.'" The NCRR stressed the importance of empowering Japanese Americans to stand up for redress. Although the NCRR was openly attacked on several occasions, it maintained a position of never publicly fighting with any of the other Japanese American redress groups. Bert Nakano remembered that maintaining a "united front" in public was paramount, but "in private it was a whole different matter."[58]

The JACL was the only one of the three major redress groups to have paid staff. The staff included Ron Wakabayashi, the national executive director, and Carole Hayashino, the public information officer. Because of underlying interpersonal and interorganizational conflicts, their primary concern was to maintain productive working relationships between the groups. Hayashino recalled, "I kept in touch with these people [*coram nobis* team, NCRR, NCJAR]. JACL had limited contact with Sansei and community people. Both Ron [Wakabayashi] and I came from that [background]. . . . Those were our friends and partners. . . . We were open to communication . . . like a bridge . . . because redress was really a JA [Japanese American] issue, it didn't belong to JACL or NCRR . . . it was a community issue. . . . It was an issue that was so critical that we had to put these petty differences aside."[59] Despite intentions to maintain a united front, relations among the groups were often very tenuous.

One commonality between the organizations was the need to raise funds or in-kind donations. Financing the movement was expensive. Because of the technical nature of the NCJAR and *coram nobis* cases, supporters of these two groups were asked to provide money or donate legal knowledge. The JACL through its chapter structure and large membership directly solicited monetary donations from its members.[60] The NCRR raised funds from its members and supporters but focused on soliciting in-kind donations, services and time. Despite their differences all the groups agreed that the forced removal, exclusion, and incarceration of Japanese Americans were wrong. By the mid-1980s the groups agreed that an apology and monetary reparations were necessary components of redress, but they differed on the question of strategy.

Ninety-ninth Congress

As the Ninety-ninth Congress convened in 1985, a new obstacle to redress was the Balanced Budget and Emergency Control Act of 1985, commonly known as the Gramm-Rudman-Hollings Deficit Reduction Act. This act set ceilings on congressional budgets and reflected the ever-increasing deficit the country was facing. By 1983 annual federal deficit spending had risen to $207.8 billion from $73.8 billion in 1980.[61] The Gramm-Rudman-Hollings Act, signed into law on December 12, 1985, sought to create a balanced budget by fiscal year 1990 and set target limits on the federal deficit each year from 1986 to 1990. The legislation mandated that when the limits were exceeded, automatic across-the-board reductions in spending would be made in most budget categories, although exceptions could be made.[62] Some legislators used this legislation as a rationale for opposing redress and the costs it would incur.

A second obstacle to redress continued to be the structural elements of the Congress. In the Ninety-ninth Congress redress again faced the challenge of trying to reach the floor of each chamber. Majority Leader Jim Wright introduced H.R. 442 on January 3, 1985, with ninety-nine cosponsors. This bill was almost identical to its precursor, H.R. 4110, but was renamed in honor of the 442d R.C.T. Like H.R. 4110, H.R. 442 was assigned to the House Subcommittee on Administrative Law and Governmental Relations. On May 7, 1985, Representative Young introduced H.R. 2415, which was assigned to the Judiciary Committee. This bill called for the House to accept the findings of the CWRIC, implement its recommendations on the Aleuts, and increase the payments to each Aleut to $12,000.

Hearings for H.R. 442

By the time H.R. 442 was heard before the subcommittee, its number of co-sponsors had increased to 125. More important, the chair of the subcommittee was no longer Representative Hall, who had been appointed to a federal judgeship earlier in the Ninety-ninth Congress. Representative Dan Glickman, a moderate Democrat from Kansas, filled the seat.

The subcommittee hearings for H.R. 442 were held on April 28, 1986, in Washington, D.C. Representative Glickman opened the hearings with supportive words for the bill. In addition he acknowledged that the bill addressed the issue of "protection of the civil and constitutional rights of all Americans."[63]

Representative Mineta, the first of thirty-six witnesses, shared his personal story and made several points. First, he explained that the well-established principle of compensation for illegal confinement was at the heart of the bill. Second, he pointed out that while the California congressional delegation had been a political force behind the exclusion and incarceration in 1942, the California Democratic delegation now fully endorsed H.R. 442. Third, he emphasized that the fiscal cost of the bill spread out over ten years was minuscule when compared with a trillion dollar federal budget.

Representative Matsui spoke of his family's experience and of feeling the stigma of disloyalty that was thrust on all Japanese Americans. He observed, "The responsibility of war is to fight for your country with dignity, not to be put in jail by your country."[64] Representatives Lowry and Dymally also made supportive statements. Representative Dymally indicated that there was an expanding legal precedent and referred to the NCJAR class action suit. Later in the hearings Representative Wright forcefully argued, "There was a period of near hysteria. . . . But that doesn't forgive us nor justify us for violating the constitutional rights of American citizens. . . . Unreasonable seizure, detention against their will without due process of law, all of these things cried out for redress. . . . the act of apology is the act of a big nation, and refusal to apologize for a palpable wrong would be an example of pettiness on the part of a nation."[65] Representative Wright responded to allegations of possible disloyalty and the dual-citizenship status of many Japanese Americans by stating that the potential to commit a crime is quite different from probable cause to believe that one has committed a crime. Furthermore, he asserted that dual-citizenship status was a belief held by the emperor of Japan and that what the emperor believed was "wholly beside the point."[66]

Frank Sato discussed the JACL's and the community's support for the bill. He also related his experience of having been on television with Elliot Roosevelt, the eldest son of President Roosevelt, who acknowledged that the hysteria on the West Coast "resulted in probably my father making the biggest mistake of his entire career as a President. . . . He was given the wrong advice, and the system broke down, and the checks and balances were not followed."[67]

Mike Masaoka, now chairman of Go for Broke, Inc., a national Niesi veterans group, testified on behalf of Nikkei veterans: "We fought to gain what is the right of every American, the presumption of loyalty, of being a loyal American. In World War II we went to camp because that presumption wasn't granted to us, it still isn't granted to us, and we think, as veterans of our group, we're entitled to that presumption."[68]

As in the Ninety-eighth Congress, there was opposition. Representative Stratton repeated his same arguments. Representative Lungren continued to assert that individual monetary compensation should not be included in the bill. The Department of Justice presented the Reagan administration's opposition to the bill through a letter from Attorney General John R. Bolton to Representative Peter W. Rodino, chairman of the House Committee on the Judiciary: "We question the wisdom and, indeed, the propriety, of accusing leaders of the United States government during World War II, both civilian and military, of dishonorable behavior. . . . We do not believe that this bill should be the vehicle for promulgation of an 'official' version of these historical events."[69] The letter further insisted that the Japanese-American Evacuation Claims Act of 1948 already provided a "reasonable and balanced" remedy, that the provision for pardons was "completely unnecessary," and that the bill would impose heavy "administrative burdens on the Attorney General." It also argued that the Aleuts were "properly removed from a war zone" and thus did not warrant special consideration.[70] The Justice Department went so far as to argue that the bill's requirement that an agent of the federal government oversee the restoration of the community's churches was a violation of the First Amendment principle of separation of church and state.

Lillian Baker, David Lowman, and Karl Bendetsen once again criticized the work of the CWRIC. Senator Hayakawa opposed both an apology and monetary compensation and characterized the camps as being "in some ways the best thing that could have happened to the Japanese on the west coast."[71] He went on to attribute the redress movement to young Sansei radicals and to "paranoid demands about injustice and injuries of more than 40 years ago."[72] In responding to a hypothetical question from Representative Glickman regarding how he would have felt if he had been excluded, Senator Hayakawa revealed his lack of identification with the Japanese American community by stating that "having been brought up away from the Japanese community most of my life, I would not have had . . . the kind of emotional identification with the rest of the Japanese community that Californian Japanese-Americans did have."[73] Senator Hayakawa failed to acknowledge his comment made in 1980 in response to the U.S. hostage crisis in Iran. At that time the senator maintained that all Iranians in the United States should be put into camps "the way we did with the Japanese in World War II."[74]

Hearings for the Aleut Bill

Hearings for H.R. 2415 were held on July 23, 1986, in Washington, D.C., before the same House subcommittee. The hearings for H.R. 2415 were significantly different from those for H.R. 442. There were only twelve witnesses, all of whom spoke in favor of passing the bill.[75] The most controversial issue discussed was whether to separate the Aleut issue from the Japanese American issue since both were contained in H.R. 442. Representative Glickman argued that the two issues were fundamentally different. He described the issues in H.R. 2415 as being "less controversial" and acknowledged that the fiscal impact of H.R. 442 "dwarfs" the fiscal impact of H.R. 2415. Representative Glickman also stated, however, that "the advocates of the other part of H.R. 442 [the part addressing Japanese Americans], I'm sure, would be, at least at this stage, extremely reluctant to see part of it pulled out, and the rest of the bill not pass."[76] The Aleut witnesses, including Dimitri Philemonof and Father Paul Merculief, nevertheless supported separating the issues.

Although Representative Glickman's voting record was much more liberal than his predecessor's, he came from Kansas, which had few Japanese American constituents. While supportive of redress, Representative Glickman did not push for either H.R. 442 or H.R. 2415. Ultimately, neither bill passed out of the subcommittee.

Senate Inaction

Senator Matsunaga introduced S.R. 1053, the companion bill to H.R. 442, on May 2, 1985, with twenty-five cosponsors. The Senate Governmental Affairs' subcommittee, however, did not hold any hearings on the bill. The Ninety-ninth Congress came to a close without any redress legislation making it out of its assigned subcommittee. Senator Matsunaga, however, had developed a growing coalition of senators who cosponsored the bill.

The 1986 JACL Elections

In 1986 political action on redress also took place outside the halls of Congress. Within the JACL the campaign for the national president position was hotly contested. The two leading candidates were Rose Ochi, national vice president of membership, and Harry Kajihara, the finance and fund-drive chair of the LEC. Both candidates acknowledged the central importance of redress to the Japanese American community and to the JACL. While both candidates also acknowledged that the issue of the JACL's involvement with

Japan needed to be reexamined, they differed over the degree of involvement. Kajihara viewed U.S.-Japan relations as less of a priority than redress. Ochi did not see the two issues as mutually exclusive and was more willing to consider how to use U.S.-Japan relations to promote the JACL.

The election was very close. The final vote was 62½ to 59½ in favor of Kajihara. Under Kajihara's leadership the JACL focused its primary attention on the redress issue. In the months following his election Kajihara's column in the *Pacific Citizen* made little mention of U.S.-Japan relations and discussed redress and organizational affairs.

"A More Perfect Union": The Smithsonian Institution Exhibit

During the early 1980s a series of unplanned events culminated in the creation of a Smithsonian Institution exhibit about the World War II concentration camps. As with the redress effort, hard work, the rightness and framing of the issue, and luck all played significant roles.

The genesis of the Smithsonian exhibit was in 1979, at the Presidio Army Museum in San Francisco. This museum was located a little off the beaten path and was visited by approximately twenty people a day. Eric Saul, the museum's curator, had long been interested in the idea of a black soldiers' exhibit. He approached his supervisor, Lieutenant Colonel Donald R. Sims, a highly decorated African American Vietnam veteran who had been a company commander, and quickly gained his approval. The commander of the post, however, initially had reservations that the exhibit might be too controversial. As luck would have it, President Carter had appointed the first African American, Clifford Alexander Jr., to the position of secretary of the army. Secretary Alexander was planning an appearance on the post for black history week; as a result, the exhibit was approved.[77]

The response to the exhibit was enormous. There was abundant media coverage, and the African American community showed great support. The experience convinced Saul that an ethnic minority perspective on relevant topics was the key to raising attendance and stimulating public support. When planning the next exhibit, Saul's father reminded him of the 442d R.C.T. Saul approached the board president of the museum association, Retired Lieutenant General William "Ray" Peers, who had been a colonel in Burma during World War II commanding OSS Detachment 101 and had many Nisei linguists under his command. Since the war he had kept in touch with many of them. Lieutenant General Peers authorized five thousand dollars for the exhibit.[78]

Saul, faced with the challenge of finding artifacts and stories for the exhibit, did not personally know any Japanese Americans and was unsure where to look. Once again good fortune smiled on the project. Saul received an unsolicited and unexpected visit from a Japanese American veteran. Hank Oyasato, a company commander in the 442d, came in and told Saul that he enjoyed the black soldiers exhibit. He encouraged Saul to complete his plans to do an exhibit on the 442d and put him in touch with another veteran, Tom Kawaguchi.

Kawaguchi contacted Saul the following week and requested a proposal and description of the exhibit. Saul was strongly in favor of dealing with the controversial topic of the exclusion and incarceration. Kawaguchi worked with Saul on the plans for the exhibit and eventually became the project's veterans coordinator. He requested a list of the artifacts and the number of photographs that would be needed and immediately set up a national network among his veteran friends to gather the memorabilia.[79] Saul anticipated that the exhibit would use up to 150 photographs. As a result of Kawaguchi's request, Saul received many boxes of artifacts and photographs from Nisei veterans. The gathering of artifacts and photographs also led Saul to make several trips to the National Archives and the Library of Congress in Washington, D.C., as well as to numerous other cities and states that had Nisei veterans (e.g., Denver, Chicago, Hawai'i).

Early in the development of the exhibit Chester "Chet" Tanaka, a highly decorated veteran who was an original volunteer with the 442d R.C.T., became instrumental in the effort and served as a co–project coordinator and technical adviser for the exhibit.[80] Tanaka was one of the original unit historians of the 442d R.C.T. and was therefore intimately familiar with its story. He had written the original regimental history in 1944–45 and was largely responsible for writing up nominations for battle honors and individual citations for members of the 442d R.C.T. and 100th Infantry Battalion. Kawaguchi, Tanaka, and Saul contributed money to help cover the expanded cost of the exhibit and to publish Tanaka's book, *Go for Broke.* The advanced sales of *Go for Broke* were also used to help fund the exhibit costs.

Saul was familiar with the history of the concentration camps and promoted this as an integral part of the story. The exhibit was eventually divided into five parts. It originally had only three sections: racism in California and why the incarceration happened, the exclusion and the WRA camps, and the 100th Infantry Battalion and the 442d R.C.T.[81] In the summer of 1981 the exhibit expanded to include the history of the Military Intelligence and Language Service and its contribution to the Allied victory in the war in the Pacific. The fifth section explained the postwar impact of the Nisei veterans on the political history of Japanese Americans on the West Coast. The exhibit opened on March 7, 1981. Over two thousand people attended the exhibit opening, including Mike Masaoka and Senators Inouye and Matsunaga.

In the fall of 1981 Lieutenant General Peers and the secretary of the

Smithsonian Institution, Dillon Ripley, corresponded about having the exhibit placed in the Smithsonian. Ripley had been a captain in Lieutenant General Peers's unit and had worked closely with the Nisei linguists. Ripley came up with the idea of tying the exhibit in with the upcoming constitutional bicentennial celebration. Ripley assigned the exhibit to Roger Kennedy, director of the National Museum of American History, with the intention of placing it in that museum. Saul provided an extensive proposal to Kennedy, who then viewed the exhibit, which was being shown at the Los Angeles County Museum of Natural History.[82] Kennedy met with Saul, Kawaguchi, Tanaka, and Hiro Takusagawa and eventually brought in Tom Crouch to be the curator of the Smithsonian exhibit.[83]

Crouch was given the task of framing the exhibit so that it would strike at the heart of the Bill of Rights. Crouch recalled telling Kennedy about the potential of the exhibit: "I told him, 'If we were to take the story of the 442d to its natural extension, if we were to talk about the experience of Americans of Japanese ancestry during the war years, we would have the show you're talking about. It would be a gutsy thing to do . . . it would speak to what can go right and what can go wrong with the Bill of Rights.'"[84]

The Smithsonian Institution's initial attempts to gather artifacts were not very successful. In response Tanaka and Saul worked with the JACL in organizing local "swap meets." People were asked to bring their artifacts to the local community center, church, or temple, where members of the exhibition team could meet with them and select objects for display. Crouch and Jennifer Locke, the research assistant on the project, would then pick out appropriate artifacts. In designing the exhibit Crouch relied heavily on his advisory board. Crouch recalled, "The advisory board was very important. Especially Aiko Herzig-Yoshinaga, who I could go to for a thorough historical review."[85]

The exhibit had its opponents. Because the Smithsonian needed to collect artifacts from the community, news of the proposed exhibit circulated quickly. The negative mail began early. The Smithsonian received scores of opposition letters protesting the exhibit's creation. An opening day protest was promised by Lillian Baker but never materialized.

According to Crouch private fund-raising for this project would have been very difficult because of its controversial and unresolved political nature. Representative Mineta, a regent of the Smithsonian, secured a congressional line item in the budget that ultimately provided for three-quarters of the exhibit's budget.[86] In an era when the Office of Management and Budget was trying to eliminate these sorts of line items from the Smithsonian's budget, Representative Mineta and other legislators fought to maintain it.[87]

The exhibit opened on October 1, 1987, and was titled *A More Perfect Union*.[88] The opening event was well attended by congressional members and many individuals from the Japanese American community. Planning and implementing the Smithsonian exhibit served as an unintended dress rehearsal for passing the upcoming redress bill. The Smithsonian exhibit addressed an unresolved political question. It helped educate congressional members about the wartime treatment of Japanese Americans, the heroism of the 442d R.C.T., and the importance of an apology and monetary redress. Representative Mineta, describing the exhibit's contribution to redress, observed that "it verified that what we were doing was right and that we were on the right course . . . the bill had been about things nobody could see or feel or touch. The exhibit made it real."[89]

Crouch believed that the inherent quality of the story and of the imagery is what made the show work: "It was not a special interest exhibit. It was not an ethnic minority exhibit. It was an exhibit about an American ideal. . . . When people first see the exhibit, it looks like a negative story. But when you stop and think about it, this is ultimately a story about fifty years worth of citizen involvement with the Constitution."[90] *A More Perfect Union* provided the lesson of how redress needed to be framed as an American issue and its potential as a positive political issue.

9 The Aligning of the One-hundredth Congress (1987–88)

By 1987 Japanese Americans were energized around redress (+). The success of the California redress bill and the anticipation of the opening of the Smithsonian exhibit contributed to a growing impetus for redress. The general U.S. society gained a heightened awareness of the redress movement through media coverage. Barriers to redress existed, however. The country was experiencing an economic recession, the stock market crashed in October of 1987, and the federal budget was facing an unprecedented debt of $2.3 trillion.[1] Overall, however, the general U.S. society remained better than neutral in its reception to redress (N+).

The *coram nobis* cases and the NCJAR class action suit were completed by the end of 1988, which provided a judicial source of influence on the legislative effort. The *coram nobis* decisions contributed to understanding that the exclusion and incarceration were not based on military necessity and clearly identified the government's manipulation of evidence that led to the camps.

The NCJAR case advanced the redress movement in two significant ways. First, while never having its merits heard in court, the class action suit led to an increased awareness of the constitutional violations of the exclusion and incarceration. Second, the NCJAR case presented an extremely costly resolution, and by comparison the legislative bill appeared to be a more moderate option (N+).

Changes in pivotal congressional positions occurred in the legislative branch. The Democrats resumed control of the Senate and House, and important changes were made in the chairs of key subcommittees. The Nikkei members of Congress were nearing the height of their collective political influence. Senator Inouye had seniority and a very powerful presence in the Senate. Senator Matsunaga was in his second term and had established himself as a very popular senator. On the House side Representatives Mineta and Matsui were entering their seventh and fifth terms, respectively, and were well respected by their colleagues. The One-hundredth Congress presented a golden window of opportunity for legislative action (+).

The executive branch, however, remained out of alignment with the other policy streams. While President Reagan had said nothing, the Department of Justice's testimony at previous congressional hearings had been strongly negative (-). Nonetheless, the different policy streams were beginning to form a strong positive alignment for redress (see table 7).

Changes in the General Society

Between 1986 and 1988 a shift occurred in public opinion concerning the redress bill. In 1986 Carol Stroebel, Representative Mineta's legislative director, received a number of calls from reporters asking, "Why should we help our enemies?" and "Why do you care about redress?"[2] These questions reflected widespread ignorance about the camp experience and the legal and constitutional issues involved. During the ensuing two years various community groups launched effective public education campaigns to increase the U.S. public's understanding of the incarceration.

An example of this increased awareness was a 1987 *People* magazine article about Representative Mineta's boyhood experience in Heart Mountain. The article did not go into depth about the nature of the constitutional violation; it simply started with the premise that an injustice took place. Representative Mineta recounted the incarceration experience through the eyes of a child: "We gathered at the train station carrying just a few belongings—clothing, bedding and kitchen utensils. I wore my Cub Scout uniform and took along my baseball bat and catcher's mitt, but I had to leave my bat behind. I guess they thought it was a dangerous weapon."[3] Representative Mineta's family left Heart Mountain in late 1943. The congressman described that

Table 7.

Years	History		Legislative Branch		Judicial Branch	Executive Branch
	Community	U.S. Society	Senate	House		
1987	+	N+	+	+	N+	−
1983–86	+	N+	N	N	N+	−
1979–82	N+	N+	N	N	N	N-
1970–78	N+	N	N+	N+	N	N+
1945–69	N	N	N	N	N	N
Pre-WWII/Exclusion/ Incarceration	−	−	−	−	−	−

experience: "There was no big opening of the gates, no mass exodus. . . . We had dinner that night in a restaurant across the street from the hotel. After my mother and I ate, I stood up and began stacking the dishes the way I always did. In the camp mess hall we always had to bus our own tables. My mother watched me for a moment and then said very softly, 'Norman, you don't have to do that anymore.' At that moment, for the first time, it hit me that I was free."[4] By 1988 Stroebel was receiving calls from younger reporters and congressional staff expressing their disbelief that anyone could oppose H.R. 442.

The One-hundredth Congress Brings Changes

While redress support came from both sides of the aisle and from all regions of the country, the legislation originated with Democrats. In the 1986 elections the Democrats recaptured control of the Senate (54 to 46),[5] and they maintained their majority in the House (258 to 177). Representative Patricia F. Saiki (Republican from Hawai'i), a fifth Nikkei supporter of redress, was among those elected to the Congress in this election. With these changes the legislative branch was advantageously positioned to pass redress.

There were five leadership changes in the Senate. Senator Robert C. Byrd (Democrat from West Virginia) replaced Senator Robert Dole (Republican from Kansas) as the Senate majority leader. This replacement was a minor setback. Senator Byrd was not an active redress supporter, while Senator Dole was an original cosponsor of the bill. Senator Alan Cranston (Democrat from California) replaced Senator Alan K. Simpson (Republican from Wyoming) as the majority whip. Both senators were redress cosponsors, but Senator Simpson opposed monetary payments. Senator Daniel K. Inouye (Democrat from Hawai'i) replaced Senator John H. Chafee (Republican from Rhode Island) as secretary of the majority. This was a major gain because Senator Chafee opposed redress. Senator John H. Glenn Jr. (Democrat from Ohio), an original cosponsor, replaced Senator William V. Roth Jr. (Republican from Delaware), a redress opponent, as chair of the Governmental Affairs Committee, which had charge of redress legislation. Finally, Senator David Pryor (Democrat from Arkansas) replaced Senator Ted Stevens (Republican from Alaska) as the chair of the Governmental Affairs Subcommittee on Federal Services, Post Office, and Civil Service. This change was a partial loss. Although Senator Pryor became a cosponsor, he expressed little interest in redress, while Senator Stevens was an active supporter. Together, however, these changes formed a unique window of opportunity for redress.

Pivotal changes in the House leadership ushered in strong support for redress. Representative Jim Wright (Democrat from Texas), became Speaker. Representative Thomas S. Foley (Democrat from Washington) became majority leader, and Representative Tony L. Coelho (Democrat from California) took on the position of majority whip. Both Representatives Foley and Coelho were from West Coast states, understood the issue, and were very supportive of redress.

The most significant change in the House was Representative Barney Frank's assumption of leadership of the Subcommittee on Administrative Law and Governmental Relations of the House Judiciary Committee. The previous chair, Representative Dan Glickman (Democrat from Kansas), left it for a seat on the Agriculture Committee. Representative Barney Frank (Democrat from Massachusetts) had a reputation for being sharp-witted, intelligent, and a champion of liberal causes. He was the national chair of the Americans for Democratic Action and the only openly gay member of Congress. Representative Frank personally knew the pain of discrimination and prejudice and saw the parallels between what had happened to Japanese Americans in World War II and the current discrimination against all minorities.

In contrast to Representative Hall, who opposed redress, and Representative Glickman, who did not make it a top priority, Representative Frank was an ardent supporter of redress from the beginning. Stroebel recounted that Representative Mineta set a meeting with Representative Frank to approach him about redress. Representative Frank caught Representative Mineta in the hall earlier in the day and said, "If you are seeing me about the redress bill, don't bother to come by. Of course I'll support it."[6] Representative Matsui also received the same assurances when he approached Representative Frank. As chair of the Judiciary Committee's subcommittee, Representative Frank was in a pivotal position to push the bill out of the subcommittee.

Representative Frank reflected on his commitment to redress:

> The first I learned about this [issue] was in a college undergraduate class on American constitutional law. I remember learning about the Korematsu case and being appalled. I said, "How can this be? This is so crazy." . . . I came to Congress with a sense that this is one of the worst things the American government had ever done. . . . As soon as I heard about the bill, I became a cosponsor, and I talked about it to both Bob [Matsui] and Norman [Mineta]. . . . When I became chairman of the subcommittee . . . I found out how come this wasn't going anywhere. Some of those who had cosponsored it were afraid to bring it out. . . . I have a different view than some subcommittee chairmen here who will never bring a bill to the floor unless they are sure it's going to win. If you've never brought a bill to the floor and lost, you clearly have also failed to bring bills to the floor that could've won. You've clearly drawn the line too closely. My view is that you go up to the line . . . if it lost, it can't be worse off than if we never brought it up at all.[7]

The Lobbying Efforts Intensify

Effective lobbying often required a combination of outside pressure from hometown constituents and internal pressure from fellow legislators and political insiders. Along with the proper framing of the issue, personal appeal, friendships, and economic and political working relationships went a long way in convincing some legislators. Given the positive changes in the 100th Congress, Grayce Uyehara focused her efforts on the membership of the House Subcommittee on Administrative Law and Governmental Relations.[8] She learned of a Nikkei woman, Gene Doi, who lived in Stone Mountain, Georgia, the congressional district of Patrick L. Swindall. Uyehara contacted Doi and told her the importance of Representative Swindall's vote on the committee. Doi understood the challenge and personally discussed the exclusion and incarceration with the congressman.

Through her personal discussion of her family's experiences Gene Doi helped to put a human face on this issue and began to positively sway the congressman's thinking. Representative Swindall, a self-avowed conservative and strict constructionalist, began to view the exclusion and incarceration as the federal government's having impinged on individual rights without due process and having denied equal protection under the law. To Representative Swindall this was a clear violation of the original intent of the Constitution.

In addition to Doi's lobbying of Representative Swindall, Grant Ujifusa utilized his inside-the-beltway network to influence the representative. Ujifusa enlisted the assistance of David Brodie, chief lobbyist for the B'nai B'rith in Washington, D.C. Brodie strongly supported redress and agreed to help obtain Swindall's vote. As a professional lobbyist, Brodie knew Swindall well, and they shared a mutually beneficial working relationship.

Brodie's relationship with Swindall included two commonalities. First, they represented a shared constituency since a significant portion of Swindall's constituency was made up of American Jews. Second, Brodie, an American Jew and a lobbyist for a Jewish organization, and Swindall, a born-again Christian, shared a common interest in Israel. Representative Swindall believed (as did many born-again Christians) that the second coming of Jesus Christ would not occur until the state of Israel had been fully reestablished. As part of their working relationship, Brodie had arranged for Representative Swindall to visit Israel on "fact-finding missions." Their relationship was one Representative Swindall valued very much.

Brodie set up a meeting with Representative Swindall and Ujifusa. Ujifusa recalled the meeting: "Dave, Swindall, and I talk. Swindall says he thinks he can support us. I couldn't believe it. . . . Dave plugged redress into the Jewish/born-again [Christian] coalition." Brodie's working relationship with

Swindall served as an impetus for securing Representative Swindall's vote. "Would you believe the hoped-for return of the Messiah pushed redress along?" reflected Ujifusa, "Only in America."[9]

Another example is the lobbying of Representative Al Swift (Democrat from Washington). Cherry Kinoshita of the Seattle JACL met with him often. Her strategy was to make herself known personally to the congressman. On one visit she brought a Nisei woman who had a common acquaintance ("a beloved teacher").[10] On another visit she brought the local president of the American Jewish Congress, an old friend of the congressman. At the same time, Representative Matsui's wife, Doris, also talked with Representative Swift. She was seated next to him at a dinner party when he asked, "Doris, were you in the camps?" She replied that she had been, and a long conversation followed. Representative Swift finally asked her what she thought about the redress bill. She replied, "I think that we should close the final chapter on this, and that's why we need to have this bill passed."[11]

On July 6, 1987, Representative Swift announced his support for the bill and indicated to Representative Matsui that his discussion with Doris Matsui had influenced his decision. Representative Swift eventually voted for the redress legislation, and on the day of the vote he made a personal phone call to Kinoshita to tell her.[12]

At times lobbying was based on the good fortune of long-standing relationships. Such was the case with Senator Alan Simpson, a noted conservative. Hollywood scriptwriters could not have thought of a better story line through which to introduce Senator Simpson to redress. In 1943, as a young boy growing up in Wyoming, Senator Simpson's Boy Scout troop participated in a joint camping trip with Boy Scouts from the Heart Mountain WRA Camp. He was paired up with none other than Norman Mineta. Representative Mineta recalled their first joint effort:

> I was assigned to a pup tent with Alan Simpson. When you build a tent, you always build a moat around it in case it rains. Then you have a place where you cut out for the water to escape. So he said, "You know there's a kid in my troop that I really don't like, what about cutting it so the water goes that way [toward that kid's tent]." I said, "Yeah that's okay with me. Let's do it." So we cut it and as luck would have it, it rained that night. Our tent was high and dry, and the water ran off to the tent below us, the tent pegs pulled, and the tent came down. All night long Alan Simpson was laughing.[13]

Throughout junior high school, high school, and college the two Boy Scouts wrote to each other. They lost contact after college but resumed their friendship in 1978, when Senator Simpson was elected to the Senate. Although Senator Simpson did not support the monetary portion of the bill, he was a cosponsor, largely because of his relationship with Representative Mineta.

Other members represented districts that had historical connections to the exclusion. Representative William J. Hughes (Democrat from New Jersey) was one such legislator. He had a large constituency of Japanese Americans who came to New Jersey from the concentration and internment camps to work for Seabrook Farms during the war and decided to stay. Japanese Americans, such as Tom Kometani and Charles Nagai, coordinated personal lobbying visits from Japanese American constituents to each of New Jersey's representatives.[14]

The Nikkei veterans groups continued to get veterans groups to pass resolutions supportive of redress and to lobby their legislators to vote for the bill. They also worked to neutralize opposition on the part of other veterans who might oppose the bill. Other community lobbying efforts intensified. The NCRR rallied Japanese Americans to write letters to their own senators and representatives and to legislators who sat on important committees. Personal letters to one's own legislators were more effective than mass form letters, but the large number of community letters sent the important message to the Nikkei legislators and other redress supporters that the Japanese American community wanted this bill.

H.R. 442's Legislative Journey

Representative Tom Foley introduced H.R. 442 on January 6, 1987, in the first session of the One-hundredth Congress. The bill had an additional 119 cosponsors (106 Democrats and 13 Republicans) and was similar to earlier bills in the Ninety-eighth Congress and Ninety-ninth Congress. Representative Don Young introduced H.R. 1631, an Aleut redress bill, on March 17, 1987. On April 29, 1987, hearings on H.R. 442 and H.R. 1631 were held by the House Judiciary Subcommittee on Administrative Law and Governmental Relations. Representative Frank framed the discussion before the subcommittee to focus on whether H.R. 442 provided the best means of redress, not whether a wrong was committed. He opened the hearings by noting, "I think there is a consensus in the country that what the Federal Government did in the 1940's was simply wrong . . . and the question before us is, what is an appropriate response for the Nation to take."[15] He later bluntly stated, "Let me just say that I agree absolutely that the people involved . . . have a right to the relief that is in the legislation, but I can't guarantee that. What I can guarantee as chairman is that this subcommittee will vote on both these bills . . . and I can promise you that these will be voted on in this subcommittee within the next couple of months."[16]

Throughout the hearings Representative Frank spoke with his usual rapid-fire pace, advised witnesses to keep their testimonies focused, challenged testimony, and unapologetically shared his own perspective. The congressman understood the importance of his role in giving the bill its hearing and his responsibility to have the issue come to a vote.

Representative Mineta offered timely testimony that a Department of Justice task force was currently proposing as "legal and appropriate the mass round-up and incarceration of certain nationalities for vague national security reasons."[17] Representative Mineta's point was well taken. Redress was not only about the suspension of liberty and justice forty-five years earlier but also about the constant need to protect these rights.

Representative Matsui refuted the claim that the bill would set a precedent for other groups with long-standing histories of oppression. He asserted that the number of potential recipients would be strictly limited by the bill's provisions. He added a personal account of how his mother had continued to have nightmares of the camps throughout her life, and he candidly stated that her suffering "can't be compensated by a mere $20,000."[18] Representatives Young and Saiki also gave supportive testimony.

The only opposing testimony came from Richard K. Willard, assistant attorney general, Civil Division of the Department of Justice, representing the Reagan administration. The Department of Justice opposed redress on three counts. First, Willard alleged the Japanese-Americans Evacuation Claims Act of 1948 already served as a remedy. Second, he maintained it was not "the proper function of our Government to adopt an official version of these historical events. . . . we oppose spending hundreds of millions of dollars to educate the American people to accept this official interpretation of our history." Third, Willard claimed that the Aleuts were "properly removed from a war zone" and that the "wartime hardships" they suffered did not "provide any factual predicate" for redress.[19]

Representative Frank labeled the Reagan administration's perspective "disappointing" and "a real failure of moral vision."[20] He also characterized it as coming "close to being exculpatory of . . . a very, very sad act in our history."[21] In response Willard acknowledged that he believed the decision to exclude and incarcerate was wrong and tainted by racial prejudice. "But," he added, "I do believe that the historical record is a complex one. There are a variety of factors that entered into it."[22]

Representative Frank immediately responded, "Complexity is not a reason to withhold judgment. Pleas of complexity as a reason for withholding judgment always come from the people who have some kind of a weak case. . . . Of course the world is complex. That's no reason not to judge."[23] Representative Frank went on to press the point that he believed the incarceration to be the result not only of the racial prejudice and failed leadership of governmental officials but, more important, of the racist society in which it took place.

Representative Howard L. Berman (Democrat from California) also challenged the administration's contradictory and seemingly disingenuous actions in attempting to influence both the judicial and legislative branches. Referring to the NCJAR class action suit, he stated that "there is something funny about the Department of Justice going to court [in the NCJAR case] and saying the claim may be very legitimate, but it does not provide a legal basis for recovery, Congress has to deal with that, and then come to Congress and oppose efforts to legislate a remedy [H.R. 442]."[24]

With Representative Frank's guidance, H.R. 442 made it out of the House subcommittee for the first time on May 13, 1987. The bill then went to the full House Judiciary Committee, chaired by Representative Peter W. Rodino. The committee passed the bill on June 17, 1987, by a roll call vote of 28 to 6.[25] On August 6, 1987, the House Judiciary Committee reported out H.R. 442 to the full House of Representatives.

H.R. 1631 was also passed out of the House subcommittee on May 13, 1987. It passed out of the House Judiciary Committee on September 29, 1987 by a voice vote. H.R. 1631 was reported out of the House Judiciary Committee on October 15, 1987 but was not debated on the floor of the House.

As the day of the House floor vote on H.R. 422 approached, lobbying efforts and attempts at internal influence continued. A number of "Dear Colleague" letters were sent in the House. Among them was a letter from an influential bipartisan group of nine representatives urging their colleagues to support H.R. 442 and in so doing to "reaffirm that the Constitution applies to all Americans."[26]

Some "Dear Colleague" letters opposed redress. Representative Norman Shumway (Republican from California), a JACL member from the Stockton, California, chapter, informed members of three amendments he planned to offer to the legislation. He thought that "the compensation [H.R. 442] provides is entirely too arbitrary and, worst of all, the measure threatens to revive anti-Japanese sentiment."[27] Representative Lungren's letter, dated September 16, 1987, just one day before the House floor debate, indicated that President Reagan might veto the legislation if it included individual monetary payments.[28] He misrepresented the CWRIC report by taking its words out of context and claiming that *Personal Justice Denied* "challenges the foundation of monetary payments."[29] He quoted the part of the report that noted that "injustices cannot neatly be translated into dollars and cents. . . . History cannot be undone; anything we do now must inevitably be an expression of regret and an affirmation of our better values as a nation, not an accounting which balances or erases the events of the war. That is now beyond anyone's power."[30] He also enclosed the letter from Assistant Attorney General John R. Bolton that outlined the Justice Department's objections to the redress bill and the Office of Management and Budget's approval of Bolton's report.[31] Representative Lungren, however, conveniently failed to mention that the CWRIC had recommended individual payments of $20,000.

Aware of the fact that Representative Lungren and others were going to propose amendments to eliminate monetary compensation, Representatives Rodino, Frank, Henry J. Hyde (Republican from Illinois), and Hamilton Fish Jr. (Republican from New York) wrote to their colleagues and argued, "To remove the compensation included in this bill would be to remove the real substance of this legislation and literally to discount the rights of thousands of Americans."[32]

S.R. 1009 Works Its Way through the Senate

As H.R. 442 was being debated in the House, Senator Matsunaga led the lobbying campaign for redress in the Senate. He spoke personally to each of the ninety-nine other senators at least once.[33] The Senate was more collegial than the House, and Senator Matsunaga was extremely well liked by his fellow senators. He had his own table in the Senate dining hall, complete with a bottle of *shoyu* (soy sauce) for his many visitors from Hawai'i. He also had a deep pride in his ethnic background and a sense of humor. An example of these two characteristics was his desk, which was once used by President John F. Kennedy. As a senator, President Kennedy had carved his initials into the desk drawer. Senator Matsunaga followed this example by carving the Japanese *kanji* character for his name underneath the president's initials. He found it humorous that someday some senator might be perplexed by this carving.[34]

Senator Matsunaga's persona put a human face on the redress issue. For many senators redress was an issue about which their friend and colleague cared very deeply. His personal appeal was at times as effective an argument as any discussion of constitutional violations.

Senator Matsunaga's motivation to pass the redress legislation with a veto-proof margin also came from his relationship with Hawai'i's other Democratic senator, Senator Inouye. In some ways both men were very similar. Both were Japanese Americans, Democrats, World War II veterans, and career politicians. Their personalities, however, were very different. Although they were colleagues, an unstated rivalry existed between the two.[35] It was the type of rivalry often seen in senators of the same party from the same state. As the number of cosponsors Senator Matsunaga gathered would increase, Senator Inouye, the politically senior of the two, would indicate that it was not enough. At first Senator Matsunaga responded by attempting to gather fifty-one cosponsors to ensure passage. He then "upped the ante" by going after at least sixty-seven cosponsors to make the passage veto-proof.

Senator Matsunaga introduced S.R. 1009 on April 10, 1987, with seventy cosponsors. Forty-three of the cosponsors were Democrats, and twenty-seven were Republicans. S.R. 1009 was assigned to the Governmental Affairs Subcommittee on Federal Services, Post Office, and Civil Service. By the time the bill reached the subcommittee its number of cosponsors had increased to seventy-four (including Senator Matsunaga). This was seven more than was necessary to override a veto and many more than the sixty needed to prevent a filibuster by invoking cloture. Senator Matsunaga's efforts ensured that S.R. 1009 would not only be brought to the floor of the Senate but also would pass by a veto-proof margin.[36]

As in the House, the Senate subcommittee's climate was favorable. There were just twelve witnesses, none of whom were redress opponents. The subcommittee chair, Senator Pryor, opened the hearing on June 17, 1987, by stating that he had participated in the dedication of monuments at the two WRA camps located in Arkansas.

Both Senators Matsunaga and Inouye shared their personal accounts of World War II. Senator Inouye repeated his story of coming back from the war only to be denied a haircut in San Francisco because according to the barber, "We don't cut Jap hair."[37] At the close of their testimonies, Senator Pryor asked Senator Matsunaga to join the committee at the dais and announced to Senator Matsunaga that he would like to become the seventy-fifth cosponsor of the bill. Senator Matsunaga, of course, readily accepted the offer.

The Japanese American community was represented by Harry Kajihara, Grayce Uyehara, Mike Masaoka, and William Hohri.[38] Although the deck was now stacked in favor of redress, supporters still needed to exercise a measure of political caution. In his testimony Masaoka belittled Senator Hayakawa, who was no longer a member of the Senate. Senator Stevens, the ranking minority member of the subcommittee, responded, "Sam is one of my great friends and I think you and your colleagues ought to be advised not to tilt at windmills. Sam has lots of friends out there on the floor of the Senate and what you have just said is going to make it very difficult for me to get this bill that I cosponsored through the Senate."[39]

Along with the testimony of witnesses the American Civil Liberties Union, the Friends Committee on National Legislation, the American Friends Service Committee, the B'nai B'rith Anti-Defamation League, the American Bar Association, the International Longshoremen's and Warehousemen's Union, and Cook Inlet Region, Inc. submitted supportive statements into the record. S.R. 1009 was reported out of subcommittee and was debated by the full Committee on Governmental Affairs on August 4, 1987. Senator Roth introduced an amendment during the markup that sought to extend payments over a five-year period. The $1.3 billion would be allocated according to the following timetable: $500 million in 1989; $400 million in 1990; $200 million in 1991; $100 million in 1992; and $100 million in 1993. The committee also clarified that an "'eligible individual' must be a United States citizen or permanent resident alien on the date of enactment of the Act" and that redress payments would not be included in determining eligibility in "certain income-based Federal benefits." The committee approved the bill by a voice vote.[40]

The NCRR's Lobbying Trip

Since the Senate and House redress bills had the most favorable legislative context to date, the NCRR organized a lobbying trip for the summer of 1987. The original strategy was to send a few individuals to lobby legislators and their staffs. Bert Nakano remembered, "As the summer started to come around and as the news [started to spread] about new Congressmen getting on board, [and] Senators getting on board. . . . There was a sense of excitement [that] this may be the year."[41] By July over 120 Japanese Americans were ready to descend on Washington, D.C. This group, representing all three generations of Japanese Americans (ages six to eighty), different parts of the country, different community groups, veterans, and World War II draft resisters, was united in its effort to speak directly to the legislators about redress. These community lobbyists made their visits between July 25 and July 29.

The visits with the members of the House or Senate (or their staff) were carefully planned by a committee headed by Miya Iwataki, the legislative chair of the NCRR and a legislative aide to Representative Mervyn Dymally (Democrat from California). The committee carefully directed the volunteers to key legislators. Geographical considerations (e.g., residence in the legislator's district) and shared life experiences (e.g., being a veteran in World War II) were key determinants in making assignments. The NCRR's lobbying efforts were targeted mainly at members of the House, since Senator Matsunaga told NCRR members that he would take care of the Senate.[42]

The nature of the lobbying visits was based primarily on personal experiences. Nakano recalled, "These people . . . wanted to tell their story . . . from their heart. And it came from the gut. . . . These were actual victims going there to tell their story."[43] Iwataki concurred, "The Issei and Nisei that went, all of them said, 'Oh, we can't talk, we can't talk.' But once you got them in there and they started talking, they were the most articulate, eloquent, moving people." Apart from the efforts of the former inmates, Iwataki pointed out that members of "the 442d were invaluable in our visits to members of Congress who were veterans."[44]

Persuading legislators required a strategy that highlighted political ideology or constituency interest and included a human element. An example was the role that Rudy Tokiwa, a decorated member of the 442d Regimental Combat Team, played in influencing the votes of four representatives from Florida. Representative Charles Bennett, a Democrat, was the senior congressman from Florida. Although Representative Bennett did not have a large Japanese American constituency in his district, he was a World War II veteran. To take advantage of this, Tokiwa was asked to help persuade Bennett to vote for the bill. Tokiwa, who was wounded during World War II,[45] met with Bennett and appealed to his sense of camaraderie with other veterans.

Initially, Tokiwa and several other NCRR members received an unfriendly reception from Representative Bennett. Representative Bennett, in very clear and colorful language, proclaimed that he had no intention of supporting any bill that required the U.S. government to apologize. Unfazed by this initial response, Tokiwa proceeded to thank the congressman for his service (as a veteran and as an elected official) to the country. Tokiwa skillfully wove into the discussion the commonality they shared as veterans with similar combat wounds. Tokiwa left this initial meeting without Representative Bennett's support for the bill but with the congressman's acknowledgement of respect. Through several more contacts Tokiwa was eventually able to obtain Representative Bennett's support for the redress bill.

In the time between Tokiwa's contacts with Representative Bennett and the introduction of the redress bill on the floor of the House, Representative Bennett's support for redress dissipated. Bennett was concerned with the fiscal implications of the bill and no longer planned on voting for it. As a senior representative from his state, Bennett instructed three other representatives from Florida to follow his vote on the floor. As the debate wore on, Representative Mineta approached Representative Bennett and asked him to look up at the balcony. Looking to the balcony, Representative Bennett saw Tokiwa sitting in the front row. One can speculate what Representative Bennett felt in that moment. His behavior, however, was clear; he and his three junior colleagues voted for the bill. Shortly after the bill's passage Tokiwa spoke to Representative Bennett by telephone, and using the congressman's same colorful language, he thanked him for his vote.[46]

During that summer the NCRR volunteers visited 101 congressional offices and received various responses, including definite noes, requests for more information, indications of possible support, and assurances of support. The NCRR effort was the largest Asian American lobbying campaign to ever descend on Washington, D.C., in such a concentrated period of time.

The House Vote

Redress supporters' hard work and persistence culminated on September 17, 1987, when H.R. 442 came to the floor of the House. Early in the One-hundredth Congress Representative Mineta arranged for the bill to come up for a vote on September 17, the two-hundredth anniversary of signing of the Constitution. This had both advantages and disadvantages. The obvious advantage was that the timeliness naturally facilitated the focus on the constitutional issues. The major disadvantage was that many members had scheduling conflicts with the numerous celebrations in Philadelphia, Washington, D.C., and their own districts.

Since the House leadership was supporting the bill, members were pressured to stay and participate in the vote. Representative Matsui recalled, "We almost did not take the issue to the floor on September 17, because it was the anniversary of the Constitution and many members wanted to get on with the recess. Several members approached me the day before asking why we had to vote on this day. Tony Coelho [the majority whip] actually grabbed a fellow member by the lapel and in no uncertain terms told them him that he was to stay and vote on this bill."[47]

A few days before the vote Representative Mineta's office counted 180 votes in favor of the redress bill, not enough to ensure its passage. The leadership and some of the key members supporting the bill discussed whether to pull the bill. According to the majority whip's counts, however, undecided members were breaking more than 2 to 1 in favor of the bill. Stroebel recalled that "to call off the vote would be a show of weakness . . . and we would miss the emotional impact of the [anniversary of the] Constitution. . . . Our supporters were all gearing up for the vote on that day."[48] The decision was made to go with it. Stroebel was only one of many who went into the vote with butterflies in their stomachs. Several members thought the debate was the best and most emotional they had ever heard on the House floor.[49] Many thought the outcome would be closer than it ended up being.

Representative David Bonior (Democrat from Michigan) opened the debate: "This day, September 17, 1987, is significant for we celebrate today the two-hundredth anniversary of the signing of the U.S. Constitution. . . . Many Americans would rather forget the torment of those thousands of people who were incarcerated, but forgetting is not the answer. To forget, I think, is to fail once again. What we must do is admit our errors, work to correct them, and ensure they are never allowed to happen again."[50] Representative Bonior later described the nature of the issue by quoting the author Susan Faludi:

> A hallucinatory quality clings to the story of the internments of the Japanese-Americans, as if the events themselves make sense only when perceived as imaginary. . . . There are the contradictions of stripping civil liberties from people—two-thirds of them U.S. citizens—as a way of safeguarding American freedoms. There are the contradictions of incarcerating an entire race while fighting a war against a nation incarcerating an entire race. When the Jews were freed from Dachau, it was the Japanese-American 442nd Regiment, the most decorated U.S. Army regiment in World War II, that threw open the gates— while their relatives waited for them at home behind barbed wire.[51]

The debate on the House floor lasted more than five hours. Three amendments were offered, and strong opposition to redress was voiced by some members of the House, who focused on the 1948 Japanese-American Evacuation Claims Act, the risk of setting a very dangerous precedent, and the establishment of a monument or a trust fund instead of individual payments of $20,000.[52] Representative Shumway drew the comparison with the desegregation policies in the South: "I do not know anyone . . . who is advocating that we go back and pay $20,000 to each of the black schoolchildren of this country who may have been victimized by the separate but equal education policies that prevailed in the South before the Supreme Court decision in 1954 declaring that to be unconstitutional."[53]

Representative Samuel S. Stratton (Democrat from New York) went so far as to argue that "Franklin Roosevelt did the right thing. In fact as Commander in Chief, if President Roosevelt had not done this he would have been derelict in his duty."[54] Not many in the House held this view. Most, even Representative Lungren, agreed that there had been an injustice. Representative Lungren, however, was the most enigmatic member of the House. He spoke seven times for a total of over forty minutes and often seemed to argue both sides of the issue. In the opening hour and a half he spoke twice regarding the inappropriateness of placing the bill on the calendar on Constitution Day, the presence of the Magic cables, and the Japanese-American Evacuation Claims Act of 1948.

Nearly two hours into the debate Representative Lungren introduced his first of two amendments, which added to the text of the bill the phrase "failure of political leadership," a quotation from *Personal Justice Denied,*[55] as a contributing factor for the WRA camps. Representative Lungren's logic was confusing, at best. He used the Magic cables in 1941 as rationale for this amendment. Representatives Barney Frank and E. Clay Shaw Jr., the ranking minority member of the Administrative Law and Governmental Relations Subcommittee, seized the moment and supported the amendment. The amendment passed on a voice vote.[56]

Representative Lungren then offered his second amendment, which eliminated individual reparations while maintaining the funding for public education. He was concerned about the precedent-setting nature of the bill. Representative Lungren argued that it was impossible to put a price tag on "misbegotten policies of the past" and that the legal statute of limitations should not be extended to something that happened forty-five years earlier.[57] He reminded the House that "prime sponsors of the legislation in the Senate to establish the Commission said they would not support the establishment of the Commission if monetary reparations were the outcome of that legislation."[58]

A heated debate ensued, with some other members speaking in support of the amendment.[59] Representative Ron Packard (Republican from California), in supporting the amendment, offered a personal story of his father's detainment on Wake Island by the Japanese military during World War II.

This account, while emotionally moving, exemplified the continued inability to distinguish actions of an enemy nation from those imposed by a nation on its own citizens.

The voices in opposition to the Lungren amendment were far from silent. Representative Ron Dellums (Democrat from California) described a court case in which he was the plaintiff (*Dellums v. Powell*) to demonstrate that economic recompense was an appropriate and practiced principle. Representative Swindall spoke against the amendment on the basis that the incarceration violated the fundamental principles of "justice and liberty" for all people. Representative Swindall, a "prolife" advocate, drew a parallel between the violations of Japanese Americans' civil liberties and those of an unborn person's: "I would say it to my prolife friends who argue consistently that the Constitution guarantees the right not to be deprived of life or liberty or the pursuit of happiness without due process of law, that that is precisely the issue which we debate here today. It is a very important point if we are to be consistent in our fight to make certain that those constitutional protections are recognized for all Americans, equal justice under the law."[60] Other representatives, such as Dan Glickman, Howard Berman, Bruce Morrison (Democrat from Connecticut), Steny Hoyer (Democrat from Maryland), and Sidney Yates (Democrat from Illinois), also voiced their opposition to the amendment.

Three hours into the debate Representative Matsui delivered what would be the first of a "one-two combination" of powerful speeches by him and Representative Mineta. Representative Matsui recounted his own experiences and the fundamental issue of the deprivation of constitutional rights. Despite the ease and conviction with which he spoke Representative Matsui recognized the historic importance of the moment: "My great fear during the debate was that I would not be able to finish my speech. I told this to Tony Coelho, who stayed on the floor all day. Tony said, 'If you choke, pause, and then leave the hall, and I will stand up and give you a standing ovation and everyone else will, too.'"[61] Representative Matsui began by acknowledging the difficulty he faced in remaining objective. He spoke of his parents and how they lost their house, their car, their small produce business, and their dignity:

> My father was not able to talk about this subject for over forty years . . . when he finally was able to articulate he said, "You know what the problem is, why I can't discuss this issue, is because I was in one of those internment camps, a prisoner of war camp and if I talk about it the first thing I have to say is look, I wasn't guilty, I was loyal to my country, because the specter of disloyalty attaches to anybody who was in those camps." And that stigma exists today on every one of those sixty thousand Americans of Japanese ancestry who happened to have lived in one of those camps.

Representative Matsui went on, "How could I as a 6-month-old child born in this country be declared by my own Government to be an enemy alien? How can my mother and father who were born in this country also be declared a potential enemy alien to their country? . . . They did not go before a court of law, they did not know what charges were filed against them. They were just told, 'You have 3 days to pack and be incarcerated.' That is the fundamental issue here."[62]

Immediately after Representative Matsui spoke Representative Mineta rose in opposition to the Lungren amendment. He also acknowledged the emotional nature of the issue and discussed the effect of the incarceration on his family and him. He recounted his experience as a ten-year-old boy, who, dressed in his Cub Scout uniform, was "herded onto a train under armed guard in San Jose, CA, to leave for Santa Anita, a racetrack in southern California."[63] He pointed out, "It is only in this kind of a country, where a 10½-year-old can go from being in a Cub Scout uniform to an armed-guard-guarded train to being a Member of the House of Representatives of the greatest country in the world."[64]

Representative Mineta described the importance of monetary compensation: "H.R. 442, including compensation, will reaffirm and strengthen this very, very vital document that we are celebrating today. . . . this authorization is not only just but long, long overdue. . . . By keeping compensation in H.R. 442, the House will tell the world that this body is genuine in its commitment to the Constitution and we will be putting our money where our mouth is."[65] The congressman wiped away a tear from his eye as he read from a letter in which his father described his feelings as the train pulled out of the station: "'I looked at Santa Clara's streets . . . I thought this might be the last look at my loved home city. My heart almost broke, and suddenly hot tears just came pouring out, and the whole family cried out.'" Representative Mineta continued, "We lost our homes, we lost our businesses, we lost our farms, but worst of all, we lost our most basic human rights. Our own Government had branded us with the unwarranted stigma of disloyalty which clings to us still to this day. So the burden has fallen upon us to right the wrongs of 45 years ago. Great nations demonstrate their greatness by admitting and redressing the wrongs that they commit, and it has been left to this Congress to act accordingly."[66] Representative Mineta closed with a heartfelt plea. His voice resonated with his personal emotion and the emotion of a whole community: "And so my dear colleagues, with all my heart, I urge you to oppose this amendment and to support H.R. 442, the Civil Liberties Act of 1987, and in so doing, to reaffirm our Constitution on this very historic day."[67]

Representatives Matsui's and Mineta's speeches were interrupted only once each by the customary five-minute rule. Once they were given extensions, neither was interrupted again, despite speaking well over the extended time period. Stroebel recalled that "our opponents could have objected but they knew that they would look bad if they did on such a personal issue . . . so they let Norm go on . . . it had an affect on the mood on the floor."[68] Both received robust applause from the members of the House. At the close of Representative Mineta's speech, even one of the House clerks, who normally are neutral in response, applauded.

Speaker Jim Wright also spoke out against the Lungren amendment. Drawing a comparison between the wrongs committed by the United States and by Germany, he repeated the words of Konrad Adenauer, head of the Federal German Republic in the 1950s: "'The atonement we owe not to others, but to ourselves.'"[69] The House voted down the Lungren amendment by a vote of 237 to 162.[70] This vote was as important as the final vote on H.R. 442. Had the authorization for individual payments been removed, the bill would have been withdrawn.[71] In addition the authorization of payments forced a genuine examination of the issues and a real debate on the floor.

Immediately following the defeat of the Lungren amendment Representative Shumway offered a final amendment. He asserted that since not all the inmates spent the same amount of time in camp and were incarcerated at different life stages, they did not suffer equally. His amendment provided monetary redress payments based on a per diem formula. Adults who were incarcerated for three years or more would receive $20,000. Other adults who had spent less than the three years would receive redress at a rate of $18 a day. Minors who had been under the age of eighteen would receive redress payments calculated at $1 a day times the age of the inmate. Representative Shumway claimed that the purpose of his amendment was not to cut costs but rather "to achieve some measure of fairness in the bill."[72] The motivation for Representative Shumway's amendment was suspect since he had opposed monetary payments less than an hour earlier: "Mr. Chairman, I cannot yet see a case having been made for the payment of money damages. Why is it we cannot say that we are sorry without paying money with it? . . . I just do not know of any precedent for compensation of money in cases like this."[73] His amendment served simply to complicate the logistics of a procedure that he did not support in principle.

After the introduction of the Shumway amendment, a number of representatives voiced their support of H.R. 442 and their opposition to the amendment.[74] Representative Frank reminded his colleagues of the pending NCJAR lawsuit that threatened to cost the government even more money. Representative Frank explained that H.R. 442 contained an extinguishment clause that made plaintiffs in the lawsuit ineligible to continue with their lawsuit if they accepted the individual payment of $20,000 from Congress.

In the final speech of the debate Representative Dellums spoke out against the Shumway amendment. He delivered an eloquent and moving account of his experiences of the exclusion as an African American child:

> My home was in the middle of the block on Wood Street in West Oakland. On the corner was a small grocery store owned by Japanese people. My best friend was Roland, a young Japanese child, same age. I will never forget, Mr. Chairman and members of this body, never forget, because the moment is burned indelibly upon this child's memory, the day the six-by trucks came to pick up my friend. I will never forget the vision of fear in the eyes of Roland, my friend, and the pain of leaving home. My mother, bright as she was, try as she may, could not explain to me why my friend was being taken away from me as he screamed not to go, and this six year old Black American child screamed back, "Don't take my friend." No one could help me to understand that, no one, Mr. Chairman.
>
> So it wasn't just Japanese Americans who felt emotions. Because they lived in the total context of community, and I was one of the people who lived in the community. . . .
>
> So this formula that if you were in for one day you get a few nickels, if you're in for three years you get the whole twenty thousand dollars, as if we could play that game. This is not about how long you were in prison. It is about how much pain was inflicted upon thousands of American people who happened to be yellow in terms of skin color; Japanese in terms of ancestry. But this Black American cries out as loudly as my Asian American brothers and sisters on this issue.
>
> So this formula, while well intended, does not in any way address the reality of the misery, Mr. Chairman. It must be rejected out of hand. Vote for this bill without this amendment. And let Roland feel that you understood the pain in his eyes and sorrow in his heart as he rode away screaming, not knowing when and if he would ever return.[75]

The House rejected the amendment with a resounding voice vote. The vote on H.R. 442 followed immediately. Initially a voice vote was called, but Representative Lungren requested a recorded vote. As the members began to vote, redress supporters anxiously waited. In the first few minutes of the vote Representatives Mineta and Matsui shared congratulatory hugs and handshakes with each other and other members of the House. The exchanges reflected both the hopeful anticipation of what possibly was about to be achieved and the deep appreciation of what had already been accomplished. Throughout this time both Representatives Mineta and Matsui stole anxious glances at the vote count. As the yea votes approached 200, more members gathered around the two Nikkei representatives. Fifteen minutes after the call for the vote, the yea count passed the 218 mark. H.R. 442 was adopted. Representative Matsui recalled the moment that the bill passed: "I will never forget that moment when my colleagues were watching the voice count and we reached that magic number of 218, which is the majority. Members were coming up to Congressman Mineta and myself embracing us with tears in their eyes saying, 'We did it. We did it.'"[76] The results of the recorded vote were 243 votes in favor, 141 votes against, and 1 "present" vote.[77]

Despite the jubilance over the passage of the bill, several legislators received harsh criticism from their hometowns for their supportive votes. Representative Matsui recalled Representative Martin Frost (Democrat from Texas) told him a week after the vote: "'I caught hell because of you. . . . I met with my chamber of commerce, and they were beating the devil out of me over this redress issue.' I told him I was sorry to hear that. He responded, 'I told them where to go.'"[78]

A sidebar to the redress vote came a month later in California. In November 1987 California's Governor George Deukmejian, a Republican, named Representative Lungren to fill a vacancy as state treasurer. Although the required confirmation by the state legislature seemed routine, it was defeated as a result of a lobbying campaign led by activists in the Japanese American and broader Asian American community who had not forgotten Representative Lungren's opposition to the monetary portion of the redress bill.[79]

The coalition of activists who opposed Representative Lungren's nomination was diverse. Vocal leaders included Donald Tamaki of the Asian Law Caucus, Henry Der of Chinese for Affirmative Action, John Ota of the NCRR, and Hoyt Zia of the Asian Pacific Bar Association. Civil rights, environmental, labor, housing, peace, and other progressive organizations banded together to form the Californians for Responsible Government, which opposed the Lungren nomination. These individuals and groups disseminated detailed accounts of Representative Lungren's conservative voting record on civil rights, education, environmental, defense, and women's issues.

Members of the Asian Pacific community and other interested groups testified at state senate and assembly hearings prior to the final confirmation vote.[80] On February 25, 1988, both the state senate and assembly voted. While the assembly, by a vote of 43 to 32, confirmed Representative Lungren's nomination, the senate, by a vote of 21 to 19, denied it. A key vote in the senate belonged to Quentin Kopp (Independent from San Francisco), who had pledged to vote for the confirmation. Prior to the vote, however, Senator Kopp's office was inundated with numerous letters opposing Representative Lungren. Senator Kopp responded to these letters by voting against the confirmation.[81]

In response to the legislative defeat Representative Lungren filed a lawsuit claiming that he needed only one branch of the state legislature to confirm his nomination. On June 23 the California Supreme Court denied his petition and upheld the Senate's decision.

The political might the Asian Pacific community displayed in its opposition to Representative Lungren's nomination put it on the political map. "In the future, I don't think politicians are going to take the Asian-American community as lightly as Lungren did," said Representative Matsui.[82] These words rang true as the redress movement progressed.

The Senate Vote

The Senate version of redress (S.R. 1009) was slightly different from the one passed by the House. It had three titles. Title I was an apology on behalf of the United States. Title II included authorization for the payment of $20,000 to each survivor, the establishment of a trust fund and a civil liberties public education fund, a requirement that the attorney general review all convictions of Japanese Americans growing out of their wartime experiences, and an extinguishment clause. Unlike the House's extinguishment clause, the Senate's version extinguished claims ten years after the final passage of the act or on the date an eligible individual received the total amount of payments under the act. Title III authorized $21.4 million for the Aleuts and Pribilof Islanders. Each survivor would receive $12,000, with the remainder to be used to restore community losses.

Going into the Senate vote, Senator Matsunaga was confident of the bill's passage. During the previous months he had increased the total number of cosponsors to seventy-six (though five cosponsors eventually withdrew their support).[83] The only concern was the rumor that Senator Jesse Helms (Republican from North Carolina) would be introducing a number of unfriendly amendments.[84]

On April 19, 1988, the Senate considered S.R. 1009. Senator Glenn reviewed the changes made in the Governmental Affairs Committee, which addressed budgetary concerns. The principal change was to establish a five-year period in which individual compensations would be made. Other modifications clarified that payments would be made only if funds were available to appropriate and that Title II and Title III would not set up new entitlement funds. Senator Glenn concluded by praising Senator Matsunaga's efforts on the bill: "Spark . . . deserves full credit for the success of this legislation. I do not believe . . . I have ever seen anyone pursue a particular piece of legislation, buttonhole Senators more effectively, call on them in their office, make certain he had their support for a particular piece of legislation . . . as well as Spark Matsunaga has done on S. 1009. . . . He has convinced those Senators of the rightness of his position."[85] At the end of his remarks Senator Glenn relinquished his position as floor manager to Senator Matsunaga.

Senator Matsunaga reminded those present of the recent bicentennial of the U.S. Constitution and fought back his tears as he defined the "wholesale relocation and incarceration in American-style concentration camps" of Japanese Americans as a tragic turning point in their lives.[86] Senator Matsunaga reviewed the findings of the CWRIC hearings, submitted a list of over 160 different organizations supporting redress, outlined the rationale behind S.R. 1009, and countered anticipated opposing arguments.

Senator Matsunaga set the tone and stage for the debate. Many senators drew from their personal experiences during the war or those of their constituents. Senators heard how Senator Paul Simon (Democrat from Illinois) was shunned after his father, a Lutheran minister, protested the treatment of Japanese Americans. Senator Cranston recounted how, in his work in the Office of War Information, he attempted to dissuade President Roosevelt from excluding and incarcerating Japanese Americans. During the first day Senator Ernest Hollings (Democrat from South Carolina) was the lone voice of opposition, both on budgetary and philosophical grounds. His arguments echoed Representative Lungren's objections to attaching a price tag to the suffering of the Japanese Americans and setting a dangerous precedent: "Where do we draw the line against reparations to the countless other groups of Americans who have suffered because of actions of the U.S. Government? Or do we tell those other groups that their suffering was somehow less meaningful, less tragic, less deserving of recompense?"[87]

The Second Day of the Senate Floor Vote

The debate resumed on April 20 and lasted seven hours. Senator Chic Hecht (Republican from Nevada) offered the first of five amendments. It deleted the authorization of all appropriations and expenditures under the bill. He stressed that the United States already made adequate restitution under the Japanese-American Evacuation Claims Act of 1948 and claimed that this $1.3 billion bill was too expensive given the huge federal deficit.

Senators Inouye, Matsunaga, and Stevens rose in quick succession to oppose this amendment. Senator Inouye argued, "How do you compensate a child who had just lost his mother, who committed suicide because of depression and anguish? . . . the goal of S. 1009 is to benefit all citizens of our Nation by educating our citizens to preclude this event from occurring again to any other ethnic or religious group or any person suspected of being less than a loyal citizen. This bill reinforces the strength of our Constitution by reaffirming our commitment to upholding the constitutional rights of all our citizens."[88]

Senator Harry Reid (Democrat from Nevada) joined in opposing the Hecht amendment. Senator Reid highlighted the blatantly racist action of incarcerating Japanese Americans and told the story of the 442d veteran Wilson Makabe. Makabe, whose family was incarcerated, had lost his leg as a result of war injuries. Upon returning to California, he found that his former neighbors had burned down his family home.

Opposing opinions emerged. Senators Warner (Republican from Virginia),

Helms, and Hecht acknowledged a wrong was committed, but they articulated four main reasons to support the Hecht amendment. First, the bill was fiscally irresponsible in view of the huge budget deficit. Second, the idea of providing tax-free individual compensation was inappropriate and arbitrary. Third, the indictment of the three branches of government for "failure of political leadership" was objectionable and based on hindsight. Finally, President Gerald Ford had already "set the record straight" when he rescinded Executive Order 9066.[89] Senator Hecht went so far as to question why we would compensate multimillionaires. Before Senator Hecht could complete this thought, Senator Stevens objected to the depiction of Aleutians and Japanese Americans as multimillionaires.

Senator Helms claimed that President Roosevelt was provided intelligence reports during the war that pointed to widespread espionage and possible sabotage on the part of Japanese Americans. He reported that representatives of the Veterans of Foreign Wars and the American Legion told him that their organizations had no position on the redress bill. Senator Matsunaga countered this claim by listing eleven different veterans groups that had adopted resolutions endorsing S.R. 1009 (including the American Legion, Sixty-sixth National Convention; the Jewish War Veterans of the USA; and the Veterans of Foreign Wars, USA, Eighty-fifth National Convention).[90] The Hecht amendment was defeated by a vote of 67 to 30.

The First and Second Helms Amendments

Following the Hecht amendment the debate continued. Senator Chafee stressed that while he supported the apology, other issues, such as maternal and child health care, the war on drugs, and homelessness, should be higher national priorities. Senator John Exon (Democrat from Nebraska) admitted that as a child he had thought it was proper to incarcerate Japanese Americans, until his father and grandfather told him of the treatment of Germans in South Dakota during World War I. "Shame on us," Senator Exon declared, "for assuming just because we did not have German names in 1917, shame on us as Americans just because we did not have Japanese names in 1941 that we took it upon ourselves to decide what was right and what was wrong regardless of the rights of the individual."[91]

Shortly thereafter Senator Helms offered his first amendment to prohibit redress funds from being appropriated in any year when there would be a budget deficit (the Senate had just passed a budget with a $140 billion deficit).[92] He called on his colleagues to be fiscally responsible. Senator Helms quoted former Senator Hayakawa's claims about the understandable terror Americans felt following Pearl Harbor. Despite his arguments the first Helms amendment was defeated by a vote of 61 to 35.

Senator Simpson, an original cosponsor of the bill, voted for the first

Helms amendment. After its defeat he recounted his personal memories of the Heart Mountain camp, and how he met Congressman Mineta. Senator Simpson explained that he supported an apology but was against the monetary payments because it made the apology less sincere. However, he stressed he would vote for the final bill because the "conflict of the actual money appropriation is overcome in the final analysis by the humanity of what happened."[93]

Senator Helms then offered a second amendment, which had two purposes: (1) to guarantee that the redress legislation would not be used as a precedent for the United States to give away any more of its national territory to any person or country; (2) to compel the president to pursue compensation from the Soviets for the descendants of the Aleut Indians they had removed from Wrangell Island against their will in 1924. Senator Helms stated that Mexican citizens had pending law suits seeking the return of several U.S. states to Mexico. This amendment would preclude these types of claims. Eventually, Senator Helms dropped the second provision when Senator Stevens informed him that Alaska had never claimed the Wrangell Islands as part of its territory. With this information the modified amendment was passed.

The Hatch Amendment

Senator Orrin Hatch (Republican from Utah), a cosponsor of the bill, offered an amendment dropping the requirement that five members of the public education fund's board of directors be of Japanese ancestry. Senator Hatch stressed that this requirement violated the Fifth Amendment, which prohibits Congress from using national origin to make distinctions between people. Senator Matsunaga readily agreed to this amendment since he was concerned that the president would have good reason for vetoing the original bill on the grounds that it might be construed as unconstitutional. The Hatch amendment was accepted without further debate.

The Third Helms Amendment

Senator Helms's third and final amendment required the Japanese government to pay families of those killed in the Japanese bombing of Pearl Harbor before redress payments could be made. The opposition to this amendment was especially fierce. Senator Stevens stressed that such a provision was unacceptable. Senator Matsunaga emphasized that Helms's amendment "presumes that we Americans of Japanese ancestry had something to do with the bombing of Pearl Harbor. That is absolutely false. . . . The [Helms] amendment . . . would obscure this distinction [between Japanese and Japanese Americans] by denying compensation to Americans for what the Japanese Government did at Pearl Harbor."[94] The Helms amendment was based on the same lack of distinction between Japanese Americans and Japanese nationals that had fueled the incarceration experience nearly fifty years earlier. Helms's third amendment was soundly defeated by a vote of 91 to 4.[95]

Final Debate and Vote

The debate closed with Senator Helms's reiterating all the arguments redress foes had used in the previous decade (e.g., statute of limitations, Magic cables, inappropriateness of making the present generation pay for another generation's action). Senator Helms's speech swayed few if any of the senators. At the conclusion of his speech the title of S.R. 1009 was changed to H.R. 442 with unanimous consent. Senator Matsunaga called for the vote. The Senate passed H.R. 442, with amendments, on April 20, 1988, by a vote of 69 to 27.[96]

Conference Committee and Resulting Bill

The Senate's passage and renaming of its bill created two versions of H.R. 442 (the House's and the Senate's), which needed to be reconciled in a conference committee.[97] One of the major discrepancies to reconcile concerned the vesting clause for individuals who died after the bill became law. The House version made individuals eligible if they were alive at the time of the enactment of the law. The Senate version required that individuals needed to be alive at the time their redress payment was made. This issue, identified by Cherry Kinoshita after carefully reading both bills, was eventually resolved in favor of the House version.

The Senate agreed to the compromise on eligibility but demanded that if an individual died, inheritance would be limited to three beneficiary categories: a surviving spouse; if no spouse, then equal shares to all children living at the time of the payment; if no children, then equal shares to parents living on the date of the payment. If a deceased individual had no one in any of these categories, the money would be returned to the trust fund. The conference report also instructed the attorney general's office to attempt to provide payments to the oldest inmates first.

The joint explanatory statement of the Committee of Conference included other changes to H.R. 442.[98] First, the Aleuts were included at $12,000 for each surviving Aleut (as per the Senate version). Second, Congress was given ten years to make all monetary payments to eligible recipients (as per the House version). Third, Congress could not appropriate more than $500 million for redress per fiscal year (as per the Senate version). Finally, the payments were subject to the availability of appropriated funds (as per the Senate version), and there was an immediate extinguishment of claims (as per the House version) (see table 8).

Table 8.

House Version	Senate Version	Conference Version
Redress limited to Japanese Americans.	Redress for Japanese Americans and Aleuts.	Redress for Japanese Americans and Aleuts.
Payment schedule of ten years.	Payment schedule of five years.	Payment schedule of ten years.
Must be alive at time of signing of bill into law.	Must be alive at time payment made.	Must be alive at time of signing of bill into law.
No specific language for beneficiaries.	Spouse, children, parents as beneficiaries.	Spouse, children, parents as beneficiaries.
No specific language for annual expenditures.	Limit of $500 million appropriations per year.	Limit of $500 million appropriations per year.
No specific language for availability of funds.	Payments subject to availability of appropriated funds.	Payments subject to availability of appropriated funds.
Immediate extinguishment of claims.	Possible ten-year period before extinguishment of claims.	Immediate extinguishment of claims.

Prior to the vote on the conference report, four conservative representatives distributed a "Dear Colleague" letter that urged members to support the conference report. Representatives Jack F. Kemp (Republican from New York), Swindall, Gingrich, and Hyde highlighted the fact that the forced exclusion and incarceration of Japanese Americans during World War II violated the Fourth and Fifth amendments of the U.S. Constitution. They concluded, "We, as Americans, are enlightened enough to learn from our mistakes and courageous enough to admit it. . . . If our Constitution is truly our guiding document both in letter and in spirit, then this redress must be made."[99] This letter reinforced the bipartisan support for the redress issue.

The conference report was submitted to both chambers in late July. The Senate agreed to the conference report on July 27, 1988, by a unanimous voice vote. The House agreed to the conference report on August 4 by a vote of 257 to 156, not a wide enough margin to override the veto that many expected. The House vote included seven ayes from California Republicans. Four of these votes came from Republican members who voted against H.R. 442 on September 17, 1987.[100] Even Representative Lungren voted in favor of the conference report, seemingly contradicting his longtime opposition to the bill. Representative Matsui interpreted these additional votes as the result of the political strength the Asian American community had displayed in defeating Representative Lungren's appointment as California treasurer.[101]

Understanding How the Bill Passed Congress

The speeches of various members on the House and Senate floors point to some of the reasons why H.R. 442 finally passed, but they do not tell the whole story. No one element made redress successful; the integration of a number of factors facilitated the passage of redress through Congress. The CWRIC's documentation of the injustices, the creation of a coalition of diverse groups backing redress, and the framing of the bill as a constitutional issue about equal opportunity and justice elevated the bill, as Carol Stroebel put it, "beyond pork barrel issues or something we are giving to some special interest group . . . it really was about the Constitution."[102]

Japanese Americans had developed personal relationships with and access to the congressional legislators during the redress campaign. This greatly facilitated the passage of the redress bill, especially through the House. While mass letter-writing campaigns were a way to involve large numbers of Japanese Americans, the effectiveness of such a strategy was minimal. Letters and personal visits from constituents were the key to gaining individual members' support, especially those from areas with little or no Japanese American constituency. One of the most important legacies of the redress movement was the development of the Japanese American community's access to legislators. As John Tateishi recalled:

> One of the things I always felt was of real value about the campaign was the empowerment of Japanese Americans. When we first started trying to get some public recognition . . . I realized . . . that our folks had never even been involved in anything political. They didn't even know how to find their [local] council members. . . . By the end . . . I could call up people all over the country and say, "Can you talk to your Congress members about such and such?" and they would say "Yeah, I'll give Pete a call today." You'd think these people were old hands at this. They literally could get in the front door of their congressperson's office, on a first-name basis . . . What a weapon.[103]

Equally important to Washington, D.C., politics were the contributions of the community groups. The ideological differences between the JACL and the NCRR, while a potential source of dissension, broadened the support for redress. Ultimately, the two groups complemented each other. By the One hundredth Congress both groups agreed on the need for monetary redress. Both groups were also keenly aware of the pressure to obtain redress before too many more Issei died. Every month roughly two hundred Issei were dying, two hundred people who would not have their dreams of justice fulfilled.

In general the JACL, with its access to the Congress, greater name recognition, long-standing involvement with other civil rights organizations, and preestablished credibility, embodied the strategic considerations of the movement. The NCRR was the expressive voice of the movement and helped broaden the support for redress, both inside and outside the Japanese American community. Their nonredress activities (e.g., opposing Dan Lungren's appointment as state treasurer of California) helped expand the coalition of outside support for redress.

Two additional elements that greatly facilitated the passage of H.R. 442

were the appointment of Representative Barney Frank to the chair of the House Judiciary Subcommittee on Administrative Law and Governmental Relations and the vote-marshaling efforts of Senator Spark Matsunaga. Representative Frank's leadership provided redress with its first legislative opening for a vote by the full House. Senator Matsunaga's efforts all but guaranteed that the bill would pass in the Senate by a veto-proof margin.

The passage of H.R. 442 was a noteworthy accomplishment. The bill was passed by both chambers of the Congress with all of its major components intact. This was quite remarkable, especially since it passed when the economy was not very healthy. Now all that was left was to convince the president to sign H.R. 442 into law.

10 The President's Signature and the Fight for Appropriations

After nearly nine years of congressional labor H.R. 442 was ready to be sent to the president of the United States. Throughout the legislative battle it was uncertain whether President Ronald Reagan would sign the legislation. While the president himself never publicly spoke against redress, his administration consistently opposed the notion of redress in general and H.R. 442 in particular. The Department of Justice's earnest contesting of the judicial cases and its opposing testimony in congressional hearings, along with the negative strictures of the Office of Management and Budget (OMB), all reflected the administration's opposition. Through his veto power President Reagan could prevent H.R. 442 from becoming law, because there were not enough votes in the House to override such an action.

Lobbying the President

Efforts to lobby President Reagan began in the mid-1980s and overlapped with the congressional action. Understanding the president's thought processes and what motivated him to action were crucial components of the lobbying effort. The Japanese American community was at a disadvantage in its efforts to lobby President Reagan. There were no Japanese Americans in the upper levels of the Reagan administration, and the most prominent Japanese American Republican, former Senator S. I. Hayakawa, was adamantly against redress.

Between 1984 and 1986 Frank Sato, the national president of the JACL, was employed as an inspector general for the Veterans' Administration. Sato took advantage of his relationships with White House officials. He disseminated packets of information supporting redress to key officials, including John A.

Svahn, the president's chief domestic policy adviser. During the One-hundredth Congress Sato also arranged for redress information to be included in President Reagan's briefing material on a weekend visit to Camp David.

Before the vote on H.R. 442 Grant Ujifusa asked a White House pollster to inquire about the level of support for the bill among members of the Reagan administration. Ujifusa was told, "I've got very bad news. . . . People over at the White House say they've drawn their wagons in a circle and they don't want this [bill] at all."[1] The pollster advised Ujifusa to wait until another session of Congress to press for the bill.

Meanwhile, Grayce Uyehara and others across the nation were organizing grass-roots letter-writing campaigns to the president.[2] As numerous as these support letters were, they were outnumbered by letters urging President Reagan to veto the legislation. Ujifusa reported that Anne Higgins, a White House aide who reviewed the incoming mail, told him that they "were swamped by the negative mail . . . four or five or six to one, particularly from outraged veterans."[3] Lillian Baker and her "Americans for Historical Accuracy" and groups of "Concerned Americans" placed opposition ads in California papers, the *New York Times,* and the *Boston Globe.* The *Pacific Citizen* urged supporters to write letters and use a prepaid hotline mailgram to send their message of support to President Reagan.[4]

While many influential Japanese American Republicans wrote to the president, there was no Japanese American who could personally persuade President Reagan. The lobbying effort needed to include non–Japanese Americans who were trusted by the president and could influence him.

Opponents of Redress in the White House

As redress supporters worked to obtain the president's support, redress opponents were actively trying to dissuade the president from signing the bill. On May 5, 1988, former Senator S. I. Hayakawa sent a handwritten note to Howard Baker, the president's chief of staff. In the letter Senator Hayakawa described Japanese Americans as "just rolling in prosperity." He went on to state, "They are a damn sight better off than whites, but they play on the widespread assumption that non-whites are all more-to-be-pitied than whites. Makes me damn sick to listen to those skillful hustlers. I crawl with embarrassment at their gimme/gimme attitude towards government. Best wishes to you. Best wishes to the President."[5]

Inside the Reagan administration the Department of Justice and the OMB favored a presidential veto. Richard Willard, the assistant attorney general from the Civil Division of the Department of Justice, had presented strongly worded testimony against the redress bill during the House Judiciary Subcommittee on Administrative Law and Governmental Relations hearing. Willard later stated that the Civil Division of the Justice Department based its opposition on its analysis of the legislation, the CWRIC report, and the litigation brought by the *coram nobis* team.[6]

Ujifusa wrote a letter to Willard on May 7, 1987, and subsequently visited him. Ujifusa argued that the original intent of the Constitution was grossly violated by the exclusion and incarceration of Japanese Americans. He also stressed the political argument that the Japanese American and the Asian American communities were "emerging natural Republican constituencies" that voted Republican in both 1980 and 1984.[7] This argument was especially important since the prominent Japanese Americans in Congress were Democrats. For many in Washington, D.C., Senators Inouye and Matsunaga and Representatives Mineta and Matsui were the Japanese American community.

On September 10, 1987, one week before the vote on the House floor, the Reagan administration released a "Statement of Administration Policy," which outlined its opposition to H.R. 442 and the intention of the president's senior advisers to recommend a presidential veto. It cited the Japanese-American Evacuation Claims Act of 1948 and the bill's inclusion of persons who repatriated to Japan during the incarceration period as reasons for opposing the bill.[8]

Immediately after the bill was passed, the OMB, the Domestic Policy Council, and other White House staff recommended a veto.[9] The fall of 1987 was a bleak time in the economy because of a plunge in the stock market and the ever-growing budget deficit. Moreover, President Reagan had already targeted a large amount of money to wage a "war on drugs." Any funds for redress would have to come from the same pot of money used to wage this war.[10] These factors provided fuel for the opponents of redress on fiscal grounds.

Governor Thomas Kean and Kazuo Masuda

Ujifusa was keenly aware of the need to reach President Reagan through key individuals. President Reagan planned to travel to New Jersey in October 1987 to lend support to Republican candidates running for the state legislature. Ujifusa was aware that Thomas Kean, the Republican governor of New Jersey, would "host" the president's visit and would have personal access to the president. Ujifusa knew Governor Kean from editing his book, *The Politics of Inclusion*, and urged the governor to lobby the president to sign the redress bill.

Governor Kean was no stranger to political controversy and protecting the rights of racial minorities. In one instance Governor Kean intervened on behalf of Asian Indians who were being persecuted and physically attacked by a white hate group named the Dot Busters. In response to another incidence of racial hatred he personally washed off a swastika that had been spray painted on the walls of a Jewish synagogue.

During a private limousine ride with President Reagan and Deputy Chief of Staff Ken Duberstein, Governor Kean spoke to the president.[11] Governor Kean was aware that members of the Domestic Council advised the president to oppose the legislation. During the conversation he learned that the president had received the same advice from other sources: "The President said he had been advised to veto it and one of the main ones advising him, interestingly enough, was that fellow that used to be head of the University out there during the riots, a Japanese American [S.I. Hayakawa]. . . . Hayakawa had been the senator from the president's home state, so that had quite a bit of influence."[12]

The governor urged President Reagan to reconsider his stance on the redress legislation since it was compatible with the president's philosophy of redressing a wrong.[13] Governor Kean recalled, "I told him that I thought Hayakawa was wrong, and that members of the community felt very differently about the bill. I told him that it was a blot on the nation, that he had a great opportunity to purge. And he said to me, 'You know I kind of felt that way . . . I was getting all this advice, but before I got it all I was inclined to sign it.' He said he was glad that I was making another argument."[14]

Despite this sympathetic perspective President Reagan would not commit his administration to redress at that point. The president expressed two primary concerns. First, he wondered whether the issue was adequately dealt with by the Japanese-American Evacuation Claims Act of 1948. Second, the president questioned whether the incarceration was a form of protective custody for the Japanese American people.

Governor Kean's forthright expression of support for redress, however, persuaded the president to take another look at the issue.[15] Governor Kean was the only person outside the Reagan administration to have spoken at length with the president about redress. Reflecting on his own support of the bill, Governor Kean stated, "I believed very much in the bill. . . . I believe that when a great people do something wrong you admit it and you try to make redress. And this was a chance for us to admit a mistake which I think is a sign of a country's maturity."[16]

On February 6, 1988, approximately four months after the limousine meeting, Governor Kean sent a letter to President Reagan urging him to sign the redress legislation. He reminded President Reagan of his participation in the wartime medal ceremony for a dead Nisei soldier from the 442d R.C.T. who was awarded the Distinguished Service Cross. He went on to write, "Given your life-long commitment to the cause of equal rights, and the esteem in which Japanese-Americans now hold you, I feel it would be very fitting for you to sign the redress legislation. It would show the world that America is big enough to admit when we make mistakes, and still true to the values on which we were founded."[17] President Reagan read the letter, and a White

House aide informed Governor Kean that the president recalled the story and was "glad to hear it again."[18]

The World War II veteran about whom Governor Kean reminded President Reagan was Kazuo Masuda. Masuda was a young Nisei staff sergeant in the 442d R.C.T. Despite his family's incarceration in Arizona he wanted to fight with the 442d R.C.T. He survived numerous military campaigns until he was killed in Italy on August 27, 1944. A mortar had lost its base plate, and Masuda filled his helmet with dirt and fired the mortar long enough to repel a German patrol that was bearing down on F Company. Several days later Masuda was killed as he was on patrol. He was awarded the Distinguished Service Cross posthumously.

In 1945 Masuda's family received threats of physical violence when it attempted to resettle in Santa Ana, California. The local community also refused to allow Masuda's body to be buried in the cemetery. In response the U.S. Army sent a group of officers to present formally the Distinguished Service Cross to Masuda's family. This was part of an intensive government campaign to defuse anti–Japanese American tensions as Japanese Americans returned home from the camps. Heading this contingent was General Joseph W. "Vinegar Joe" Stilwell. Among the other officers was none other than Captain Ronald Reagan. Captain Reagan read a statement prepared by the U.S. Army and the Office of War Information, which said in part, "Blood that has soaked into the sands of a beach is all of one color. America stands unique in the world, the only country not founded on race, but on a way—an ideal. Not in spite of, but because of our polyglot background, we have had all the strength in the world. That is the American way. Mr. and Mrs. Masuda, just as one member of the family of Americans, speaking to another member I want to say for what your son Kazuo did—Thanks."[19]

Accompanying Governor Kean's letter to President Reagan were two carefully chosen letters from Grant Ujifusa and Jane Masuda Goto, Kazuo's sister. Ujifusa's letter to President Reagan clarified that Japanese Americans did not leave their homes voluntarily and that the Japanese-American Evacuations Claims Act of 1948 did not adequately compensate Japanese Americans. June Masuda Goto's letter included a photograph of the medal ceremony. She recalled the moving remarks the president delivered and his participation in honoring her brother. She wrote, "Our family feels that what you and General Stilwell said in 1945 are as true and important as ever: the ideals for which all good Americans should be willing to fight and die. My brother did both, even though his parents and family were stripped of all their American rights, and placed in an Arizona internment camp."[20]

By mid-February 1988 Ken Duberstein indicated to Ujifusa that the president was going to sign the bill.[21] Secretary of Education William Bennett and President Reagan's domestic policy adviser Gary Bauer (a prominent antiabortion, family values advocate), also spoke to Ujifusa about their support for redress.[22] Ujifusa approached others, such as Burton Pines from the conservative Heritage Foundation and Paul Weyrich from the Committee for the Survival of a Free Congress. Having support from such conservative individuals and organizations made it politically more feasible for President Reagan to back the legislation.[23]

A March 28, 1988, internal OMB memo questioned the appropriateness of threatening a veto.[24] The next day Chief of Staff Howard Baker sent a memo to the president recommending that the administration "withhold any further threat of a veto and explore with Congress the possibility of reducing the potential costs while making it clear we expect any subsequent appropriations to be in accord with our budget agreement."[25] With his initials President Reagan approved the recommendation and set a new direction for the administration's policy.

The 1988 Presidential Campaign

Concurrent with President Reagan's decision to support redress, the 1988 presidential campaign was proceeding. Early in the campaign the major candidates, Vice President George Bush, Governor Michael Dukakis of Massachusetts, and Reverend Jesse Jackson, endorsed the redress legislation. The vice president stated, "It is only fair that our country provide apologies and reparations to those innocent Japanese Americans interned in prison camps during World War II."[26] Excerpts from a statement released later by Vice President Bush's press secretary described the wartime incarceration as "an unfortunate chapter in our nation's history. . . . During times of war, it is often difficult to resist succumbing to hysteria. However, we should always try to remember our basic purpose—to defend freedom and civil rights for all."[27]

Budgetary Concerns

Despite President Reagan's and the presidential candidates' general support the Reagan administration continued to have budgetary concerns about the bill. As H.R. 442 passed on the Senate floor, the Reagan administration preferred that the payment period be extended from five to ten years, the amount appropriated be limited to $500 million annually, and an immediate extinguishment clause be adopted. Joe Wright, the director of the OMB, and Ken Duberstein suggested that members of the House-Senate conference committee address these issues. Duberstein recalled, "There was a lot of give and take. We essentially signaled to Congress that if they made these accommodations to the president's concerns the president would look favorably on it and in all likelihood sign the legislation."[28]

Once the president was convinced that the conference bill addressed his concerns, he sent a public letter to Speaker Jim Wright two days before the

House was scheduled to vote on the conference committee's bill. The letter, dated August 1, 1988, stated:

> We welcome the action of the House-Senate conference on H.R. 442, a bill to provide compensation for Americans of Japanese descent interned in the United States during the Second World War. The bill reported from the conference and passed by the Senate on July 27 is substantially improved over the versions of the bill previously considered.
>
> We are particularly pleased that the bill provides for a measured disbursement of the amounts authorized for the trust fund and ensures that acceptance of compensation under the legislation fully satisfies claims against the United States based on the unique circumstances of the internment. The enactment of H.R. 442 will close a sad chapter in American history in a way that reaffirms America's commitment to the preservation of liberty and justice for all. I urge the House of Representatives to act swiftly and favorably on the bill.[29]

With the threat of a presidential veto publicly removed, the Congress passed H.R. 442.

The Signing of H.R. 442

After the president decided to sign the bill, the question remained about whether there would be an official signing ceremony. Some in the president's administration were in favor of a ceremony, while others were opposed, feeling that he should sign the bill without any fanfare.[30] The president thought that a signing ceremony would be the appropriate thing to do. The Civil Liberties Act of 1988 became law on August 10, 1988, when President Ronald Reagan signed Public Law 100-383 in Room 450 of the Old Executive Office Building. Before signing the bill President Reagan remarked that "we gather here today to right a grave wrong. . . . More than forty years ago . . . 120,000 persons of Japanese ancestry living in the United States were forcibly removed from their homes and placed in makeshift internment camps. This action was taken without trial, without jury. It was based solely on race."[31] He described the concentration camp experience by citing Congressman Norman Mineta's personal story. The president captured the essence of the bill by stating that "no payment can make up for those lost years. So, what is most important in this bill has less to do with property than with honor. For here we admit a wrong; here we reaffirm our commitment as a nation to equal justice under the law. . . . the ideal of liberty and justice for all—that is still the American way."[32]

The president mentioned his personal recollection of the Masuda story. He credited Rose Ochi with sending him a December 1945 newspaper clipping from the *Pacific Citizen* about the medal ceremony. The president injected a bit of wit by alluding to a speech made by a young actor on that day.

He humorously remarked, "The name of that young actor—I hope I pronounce this right—was Ronald Reagan."[33] He concluded by acknowledging that the bill was fittingly named in honor of the 442d R.C.T.

The signing ceremony was a memorable moment. Ken Duberstein acknowledged that the signing "was one of the most moving moments in my White House career . . . the [signing ceremony sent] chills up and down my spine. . . . The tears that flowed at that signing ceremony reinforced [to those of us on the White House staff] that President Reagan had done the right thing. This was not a question of a bailout . . . this was a question of doing the right thing in a measured way to redress a wrong and to be up front about it."[34]

June Masuda Goto was in the audience. At the conclusion of President Reagan's remarks several veterans rushed her up to meet the president. When President Reagan realized who she was, he stopped and extended a heartfelt handshake.

Many of those who played a significant role in the redress struggle were in the audience, including key congressional members, White House staff, and numerous members and friends of the Japanese American community. One key player, however, was noticeably absent: Representative Mike Lowry. Representative Lowry's invitation was mistakenly sent to Representative Bill Lowery (Republican from California), who accepted the invitation, attended the signing ceremony, and posed behind President Reagan in photographs of the event. Representative Bill Lowery's attendance was, at best, a curiosity, since he voted against H.R. 442 on every single House vote.

The reception held after the signing ceremony was a joyous and festive occasion. Hugs, congratulatory slaps on the back, and tears filled the room. Ron Wakabayashi recalled being physically picked up off the floor by a hug from Representative Matsui.[35] The mood of the day was best captured by Thomas Shimasaki, who declared, "The ceremonies today made me feel that for the first time in the past forty-six years that I was an American, like the rest of the people."[36]

Understanding Why President Reagan Signed

The process by which President Reagan was persuaded to sign the legislation is a critical component of the redress movement. Early in the redress process all indications were that President Reagan would veto the redress bill. If President Reagan vetoed H.R. 442, the House of Representatives would not have had the votes needed to override the veto. A combination of factors influenced President Reagan to sign the bill: the manner in which the issue was presented to the president, the relative importance of the bill to the president and his administration, and the willingness of the Congress to work toward a compromise on key aspects of the bill.

The strategy of the JACL LEC was to present redress to President Reagan on an anecdotal level. Ujifusa reasoned that reminding President Reagan of his personal connection to the issue (i.e., by using the words from his 1945 speech) would be a persuasive strategy. Although the words spoken at Kazuo Masuda's medal ceremony were written by army superiors and performed by a young officer on active duty, they could be used to remind the president of his involvement.

Ken Duberstein and Ed Meese, the U.S. attorney general, described President Reagan as a president who used anecdotes to communicate his philosophical views and convictions but who liked to make decisions based on facts. He had very strong beliefs and goals, and when the facts fit the beliefs and goals, he could be convinced.[37] To persuade President Reagan on the redress issue, it was important to highlight the injustices of the camp and the heroics of the 442d R.C.T. and the 100th Battalion. He was aware of the contributions of the 442d/100th and often mentioned them when talking about World War II.[38] The Masuda story did all of these things. It connected President Reagan personally to the issue and provided him with an anecdote through which to communicate his conviction. It also supported the facts that Japanese Americans were loyal Americans who were unconstitutionally denied their civil liberties during that period.

A second factor in the president's decision to sign the legislation was that although the redress bill was momentous for members of the Japanese American community, it was not a major bill for the Reagan administration.[39] The scope of the individuals affected and the amount of money required were much smaller than for other issues before the president. President Reagan frequently used meetings with members of his cabinet to make decisions on controversial issues. There was no cabinet meeting on the redress issue. Internal White House communication on redress occurred through memos or conversations with key staff members. President Reagan did not mention the redress legislation in his memoirs.

The final factor was the willingness of the House-Senate conference committee to make concessions to the administration. The negotiations to find common ground on the issues that concerned the Reagan administration overcame the final obstacle to signing the bill. By August 10, 1988, President Reagan was in favor of the legislation. The president felt that Congress had met his administration's concerns halfway, and he recognized that since H.R. 442 was an authorization bill, further concerns could be addressed in the subsequent appropriations bill. According to Duberstein, "From an ideological standpoint I think that the President was convinced months before [the conference committee] that a blanket veto signal was a mistake." Furthermore, on August 10, President Reagan believed that signing the redress bill "was the right thing to do."[40] With that belief, the various streams of influence became properly aligned (see table 9).

Table 9.

Years	History		Legislative Branch		Judicial Branch	Executive Branch
	Community	U.S. Society	Senate	House		
1988	+	N+	+	+	N+	+
1983–86	+	N+	N	N	N+	–
1979–82	N+	N+	N	N	N	N-
1970–78	N+	N	N+	N+	N	N+
1945–69	N	N	N	N	N	N
Pre-WWII/Exclusion/ Incarceration	–	–	–	–	–	–

A Message for Deaf Ears

Ironically, on the same day that President Reagan signed the bill a debate in the California Assembly demonstrated that not everyone understood the message of the Civil Liberties Act of 1988. In a debate over a bill to exempt redress payments from state taxes,[41] Assemblywoman Marian La Follette (Republican from Northridge) argued, "I was a child when the Japanese bombed Pearl Harbor in their surprise attack. Many of the young men that I went to school with also died in that war. . . . I'll tell you, I would like to see an apology from the Japanese government at that time for the maiming and killing of so many of our better citizens . . . our strong men who were willing to go and fight for this country and I really cannot see that we should be in a point of apologizing for protecting the integrity of this democracy."[42]

Members of the assembly rose quickly to rebut La Follette's arguments. Assemblyman Richard Floyd (Democrat from Gardena) stated, "What we are talking about, reparations, has not a damn thing to do with the Japanese government. . . . What we are apologizing for is that we, as a country, took our own citizens and put them in concentration camps. . . . We're not talking about the Japanese Army or Navy. We are not talking about the people that bombed Pearl Harbor. We are talking about U.S. citizens and you are damn right, it is time we apologize."[43] The bill passed, with 57 ayes and 9 noes. The victory, however, was a sobering reminder that some people still did not understand.

The Supreme Court Rules on the NCJAR Case

While H.R. 442 was in the final stages of being passed by the Congress and signed into law by President Reagan, the NCJAR petitioned for a final hearing by the Supreme Court. Even after redress became law, the NCJAR case was still on the Supreme Court's docket. For most of the community, however, the case was now a moot issue. The extinguishment clause in the act barred those who accepted the $20,000 payment from pursuing any further claims against the government. Only those who did not accept the redress money would be eligible to continue in the lawsuit. On October 31, 1988, the Supreme Court rejected the NCJAR's petition to hear the case. The decision by the Court was final.

The Supreme Court was not unanimous in refusing to consider the NCJAR's case. Justice Thurgood Marshall's papers reveal that he wanted the Court to hear the NCJAR's case and revisit its decision on *Korematsu* in 1944: "It seems clear that this case offers this Court an opportunity to vacate the *Korematsu* case, one of its greatest blunders and a shameful stain on the record of the institution of the Supreme Court. This case is a grant."[44] The opportunity went unused.

Authorization: Only a Promise to Pay

With the signing of the Civil Liberties Act of 1988 the Japanese American community quickly learned the difference between "authorization" and "appropriations." Authorization bills simply permit the government to spend money on a particular issue. A separate appropriation bill is necessary to fund enacted laws. The Civil Liberties Act of 1988 was an authorization bill and provided no money to fund its provisions. It was only a promise to pay.

Office of Redress Administration

The Civil Liberties Act of 1988, however, created the Office of Redress Administration (ORA) within the Department of Justice. It was given a ten-year life in which to identify, register, verify, and administer payments to eligible individuals. The ORA's influence rested in its interpretation of the law. Robert K. Bratt became the first director of the ORA.[45] The ORA worked diligently with the NCRR and the JACL to disseminate information regarding redress in a "community friendly" manner through Japanese American newspapers, community meetings, and organizational newsletters. Many community activists agreed that the ORA and its leadership brought a sympathetic openness to the interpretation of the legislation.[46] The tightly knit structure of the Japanese American community facilitated the dissemination of redress information through word of mouth. The ORA minimized the need for excessive paperwork in applying for redress eligibility. Within six months of the signing of the Civil Liberties Act of 1988 the ORA had identified over 48,000 potential recipients.[47]

In January 1989, as he was about to leave office, President Reagan released his budget for fiscal year 1990 (October 1, 1989–September 30, 1990). His budget allocated $300,000 to Aleuts and $20 million to Japanese Americans for redress payments. This appropriation represented only 1.6 percent of the amount authorized for Japanese American redress and would compensate only 1,000 of the then estimated 60,000 eligible Japanese Americans. At this rate the completion of redress payments would take sixty years. The redress appropriation figure was based on the assumption that $171 million would be appropriated each year thereafter. Defending the Reagan budget appropriation, OMB director Joe Wright stated the funding was appropriate "because the Justice Department is not geared up to begin verifying and processing claims for the fiscal year that begins next Oct. 1."[48] Barbara Clay, spokesperson for the OMB, amplified this, alleging, "The key issue is how fast the Justice Department can spend this money. They must pay off the oldest people first, so they cannot pay out the money until they find out who the oldest people are."[49]

Both justifications were incorrect. The ORA had already identified approximately 48,000 potentially eligible individuals.[50] There also was no implicit or explicit requirement to delay compensation until everyone was located. The law simply stipulated that the oldest identified individuals be paid first.

As the pursuit for appropriations continued, redress supporters reiterated the theme that "justice delayed was justice denied." With every passing month approximately two hundred elderly Japanese Americans died without having the promise of redress fulfilled. With that broken promise came renewed cynicism and skepticism in the community. Bill Yoshino, acting national director of the JACL, echoed the sentiment of the community that "any delay in the distribution of payments will deny many victims a measure of justice under the Civil Liberties Act."[51] Representative Mineta also clearly voiced his displeasure with the Reagan budget and his concern for what President Bush would do. He asked, "As president in 1988 and as a veteran of World War II in 1945, Ronald Reagan said that his idea of liberty and justice for all is 'the American Way.' Why has the president's vision narrowed now? . . . On behalf of the thousands of loyal Americans still living who have waited most of their lives for justice after the tragic evacuation and internment, I ask President-elect [George] Bush, 'How much longer must they wait?'"[52]

The Struggle for Appropriations

The fight for redress appropriations occurred primarily during President George Bush's first year in office. Conciliation and compromise were the pledged cornerstones of President Bush's first year fiscal strategy. This "kinder and gentler" administration was reportedly interested in working with the Congress and avoiding the annual deficit wars.[53] President Bush's interest in and the Democrats opposition to a reduced capital-gains tax and no new taxes, the growing federal deficit, and the 1985 Gramm-Rudman-Hollings Deficit Reductions Act all colored the setting in which the fight for redress appropriations took place. As Bush took office in January 1989, Japanese Americans and other supporters of redress were encouraged to thank him for being the first Reagan administration official to support redress publicly and to urge him to recommend larger appropriations.

Bipartisan groups of legislators sent letters to President Bush urging an increased level of funding. One letter from ten members of Congress stated, "We should not encourage the sad and ironic situation where someone who waited decades for justice, and who survived at least until August 10, 1988, would never see the compensation because funds had not been appropriated before they died. Yet that is exactly the situation this [President Reagan's] current proposal creates."[54]

President Bush, however, did not add any money for redress in his fiscal year (FY) 1989 supplemental budget. The president's FY 1990 budget released in February 1989 was little better. It provided $20 million in redress payments and $3.5 million for administration of the redress program.

The appropriations battle took place in the trenches of the Congress: the committees and subcommittees. In 1989 the House had two avenues through which to secure appropriations for redress payments: the FY 1989 supplemental budget and the FY 1990 budget. Hearings for both budgets overlapped and campaigns were waged inside and outside of Congress.

The community sent letters to the president, his budget director, and members of the appropriate committees and subcommittees. Grant Ujifusa reminded the community, "We are not taking on the entire Congress this time, only targeted members of two full committees and two subcommittees."[55] The NCRR actively encouraged its members to send letters. In the next six months over twenty thousand letters were sent from the San Francisco area. Thousands more poured out of Los Angeles, San Jose, New York, and other areas.[56] The cascade of letters was the result of tireless efforts of Japanese Americans and friends across the nation. One example of particular note was Tsuyako "Sox" Kitashima, a Nisei NCRR activist in San Francisco, who personally compiled and mailed over eight thousand letters to Congress.[57]

Fiscal Year 1989 Supplemental Appropriations

The fiscal year supplemental appropriations bill for 1989 provided the first opportunity to secure immediate funding. President Reagan's FY 1989 budget included only $2.1 million for administrative costs. On April 5, 1989, the House Appropriations Subcommittee on the Departments of Commerce, Justice, and State, the Judiciary, and Related Agencies held hearings for supplemental appropriations for the remainder of FY 1989.[58] Included in these supplemental appropriations were funds for redress payments. During the hearing subcommittee member Representative Jim Kolbe (Republican from Arizona), who had voted against H.R. 442, argued that there was a congressional obligation to fund and carry out the bill: "After a great deal of personal anguish, I did not support this legislation on the floor of the House of Representatives . . . because I had doubts about whether we could make right that injustice with the payment of a sum of money. . . . But that issue, in my opinion, has been decided. . . . This committee, this subcommittee, this body now has an obligation to meet the law that we passed. . . . And this member of the subcommittee, although I had not supported this legislation, will support that."[59]

Many of the same redress legislation supporters were present to repeat their same arguments in order to secure appropriations. In her written testimony Rita Takahashi, the acting executive director of JACL LEC, stressed that "to delay redress payments would be to deny justice. After forty-seven years, many will not receive redress because many will pass away before the monies are appropriated. . . . with each passing day, fulfilling this intent [of the Civil Liberties Act] becomes more and more remote."[60]

The opposition's arguments were essentially the same as the ones they posed in their opposition to the Civil Liberties Act. Committee members, however, sharply rebuked the redress opponents. In response to one redress opponent's testimony Representative Kolbe remarked, "I have to say that I find parts of this statement really repugnant to me. [Especially] The statement that we are talking about a group including enemy aliens, traitors, draft dodgers."[61] Representative Kolbe went on to reiterate his support for the bill. The next day the subcommittee recommended $250 million in redress payments and $6.4 million for related administrative expenses for FY 1989,[62] a vast improvement over the Reagan and Bush budget proposals.

On May 24, under the threat of a presidential veto, House leaders stripped the $250 million from the supplemental spending bill before passing it. The supplemental bill approved $3.7 billion for other expenditures but nothing for redress. Representative Matsui, acknowledging his disappointment, stated, "The money was there and ready to go before it was stripped by a veto threat from the same team that made redress a campaign issue last year [referring to then Vice President Bush's campaign]. When an election was on the line, they couldn't say enough about their support for reparations. Now that 200 survivors are dying each month without the benefit of seeing their dreams completed, they want to block the funding."[63]

The Senate passed its version of the supplemental appropriations bill on June 7, 1989. The Senate's version contained only $1 million for redress administrative costs and nothing for payments. On June 22 and 23 the Senate and House adopted a supplemental appropriations bill (H.R. 2402) for FY 1989, which was signed into law by President Bush on June 30.[64] It provided only the $2.1 million for administrative costs that President Reagan's FY 1989 budget had originally proposed.[65]

Fiscal Year 1990 Appropriations

The budget bill for FY 1990 presented an opportunity for appropriating funds for redress payments that would become available on October 1, 1989. During March 1989 the House bill was heard before three different committees. Testimony at these hearings stressed the efficiency of paying recipients immediately instead of having to search for heirs later. On May 11 Senate and House negotiators agreed on a $1.17 trillion budget resolution for FY 1990, which included $150 million in redress payments. These figures, however, were only recommendations. In July 1989 the House Appropriations Subcommittee on the Departments of Commerce, Justice, and State, the Judiciary, and Related Agencies cut this amount to $20 million.

Representatives Matsui and Mineta, along with redress supporters, immediately began to work to increase this amount. As with the passage of the Civil Liberties Act of 1988, the framing of the issue was crucial in maintaining support through the appropriations process. On July 18, 1989, Ujifusa met with Representative Newt Gingrich, the House Republican whip, on his morning walk. During this talk Representative Gingrich agreed to work to amend the subcommittee's $20 million figure. Gingrich stated that because "redress speaks to the deepest values of the nation, we must try to do something in the House, even though every dime in an Appropriations bill has powerful political protectors."[66] For Representative Gingrich the incarceration was an example of big government's infringement on the rights of individual citizens. Ujifusa capitalized on this perspective to win Gingrich's support.

On July 25, 1989, in the full House Appropriations Committee several amendments to raise the amount for redress were offered. Representative Vic Fazio (Democrat from California) moved that the funding level be increased from $20 million to $50 million. The support from Representative Fazio, a member of the new Democratic leadership, was symbolically important since many of the powerful longtime redress allies were no longer in Congress (e.g., Representatives Wright and Coelho).[67] A second amendment from Representative Neal Smith (Democrat from Iowa) proposed to increase the redress funding to $100 million by transferring funds from the Census budget. This amendment reflected a political irony: to fund redress, supporters would have to dip into the Census Bureau funds, which was one of the highest priority issues for the Asian American community. Representative Sidney Yates (Democrat from Illinois) offered a third amendment, which sought to raise the funding level to $500 million and make redress an official entitlement program. This amendment was immediately rejected by representatives, who cited the establishment of an entitlement program was prohibited this late in the process.

The speeches that followed included impassioned and emotional reminders that the Congress had an obligation to fulfill its promise. Representative Gingrich's promise to deliver conservative support became evident when Representative Vin Weber (Republican from Minnesota) supported the Fazio amendment. The fact that Representative Weber, a staunch conservative, spoke in favor of the amendment was a testimony to the bill's bipartisan support. The speeches, however, were not all in favor of the appropriations. Representative Bob Livingston (Republican from Louisiana) stated that he believed higher priorities existed. He cited poor shrimping families in his home state. Representative Weber immediately responded and silenced Representative Livingston by stating, "We cannot deny due process."[68] Fellow committee members observed as one staunch conservative took on another over the issue of funding redress.

The vote was called for the first two amendments, and both suffered defeat. The Smith amendment lost, 18 yeas to 27 nays. The Fazio amendment was closer but still lost, 23 yeas to 24 nays. Representative Steny Hoyer (Democrat from Maryland) immediately offered a fourth and final compromise amendment, which would transfer $30 million from the Census budget to increase the redress funding to $50 million. This amendment passed on a voice vote and was an act of political courage for Representative Hoyer, whose district was among those that would have benefited the greatest from additional Census funding.

On August 1, 1989, the full House adopted the committee's bill (H.R. 2991) with a vote of 258 to 165. The $50 million for redress would be enough to provide payment only to individuals who were eighty-seven and older (an estimated 2,500 former inmates). The day after the passage of H.R. 2991 the ORA released figures indicating there were nearly 16,000 surviving inmates who were seventy years of age or older. Realizing that many of the eligible recipients were elderly, the JACL and NCRR stepped up their campaign to influence key senators, especially Senator Inouye, to appropriate a higher figure.

The Senate and the Fiscal Year 1990 Budget

On February 23, 1989, the Senate Appropriations Subcommittee on Commerce, Justice, and State, the Judiciary, and Related Agencies held hearings. Three days earlier Senator Hollings, the chair of the subcommittee, had sent a letter to the JACL stating:

I opposed the enactment of the Wartime Reparations Act because I believe we should not attach a monetary value to human suffering. How then do we monetize the suffering of, for instance, the soldier killed in action, or the black man who fought on the front line yet returned home to sit in the back of the bus? In contrast, I believe there can be no more meaningful and valuable compensation to internees than the solemn apology of the American people expressed by their Congress and President. . . . I am not convinced that implementing this legislation is a wise and prudent decision.[69]

Such opposition from a key senator underscored the difficulty in obtaining a higher level of appropriations. The appropriations process in Congress is very much an "insider's game," in which key players who sit on the appropriations committees hold tremendous influence and power. Grant Ujifusa was aware of this and knew that Senator Inouye was such a player. On July 17, 1989, Ujifusa released a press statement: "For us there is one person with the internal institutional clout to put a bigger redress number on the table, and that person is Daniel K. Inouye: the powerful number two Democrat on the full Senate Appropriations Committee, the Chairman of the Senate Defense Appropriations subcommittee . . . and most important, the number two Democrat in the appropriations Subcommittee where the Senate decision on redress money will be made. . . . Senator Inouye is the man of the hour."[70] In a subsequent release Ujifusa continued to identify the importance of Senator Inouye: "Our community must recognize that at the appropriations stage, politics is not patty cake or public relations, but inside, subcommittee hardball. This means that a single individual inside the single relevant subcommittee must champion our cause."[71]

Redress supporters also tapped into the senator's personal loyalties. One group outside of Senator Inouye's Hawaiian constituency to which he responded was his fellow 442d R.C.T. veterans. Members of the 442d were encouraged to call and write the senator. One veteran even called Senator Inouye at home to urge him to advocate higher funding. Redress supporters had a growing sense that the responsibility for appropriations rested largely on the senator's shoulders.

The JACL LEC provided form letters to send to the senator. Ujifusa hoped these letters and his memos would prompt the senator to act.[72] By identifying him as the one person who could obtain greater appropriations for redress, Ujifusa hoped to put Senator Inouye in a "must do" situation. The senator's office took notice. Shortly after the memos were issued Ujifusa received a call from Marie Blanco, Senator Inouye's legislative assistant, asking him why he was releasing these memos.[73]

Any concern that Senator Inouye needed to be prompted to act was unfounded. In the very early stages of the FY 1990 appropriations process, Senator Inouye, well aware of his important position, had already begun seeking means of obtaining a higher level of appropriations. Senator Inouye and his staff engaged in discussions with members of the Senate Appropriations Committee and their staff about the possibility of various funding alternatives, including the establishment of an entitlement program.

Entitlement

Senator Inouye approached Senator Hollings with the idea of making the redress program an entitlement. Senator Hollings was not inclined to back the idea, but after some discussion he agreed to support it. Senator Hollings, however, requested that Senator Inouye not ask for any appropriations for FY 1990. Senator Inouye agreed. As an entitlement program, redress would become a legally binding commitment of the federal government, similar to social security or medicare funding. Because of the legal obligation, the appropriation process for entitlements is a formality; the money is automatically appropriated at the amount that is legally obligated. It is a form of nondiscretionary funding that is not subject to changes in funding levels or political whims.

Senator Inouye sent a "Dear Colleague" letter to all the senators on the Senate Appropriations Committee pointing out that "my participation in these debates, as you may have been aware, has been minimal. It is most difficult for me to admit that I have been inhibited and reluctant to say much in these debates because of my ethnic background."[74] Senator Inouye went on to describe his wartime experiences and how he learned of the incarceration camps. He described the heroism of his fellow soldiers in the 442d whose families had been incarcerated. The letter concluded with an impassioned request for the support of his fellow senators:

> I am certain you must have concluded that this letter has been most difficult to compose. It is with some measure of reluctance that I share it with you. I hope that when the time for decision is upon us, you will join me in remembering those men from the internment camps who proudly and courageously demonstrated their "last full measure of devotion" in the defense of their country. Although these men will not receive benefits from the provisions of this bill, I am certain that they will gratefully rest in peace.[75]

On September 12, 1989, the Senate Appropriations Subcommittee on Commerce, Justice, and State, the Judiciary, and Related Agencies approved Senator Inouye's proposal to convert the redress program into a federal entitlement program. This entitlement provided annual funding of $500 million beginning in FY 1991 (October 1, 1990), which would complete redress payments within three years. In making this recommendation, however, it eliminated all funding for FY 1990.

Senator Hollings's action on the subcommittee was critical to redress becoming an entitlement. When Senator Inouye approached Senator Hollings with the idea, Senator Hollings indicated he would not exercise any undue measures. "He said, 'I'll just vote against it and you'll report it out [of conference],'" recalled Senator Inouye, "He could have very easily done something to stall it and there wasn't much I could do about it. In our fraternity . . . that's really decent."[76]

The subcommittee's action was an instrumental step in the fulfillment of the redress promise, but reaction to it was mixed. Some Japanese American newspapers and mainstream press focused more on the absence of funding for FY 1990 than on the establishment of the entitlement. "Senate Subcommittee Kills 1990 Redress Funds" and "Panel Votes Not to Fund Payments for Internees" were examples of headlines focusing on the lack of 1990 funding.[77] Jerry Enomoto, board chair of the JACL LEC, stated, "We cannot accept more broken promises. The prospect of redress becoming an entitlement program gives us hope, but our concern continues to be that next year will be too late for many people." JoAnne Kagiwada, LEC executive director, called on constituents to urge the House and Senate conference committee to maintain the $50 million appropriation funding for FY 1990.[78]

Grant Ujifusa aptly described the dilemma: "What we are looking at pits the arithmetic of the head against the anguish of the heart. If our bill, with a ten year authorization can be guaranteed full funding in four years time the community as a whole is ahead, but any eligible individual who dies without receiving the full measure of justice represents a wrenching community and personal tragedy."[79]

On September 29, 1989, the full Senate debated whether to make redress a federal entitlement program.[80] During the debate Senator Jesse Helms raised a point of order that no new entitlement program could be created if there was not yet an approved budget for that year. He argued that it was unfair to create an entitlement program for Japanese Americans when entitlements were not available for other disadvantaged groups, such as veterans and babies born with AIDS. In response to this argument Senator Hollings called on the Senate to waive this restriction because of the extraordinary circumstances surrounding this issue.

Senator Inouye then addressed the Senate, "I believe the time has come for me to tell my colleagues what has been in my heart for all these many years." He described the wartime experiences of his fellow Japanese American soldiers who were fighting for justice and freedom in Europe while their families were incarcerated behind barbed wire back home. He spoke with uncharacteristic emotion as he described his fellow Japanese American soldiers, whose "only crime was that they were born of parents of Japanese ancestry." Senator Inouye, a respected decorated war veteran, stated, "Mr. President, I have oftentimes asked myself the question: Would I have volunteered under these circumstances? In all honesty, I cannot give you a forthright answer."[81]

After concluding his remarks Senator Inouye continued to display his emotions. As Senator Warren B. Rudman (Republican from New Hampshire) spoke of Senator Inouye's war service and loss of an arm in battle, Senator Inouye wiped away the tears welling in his eyes. Senator Rudman, coauthor of the Gramm-Rudman-Hollings Deficit Reduction Act, which set ceilings on congressional budgets, stated that "there are times that we deal with fiscal reality. . . . But there are also times . . . that one must set fiscal reality aside . . . and look at what is the right thing to do."[82]

Senator Bill Bradley (Democrat from New Jersey) demonstrated his moral and emotional commitment to redress by directly confronting Senator Helms. Members of the Senate, in an attempt to maintain civil debate, adhere to Senate rules, which require that members address each other indirectly through the presiding officer. On this occasion, however, Senator Bradley looked directly at Senator Helms and stated, "I would hope we would not continue to reopen old wounds. . . . I would implore you to use some restraint when it comes to issues as sensitive as this."[83] Senator Helms left shortly afterward and did not return until Senator Bradley concluded his remarks.

Senator Dale Bumpers (Democrat from Arkansas) addressed the Senate in support of the entitlement. Senator Bumpers, who had received mail from his constituents opposing redress, concluded his remarks by stating that "in the future when I get mail from my constituents on this issue, I intend to have copies of Senator Inouye's speech printed, and say, 'Enclosed is the reason I voted as I did.'"[84]

Senators Brock Adams (Democrat from Washington), Arlen Specter (Republican from Pennsylvania), Paul Simon (Democrat from Illinois), Spark Matsunaga (Democrat from Hawai'i), Tim Wirth (Democrat from Colorado), and Pete Domenici (Republican from New Mexico) also spoke in favor of an entitlement. The Senate voted to make redress an entitlement (74 to 22, a larger margin than the 69-27 vote for the passage of the H.R. 442).

After the vote Senator Inouye expressed how "surprised, and very pleased" he was with the margin of victory. He acknowledged, "I thought that we would get a comfortable margin, about 60 or more."[85] The Senator, however, knew that the action would pass. Senator Inouye stated, "I spoke to the other senators one-to-one. There were a lot of chits involved."[86] Senator Inouye was fully aware of the virtues and trade-offs involved in this plan: "Of course this means that this year some of the old folks will die, and they will not have the good feeling of receiving their redress payments. But in the decades following the war, many others have preceded them. By making it into an entitlement program, we will be assured to pay off everyone in three years. . . . Otherwise, it might take 50 years—$20 million one year, $10 million the next. . . . Each year, we would have to fight the same battle over and over again."[87]

With the passage of the Senate's version of the appropriations bill (entitlement starting in FY 1991), a House-Senate conference committee was necessary to resolve the differences with the House's version ($50 million appropriated payments in FY 1990). Once again bipartisan "Dear Colleague" letters and community letters were sent to key players on the conference committee. The hope was to obtain the best from both versions: the House's $50 million for FY 1990 and the Senate's entitlement program starting in FY 1991.[88]

A letter to legislators from the Leadership Conference on Civil Rights stressed the urgency of obtaining redress funds immediately:

> We just heard about the case of Joe Kosai of Puyallup, Wa, whose 92 year old aunt received notification regarding her potential eligibility from the ORA on the very day she died. Mrs. Kinuyo Hokoda, a Los Angeles retirement home resident, has not received her letter from the ORA because at age 87, she is not old enough to be included in the first round of correspondence. After 45 years, she is still waiting for the government to make good on its promise. She remarked, "We trust America, but we doubt. . . . we doubt. We are not sure now."[89]

On October 19, 1989, the House-Senate conference committee accepted both parts of the Inouye-Hollings compromise. Redress funding would become an entitlement in FY 1991, but no funds would be appropriated for FY 1990.

The agreement both pleased and disappointed Representatives Mineta and Matsui. Representative Mineta stated, "I am pleased that the conferees agreed to fund the redress program fully beginning next fall. . . . But there's no disguising my frustration and disappointment that by the time the first check is delivered more than two years will have come and gone since the Civil Liberties Act was signed into law."[90] Representative Matsui also clearly stated his mixed feelings: "While I am grateful the conferees saw fit to make redress an entitlement program, my heart sinks for the many internees who won't live to see their payment. Once again, we have been forced to accept a post-dated check—one that unfortunately will never reach thousands of internees who will die before the first payments are made."[91]

With the approval by the House-Senate conference committee, the conference bill was sent back to the House and Senate for their full approval. The House debated the bill on October 26, 1989. As with other steps in the redress process, this procedure had its anxious moments. Three votes were taken that affected the entitlement program. The first vote was whether to adopt a rule that would waive certain points of order to set up the entitlement program. The rule was adopted by a vote of 226 to 189. This margin of victory was the slimmest of any floor vote on redress in the Congress. The funding for redress came very close to being completely derailed at this point. Had the amendment been voted down, there would have been no money appropriated for FY 1990 or 1991.

The second vote was to approve the conference report, which appropriated $17.2 billion for the Departments of Commerce, Justice, and State, the judiciary, and related agencies in FY 1990. The report passed 323 to 81. Upon the adoption of the waiver and the conference report, the third vote was whether to approve the Senate's amendment to create an entitlement program for redress. Representative Mineta set the tone of the debate by stating, "This body cannot prevent the deaths of these elderly loyal Americans. But Congress can make the effort to disburse the redress compensation as quickly as possible."[92]

Representative Frank noted that this entitlement program would not expand because there was only a limited number of eligible individuals. Representative Ron Dellums, as he had done in the House floor debate for the original bill, delivered an impassioned plea: "There were tears in the House Chamber, and there was conflict, agony, and pain in this Chamber [during the 1987 debate]. Let that same spirit that allowed us to pass that legislation allow us to agree to this amendment. Let us not hide behind the technical, the earthbound, and the pedestrian."[93] Representative Gingrich stated that the entitlement was "trying [to] make sure that those who are now elderly, who once suffered a grievous harm, are given a chance to have their Government and the country they love repay that harm before they pass on."[94]

The opposition to an entitlement program spoke as well. Representative Gerald Solomon (Republican from New York) criticized the waiver as a "breach of fiscal discipline."[95] Representative Harold Rogers (Republican from Kentucky) questioned whether payments to Japanese Americans should take priority over other national needs, such as child care and education. The entitlement amendment, however, was approved (249 to 166). The conference report with the entitlement amendment now moved on to the Senate for approval. Through a series of technicalities unrelated to redress the Senate returned the bill to the House, resulting in a week's delay. On November 7 the House approved the final compromise appropriations bill by voice vote. The next day the Senate followed suit.

On November 21, 1989, President Bush signed into law H.R. 2991, which guaranteed funds to carry out redress payments to Japanese Americans. At the signing ceremony the president described the appropriations measure as primarily focused on funding the war on drugs and violent crime. He mentioned his concerns over the lack of funding for U.S. contributions to international organizations and peacekeeping and to the Christopher Columbus Quincentennial Celebrations. He praised the inclusion of the promotion of international trade and advanced technology, U.S. diplomacy, and the initiative to protect sea turtles. Absent from his remarks was any reference to Japanese Americans or the entitlement program.[96]

Japanese Canadians: A Faster Parallel Process

At the same time that Japanese Americans were fighting for redress, Canadians of Japanese ancestry were engaged in a similar struggle. Japanese in Canada, three-quarters of whom were Canadian citizens, were excluded during the war from western Canada on the basis of their ancestry. Beyond the loss of their civil liberties, much of their property was confiscated by the government, and they were not allowed to return to coastal British Columbia until April 1, 1949. The total economic loss suffered by Japanese Canadians was estimated to be no less than $443 million.[97] Japanese Canadians began to speak out about redress in the mid-1970s, and by the summer of 1982 the National Association of Japanese Canadians (NAJC) began to talk formally about Japanese Canadian redress. Encouraged by the CWRIC's findings and recommendations, the NAJC passed a resolution in January of 1984 to pursue an official apology, monetary compensation, and a review of the War Measures Act.

In 1984 the prime minister of Canada, Pierre Elliott Trudeau, spoke out against redress. He used arguments similar to those used by redress opponents south of his border. Prime Minister Trudeau stated, "I am not quite sure where we could stop the compensating. I know that we would have to go back a great length of time in history."[98] It was an election year, and Trudeau was replaced by Brian Mulroney, who declared his support for Japanese Canadian redress during his campaign. Under the Mulroney administration three Tory ministers for multiculturalism incrementally increased their offers of redress to an apology and a $12 million foundation to study and promote race relations. All of the offers were considered unacceptable by the NAJC since they did not include individual payments.

In 1988 the Mulroney government agreed to an apology; a monetary payment of $21,000 (Canadian dollars) to individuals; $12 million to promote the educational, cultural, and social interests of the Japanese Canadian community; $24 million to create a Canadian race relations foundation; citizenship to those expelled from Canada or whose citizenship had been revoked; and the clearing of the names of all persons of Japanese ancestry who had been convicted under the War Measures Act.[99] The agreement was reached through negotiations between Gerry Weiner, the fourth Tory minister of multiculturalism, and Art Miki, president of the NAJC. On September 22, 1988, forty-three days after President Reagan signed the U.S. redress bill, the Mulroney government's settlement was announced to the Canadian Parliament. Leaders of the other two major Canadian political parties immediately announced their support.

The U.S. actions no doubt facilitated the Canadian version of redress. In Canada, however, there is no distinction between authorization and appropriation in the legislative process. Payments therefore began almost immediately. By the end of 1990, 18,233 redress applications had been received, 17,154 applications verified, and over $360 million (Canadian) expended.[100]

Understanding How Entitlement Was Obtained

The redress story in the United States is incomplete without an appreciation of the process that secured entitlement. The major element in securing entitlement was influential inside political power. This power was embodied in Senator Daniel Inouye, and the credit for this chapter of the redress story falls squarely in his corner. Senator Inouye created the "bookends" of the redress process. In the beginning he urged the creation of the congressional commission that initiated congressional involvement with redress. At the end he obtained the guarantee of funding through the entitlement program. The senator's understanding of the power structure of the Congress and his personal power base were critical to these two accomplishments.

Senator Inouye's suggestion to establish the congressional commission was in some ways a "hedged bet." However, his contribution to the establishment of the entitlement program necessitated political risk and involvement. Senator Inouye was the only member of Congress able to obtain the entitlement status. He had the necessary seniority in the Senate, a position on the Appropriations Committee, and enough political chits to "call in." Most important, he had the necessary desire to take the political risk.

The obtaining of the entitlement status is a good example of how the "rightness" or "appropriateness" of an idea is not sufficient for its adoption. Representative Yates introduced in the House Appropriations Committee an amendment to make redress an entitlement program. Despite being a senior member of that committee Representative Yates was unable to persuade his colleagues to adopt the amendment. Senator Inouye was the person who made entitlement happen. The senator, reflecting on his contribution, commented, "I see it simply as a division of effort. The man who should take nearly all of the credit for the passage of the redress bill is Senator Sparky Matsunaga. . . . In the House, Mineta, Matsui, Saiki, and Akaka, along with others, did all of the work. But when it came to appropriations, I am the one on the appropriations committee. They had a right to expect more from me at this point than from Sparky or the others."[101]

The establishment of the entitlement program was a brilliant move. It was, however, not without its casualties (those who died in that extra year). Senator Inouye and his fellow legislators received some criticism for this shortcoming, but overall the extra year was an acceptable price for the guarantee of the bulk of the payments within four years.

11 Delivering on the Promise

Nearly fifty years after being forcibly excluded and incarcerated, the Japanese American community experienced an exuberant moment when the first Japanese Americans received redress from the U.S. government. On October 9, 1990, Attorney General Richard Thornburgh presented a formal apology signed by President Bush (see figure 2) to nine elderly Japanese Americans on behalf of the nation and presented them with redress checks of $20,000 each.[1] The ceremony was held in the Great Hall of the Justice Department in Washington, D.C., an ironic location since the Justice Department actively supported the exclusion and incarceration of Japanese Americans during World War II and fought the redress movement in Congress and the courts.

The ceremony was emotional. The nine individuals ranged in age from 73 to 107 and were wheeled onto the stage one-by-one in their wheelchairs. A tenth recipient, who was one month short of her 108 birthday, was ill and could not make the trip to Washington, D.C. The opening invocation was given in Japanese by Mamoru Eto, a 107-year-old former minister who had been incarcerated at Gila River. As the attorney general knelt beside Eto and presented him the check, he stated, "[Even when the American] system failed you, you never lost your faith in it. By finally admitting a wrong, a nation does not destroy its integrity but, rather, reinforces the sincerity of its commitment to the Constitution and hence to its people."[2] During the ceremony tears came to the eyes of Senator Inouye and Representatives Mineta and Matsui. Representative Mineta was moved to speak: "Americans of Japanese ancestry now know in their hearts that the letter and spirit of our Constitution holds true for them."[3] Senator Inouye declared that by providing redress, "We honor ourselves and honor America. We demonstrated to the world that we are a strong people—strong enough to admit our wrongs."[4]

THE WHITE HOUSE
WASHINGTON

A monetary sum and words alone cannot restore lost years or
erase painful memories; neither can they fully convey our Nation's
resolve to rectify injustice and to uphold the rights of individuals.
We can never fully right the wrongs of the past. But we can take a
clear stand for justice and recognize that serious injustices were
done to Japanese Americans during World War II.

In enacting a law calling for restitution and offering a sincere
apology, your fellow Americans have, in a very real sense, renewed
their traditional commitment to the ideals of freedom, equality, and
justice. You and your family have our best wishes for the future.

Sincerely,

GEORGE BUSH
PRESIDENT OF THE UNITED STATES

OCTOBER 1990

Figure 2. The presidential apology.

For some it was hard to believe that the day had finally come. Kay Ochi, a longtime NCRR member, was present at the ceremony and recalled, "I will never forget Mrs. Kiriyama [a 100-year-old woman from West Los Angeles who had been at Manzanar and Tule Lake]. . . . She looked so fragile and tiny in the midst of that cavernous room. Her serenity and grace were captivating. . . . Her hands were pressed together as in prayer, her eyes downcast. She represented to me all of the Issei who had endured so much hardship."[5]

The symbolic significance of the monetary payment was reflected by one woman who slept that first night holding onto the purse that contained her redress check.[6] In the coming months other Issei and older Nisei began to receive their checks. Ron Wakabayashi recalled accompanying his mother to the local bank in the J-Town area of Los Angeles, where they saw a line of elderly Japanese Americans waiting to deposit their checks. Wakabayashi struck up conversations with several of the Issei and inquired what they planned to do with the money. He received an unexpected answer from one elderly Issei woman who said, "You know what I'm going to get? Teeth!" as she gleefully pointed to her mouth and flashed a toothless smile.[7]

The Office of Redress Administration (ORA) worked to identify potential recipients and verify their eligibility. Community activists contributed greatly to this effort. Tsuyako "Sox" Kitashima, for example, assisted the ORA in tracking some difficult to find persons, informing them of their eligibility, and in some cases assisting them in applying for redress. Some of the people Kitashima found were living in desperate conditions on the streets or in retirement homes. Kitashima located one man who had originally applied for redress but later could not be located because he was incarcerated in northern California. Undeterred, she and her attorney friend, Jeff Adachi, went into the jail to help him reapply for redress and get his check.[8]

Amendments in 1992

The redress movement, however, was not finished. Unresolved aspects, such as an underestimation of the number of eligible individuals, overly restrictive definitions and interpretations of the eligibility criteria, and ambiguous taxation status, became apparent in the bill. During the One-hundred-and-second Congress it became apparent that the existing appropriations would not cover all eligible individuals. At the time of the original Civil Liberties Act of 1988, the Justice Department had estimated that there would be approximately 60,000 individuals eligible for redress payments. By 1992, however, it was clear that many more Japanese Americans were eligible. The difference was because the number of eligible people alive at the time the bill was signed into law was underestimated and the Justice Department found some new categories of eligible individuals. Community members began to lobby their legislators to push for increased appropriations for redress payments.

H.R. 4551, which increased redress appropriations by $400 million, was introduced in the House on March 24, 1992, by Representative Richard Gephardt (Democrat from Missouri) with a bipartisan group of fifty-two other cosponsors. After a final markup on April 1, 1992, the subcommittee recommended the bill favorably to the full committee with a single substitute amendment offered by Representative Barney Frank. The amendment gave claimants the benefit of the doubt in cases where the evidence supporting their eligibility was inconclusive. The U.S. Claims Court was also given exclusive judicial review of decisions made by the Justice Department concerning eligibility.[9] On July 30, 1992, the Justice Department estimated that a total of 80,000 individuals would be eligible for redress payments.[10]

The Committee on the Judiciary passed H.R. 4551 with a voice vote. Representative Jack Brooks (Democrat from Texas) presented the committee's favorable report on the legislation to the full House. It contained the following provisions:

1. To increase the amount authorized for the Civil Liberties Act of 1988 from $1.25 to $1.65 billion. This amount provided for an additional 20,000 redress payments, while maintaining the original reserve of $50 million to be made available for educational purposes;

2. Individuals not of Japanese ancestry would become eligible for redress if they had been incarcerated with their spouse or children. These payments would come from discretionary appropriations;

3. The U.S. Claims Court would have exclusive judicial review over decisions concerning eligibility of individuals;

4. The benefit of the doubt in determining eligibility would be given to claimants by the Justice Department;

5. Redress payments would not be viewed as income when making eligibility determinations for veterans' benefits; and

6. The Justice Department's ORA would be given 180 days to complete its administrative activities following termination of the Civil Liberties Public Education Fund.

The House briefly debated H.R. 4551 on September 14, 1992. All of the representatives who spoke supported the bill.[11] Representative Matsui put the bill in context: "The issue cuts to the heart of the foundation of freedom and liberty in American society. Today we are seeking to fulfill the congressional intent of the redress law and to complete the healing process that is so important to Americans of Japanese ancestry."[12]

Representative Mineta argued that an important function of the Civil Liberties Act of 1988 was to educate the American public. He cited the FBI's singling out and investigating Arab Americans as alleged terrorists during the Persian Gulf War as an example of the need for education. He recounted how he had attended meetings with the FBI to discuss concerns about their treatment of Arab Americans. Representative Mineta stressed, "There is no doubt in my mind that a heightened awareness of what happened to Japanese-Americans during World War II was a powerful weapon in fighting discrimination against Arab-Americans this time. But it is clear that the attitudes and the prejudices that led to the internment are still with us."[13] On September 14, 1992, H.R. 4551 was passed by a voice vote.

On the Senate side Senator Inouye introduced S.R. 2553 on April 8, 1992, which was referred to the Governmental Affairs Committee.[14] The bill was reported out by a voice vote and submitted to the full Senate by Senator John Glenn on September 8, 1992. S.R. 2553 contained essentially the same provisions as the House version, except that the Senate authorized only an additional $320 million in redress payments. The Senate indefinitely postponed consideration of S.R. 2553 and supported the House figures by passing H.R. 4551 on September 16, 1992.

On September 27, 1992, President George Bush signed the Civil Liberties Act Amendments of 1992 into law (Public Law 102-371). President Bush stated that the technical amendment would "help to ensure fair treatment of claimants and smooth administration" of the redress program. He went on to state that he found the additional funds to be "compelled by justice" and that they would fulfill the promise made by the Civil Liberties Act of 1988.[15]

New Categories of Eligibility

Several categories of unclear "eligibility" emerged and were resolved after the passage of the Civil Liberties Act of 1988. The NCRR and local JACL chapters held meetings in the community, assisted individuals in gathering evidence and writing their appeals, contributed to the ORA's research on specific categories of claimants, and urged a broad interpretation of the law. At times the process was cooperative; at other times the community groups, especially the NCRR, aggressively advocated approval of the claimants' eligibility. These categories included the children of parents who were excluded but not incarcerated; the children born outside of camp whose mothers left camp under the "indefinite leave" program or "voluntarily" reentered before or just after giving birth; individuals and their children relocated from the concentration camps to teach in the naval language schools; children whose fathers were in the 442d and whose mothers voluntarily returned to camp; children who accompanied parents who were sent to Japan in exchange for American civilians (most of whom were white Americans); individuals in Phoenix and Glendale, which were split down the middle by the exclusion zone; individuals born outside of the military and exclusion zones after January 1945; Japanese Latin Americans; railroad and mining employees; and individuals affected in Hawai'i.

Children of Parents Who Were Excluded but Not Incarcerated

During the spring and summer of 1995 there were legal victories for children of parents excluded from the West Coast but not incarcerated in a concentration camp. These families moved to the interior regions of the country in response to the issuance of Executive Order 9066 and before the forced removal of Japanese Americans by the military. These families are colloquially known as "voluntary evacuees." The decision by these families to move was "voluntary" in that they picked the time and location to which they moved. The question of whether to move was determined by the government.

On March 31, 1995, Judge Kenneth Harkins of the U.S. Court of Federal Claims ruled that Howard Den Motoyoshi, who had been denied redress by the ORA, was eligible for redress. Motoyoshi was born in Denver, Colorado, on January 2, 1943, after his parents "voluntarily" moved from their home in the restricted zone of Santa Barbara, California. This move was the result of fear and apprehension about what the government planned for Japanese Americans on the West Coast. After his birth his family was granted permission to move to Portland, Oregon, so that his father could translate Japanese propaganda broadcasts for the Foreign Broadcast Intelligence Service.[16] When his job was finished, the Motoyoshis had to leave Oregon because of the exclusion proclamations. In rendering his decision Judge Harkins declared that the phrase "otherwise deprived of liberty" in the Civil Liberties Act of 1988 should be broadly interpreted and applied to Motoyoshi's case.[17]

Two other similar cases also upheld the eligibility of children of "voluntary evacuees." The first case was Douglas Ishida, who was born in Marion, Ohio, on November 23, 1942, after his parents were excluded from California. Ishida's case was initially denied by the ORA, and the government's decision was upheld by the U.S. Court of Federal Claims in *Ishida v. U.S.* on April 22, 1994. Ishida and his attorney, Richard Halberstein, appealed the case to the U.S. Court of Appeals for the Federal Circuit, which reversed the decision on July 6, 1995. The appeals court ruled that although Ishida was not born in one of the concentration camps, he and children like him were deprived of their liberty when they were "excluded" by Executive Order 9066 from their parents' original residence.[18]

The second case was that of Linda Yae (Kawabe) Consolo, whose personal story was similar to Douglas Ishida's. Consolo was born in Utah after her parents were forced to leave their home in Los Angeles, California. Her case was initially denied by the ORA and appealed by her attorney, Gerald Sato, to the U.S. Court of Federal Claims, the same court that denied the Ishida case. In the Consolo case, however, Judge James Turner ruled that Consolo was eligible. The Justice Department appealed the decision to the U.S. Court of Appeals for the Federal Circuit, which on July 10, 1995, affirmed Judge Turner's earlier opinion. The *Consolo* ruling was based on the same argument used in the *Ishida* case, and the Department of Justice opted not to appeal the decision to the Supreme Court. These decisions opened the door for approximately 1,300 others who fell under the category of "children of voluntary evacuees" to file for redress.

"Baby Internees"

The category of children of mothers who left camp and "voluntarily" reentered before or just after giving birth is known as the "baby internees." Some families left camp under the "indefinite leave" program and returned because of the absence of a supportive community and lack of job opportunities. Children born during this period outside of camp and then brought back by their parents were originally denied redress because the parents "voluntarily" chose to enter or reenter camp. This decision was reversed at a August 2, 1993, meeting in Washington, D.C., between Assistant Attorney General James Turner and representatives from the NCRR, JACL, and Asian Law Caucus. Turner acknowledged that these children and their mothers were subject to the same oppressive conditions and loss of liberty that the other inmates were.

Related to the "baby internees" are those babies born outside of the camps to parents who left the camps through the "indefinite leave" program. Sharon Tanihara and Grace Watanabe filed cases in the U.S. Court of Federal Claims on June 22, 1994, and July 25, 1994, respectively, claiming they were unjustly denied redress by the ORA under the Civil Liberties Act of 1988. Both women were born after their parents were released under the War Relocation Authority's Indefinite Leave Program.[19] Their lawsuits asserted that the U.S. Supreme Court's 1944 unanimous ruling in *Ex Parte Endo* held that "the 'indefinite leave' rules constituted an exercise of power beyond the lawful authority of WRA, and therefore subjected Japanese Americans to an illegal restraint of liberty."[20] In 1996 Tanihara and Watanabe received their redress checks from the government.

Children of Men in the 442d R.C.T.

The cases of children of the 442d Regimental Combat Team involved the families of men who were drafted into combat. When the draft was reinstituted on January 14, 1944, many families were affected. Nisei solders were often too far away to visit their wives in camp. As a result, wives faced the dilemma of either leaving the camps and their extended families or not being able to see their husbands. Most of the children of these families born outside of camp were found eligible.

Children of Naval Language School Personnel

Another related category involved the children of men who were ordered to teach the Japanese language to personnel at the Naval Institute in Boulder, Colorado. The adults relocated from the concentration camps to teach in language schools were found to be eligible. However, their children who were born at the Naval Language School after their parents left the camps were initially ruled ineligible. These children experienced the same loss of liberty as their counterparts in the War Relocation Authority and Justice Department camps. The legal victory in the *Consolo* case positively affected these claims. These redress claims were deemed eligible and were considered to be the same as those of the children of voluntary evacuees.

Children Repatriated to Japan

Between 1942 and 1943 over two thousand individuals of Japanese ancestry were sent to Japan aboard the MS *Gripsholm*. These individuals, many of whom were Japanese diplomats or resident aliens, volunteered for the journey. They and their families were exchanged primarily for white Americans who were in Japan.[21] Often the children (who were American-born U.S. citizens) of these individuals were left with little choice except to accompany their parents to Japan. Many of these families arrived in Japan with little money, since their bank accounts had been frozen by the U.S. government. A number of the children were not allowed to attend public schools in Japan or use public facilities.[22]

This category of minors included nearly two hundred people. Approximately 124 Japanese Americans had their applications for redress denied because the government claimed that they had relocated to Japan at a time when it was at war with the United States. Of these individuals, 108 returned to the United States after the war, the majority of whom had not entered into active military service for Japan.[23] A lawsuit, *Kanemoto et al. v. Reno,* was filed in 1992 challenging the government's denial of eligibility.[24]

On June 12, 1996, the Justice Department reversed its earlier decisions on these *Gripsholm* cases and granted them redress.[25] The decision was based on a technical interpretation of the passive and active voices in describing the eligibility and exclusionary clauses in the legislation. The eligibility clause of the Civil Liberties Act of 1988 used the passive voice by defining an "eligible individual" as a person of Japanese ancestry "who, during the evacuation, relocation and internment period—. . . *was* confined, held in custody, relocated, or otherwise deprived of liberty or property."[26] This use of the passive voice was interpreted, based on statutory precedent, to include all individuals fitting the description. However, the exclusion clause in section 108 used the active voice expressly to exclude from eligibility "any individual who, during the period beginning on December 7, 1941 and ending on September 2, 1945, *relocated* to (another) country while the United States was at war with that country" (emphasis added). The contrasting and ambiguous wording led the Department of Justice to conclude that "the contrasting use of the active voice in the exclusion clause suggests the possibility that section 108 might be read to exclude only those individuals who voluntarily relocated to an enemy country during the war. . . . Thus, the statutory language creates an ambiguity as to whether eligibility decisions should distinguish between voluntary relocatees and involuntary relocatees. . . . we believe the better interpretation is to exclude only individuals who relocated voluntarily."[27] To be eligible for redress, individuals needed to be under twenty-one years of age at the time they were sent to Japan and could not have served in the Japanese military during World War II.[28]

The Arizona Cities of Phoenix and Glendale

Some individuals in the Arizona cities of Phoenix and Glendale were also eventually found eligible for redress. These cities were split down the middle by the exclusion zone boundaries. The boundary literally ran down the middle of the main streets in both cities. Those living on the north side of the exclusion boundary were not moved or incarcerated. The exclusion boundary, however, meant that adults were unable to go to work, children were unable to attend school, and families were unable to shop, go to church, go to the hospital, or conduct other activities of daily living. The Justice Department considered these individuals to have been deprived of their civil liberties although they had not been excluded or incarcerated. Roughly 125 individuals filed claims on the basis of these conditions, of which at least 76 received redress payments.

Controversial Cutoff Date

On April 22, 1996, the ORA published proposed changes in redress regulations in the *Federal Register* that directly affected children of "voluntary evacuees" and camp inmates who left camp and settled outside the military exclusion zone.[29] The proposed changes would make such individuals eligible for redress, but only if they were born outside of the military exclusion zone by midnight of January 2, 1945.[30]

Many in the community felt the proposed cutoff date did not accommodate the reality Japanese Americans faced at that time. The community argued that the eligibility cutoff date should be June 30, 1946, to remain consistent with the wording of the Civil Liberties Act of 1988.[31] Community members argued that most individuals of Japanese ancestry were not aware of Proclamation 21 at the time and were not notified of it in a timely fashion by the government, while others thought the climate on the West Coast was still too dangerous for them to return in early 1945. The Department of Justice initially chose the January 3, 1945, date because the Western Defense Command's Proclamation 21, which rescinded the military exclusion zones on the West Coast, went into effect at midnight on January 2, 1945. The Department of Justice's position was that individuals of Japanese ancestry were no longer legally excluded from returning to the West Coast as of January 3,

1945.[32] On April 24, 1997, however, the Department of Justice published its final ruling, which extended the cutoff date to January 20, 1945. This date was chosen because there were still small designated areas from which Japanese Americans were excluded after January 3 but "after January 20, 1945, individuals were generally free under the law to decide for themselves whether and when they should return to the West Coast."[33]

Japanese Latin Americans

The term *Japanese Peruvians* was used to describe the category of over 2,260 people who were taken by the U.S. government from twelve Latin American countries. Approximately 80 percent of them were from Peru. These individuals were incarcerated in Department of Justice camps, and approximately 700 were sent to Japan, primarily in exchange for white Americans in Japan. The United States also deported over 1,100 individuals after the war because of their status as "illegal aliens." Approximately 200 individuals remained in the United States and became naturalized or permanent residents. Originally, this group was categorically denied eligibility because they were not citizens or permanent residents during the incarceration. At the urging of community groups, the Department of Justice and the Immigration and Naturalization Service reviewed individual cases and in some instances made individuals' legal immigration status retroactive to the incarceration period. Those who left the United States immediately after the war or were sent to Japan were not eligible for residency status.

The community intensified its efforts to obtain redress for Japanese Latin Americans. A group called Campaign for Justice employed judicial and legislative strategies to include Japanese Latin Americans under the Civil Liberties Act of 1988. In 1996 Carmen Mochizuki and other former inmates filed a federal class action suit, *Mochizuki et al. v. United States,* seeking redress. In June 1998 a settlement was reached. The U.S. government agreed to issue an apology and redress payments of $5,000 to each eligible Japanese Latin American or immediate heirs. Response to the settlement was mixed. Over six hundred Japanese Latin Americans applied for redress. While many appreciated the formal apology, the monetary payments were considered unsatisfactory. In August 1998 Japanese Latin Americans began to file individual lawsuits against the United States.[34]

Railroad and Mining Employees

Others initially found to be ineligible were individuals (and their families) fired by the railroad and mining companies. These people often lived near the railroad tracks, far removed from the exclusion zones. When their companies fired them, these workers were frequently left in the middle of nowhere, with few job prospects and a hostile surrounding environment. These individuals were deemed ineligible because private industry, not the federal government, created their situations. Deprivation of civil liberties (e.g., curfew and travel restrictions, confiscation of weapons) by the federal government was under the auspices of the Trading with the Enemy Act, which had been in existence for over a hundred years. Individuals affected by this act included those of German, Italian, and Japanese ancestry, and the deprivations they endured were not considered to fall under the provisions of Executive Order 9066.

In the spring of 1996 Gerald Sato, an attorney, filed a case (*Kaneko v. United States*) in Washington, D.C., for a railroad worker's widow, Emiko Kaneko, on behalf of her deceased husband. Kaneko's husband, Sotaro Kaneko, was fired from his Southern Pacific Railroad position in February 1942. He had been employed by the company for over twenty years. Evidence was discovered indicating that federal agencies, such as the FBI, influenced the actions of railroad and mining companies. On July 16, 1996, Judge Robert Yock of the U.S. District Court of Federal Claims in Washington, D.C., ruled that the wartime terminations of railroad workers were not covered under the Civil Liberties Act of 1988. While there was no question that the federal government was involved in the firing of Sotaro Kaneko, Judge Yock ruled that it was not related to the federal actions "respecting the evacuation, relocation, or internment."[35]

Despite this ruling the lobbying efforts continued. With the discovery of new evidence, such as a letter that spelled out a FBI directive to fire railroad workers of Japanese ancestry, the ORA reconsidered its original decision. On February 27, 1998, Acting Assistant U.S. Attorney General Bill Lann Lee announced that railroad and mine workers in this category would be deemed eligible for redress.

Individuals Affected in Hawai'i

The wartime situation that individuals of Japanese ancestry faced in Hawai'i differed from the one on the mainland. While the largest concentration of people of Japanese ancestry was in Hawai'i, the vast majority were not forcibly excluded or incarcerated in concentration camps. For pragmatic reasons the U.S. government did not claim that military necessity required the exclusion and incarceration of all Japanese Americans in Hawai'i. Japanese Americans made up one-third of Hawai'i's population during World War II.[36] Excluding and incarcerating them might have caused the remaining population to starve. Transportation also posed a problem, since the government lacked sufficient shipping resources to take them to camps on the mainland.[37] Instead, the government forced a smaller group of Japanese Americans from Hawai'i, those they deemed were community leaders, into two army detention camps in Hawai'i and eventually into both Justice Department and War Relocation Authority camps on the continental United States.[38] Meanwhile, hundreds of others were forcibly excluded from their homes.

In 1990 the Kanemaru family approached William Kaneko of the Honolulu JACL to discuss the family's experience in Waianae. Kaneko in turn spoke to Robert K. Bratt, administrator of the ORA, who indicated that the Hawai'i cases might be eligible. The Honolulu JACL chapter solicited stories about Japanese American families in Hawai'i during World War II and received hundreds of phone calls describing Japanese American families singled out because of their race.

The ORA hired two local Japanese Americans, Pam Funai and Jennifer Kim Mikami, to conduct research and attempt to find government documentation proving that the military discriminated against Japanese Americans on the basis of race. Funai recalled that there were literally "hundreds of boxes of [government] letters and correspondence," which were mostly concerned with food production, civil defense, and civilian operations on the island. Funai stated, "It was like looking for a needle in a haystack."[39] However, while searching through documents in the Hamilton Library at the University of Hawai'i, Funai found a letter from the Office of the Assistant Provost Marshal in Honolulu that stated, "Pursuant to the provisions of the Directive issued by the Commanding General, Hawaiian Department, dated 7 January 1943, all alien Japanese and citizens of Japanese ancestry residing in the areas hereby designated will be evacuated. . . . This order is issued in the interest of public safety."[40] Upon making her discovery, Funai, in her true Hawaiian pidgin English, yelled, "Score!" The librarian immediately rushed over and told her not to do that again. The warning did nothing to dampen her enthusiasm because Funai realized that this document would be the foundation for many of the Hawai'i Japanese American redress cases.

Other similar documents were uncovered that demonstrated racial discrimination toward Japanese Americans in other parts of Oahu. Identifying these individuals and verifying their eligibility were more difficult tasks than in the continental United States. Since Hawai'i was a site of military action, it was necessary to demonstrate not only that individuals were forcibly moved but also that such action was not simply a military necessity. Some sections of Hawai'i, which were racially integrated, were evacuated for military reasons. There were other instances, however, where all families were removed from their homes, but only the non-Japanese families were allowed to return. In other cases Japanese Americans were subject to excessive and undue restrictions when they tried to return.[41] The Civil Liberties Act Amendments of 1992 stated that the benefit of doubt would be given to the claimant in such cases. A number of individuals whose cases were initially deemed ineligible were eventually found to be eligible after community efforts by the Hono-lulu JACL, legal consultation by ACLU attorneys, and reconsideration by the ORA. The cases of hundreds of Japanese Americans from the areas of Waiau, Iwilei, Lualualei, Pauoa Valley Puuloa, McGrew Camp (next to Aiea Bay), and Thompson Corner were eventually deemed eligible.[42]

William Kaneko, the JACL's national vice president for public affairs in 1994, applauded the work of the ORA in the Hawai'i cases: "The ORA staff should be commended for conducting the additional research required to gain a more complete, comprehensive analysis."[43] Over 2,500 people from Hawai'i received redress, including approximately 1,100 individuals from categories originally deemed ineligible.[44]

Total Number of Payments

A total of 82,219 individuals were granted redress.[45] The vast majority of these individuals were either forcibly excluded, incarcerated, or both. Only 28 refused to accept their redress payments. The Department of Justice was unable to locate less than 1,500 potentially eligible people. This number was originally much higher, but through the efforts of the ORA and community groups, pri-marily the NCRR and JACL, the number was lowered. Published lists of these individuals' names appeared in the JACL's newspaper, the *Pacific Citizen,* in Japanese American newspapers across the nation, and in publications at vari-ous Japanese American and Asian American conferences.

The Civil Liberties Public Education Fund

Redress was more than an attempt to obtain monetary payments for Japa-nese Americans. Equally important was the education of the American public about what happened during World War II. Despite an official apology by the Civil Liberties Act of 1988 racism against Japanese Americans did not end. In 1991 Kimochi, Inc., a Japanese American senior service center in San Fran-cisco's J-Town, the national JACL office, and a Buddhist temple in San Fran-cisco all received a note declaring, "Death to all former internees."[46] On May 16, 1995, Kimochi, Inc. received an anonymous hate letter that stated, "May all former internees suffer eternal damnation."[47] The national JACL head-quarters was also subject to bomb threats. Clearly, while the apology had been made by the highest branches of the federal government, not all the citizenry of the nation were in agreement.

The Civil Liberties Act of 1988 created a vehicle through which to accom-plish the task of educating the public: The Civil Liberties Public Education Fund (CLPEF). Although the CLPEF was authorized by the redress legisla-tion, it faced an uncertain future through 1995. The Civil Liberties Act of 1988 authorized $50 million for the Civil Liberties Public Education Fund, yet by 1994 only $5 million had been appropriated. Nikkei legislators, the JACL, and the NCRR urged members of the community to lobby their legislators and members of the House and Senate appropriations committees to increase appropriations for the CLPEF. Senator Inouye and Representative Mineta gained the support of Senator Hollings, chair of the Appropriations Subcommittee on Commerce, Justice, State, and Judiciary, to include funding for the CLPEF for FY 1995.[48] Other members of the Senate Appropriations Committee, including Senators Patty Murray (Democrat from Washington), Dianne Feinstein (Democrat from California), and Ted Stevens lent their support.

In 1996 President William J. Clinton appointed eight individuals to sit on the board of the CLPEF, which the Senate approved. The eight were Robert F. Drinan from Massachusetts, a Georgetown University professor of law, a former U.S. representative, and a member of the CWRIC; Leo K. Goto of Colorado, the director of the Colorado Restaurant Association; Susan Hayase from California, a software development engineer at Hewlett Packard Company; Elsa H. Kudo from Hawai'i, a realtor, a former Justice Department camp inmate, and a spokesperson for Japanese Peruvian detainees; Yeiichi Kuwayama from the District of Columbia, a retired decorated World War II veteran; Dale Minami from northern California, Fred Korematsu's *coram nobis* attorney and a law partner in the firm of Minami, Lew, Tamaki, and Lee; Peggy Nagae from Washington State, Gordon Hirabayashi's *coram nobis* attorney and an attorney in the management consultant firm of PNL Consultants; and Don T. Nakanishi from southern California, the director of the Asian American Studies Center at the University of California, Los Angeles. Dale Shimasaki, a redress activist and the director of government relations at City College of San Francisco, was sworn in as the executive director in June 1996.

Nearly eight years after the signing of the Civil Liberties Act of 1988, the CLPEF board was sworn into office by Representative Matsui and held its first board meeting on April 1, 1996, in the capital.[49] At this meeting the board members elected Dale Minami as chair and Susan Hayase as vice-chair. The board of directors was charged with the following mission: "To sponsor research and public educational activities, and to publish and distribute the hearings, findings, and recommendations of the Commission, so that the events surrounding the evacuation, relocation, and internment of United States citizens and permanent resident aliens of Japanese ancestry will be remembered, and so that the causes and circumstances of this and similar events may be illuminated and understood."[50] The board members conducted outreach in their communities to inform people about the mission of the fund and solicit their input on how the money should be spent.

In March of 1997 100 recipients received grants totaling $2.7 million from the CLPEF. This number was subsequently raised to 132, which included 18 national fellowships and brought the total awards to $3.3 million.[51] The grants ranged from $2,000 to $100,000. Seven different categories of projects were funded: curriculum, landmarks and institutions, community development, arts and media, research, national fellowships, and research resources. The CLPEF also initiated and funded several of their own projects.

Among the grants $50,000 was awarded to the authors of this book to convene a conference entitled "Voices of Japanese American Redress." Held in September 1997 at the University of California, Los Angeles, the conference brought together nearly seventy highly visible redress participants. The group was made up of representatives from the different major redress groups, generational cohorts, geographic regions, and chronological stages of the movement. The conference provided an opportunity for dialogue and reflection on the lessons of the redress movement. What was evident at the conference was that a great deal of personal and organizational friction had been replaced with a sense of community accomplishment.

12   Lessons of a Movement

I wander amongst my dreams
That takes me to
    New places and hopes.

—Hiroshi John Yamashita, *Haiku Images*

What were the dreams of Japanese Americans at the end of World War II? What were the new places and hopes about which they dreamed? For many adults the dream was a pragmatic one of wanting to return home and rebuild their lives. For adolescents the dream included being able to order a hamburger, fries, and a coke or simply enjoy the attractions of a large city. For children the dream was to remain with their families and sleep in a real house, which kept the dust out and had running water. For some Japanese Americans the dream of new places and new hopes included a vision of the government's acknowledgment of the wrong it committed. However, the concentration camps remained a stark reality, and until 1988 meaningful redress was only an "impossible dream."

The eventual alignment of important policy streams allowed Japanese Americans to obtain the impossible dream. The Japanese American community, the general U.S. society, and the three branches of government aligned themselves during the One-hundredth Congress and created a brief window of opportunity for the passage of redress. In 1942 the alignment of a weak and relatively disorganized ethnic community, a historical context of racism and xenophobia, and three branches of the federal government affected by wartime hysteria and race prejudice resulted in the forced removal and incarceration of 120,000 persons of Japanese ancestry. Forty-six years later, in 1988, the alignment of a mobilized and active community, a sympathetic general public, and more enlightened branches of government produced the Civil Liberties Act of 1988.

In chapter 1 three questions were asked. First, why did it take nearly fifty years for this legislation to be enacted? Second, what were the essential factors and elements that precipitated and maintained the redress movement?

Third, what were the characteristics of the legislation and the sociopolitical context that facilitated its passage? The answers to these questions provide the lessons of the Japanese American redress movement.

From Exclusion and Incarceration to Redress

The Kitano-Maki proper alignment model provides a perspective on why it took nearly fifty years to pass the Civil Liberties Act of 1988. The model demonstrates that there was an alignment of negative influences in 1942 that enabled the U.S. government forcibly to remove, exclude, and incarcerate nearly the entire West Coast population of Japanese ancestry. The decades in between the closing of the camps and 1988 were transitional years leading to the proper positive alignment for the successful passage of redress.

The history of the Japanese in the United States, from their significant immigration in the 1890s up to World War II, unfolded amidst extreme hostility. Prejudice, discrimination, and segregation perpetuated the stereotypes of Japanese as sly, tricky, and treacherous. In the years leading up to World War II the streams of influence were aligned to take punitive action against the Japanese in the United States, whether they were citizens or aliens. This context was facilitated by the inability of many Americans to differentiate between Japanese Americans and Japanese in Japan. The mainstream society in the United States supported the policy of exclusion. The press led the way, and local politicians saw the action as a popular one. Anti-Japanese feelings and hysterical patriotism were the foundation of the U.S. society's perspective.

The Issei bore the brunt of the hostility toward the Japanese in America. They were "aliens ineligible to citizenship," restricted to segregated communities, hemmed in by prejudice and discrimination, and unfamiliar with the English language and American culture. They had limited access to the political system and were politically powerless. Meanwhile, the Nisei were a young generation. They were beginning to form their own organizations, such as the JACL, and were caught in the common generational conflict between the culture of their parents' homeland and that of their own native country. They had U.S. citizenship, but they were still dependent on the Issei for advice and leadership. It was the period of "Americanization" for the Nisei, and many of the young leaders were motivated to join the mainstream and discard the culture of their parents. It was also the time of the Great Depression, and the struggle for survival was paramount. Both generations were relatively powerless and represented only a minuscule fraction of the general society. There was therefore little organized opposition by the Issei or Nisei community against Executive Order 9066.

The overwhelming consensus in the larger U.S. society was that some form of action against the Japanese in the United States, regardless of their citizenship status, was necessary. These feelings pervaded the legislative, judicial, and executive branches of the federal government. Wartime hysteria, manipulated and biased information, poor progress in the war, and racism all created a context in which constitutional safeguards broke down. No organized civil rights group protested the treatment of Japanese Americans. As a result due process was denied and constitutional rights were violated.

The Transitional Years, 1945 to 1988

The years between the closing of the concentration camps and the passage of the Civil Liberties Act of 1988 were not idle. Significant changes occurred in each of the streams of influence in the proper alignment model. The community stream changed in the postwar decades as Japanese Americans began reestablishing their lives. Securing employment, obtaining education, and rebuilding familial and community structures were the priorities of Japanese Americans. Those who served in the armed forces used the GI bill to get a college education. Many others also went on to attain higher education and professional degrees. Job opportunities for Japanese Americans in the postwar economy, especially government jobs, became more available than before the war. The economy was booming, and the United States was on its way to becoming the most powerful nation in the world.

The decades following the war also brought political and social changes in the Japanese American community. Many began to read literary works by Japanese Americans in the 1960s, and Asian American studies programs emerged in the same decade. Increased academic attention and scholarship contributed to the awareness of the Japanese American community's experience. Community interest in remembering the concentration camps was fostered by pilgrimages to the sites of former WRA camps and the many Days of Remembrance. The Sansei emerged as a political force in the 1960s and began confronting the establishment and questioning the exclusion and incarceration experience. By the 1980s the Japanese American community was in a position to provide economic, political, and community support for a redress movement. The ten community hearings held by the Commission on Wartime Relocation and Internment of Civilians were a catalyst in reconciling the different generational viewpoints of the camp experience. The hearings provided the Japanese American community with the opportunity to have their voices heard.

There were also changes in the U.S. society. The civil rights movement, the women's movement, and the anti–Vietnam War movement increased sensitivity to the plight of women and ethnic minorities. Japan was no longer a wartime enemy but a political ally. Americans' impressions of Japan, however, were not completely positive. Japan's postwar industrial growth was so enormous that by the 1980s it had become a world economic power. The increased impact of Japan's trade policies and practices on numerous sectors of a then-weakening American economy generated a new round of "Japan bashing" in the 1980s.

The media took a more neutral if not positive view of Japanese Americans after the war and eventually became sympathetic to the redress movement. The term *model minority* was coined in 1965 to describe Japanese Americans. While not without its own symbolic problems, the term was an improvement over past stereotypes and descriptions.

In the postwar decades the three branches of government took significant judicial and legislative actions that partially addressed wartime losses from the exclusion and incarceration. Anti-Asian laws on the national and state levels were overruled or voted down. In the 1980s state, county, and city governments passed legislation and resolutions that addressed the wrongs they committed during World War II. The decisions in the *coram nobis* cases reflected judicial agreement that constitutional violations had occurred.

As Japanese Americans were elected to Congress in the late 1950s (due to Hawai'i's statehood in 1959), 1960s, and 1970s, the political might and insider access of the community grew. The redress movement spanned the administrations of six presidents: Nixon, Ford, Carter, Reagan, Bush, and Clinton. Each president influenced the process by supporting the concept of redress or by ultimately not opposing the progress of the movement.

Although there is a tendency to equate the transitional years from incarceration to redress as "wasted years," they were a necessary period between the shock of incarceration and the ability to organize community resources for ultimate action. Japanese Americans began to mobilize their resources and take a more activist stance. The general U.S. society became less hostile and more sympathetic. The three federal branches moved from a position of promoting the concentration camps to one of recognizing the injustice. The transitional years were necessary to achieve the proper alignment of influences. Such an alignment was unlikely prior to 1988 and would have been difficult to achieve in subsequent years (see table 10).

Elements of the Redress Movement

The Kitano-Maki proper alignment model tracks policy change from a macro perspective. Of critical importance to understanding redress is an appreciation of how elements within each stream of influence facilitated their alignment. Such elements as the emergent norm, sense of feasibility, timeliness, existence of preexisting organizations, and the presence of an extraordinary event that promoted solidarity all played a crucial role in the alignment of the streams of influence.

The redress movement included the *emergence of a norm* in the Japanese

Table 10.

Years	History		Legislative Branch		Judicial Branch	Executive Branch
	Community	U.S. Society	Senate	House		
1987–88	+	N+	+	+	N+	+
1983–86	+	N+	N	N	N+	–
1979–82	N+	N+	N	N	N	N-
1970–78	N+	N	N+	N+	N	N+
1945–69	N	N	N	N	N	N
Pre-WWII/Exclusion/ Incarceration	–	–	–	–	–	–

community that the concentration camps were not simply a misfortune but a carefully and purposefully constructed social injustice. This recognition, which developed during the late 1960s and throughout the 1970s, was facilitated by literary works, Asian American studies classes, Sansei's questioning of the camp experience, pilgrimages, Days of Remembrance, and the Nisei's and Issei's willingness to remember. The recognition of this injustice drove the community's desire to fight for redress.

As the understanding of the injustice grew, so did the sense of *feasibility* that something could be done to address it. By the early 1970s the Japanese American community possessed financial resources, legal knowledge, and access to both the mass media and those in key decision-making positions. The late 1960s and early 1970s were a time of activism and empowerment. Reflecting the courage, anger, and determination of this context, the initial leaders of the movement firmly believed redress was feasible.

The issue of *timeliness* presented itself in two ways. There was a sense of urgency that for the Issei this would be their "last chance" before they died to obtain a meaningful acknowledgment from the U.S. government of its wrongdoing. Second, the opportunity existed to tie redress into the two-hundredth anniversary of the signing of the Constitution. Both types of timing provided energy and momentum to the movement.

The presence of *preexisting groups* with communication networks and the ability to utilize the mass media was essential in initiating and sustaining the movement. The JACL was especially important in providing a national network of chapters through which discussion about redress in the 1970s could take place. The JACL also had an effective legislative history in Washington, D.C. Other community groups, especially the NCRR and NCJAR, while not "preexisting," were instrumental in giving a voice and a strategy to those who were not affiliated or in agreement with the JACL. While not having the same membership size or the legislative connection inside Washington, D.C., as the JACL, the NCRR was the expressive voice of the community. In the major cities in which it was present, the NCRR presented an opportunity for individuals to have a sense of involvement in the redress movement. The NCRR sent a clear message to those in Washington, D.C., that the community wanted redress.

Supportive preexisting groups were also present in the larger U.S. society. National mainstream groups, such as the Leadership Conference on Civil Rights, contributed to a broader coalition of support for redress. Such broad support facilitated the framing of redress as a fundamental concern for all Americans.

Finally, there were two *extraordinary events* for Japanese Americans that promoted solidarity in the movement. The first was the shared experience of having been incarcerated in concentration camps. This shared experience bonded those in the movement, whether one was actually incarcerated, was a member of an inmate's family, or simply knew people who were incarcerated. The second solidifying experience was the redress movement itself. As the movement progressed, it provided the community with a cathartic, synergistic, and self-empowering experience. The wounds between the generations began to be healed. The silent shame of the community was replaced by righteous demands of justice. The movement empowered the Japanese American community and promoted its solidarity.

General Elements to the Passage of Redress Legislation

The redress movement was a community effort, and no single individual, organization, or event can take all the credit for the passage of the Civil Liberties Act of 1988. The longstanding involvement of the Japanese American redress organizations was central to the redress legislation's becoming a reality. In addition a number of other general elements facilitated the passage of the bill. These elements included the findings of the CWRIC, the contributions of the *coram nobis* and NCJAR cases, the heightened awareness of the reasons for redress, the broad coalition of support, the role of the World War II Japanese American veterans, the cohesion of the Japanese American community, the framing of the issue, the personal dedication of the Nikkei legislators, the importance of political power, and the rightness of the issue.

The importance of the CWRIC and its subsequent findings cannot be overstated. The hearings were instrumental in organizing and energizing Japanese Americans to fight for redress. The hearings reinforced the idea that the camps were a social injustice, not simply an unfortunate occurrence. The findings of the commission transformed the debate from whether a wrong had been committed to what the Congress should do about this constitutional violation. In doing so, it played a pivotal role in aligning the Japanese American community, the U.S. society, and the legislative branch in favor of redress.

The CWRIC hearings also facilitated another important aspect of the redress legacy: reconciliation. The redress movement helped promote reconciliation between the U.S. government and the Japanese American community, between the different generations within the Japanese American community, between the different factions of the Japanese American community, and within the individual psyches of Japanese Americans.

The *coram nobis* cases and the NCJAR case offered additional support for passing H.R. 442. The *Korematsu* and *Hirabayashi coram nobis* cases provided judicial recognition that a constitutional violation had occurred. The *coram nobis* cases were not without risk. Had the court decisions been different, the redress effort would have experienced a significant setback. The success of the *coram nobis* cases was instrumental in aligning the judicial branch by neutralizing legal obstacles to the redress movement.

The NCJAR case clearly articulated the constitutional violations of the exclusion and incarceration. Although the NCJAR case had only a slim chance of winning because of technical barriers, the large amount of the demanded settlement figure (over $24 billion) made the legislative option appear much more palatable. After the House passed H.R. 442, Representative E. Clay Shaw Jr. told Aiko Herzig-Yoshinaga and Jack Herzig that the class action suit helped sway some votes.[1] However, to categorize H.R. 442 as an "out of court settlement" for the NCJAR case is to link the two efforts much more closely than they were. Nonetheless, their coexistence during the One-hundredth Congress created the opportunity for the NCJAR case to be used to facilitate the passage of H.R. 442 (e.g., Representative Frank's reference to the lawsuit on the House floor debate).

The media attention given to the redress movement was another element to its success in Congress. The attention was generally sympathetic and resulted in a heightened sensitivity toward redress. Throughout the 1980s and early 1990s academic textbooks increasingly included descriptions of the wartime exclusion and incarceration experiences. National magazines and local newspapers provided sympathetic coverage of the redress movement. The Smithsonian Institute's exhibition *A More Perfect Union* provided many members on Capitol Hill with important exposure to the incarceration experience. The successful effort to fund the exhibit demonstrated that redress was not a political liability. This was critical in securing the proper alignment of the legislative branch.

The heightened awareness by itself was not sufficient to ensure legislative success. Transforming this knowledge into a broad base of support was necessary to advance redress as a legislative item. A broad coalition of support made it easier to find common ground to appeal to individual legislators. Japanese American involvement with other national civil rights groups, religious organizations, ethnic minority groups, and professional associations produced this broad coalition. Forming a coalition with the Aleutian and

Pribilof Islanders also added support from the Alaskan congressional delegates, all of whom were Republicans. Such cross-cutting support elevated redress from being a special-interest issue to one with more national significance.

The role of the World War II Japanese American veterans was another important element in the passage of H.R. 442. Their wartime accomplishments were undeniable proof of the loyalty of Japanese Americans. They were invaluable in convincing many members of Congress to vote in favor of the bill. As Senator Inouye stated, "Without the 442d, we would still be debating the issue. To many of the doubters, one could say notwithstanding the indignities, the unconstitutionality, the open prejudice and discrimination, these men volunteered from behind barbed wires and gave their lives. You could almost look at the other guy and say 'Where were you?'"[2]

The contributions of the Nikkei veterans went beyond their wartime experiences. Their contemporary efforts to gain the support of some national veterans groups and to neutralize the opposition of other veterans groups paved the legislative road to passage. Grant Ujifusa put it succinctly when he observed, "No veterans, no redress."[3] Art Morimitsu, the JACL LEC's veterans liaison, stated:

> We appreciate all of the AJA [Americans of Japanese Ancestry] veterans and all the other veterans organizations across the country who responded to our call for help. Special thanks go to Go For Broke Nisei Veterans Association, 34th Infantry Division Association, Seattle NVC veterans, Denver American Legion Nisei Veterans, Nisei 14–Post VFW Coalition of California, Southern California Nisei Veterans Coordinating Council, and Illinois veterans groups. Especially we don't want to forget Mits Kasai of Salt Lake City and Sam Yada of Arkansas, who have done so much to get support in their states.[4]

The cohesion of the Japanese American community was a crucial element in bringing the redress issue to the Congress and ensuring support for the redress bill through the legislative process. Even though Japanese American organizations advocated different paths and objectives, the Japanese American community agreed that redress was an appropriate goal. There was no formal opposition in the Japanese American community or among the Japanese American legislators in the One-hundredth Congress. Such cohesion created a situation in which the supporters were not pitted one against the other and legislative support was not split between two options. Although there were interpersonal and interorganizational differences and tension, they were well managed. In some cases the differences served to compel different individuals to "blaze their own trail," which ultimately helped propel the movement forward.

The personal dedication of the members and friends of the Japanese American community was critical. The community activists who initiated and maintained the redress movement were mainly volunteers. Even the few individuals who were paid put in countless hours of unpaid overtime. Early morning hours, late evening hours, entire weekends, and personal vacation time were when redress activists worked for the cause. Without the energy provided by individuals in the Japanese American community, redress would never have been placed on the national agenda.

The dedication of community members was often complemented by the heightened roles for women in community organizations. The redress movement provided an opportunity for increased activism by Japanese American women. Lillian Nakano recalled being challenged by the question of what the role of women should be in society, the Japanese American community, and the redress movement. She answered the question by becoming an outspoken activist in the NCRR.[5] Chizu Iiyama, a Contra Costa JACL member, indicated that another important factor was the upward mobility of many Nisei families. She noted, "By the 1970s, women were more free to participate in civil rights activities and play an active role in redress."[6]

The educational levels, socioeconomic status, and social approval of activism of women had all increased. While sexist notions and male chauvinism still existed in society and in the Japanese American community, many Japanese American women played key roles as leaders, organizers, and activists. Sue Embrey, Mollie Fujioka, Carole Hayashino, Aiko Herzig-Yoshinaga, Chizu Iiyama, Miya Iwataki, JoAnne Kagiwada, Cherry Kinoshita, Tsuyako "Sox" Kitashima, Sumi Koide, Kathy Masaoka, Lillian Nakano, Kay Ochi, Rose Ochi, Mae Takahashi, Rita Takahashi, Chiye Tomihiro, and Grayce Uyehara were just a few of the many women who provided leadership and support throughout the movement. It is doubtful that women could have contributed to the same degree if the redress movement had peaked in the 1950s.

The framing of the issue was an important element throughout the redress movement, particularly in securing votes in the House. The actual drafting of the bill was important because it ensured that the bill had to go before only one House committee. Naming the bill the "Civil Liberties Act" was a brilliant stroke because it reflected the notion that it was not about property losses for a specific minority group but was about the violations of the constitutional rights of Americans. Focusing on the government's role in the denial of equal opportunity brought conservatives and liberals together. It is unlikely that a partnership between conservatives and liberals would have occurred with a title like "Japanese American Redress for World War II." With such a title the redress bill would have been labeled a liberal, special-interest, minority bill, and it would not have passed.

The timing of the bill in the One-hundredth Congress was another important element. It would have been futile to push for legislation if the variables making up the "proper alignment" had been negative. For example, when there was a move to repeal the Chinese Exclusion Act during World War II, Owen Lattimore, an advocate for the repeal, suggested that Japanese exclusion also be repealed. The suggestion did not receive any further discussion because the timing was inappropriate.[7]

The One-hundredth Congress offered an unique window of opportunity for the passage of H.R. 442. The Nikkei legislators were at the peak of their collective political power, and Senator Hayakawa was no longer in office. The Democrats had recaptured the Senate, and sympathetic Democrats were leaders in the House. Representative Barney Frank became the chair of the subcommittee to which the legislation was assigned. Finally, the scheduling of the House vote on the two-hundredth anniversary of the signing of the Constitution took political advantage of a once-in-a-century anniversary.

The personal dedication of the Nikkei legislators cannot be ignored. Beyond the sophistication of their political strategy and maneuvering, the four men possessed a combination of power and charisma. Through their use of political chits and personal appeal, they were successful in garnering enough votes to pass the bill. These legislators paralleled the community's growth and commitment to the redress issue. At their initial meeting with the JACL in 1979 not one of them was willing to lead the "charge up the hill." Their initial reaction can be described as, at best, cautiously supportive. As the movement grew, so did their willingness to commit themselves personally and politically to the effort. Cautious support eventually transformed into an absolute commitment to the passage of the redress bill. These were not the same legislators who met in 1979. As the redress movement evolved, so did the legislators' support, leadership, and use of political power.

The element of political power became most evident in the struggle to secure appropriated funds and eventually to make redress an entitlement. Mass community lobbying was less effective during this stage of the process, and the need for strategically placed political power was obvious. Senator Inouye held that power. Without him the funding of the redress payments would have been an annual struggle, with no guarantees of success. His use of his power and position guaranteed funding.

The final overall element was simply the rightness of redress. Representative Matsui clearly articulated this in his observation that "once a person understood what happened to Japanese Americans during World War II, it became almost impossible to really oppose the idea . . . even Dan Lungren had to understand the injustice that occurred. So from the larger perspective, once this issue was out there in the public eye, it almost couldn't be opposed."[8] It would be naive to think that the bill passed solely because it was the right thing to do. However, the rightness of the bill helped transcend a strictly bipartisan debate and played a significant role in convincing legislators to vote for it.

Important Elements in the House

In the House there were key elements that specifically affected the passage of the bill. These included the strategic lobbying efforts of the Japanese American community and the use of non–Japanese American proxy advocates. The lobbying efforts of the JACL LEC and the NCRR were essential for two reasons. The first was that they either prompted uncommitted legislators to consider supporting the bill or solidified the support of legislators already in favor of the bill. Second, the support from the community sent a strong message to Representatives Mineta and Matsui that the community wanted this bill to pass. The unwavering message was a constant reminder that this bill was of the highest priority to the community.

The community's lobbying efforts faced difficult obstacles. Legislators received far more opposition letters than letters supporting redress. Since most Japanese Americans resided along the Pacific Coast and in Hawai'i, it is naive to believe that the representatives and senators were influenced simply by letters and telephone calls from people outside their districts. Letters, mailgrams, and telephone calls from individuals were most effective when used to target their own legislators. The use of "proxy" Japanese Americans to lobby legislators was productive in districts that had few or no Japanese American constituents. In addition what made the letters effective was the channeling of lobbying energy toward key legislators and committees.

Important Elements in the Senate

In the Senate there was one unique element that facilitated the passage of H.R. 442: Senator Spark Matsunaga. Senator Matsunaga's personal solicitation of over seventy cosponsors and his effort to speak to each U.S. senator was unprecedented at the time. The collegial nature of the Senate and the popularity of Senator Matsunaga made him the right person in the right place at the right time. The high priority he gave to redress and his appeal to fellow colleagues coalesced, and as a result the Senate vote was never in doubt.

Senator Inouye described Senator Matsunaga's contribution best by stating, "The man who should take nearly all of the credit for the passage of the redress bill is Senator Sparky Matsunaga. He is the one who sponsored the bill and organized the vote on that in the Senate."[9]

Important Elements Affecting President Reagan

Several additional elements played a role in convincing President Reagan to sign H.R. 442 into law. These elements included the manner in which the issue was presented to the president, the relative importance of the bill to the president and his administration, and the willingness of the Congress to work toward a compromise.

Understanding the president's thought process and his values was important in approaching President Reagan. The use of the Kazuo Masuda story accomplished a great deal. It reminded the president of his personal involvement with the issue and provided him with an anecdote to convey his convictions and values. A second element was that the bill was a relatively minor item on the president's agenda. Although the bill was of major concern to the Japanese American community and to its handful of vocal opponents, it paled in comparison with such issues as international relations and tax reform. Its relatively small budget and limited visibility helped it to avoid extensive Cabinet discussions that might have diminished the chances of the president's signing the bill. Finally, the willingness of the House-Senate conference committee to make necessary concessions to the administration was a crucial element. The negotiations to compromise with the White House removed the final obstacle to the president's signing the bill.

A Final Element

A final element is the presence of luck or good fortune, which was often cited by those who were closely tied to the redress effort. The notion of *luck* is arguably ill-defined and elusive. However, throughout the movement there were a number of coincidences and other episodes of good fortune. In the redress effort luck is best understood by the athletic analogy "the harder we work, the luckier we get." For example, one fortuitous bit of timing and luck was Representative Barney Frank's becoming chair of the House Judiciary Subcommittee on Administrative Law and Governmental Relations. Had Representative Frank not assumed this position, the bill could have easily died again in subcommittee. Representative Frank's appointment to the chair of the subcommittee was neither planned nor the result of careful strategy. It was good luck.

In addition to good luck, however, the Japanese Americans were in a position to capitalize on these fortuitous events. They achieved this position through hard work and diligence. From this perspective crucial moments of luck in the redress movement (e.g., Aiko Herzig-Yoshinaga's finding a key document on the archivist's desk, Peter Irons's knowing about writ of *coram nobis,* the Mineta-Simpson relationship) can be described as "good fortune born of hard work." Had the community not worked so hard to put itself in a position to take advantage of these fortuitous events, luck would not have mattered.

Precedent for Other Groups

The success of Japanese American redress provides important lessons for other groups seeking public policy legislation. The Kitano-Maki model and the aforementioned elements are applicable in varying degrees to the causes of ethnic minorities, women, gays and lesbians, and any other group fighting for policy change. The Civil Liberties Act of 1988, however, is very specific legislation that cannot be used in toto as a precedent for redressing all injustices.

The most apparent aspect of the Civil Liberties Act of 1988 that prevents the setting of a precedent is the requirement that individuals needed to be alive at the signing of the law in order to be eligible. While this served as a cost-saving measure, the basic intent behind this provision was to prevent the act from becoming a precedent for other groups with long-standing histories of oppression. For example, any attempt by African Americans to seek legislative redress for the history of slavery could not be based on Japanese American redress since no former slaves are still alive.

A second limitation to its application to other groups is the amendment Senator Helms introduced (Title III of the Civil Liberties Act of 1988). This amendment prohibits the recognition of another country's claims to U.S. territory, which limits the applicability of the act to such movements as the Hawaiian sovereignty movement. These limitations were the result of compromises to get the bill passed.

The redress movement, however, contributes a model for getting legislation passed. The structure and the elements of the movement provide valuable lessons to groups seeking justice (e.g., women used as prostitutes by the Japanese Imperial Army during World War II ["comfort women"], gays and lesbians seeking to legalize same-sex marriage).

In 1994 survivors of an African American community in Rosewood, Florida, were granted redress by the state of Florida for an injustice that had occurred over seventy years earlier. In 1923 the small African American town of Rosewood was burned to the ground by an angry white mob. Numerous residents were killed or maimed, while state and local authorities did nothing to stop the violence and at times even facilitated it. In 1993 the survivors presented legislation to the Florida state legislature that was modeled after the Japanese American redress movement. These individuals were each awarded $150,000, and a college scholarship fund was established for the victim's descendants.

Conclusion

The redress movement benefited the Japanese American community, in particular, and the United States, in general. It is important to remember, however, that the Civil Liberties Act of 1988 simply brought *legislative closure* to the injustice of the exclusion and incarceration. For many Japanese Americans the personal anguish and painful memories remain. No act of Congress can change the past; it can only acknowledge it.

Beyond the formal legislation Japanese Americans achieved a greater sense of pride by standing up for themselves. The Japanese American community initiated and spearheaded the redress movement. A healing process occurred through the increased communication and understanding between the Japanese American generations. All Americans were exposed to the frailties of the Constitution and Bill of Rights and were reminded of the need to be ever vigilant in safeguarding every American's civil liberties.

Finally, redress is not just a great Japanese American story. It is a great American story. The story includes the nightmare of the World War II concentration camps and the subsequent dream of an apology and compensation for unjust treatment. It includes pain, humiliation, and suffering, along with acknowledgment, accomplishment, and redress. It is a story of how an impossible dream became a reality.

Notes

Introduction

1. Quoted in Witt, "Japanese-Americans Seek Redress from Court," 724.
2. Ornstein, Mann, and Malbin, *Vital Statistics on Congress*, 155–60.
3. Definition from *The New Lexicon Webster's Dictionary*, 327.
4. *The New Lexicon Webster's Dictionary* defines *concentration camp* as "a place of arbitrary internment, not subject to courts and processes of law." The term was used by President Roosevelt and members of his cabinet in describing the War Relocation Authority's centers. Opponents of the redress movement often decried that the use of the term *concentration camp* unjustly equated the American camps with those of Nazi Germany. The inmates and survivors of the Nazi camps did not refer to the Nazi camps as "concentration camps" but more accurately as "death camps."
5. Civilian Exclusion Order No. 5, posted notice.
6. Daniels, "Internment of Japanese Nationals in the United Stated during World War II," 66. Daniels notes that more than 8,000 Japanese were interned at one time or another in Justice Department INS camps.
7. Japanese Americans have distinct terms for different generational cohorts. The immigrating generation is referred to as the first generation, or *Issei*. The children of the Issei (the first American-born generation) are the *Nisei*. The *Sansei* are the third generation. The *Yonsei* are the fourth generation. The term *Nikkei* refers to individuals of Japanese ancestry outside of Japan.
8. Kitano, interview by authors, March 12, 1996.

Chapter 1: Theoretical Perspectives

1. Kingdon, *Agendas, Alternatives, and Public Policies*, 1.
2. Campbell, *How Policies Change*, 49–50.
3. Ibid., 50.
4. In various documents and speeches the commission was referred to as the Presidential Commission, while at other times it was referred to as the Congressional Commission.

5. Cohen, March, and Olsen, "Garbage Can Model of Organizational Choice."

6. Morris, *Origins of the Civil Rights Movement.*

7. Turner and Killian, *Collective Behavior.*

8. Kingdon, *Agendas, Alternatives, and Public Policies,* 89–90.

9. Ibid., 90.

10. Ibid., 21.

11. Ibid., 20.

12. Ibid., 90–91.

13. Morris, *Origins of the Civil Rights Movement,* 275.

14. Ibid.

15. Turner and Killian, *Collective Behavior,* 77–78, 241–61.

16. Turner, interview by authors, February 26, 1996.

17. Turner and Killian, *Collective Behavior,* 300–304.

18. Ibid. 105, 300–304.

19. Mineta, interview by authors, August 6, 1994.

20. Kingdon, *Agendas, Alternatives, and Public Policies,* 188.

Chapter 2: Historical Factors prior to World War II

1. Daniels, *Prisoners without Trial,* 6.

2. U.S. Census of the Population, cited in Kitano, *Japanese Americans,* 211. In 1920 roughly 26.7 percent of the Japanese on the continental U.S. were American-born. In 1930 this percentage rose to 49.2 percent. By 1940 the percentage of American-born individuals was 62.7 percent. U.S. census data, cited in Kitano and Daniels, *Asian Americans,* 59.

3. Self-proclaimed nativists during this era were generally white Americans whose families had lived in California for at most a few generations. Although not truly "native" to the area, these individuals often promoted what they perceived as their indigenous rights.

4. Gulick, *American Japanese Problem,* 216–46.

5. Quoted in Kitano, *Japanese Americans,* 18

6. Daniels, *Prisoners without Trial,* 13.

7. Ibid., 13–14.

8. Quoted in Gulick, *American Japanese Problem,* 189. Webb made this statement in front of the Commonwealth Club of San Francisco on August 9, 1913.

9. Kitano, "Japanese Americans," 563.

10. Matsumoto, *Farming the Home Place,* 10.

11. Daniels, *Politics of Prejudice;* Ichioka, *Issei.*

12. Kazuo Kawai, "Three Roads and None Easy," 165, quoted in Strong, *Second-Generation Japanese Problem,* 12.

13. Ibid.

14. Kay Yasui, "Jap!" "Jap!" "Jap!" from the *Japanese-American News* and reprinted in *Pacific Citizen,* January 15, 1931, as quoted in Strong, *Second-Generation Japanese Problem,* 20.

15. Aiji Tashio in *New Outlook,* September 1934, quoted in McWilliams, *Prejudice,* 99. Tashio's parents were probably better educated than the average Issei, since they read to him in English.

16. Strong, *Second-Generation Japanese Problem,* 64.

17. Ernest Iiyama, interview by authors, October 10, 1995.

18. Hosokawa, *Nisei,* 191–205. The JACL's founding convention was held during the summer of 1930. Initial organizing occurred during the late 1920s.

19. Division of Far Eastern Affairs to State Department, S.D.F. 894.20211-131, N.A., August 24, 1934, quoted in Kumamoto, "Search for Spies," 49.

20. Irons, *Justice at War*, 20.

21. Roosevelt to Chief of (Naval) Operations, August 10, 1936, Box 216, Folder A8-5, Record Group 80—General Records of the Navy Department, National Archives, Washington, D.C., as cited in Irons, *Justice at War*, 374.

22. Kitano, interview by authors, October 20, 1995.

23. Kumamoto, "Search for Spies," 58.

24. Irons, *Justice at War*, 22.

25. Ibid., 23.

26. Kitano, *Generations and Identity*, 39.

27. Reginald Sweetland, "Japan Pictured as Nation of Spies," *Los Angeles Times*, December 23, 1941, part 1, 3.

28. "Eviction of Jap Aliens Sought," *Los Angeles Times*, January 28, 1942, part 1, 1.

29. "Lincoln Would Intern Japs," *Los Angeles Times*, February 13, 1942, part 1, 6.

30. "Jap Roundup" (editorial), *Los Angeles Times*, February 2, 1942, part 2, 4.

31. "Lincoln Would Intern Japs," *Los Angeles Times*, February 13, 1942, part 1, 6.

32. *San Francisco Examiner*, January 29, 1942, quoted in Conrat and Conrat, *Executive Order 9066*, 52.

33. Quoted in Conn, Engelman, and Fairchild, *United States Army in World War II*, 118.

34. U.S. Department of War, *Final Report*, 33–34, quoted in Irons, *Justice at War*, 377.

35. Warren, statement in U.S. House Select Committee Investigating National Defense Migration, *Hearings Pursuant to H. Res. 113*, February 21, 1942, 11011–12.

36. Quoted in Daniels, *Concentration Camps USA*, 55–56.

37. Telephone conversation between Gullion and Mark W. Clark, National Archives, Record Group 389, quoted in Daniels, *Concentration Camps USA*, 58.

38. The telephone conversation between President Roosevelt and Secretary of War Stimson was not recorded. The reported statement was made by McCloy to Bendetsen in describing the president's statement. Conn, "Notes," as quoted in ibid., 65.

39. Letter from Attorney General Francis Biddle to Franklin D. Roosevelt, February 17, 1942, Franklin D. Roosevelt Library, Hyde Park, N.Y., quoted in ibid., 70.

40. Irons, *Justice at War*, 61–62.

41. Biddle, *In Brief Authority*, 226.

42. Irons, *Justice at War*, 57–58.

43. Executive Order 9066, 1407.

44. *Congressional Record*, 77th Congr., 2d sess., vol. 88, part 2, February 23 to March 25, 1942, 2726.

45. U.S. Congress, *Fourth Interim Report of Select Committee Investigating National Defense Migration*, 318.

46. Among the first persons to be evicted from their homes were the nearly five hundred Japanese American families living on Terminal Island. This action was not a result of Executive Order 9066 but was a U.S. Navy action. Terminal Island was a small piece of land situated across the channel from San Pedro, California, near the Port of Los Angeles and the Long Beach Naval Station. These families received notices on February 14 and February 25, 1942, that they were to vacate the island by midnight on February 27, 1942. The original notice on February 14, 1942, indicated that the families had until March 14 to leave. The notices on February 25 gave the families that had not evacuated a little over forty-eight hours to evacuate. The evacuation notices did not state where the families had

to go since no firm evacuation plan had been made at that time. Once evicted, the Japanese American families were free to go where they wanted. However, this freedom was temporary because the forced exclusion of all Japanese Americans from the West Coast would soon occur.

47. Hosokawa, *Nisei,* 310.

Chapter 3: World War II (1941–45)

1.Issei are referred to as "resident aliens" rather than Japanese Americans, since they did not have U.S. citizenship. Some assembly centers, such as Manzanar, became permanent relocation centers.

2. Unlike the WRA camps, the Justice Department camps were internment camps.

3. Masaoka, *They Call Me Moses Masaoka,* 92.

4. In January of 1943 the army decided to form an all-Nisei combat unit, thus necessitating the need to recruit Nisei males from the camps. Simultaneously, Dillon Myer, the national director of the WRA, was convinced that "loyal" inmates should have their freedom restored. In an attempt to address both issues the WRA composed a questionnaire that served as the Application for Leave Clearance. Included in this questionnaire were the notorious "loyalty questions."

5. Those who refused to answer or answered no to either question 27 or question 28 on their leave clearance questionnaires were presumed to be disloyal by the War Relocation Authority. Question 27 asked, "Are you willing to serve in the armed forces of the United States on combat duty, wherever ordered?" and question 28 asked, "Will you swear unqualified allegiance to the United States of America and faithfully defend the United States from any and all attack by foreign or domestic forces, and foreswear any form of allegiance to the Japanese Emperor, or any other foreign government, power, or organization?"

6. Telegram to U.S. Attorney General Francis Biddle, February 16, 1942. Organizations to sign the telegram were the Los Angeles City and County Citizens of Japanese Ancestry; Perry Post, American Legion; Southern California Christian Church Federation; Los Angeles Citizens League; Japanese YMCA; Fruit and Vegetable Workers Union, Local 1510 American Federation of Labor; Young Men's Buddhist Association; Young Women's Buddhist Association; Flower Market Association Junior Produce Club; Japanese YWCA; and the Southern District Citizens League.

7. Irons, interview by authors, October 26, 1994.

8. Quoted in Irons, *Justice at War,* 84.

9. Statement by Gordon Hirabayashi found in Special Agent in Charge, Seattle, to Director, FBI, Memo, May 23, 1942, File 146-42-20, Department of Justice, quoted in Irons, *Justice at War,* 88.

10. Hirabayashi was originally sentenced to thirty days for each conviction to be served one after the other. To qualify for "road duty," Hirabayashi requested a longer sentence and was granted the sentence of ninety days per conviction to be served simultaneously. Hirabayashi, interview by authors, August 26, 1996.

11. *Hirabayashi v. United States,* 320 U.S. 81, 102 (1943).

12. Ibid., 103–4.

13. *Yasui v. United States,* 320 U.S. 115, 117, 63 S. Ct. 1392 (1943).

14. *Korematsu v. United States,* 323 U.S. 214, 225–26 (1944).

15. Ibid., 233.

16. Ibid., 239.

17. Ibid., 242.

18. Ibid., 242–43.

19. Quoted in Hosokawa, *Nisei,* 337.

20. Yuri Tateishi, quoted in Tateishi, *And Justice For All,* 26.

21. Ibid., 145.

22. Kitano, "In Search of an Identity," 130, 132.

23. Quoted in Thomas and Nishimoto, *Spoilage,* 368.

24. Quoted in Thomas, *Salvage,* 281.

25. Hohri, *Repairing America,* 29–30.

26. Kurihara, letter to Yoshiko Hosoi (entitled "Niseis and the Government"), circa 1942.

27. The JACL officials included Min Yasui and Joe Grant, Mike Masaoka's older brother.

28. An additional, albeit lesser-known, all-Nisei unit was the 1399th Engineering Construction Battalion, which was responsible for completing fifty major construction projects in Hawai'i during World War II. This unit was made up of both drafted and enlisted men and received the Meritorious Service plaque for their contributions to the war effort.

29. Hosokawa, *Nisei,* 415–16.

30. Roughly one hundred Nisei women joined the Women's Army Corps during World War II. Unlike the Nisei men, these women did not serve in strictly segregated units. Like the men, Nisei women were allowed to serve only in the army. For more information, see Hirose, "Japanese American Women and the Women's Army Corp"; and Yanamoto, "Nisei WAC Has No Regrets about Enlistment."

31. Masaoka, *They Call Me Moses Masaoka,* 123.

32. Ibid., 124.

33. Kitano, interview by authors, March 14, 1996.

34. Quoted in Tateishi, *And Justice For All,* 181.

35. "Potential Number of Persons of Japanese Ancestry Available for Military Service," War Department, Military Intelligence Service, March 29, 1943, Files, Military Intelligence Service, War Department, as cited in Duus, *Unlikely Liberators,* 70.

36. K.O., letter to Monroe Deutsch, March 15, 1943, President's Files, University of California Archives, quoted in Daniels, *Concentration Camps USA,* 114.

37. As a unit, the 442d R.C.T. participated in seven major campaigns and was awarded 7 Presidential Unit Citations, 36 Army Commendations, and 87 Division Commendations. Individual members of the 442d were awarded 18,143 commendations. These commendations included 1 Medal of Honor, 52 Distinguished Service Crosses, 560 Silver Stars with 28 Oak Leaf Clusters, more than 4,000 Bronze Stars with 1,200 Oak Leaf Clusters, and 9,486 Purple Hearts. Masaoka, *They Call Me Moses Masaoka,* 177.

38. Daniels, *Concentration Camps USA,* 152.

39. Inouye, *Journey to Washington,* 133.

40. Masaoka, *They Call Me Moses Masaoka,* 177.

41. Quoted in Thomas and Nishimoto, *Spoilage,* 51.

42. Kitano, *Japanese Americans,* 77.

43. Mass, "Psychological Effects of the Camps on Japanese Americans," 160–61.

44. Kitano and Daniels, *Asian Americans,* 68.

45. *Ex Parte Endo,* 323 US 283, 294 (1944)

46. Ibid., 283–310.

47. Jerome was the first WRA camp to close. It closed on June 30, 1944. On March 20, 1946, the last remaining WRA camp, Tule Lake, was closed. Although restrictions began to be lifted as early as December 17, 1944, it was not until January 20, 1945, that all categories of exclusion orders affecting individuals of Japanese ancestry were rescinded.

48. Ball, "Judicial Parsimony and Military Necessity Disinterred," 184.

49. Ibid.

50. Ibid. Ball based this statement on Hugo L. Black's Papers, Box 59, Library of Congress.

51. Commission on Wartime Relocation and Internment of Civilians, *Personal Justice Denied*, 317. For other information about the history and wartime experiences of the Aleuts, see Thill, Thill, and Philemonof, *Aleut Evacuation;* Kirtland and Coffin, *Relocation and Internment of the Aleuts during World War II;* and Kohlhoff, *When the Wind Was a River.*

52. Letter from Ernest Gruening to Harold L. Ickes, quoted in Commission on Wartime Relocation and Internment of Civilians, *Personal Justice Denied*, 327.

53. Dutch Harbor was strategically situated. Whoever controlled Dutch Harbor commanded Unimak Strait, which allowed passage through the chain of Aleutian islands and linked the Bering Sea to the Pacific Ocean.

54. In the next two months, under orders from U.S. military officials, the Aleuts were evacuated from the Pribilof Islands of Atka; St. Paul and St. George; Nikolski village on Umnak Island; Makushin, Biorka, Chernofski, Unalaska, and Kashega villages on Unalaska Island; and Akutan village on Akutan Island. These villagers were evacuated without choice to sites in southeast Alaska.

55. Kirtland and Coffin, *Relocation and Internment of the Aleuts during World War II,* 12–13; Commission on Wartime Relocation and Internment of Civilians, *Personal Justice Denied,* 328–29. Four structures remained after the implementation of the scorched-earth policy.

56. Letter from Fredrika Martin, March 1965, quoted in Commission on Wartime Relocation and Internment of Civilians, *Personal Justice Denied,* 330–31.

57. Ibid., 330.

58. Two camps were located in Funter Bay and one camp each in Killisnoo Island, Ward Cove, and Burnett Inlet. The Wrangell Institute in Alaska also housed some children.

59. Commission on Wartime Relocation and Internment of Civilians, *Personal Justice Denied,* 348–49; Kirtland and Coffin, *Relocation and Internment of the Aleuts during World War II,* 57.

60. Commission on Wartime Relocation and Internment of Civilians, *Personal Justice Denied,* 21.

61. Thill, Thill, and Philemonof, *Aleut Evacuation.*

62. Commission on Wartime Relocation and Internment of Civilians, *Personal Justice Denied,* 341. Ironically, an official prisoner of war camp was situated near Excursion inlet, forty miles from the Funter Bay camps. The 694 German prisoners of war were provided with good medical care, nutritious food, and clean and heated buildings.

63. Ibid.

64. Ernest H. Gruening, *Annual Report of the Governor of Alaska to the Secretary of the Interior for the Fiscal Year Ended June 30, 1944* (Washington, D.C.: U.S. Government Printing Office, 1944), 13, quoted in Commission on Wartime Relocation and Internment of Civilians, *Personal Justice Denied,* 345; Pribilof Log, September 13, 1943, quoted in Kirtland and Coffin, *Relocation and Internment of the Aleuts during World War II,* 99. The Pribilovian

sealers were compensated for their work on the harvest at a rate of approximately $1.00 per sealskin, while the non-Pribilovian Aleut sealers were paid $150.00 per month. They were forced to work daily under the threat that food would not be prepared for them.

65. Conn, Engelman, and Fairchild, *United States Army in World War II*, 80.

66. Kirtland and Coffin, *Relocation and Internment of the Aleuts during World War II*, 71.

67. Commission on Wartime Relocation and Internment of Civilians, *Personal Justice Denied*, 355–56.

68. Ibid., 357.

69. Quoted in Kirtland and Coffin, *Relocation and Internment of the Aleuts during World War II*, preface.

70. Ibid., 62.

Chapter 4: The Postwar Decades (1945–69)

1. Nishimoto, *Inside an American Concentration Camp*, 163.

2. Daniels and Kitano, *American Racism*, 73–85.

3. Truman, *Public Papers of the Presidents of the United States: Harry S. Truman, January 1 to December 31, 1946*, 347.

4. "President Seeks Immediate Congressional Passage of Legislation for Indemnification," *Pacific Citizen*, July 27, 1946, 1.

5. *Congressional Record*, 80th Congr., 2d sess., vol. 93, part 8, July 21 to November 17, 1947, 9872.

6. "No Opposition Recorded during Floor Discussion of Proposal to Pay for Property Losses," *Pacific Citizen*, July 26, 1947, 1.

7. Others who testified in favor of the bill at the Senate judiciary subcommittee hearings on May 21, 1948 were Dillon S. Myer, head of the Inter-American Institute and former director of the WRA; Francis Biddle, former U.S. attorney general; Edward J. Ennis, head of the Justice Department's Alien Enemy Control Unit during the war; Galen Fisher of the wartime West Coast Committee on American Principles and Fair Play; Mike M. Masaoka, legislative director of the JACL Anti-Discrimination Committee; and Maston G. White, solicitor for the Department of the Interior.

8. The most significant amendment the Senate made was a clause forbidding claims for anticipated profits or earnings.

9. The Japanese-American Evacuation Claims Act of 1948 (Public Law 80-886) provided for the U.S. attorney general to pay claims not exceeding $2,500 for damage or loss to property resulting from the evacuation orders of February 19, 1942. Claimants needed to substantiate their property and businesses losses. Any awards above $2,500 were subject to the approval of Congress. Voluntary evacuees were entitled to file claims. Applications for claims needed to be submitted within eighteen months from the date of enactment of the bill. Claims filed by or on behalf of any person who was repatriated or deported from the United States were not recognized. Similarly, claims submitted on behalf of any alien who did not reside in the United States on December 7, 1941, were not recognized. The Japanese-American Evacuation Claims Act did not specify any sum for appropriations but contained a provision allowing Congress to appropriate such sums as necessary.

10. "Pre-War Farmers Settle Eviction for $350,000," *Rafu Shimpo*, October 8, 1965, 1.

11. The state of Washington repealed its Alien Land Law in 1966, becoming the last state to do so.

12. These rights included grade, time in grade, and rate of compensation.

13. This bill was an expanded version of an original bill introduced by Representative Gordon L. McDonough (Republican from California), Representative Norris Poulson (Republican from California), and Representative George P. Miller (Democrat from California). The original bill applied only to federal postal workers.

14. Kitano and Daniels, *Asian Americans,* 5–6. The vast majority of these individuals were allowed entry under family reunification or refugee provisions in the law.

15. Harry H. Nakamura was the individual whose claim was denied.

16. Daniels, interview by authors, October 5, 1994.

17. Morris, *Origins of the Civil Rights Movement,* 4–7.

18. Ibid.

19. Ibid., 13.

20. Masaoka, *They Call Me Moses Masaoka,* 289–90.

21. Ibid. 290.

22. William Petersen, "Success Story," *New York Times,* January 9, 1966, 21.

23. Kitano, "Japanese Americans on the Road to Dissent," 107.

24. Kitano, interview by authors, October 20, 1995.

25. Quoted in "Minorities: A Wrong Partially Righted," *Time: The Weekly Newsmagazine* 89 (April 21, 1967): 25.

26. Ibid.

27. Furutani, interview by authors, October 3, 1995.

Chapter 5: The Genesis of the Modern Redress Movement (1970–78)

1. Other groups passed resolutions against redress (e.g., American Ex-Prisoners of War and American Defenders of Bataan and Corregidor, Inc.).

2. Edison Uno was a well-respected community activist who had been incarcerated at both Granada and the Justice Department camp at Crystal City.

3. Commission on Wartime Relocation and Internment of Civilians, *Personal Justice Denied,* 120. The $400 million figure was based on reported estimates made by the Federal Reserve Bank of San Francisco on the value of the property lost by Japanese Americans during the exclusion. These estimates were often referred to but remain undocumented.

4. Tateishi, "Interview by Eric Saul," 22.

5. Uchida, *Desert Exile,* 147.

6. This part of Title I was declared unconstitutional by the U.S. Supreme Court and repealed in 1968.

7. Truman, *Public Papers of the Presidents of the United States: Harry S. Truman, January 1 to December 31, 1950,* 645–53.

8. Okamura, "Background and History of the Repeal Campaign," 75–76.

9. "Reparation Campaign Underway," *Pacific Citizen,* April 30, 1976, 1.

10. The bill was introduced by Representative Spark Matsunaga at the urging of the Committee of Japanese American Yen Depositors and the JACL.

11. Nixon, *Public Papers of the Presidents of the United States: Richard M. Nixon, 1972,* 949–50.

12. The senators who were in Congress on December 8, 1941, were Carl T. Curtis (Republican from Nebraska), Hugh Scott (Republican from Pennsylvania), George D. Aiken (Republican from Vermont), Warren G. Magnuson (Democrat from Washington), Henry

Notes to Pages 68–71 251

M. Jackson (Democrat from Washington), Jennings Randolph (Democrat from West Virginia); the representatives were Robert L. F. Sikes (Democrat from Florida), Wilbur D. Mills (Democrat from Arkansas), Wright Patman (Democrat from Texas), William R. Poage (Democrat from Texas), George H. Mahon (Democrat from Texas), F. Edward Hebert (Democrat from Louisiana), Claude D. Pepper (Democrat from Florida), and Jamie L. Whitten (Democrat from Missouri). The additional senators and representatives who had served in Congress from 1943 to 1944 were Senator James O. Eastland (Democrat from Mississippi), Senator Michael J. Mansfield (Democrat from Montana), Senator John L. McClellan (Democrat from Arkansas), Senator J. William Fulbright (Democrat from Arkansas), Representative O. Clark Fisher (Democrat from Texas), Representative Chet Holifield (Democrat from California), and Representative Ray J. Madden (Democrat from Indiana).

13. "Reparations Campaign Underway," *Pacific Citizen*, April 30, 1976, 1.

14. "Evacuee Reparation a Sleepy Issue in JACL," *Pacific Citizen*, January 24, 1975, 3.

15. Four other chapters were sent the questionnaires. No response was received from Cleveland, Dayton, or St. Louis. Detroit sent back one response. "MDC Reparations Survey," *Pacific Citizen*, October 10, 1975, 1, 3.

16. Ibid.; "Reparations Campaign Underway," *Pacific Citizen*, April 30, 1976, 1.

17. "MDC Reparations Survey," *Pacific Citizen*, October 10, 1975, 3.

18. Ibid., 1.

19. Ibid.

20. Ibid.

21. Among the numerous surveys were ones conducted by the Midwest District of JACL, the Pacific Northwest District of the JACL, the Pacific Southwest District of the JACL, and the Seattle Evacuation Redress Committee.

22. "Campaign Hinges on Support," *Pacific Citizen*, October 10, 1975, 1.

23. Mike Masaoka, "Reparations for Evacuees Urged on Individual Basis, May Rally JACL Nationally," *Pacific Citizen* (holiday issue), December 19–26, 1975, D-1.

24. Norman Mineta, as told to Susan Schindehette, "The Wounds of War: A California Congressman Recalls the Trauma of World War II Internment," *People Weekly* 28 (December 14, 1987): 174.

25. Ibid., 175.

26. Barone and Ujifusa, *Almanac of American Politics, 1986*, 127–29.

27. Mineta, letter to Shig Sugiyama, January 30, 1976, 1

28. "Reparation Campaign Underway," *Pacific Citizen*, April 30, 1976, 3.

29. "The Orphan Issue: Executive Order 9066," *Rafu Magazine*, no. 25,660 (December 17, 1988): 3.

30. Ford, *Public Papers of the Presidents of the United States: Gerald R. Ford, 1976–1977*, 366.

31. Both the Senate and the House passed legislation in late August 1976 to assert congressional authority to oversee and review states of national emergency declared by the executive branch. On September 14, 1976, President Ford signed the National Emergencies Act, which terminated certain presidential powers and authorities, as well as section 1383 of Title 18 of the U.S. Code, which was the section of Public Law 503 that specifically provided the criminal penalties for Executive Order 9066. National Emergencies Act, 1255–59.

32. The members of the board of E.O. 9066, Inc. in the summer of 1975 were Paul

Tsuneishi, Sue Embrey, Phil Shigekuni, Ken Honji, Lyle Asaoka, Hana Shephard, Amy Ishii, Joan Lang, Tomoo Ogita, and Richard Yamauchi.

33. Tsuneishi, notes and rough outline on redress for panel on October 25, 1995, 5.

34. Tsuneishi, Embrey, and Shigekuni, letter to Ed Yamamoto, April 9, 1976. The following religious organizations passed resolutions in support of redress in 1975 and 1976: the Lutheran Churches of America (L.C.A.); Western Baptist State Convention of California (one hundred black Baptist churches); Southern California–Nevada Annual Conference of the United Methodist Church; Asian American Baptist Convocation; and the Board of the Japanese Free Methodist Churches of America. Tsuneishi, notes and rough outline on redress for panel on October 25, 1995, 6–7.

35. "Wilkins Urges Religious Leaders to Shun Reparations as Delusion," *New York Times,* October 22, 1969, 20.

36. "Wounded Knee Reparations: A Bad Precedent?" *Washington Post,* March 25, 1976, A19.

37. Quoted in "Wounded Knee," *Washington Post,* June 13, 1976, C8.

38. Sasaki, *Appeal for Action to Obtain Evacuation Redress.* The text can be found in "Seattle's Reparation Proposal Put on Tape," *Pacific Citizen,* January 23, 1976, 4–5.

39. Ibid.

40. "$2 Billion Seen For Evacuees," *Pacific Citizen,* May 14, 1976, 1.

41. This committee was also interchangeably referred to as the National JACL Reparations Committee, the National JACL Committee for Reparations, and REPACAMP. Members included Mike Masaoka, Mike Honda, Paul Tsuneishi, Tom Masamori, Henry Miyatake, Tom Shimasaki, and Dale Shimasaki representing the youth. Also attending the first meeting of the committee were Wayne Horiuchi, the JACL representative from Washington; Stan Kiyokawa, the Pacific Northwest regional director; and Tomio Moriguchi, the national treasurer, as liaisons with the JACL executive committee. Two individuals who provided consultation were Kaz Oshiki and Edison Uno. Advisers to the National JACL Reparations Campaign Committee were John Kanda, Emi Somekawa, James Tsujimura, James Watanabe, and Homer Yasui.

42. "$2 Billion Seen For Evacuees," *Pacific Citizen,* May 14, 1976, 1.

43. Ibid.

44. Tsuneishi, letter to Ed Yamamoto, June 3, 1976.

45. Nishikawa, letter to Paul Tsuneishi, May 10, 1976.

46. Horiuchi, "Report on Reparations Legislation For Japanese Americans," 12.

47. Justice Goldberg served on the U.S. Supreme Court from 1962 to 1965 before becoming the U.S. ambassador to the United Nations from 1965 to 1968. Present at the meeting with Justice Goldberg were Marvin J. Anderson, dean of Hastings Law School; David Ushio, national director of JACL; Floyd Shimomura; Steve Doi; and S. Stephen Nakashima. Nakashima, internal memorandum to JACL, June 14, 1976.

48. Statement made at Hastings College of the Law Bicentennial Year Program in San Francisco, January 29, 1976, as quoted in ibid.

49. Goldberg, letter to Stephen Nakashima, April 20, 1976.

50. For a fuller discussion of the parallels and differences related to justification of compensation for Japanese Americans and Jews in Nazi Germany, see Castelnuovo, "With Liberty and Justice for Some."

51. Nakashima, internal memorandum to JACL, June 14, 1976.

52. The other mistake involved reapportionment. Ibid.

53. Ibid.

54. "Editorials: Reparations Project," *Pacific Citizen,* February 25, 1977, 4.

55. Ibid.

56. "Reparations Study," *Pacific Citizen,* June 4, 1976, 1.

57. Resolution by Western Baptist State Convention of California, February 19, 1976.

58. Quoted in "VFW Urges Reparations," *Pacific Citizen,* September 10, 1976, 1.

59. Harris, news release, October 6, 1976.

60. "VFW Urges Reparations," *Pacific Citizen,* September 10, 1976, 1.

61. Samuel I. Hayakawa, "Radical Chic among the Japanese," *Seattle Times,* February 3, 1976, A12.

62. Ibid.

63. "Times Readers Have Their Say: Hayakawa Discredits Only Himself," *Seattle Times,* February 11, 1976, A13.

64. Quoted in Kutler, "Forging a Legend," 1380.

65. Ibid. Toguri d'Aquino was convicted of having broadcast this statement despite her denial of ever having done so, witnesses who corroborated her denial, and the absence of any written or tape-recorded documentation of any such statement being broadcast. This alleged statement was evidence of treason since it was supposedly intended to demoralize American troops.

66. For a fuller description of Iva Toguri d'Aquino's story, see Kutler, "Forging a Legend"; and Uyeda, *Final Report and Review;* and Lipton, "Wayne M. Collins and the Case of 'Tokyo Rose.'"

67. Murakami, telex to Ed Yamamoto, September 24, 1976.

68. "Editorials: Reparations Project," *Pacific Citizen,* February 25, 1977, 4.

69. In the first quarter of 1977 the Pacific Southwest JACL District Council reparations committee found that 93 percent of the 401 respondents favored reparations. Seventy-eight percent of the respondents were in favor of direct payment to individuals, while 31 percent favored funding for Japanese American community services, 15 percent supported funding scholarships and a legal defense fund for Japanese Americans, 10 percent supported funding for a public relations program to strengthen U.S.-Japan understanding, and 6 percent preferred their own proposals. Some 175 (43.6 percent) of the respondents preferred Plan A, which called for $5,000 per person plus a $10 for each day of incarceration, while 164 (40.9 percent) favored Plan B, or $10,000 per person. "93 percent Responding to Survey on Reparations Check 'Yes,'" *Pacific Citizen,* April 1, 1977, 1.

70. Japanese American Citizens League, *Japanese American Incarceration.*

71. The Seattle Plan, the Shimomura Plan, and the Northern California–Western Nevada Plan.

72. The Yasui Plan, the Columbia Basin Plan, and the Oshiki Plan.

73. "On Method of Redress," *Pacific Citizen,* January 6–13, 1978: 4.

74. Takeuchi, "Interview with Dr. Clifford Uyeda," 42–43.

75. John W. Dean III, former counsel to President Nixon who had worked for the Justice Department during the campaign to repeal Title II, supported the term *redress.* In a speech at the JACL Tri-District Conference in 1975, Dean proposed using the term *redress* instead of *reparations* since the redress of grievances was a right of U.S. citizens.

76. Japanese American Citizens League, *Visions,* 24.

77. Legislation had been enacted in 1952 that granted civil service credit to persons already in the civil service system at the time of incarceration. This current legislation would provide retirement credit for federal governmental employees who did not benefit from the 1972 social security retirement credit. Federal government employees do not receive social security retirement.

78. Several other bills that were similar in nature were also introduced by Representatives Robert Legget (Democrat from California), Phillip Burton (Democrat from California), and William Ketchum (Republican from California). Representative Jerome R. Waldie (Democrat from California) had introduced similar legislation in 1972.

79. *Congressional Record,* 95th Congr., 2d sess., vol. 124, part 1, January 19 to January 27, 1978, 423.

80. Carter, *Public Papers of the Presidents: Jimmy Carter, 1978, Book II, June 30 to December 31, 1978,* 1570.

81. Japanese American Citizens League, *Visions.*

82. Uyeda, memorandum to Ed Yamamoto, October 8, 1978.

83. Uyeda, interview by authors, January 20, 1995.

84. Quoted in Mike Carter. "For World War Reparations, JACL's Request 'Not Justified,'" *Salt Lake City Tribune,* July 23, 1978, B1.

85. Ibid.

86. Honda, memorandum to Harry Kitano, July 28, 1994.

87. "Senator's Statement Ires Japanese Americans," *Salt Lake City Tribune,* July 24, 1978, B1, B7.

88. Chin, oral comments during panel discussion at the Japanese American National Museum.

89. Kinoshita, Hayashino, and Yoshino, *Redress.*

90. Ibid.

91. Quoted in "'Camp Harmony' Remembered," *Pacific Citizen,* December 1, 1978, 1.

Chapter 6: The Commission on Wartime Relocation and Internment of Civilians (1979–82)

1. Tateishi met with Ernest Weiner from the American Jewish Committee in San Francisco and Samuel Samet, the director of the American Jewish Committee's domestic affairs division. Both Samet and Weiner suggested the creation of a presidential commission to educate the public about the facts of the incarceration. Tateishi, "Interview by Eric Saul."

2. Ibid., 40.

3. Ibid., 42.

4. John Tateishi specifically invited Ron Mamiya to present the Seattle Plan. Tateishi, telephone interview by authors, November 14, 1995.

5. Tateishi, telephone interview by authors, November 14, 1995.

6. Tateishi, "Interview by Eric Saul," 43–44.

7. Kinoshita, Hayashino, and Yoshino, *Redress.*

8. Mineta, interview by authors, August 6, 1994.

9. Glenn Roberts, legislative director for Representative Mineta, quoted in Naito and Scott, *Against All Odds,* 10.

10. Japanese American Citizens League National Committee for Redress, audiocassette.

11. Ibid.

12. Ibid.

13. Kinoshita, Hayashino, and Yoshino, *Redress.*

14. Bill Hosokawa, "Chapter Vote on Redress," *Pacific Citizen,* August 3, 1979, 5.

15. Uyeda, interview by authors, January 20, 1995.

16. Kitayama, *Japanese Americans and the Movement for Redress,* 47.

17. Quoted in Kitayama, *Japanese Americans and the Movement for Redress,* 48.

18. Bert Nakano, interview by authors, May 29, 1996.

19. Katsuda, interview by authors, May 29, 1996.

20. Kinoshita, interview by authors, October 8, 1994.

21. Lillian Nakano, interview by authors, May 29, 1996.

22. Kohlhoff, *When the Wind Was a River,* xiii.

23. Original cosponsors of S.R. 1647 were Alan Cranston (Democrat from California), Frank Church (Democrat from Idaho), S. I. Hayakawa (Republican from California), and James A. McClure (Republican from Idaho). Later cosponsors were Bill Bradley (Democrat from New Jersey), Mike Gravel (Democrat from Alaska), Henry M. Jackson (Democrat from Washington), Warren G. Magnuson (Democrat from Washington), Patrick Leahy (Democrat from Vermont), John Melcher (Democrat from Montana), Barry Goldwater (Republican from Arizona), and David Durenberger (Republican from Minnesota). Roger Daniels attempted to have Senator Inouye replace the word *internment* in the title of the commission with *incarceration.* However, by the time the suggestion was made, Senator Inouye had already obtained his cosponsors' approval of the stated title.

24. *Congressional Record,* 96th Congr., 2d sess., vol. 126, part 10, May 22 to June 4, 1980, S 12054.

25. Uyeda, interview by authors, January 20, 1995.

26. The original nine were Jim Wright (majority leader from Texas), John Brademas (majority whip from Indiana), Norman Mineta (from California), Bob Matsui (from California), Phil Burton (from California), Glenn Anderson (from California), Peter Rodino (from New Jersey), Sidney Yates (from Illinois), and Paul Simon (from Illinois).

27. Mineta, interview by authors, August 6, 1994.

28. Ibid.

29. Lowry, interview by authors, October 8, 1994.

30. *Congressional Record,* 96th Congr., 1st sess., vol. 125, part 26, November 27 to December 6, 1979, H 33966.

31. Matsui, interview by authors, July 11, 1995.

32. Ibid.

33. Tateishi, "Interview by Eric Saul."

34. The senators who made opening statements were Henry M. Jackson, Democrat from Washington; Daniel K. Inouye, Democrat from Hawai'i; Carl Levin, Democrat from Michigan; Spark M. Matsunaga, Democrat from Hawai'i; and Charles McC. Mathias Jr., Republican from Maryland. Those who testified in favor of the commission were Representative Jim Wright, Democrat from Texas; Representative Norman Y. Mineta, Democrat from California; Representative Robert T. Matsui, Democrat from California; Clarence M. Mitchell Jr., chairman of the Leadership Conference on Civil Rights; Roger Daniels, head of the history department at the University of Cincinnati; Jerry J. Enomoto, past president of the JACL; Mike M. Masaoka, president of the Nisei Lobby; and Diane Y. Wong, executive director of the Washington State Commission on Asian American Affairs. William Hohri, chair of the NCJAR and representative of the Methodist Federation for Social Action, was the only one who testified against the creation of a congressional commission.

35. U.S. Senate Committee on Government Affairs, *Hearing before the Committee on Governmental Affairs on S. 1647,* March 18, 1980, 17.

36. Ibid., 169.

37. Ibid., 171.

38. Ibid., 158.

39. The witnesses who testified included Representative Michael E. Lowry, Democrat from Washington; Representative Robert T. Matsui, Democrat from California; Representative Norman Y. Mineta, Democrat from California; Representative Jim Wright, Democrat from Texas; William M. Hohri, chair of NCJAR; Mike M. Masaoka, president of Nisei Lobby; Stuart E. Schiffer, deputy assistant attorney general, Civil Division, Department of Justice; John Y. Tateishi, chair of JACL NCR; Phil Tutiakoff, chair of the Aleutian Pribilof Island Association; and Mike Zacharof, executive director of the Aleutian/Pribilof Islands Association.

40. In the "markup" session the subcommittee amends a bill as the members of the subcommittee deem appropriate. The "marked-up" bill is then sent on with recommendations to the full committee, where a similar "markup" process takes place. In this case H.R. 5499 was used as the foundation bill. The other two bills included in the "markup" were S.R. 1647 (the Senate version of the commission bill, which included the Aleuts' wartime experiences as a focus of study) and H.R. 5977 (the Lowry direct monetary compensation bill). Not one of the provisions contained in the Lowry bill was added to the final product.

41. *Congressional Record*, 96th Congr., 2d sess., vol. 126, part 14, June 28 to July 21, 1980, H 18862.

42. Ibid.

43. Ibid., H 18864.

44. Ibid., H 18875. Of the 279 representatives voting for the bill, 187 (67 percent) were Democrat, and 92 (33 percent) were Republican. This distribution roughly paralleled the composition of the House (Democrats 63 percent; Republicans 37 percent). Of those opposing the bill, 49 (45 percent) were Democrat, and 60 (55 percent) were Republican.

45. Tateishi, "Interview by Eric Saul," 57.

46. Carter, *Public Papers of the Presidents of the United States: Jimmy Carter, 1980–1981, Book II, May 24 to September 26, 1980*, 1455, 1457.

47. Commission on Wartime Relocation and Internment of Civilians, *Personal Justice Denied*, 1.

48. "National Coalition to Spearhead Nikkei Redress Drive," *Rafu Shimpo*, December 4, 1980, 1, 4.

49. Kinoshita, Hayashino, and Yoshino, *Redress*.

50. Carter, *Public Papers of the Presidents of the United States: Jimmy Carter, 1980–1981, Book III, September 29, 1980, to January 20, 1981*, 2870–71.

51. *Congressional Record*, 97th Congr., 1st sess., vol. 127, part 2, February 3 to February 23, 1981, 2217.

52. Ibid., 96th Congr., 2d sess., vol. 126, part 25, December 8 to December 30, 1980, 34008.

53. Ibid., 97th Congr., 1st sess., vol. 127, part 2, February 3 to February 23, 1981, 2217, 2264.

54. Marutani, interview by authors, September 12, 1994.

55. The commission staff included Donna H. Fujioka, assistant research director; Donna Komure, legal counsel; Dr. Tom Taketa, associate director; Lois J. Wilzewske, executive administrator; Cheryl Yamamoto, assistant to the chair; Aiko Herzig-Yoshinaga, research associate; Paul T. Bannai, executive director; and Angus Macbeth, special counsel. Additional consultants and volunteers included Mark Baribeau, Kate C. Beardsley, Donald R. Brown, Jeanette Chow, Michelle Ducharme, Jack Herzig, Helen Hessler, Toro Hirose, Stuart J. Ishimaru, Gregory G. King, Key K. Kobayashi, Barbara Kraft, Alex M. Lichtenstein,

Karen L. Madden, Teresa M. Myers, Robin J. Patterson, Ardith Pugh, Mitziko Sawada, Nancy J. Schaub, Lois Schiffer, Maria Josephy Schoolman, Katrina A. Shores, Charles Smith, Fumie Tateoka, Terry Wilkerson, and Kiyo Yamada.

56. Herzig, interview by authors, October 3, 1995.

57. Tateishi, "Interview by Eric Saul," 59.

58. The appointed members of the new committee were Clifford Uyeda (associate chair), George Hara, Ben Takeshita, Chuck Kubokawa, Tom Shimasaki, Harry Kawahara, John Tameno, Henry Tanaka, George Sakaguchi, Cherry Tsutsumida, and John Tateishi (staff coordinator).

59. The Washington Coalition on Redress was a group of sixteen Japanese American organizations in the Puget Sound region that came together in the fall of 1980: the main Buddhist church; six Christian churches with significant Nikkei membership; four chapters of the JACL, including the Seattle chapter; the Washington State Commission on Asian American Affairs; Tomonokai; Nisei Veterans Committee, Inc.; Keiro Nursing Home/Nikkei Concerns, Inc.; and Japanese Community Service.

60. Wakabayashi, interview by authors, May 15, 1996.

61. "Sansei Congressman Warns JAs Not to Raise Redress Expectations," *Rafu Shimpo,* March 6, 1981, 1.

62. The hearings were held on the following dates: in Washington, D.C., on July 14 and 16, 1981, and again on November 2, 1981; in Los Angeles on August 4–6, 1981; in San Francisco on August 11–13, 1981; in Seattle on September 9–11, 1981; in Anchorage on September 14, 1981; in Unalaska on September 17, 1981; in St. Paul on September 19, 1981; in Chicago on September 22–23, 1981; in New York on November 23, 1981; and in Boston (at Harvard University) on December 9, 1981.

63. Bert Nakano, interview by authors, May 29, 1996.

64. Marutani, interview by authors, September 12, 1994.

65. Unpublished transcripts of CWRIC hearings, July 14, 1981, 5.

66. Ibid., 10.

67. Ibid., 13–14.

68. Ibid., 20.

69. Ibid., 43–44.

70. By the time of the hearings the leadership of the NCJAR decided to pursue redress through a judicial route. Once the commission was created, the NCJAR agreed to cooperate with it and share its research findings.

71. Unpublished transcripts of CWRIC hearings, July 16, 1981, 266–67.

72. Ibid., 284.

73. Ibid., 293.

74. Quoted in Commission on Wartime Relocation and Internment of Civilians, *Personal Justice Denied,* 18.

75. Letter from Eisenhower to Claude Wickard, April 1, 1942, "Correspondence of the Secretary of Agriculture, Foreign Relations, 2-1, Aliens-Refugees," Record Group 16, National Archives, quoted in Daniels, "Introduction," 3.

76. Commission on Wartime Relocation and Internment of Civilians, *Personal Justice Denied,* 18.

77. Bendetsen's original *Who's Who in America* entry described him as the "chief architect" of the exclusion and detention of Japanese Americans during World War II, but this description was dropped in later editions.

78. Unpublished transcripts of the CWRIC hearings, November 2, 1981, 7–125.

79. Bendetsen, "Written Statement for the Commission on Wartime Relocation and Internment of Civilians, July 8, 1981," 6, 10, 11.

80. Unpublished transcripts of the CWRIC hearings, November 3, 1981, 31; Marutani, interview by authors, September 12, 1994.

81. Marutani, interview by authors, September 12, 1994.

82. Unpublished transcripts of the CWRIC hearings, November 3, 1981, 32.

83. McCloy used the term *Japanese* when describing Japanese from Japan, legal Japanese residents in the United States, and Japanese Americans.

84. Marutani, interview by authors, September 12, 1994.

85. Unpublished transcripts of the CWRIC hearings, November 3, 1981, 55.

86. Marutani, videotaped interview by Mitchell T. Maki, Darcie Iki, and John Esaki, August 27, 1998.

87. Lillian Baker made these same arguments in *Concentration Camp Conspiracy; Dishonoring America;* and *American and Japanese Relocation in World War II.*

88. Unpublished transcripts of the CWRIC hearings, July 16, 1981, 378–80.

89. Ibid., August 4, 1981, 19.

90. Ibid., 24.

91. Other high-ranking government officials, including President Franklin D. Roosevelt himself, used the term *concentration camps.* President Roosevelt used the term in press conferences he gave on October 20, 1942, and November 21, 1944. Chief of Staff George C. Marshall used the term *concentration camps* in Marshall, letter to General Delos Emmons, October 7, 1943.

92. Unpublished transcripts of the CWRIC hearings, August 4, 1981, 25.

93. Judith Michaelson, "Hayakawa Jeered at Hearing on Internment," *Los Angeles Times,* August 5, 1981, part 2, 1.

94. Paul Conrad, "Play It Again, Sam," *Los Angeles Times,* August 6, 1981, part 2, 7.

95. Frank Chin, "Unfocused L.A. Hearings: 'A Circus of Freaks,'" *Rafu Shimpo,* August 21, 1981, 1.

96. Lillian Nakano, "Looking Back on the Commission Hearings," *NCRR Banner* 1 (September/October 1981): 1.

97. Unpublished transcript of the CWRIC hearings, August 6, 1981, 21.

98. Ibid., August 5, 1981, 9–10.

99. Ibid., November 23, 1981, 99–100.

100. Frank Chin, "Unfocused L.A. Hearings: 'A Circus of Freaks,'" *Rafu Shimpo,* August 21, 1981, 1.

101. Unpublished transcripts of the CWRIC hearings, August 5, 1981, 20.

102. Ibid., November 23, 1981, 67–68.

103. Ibid., August 4, 1981, 51.

104. Katsuda, interview by authors, May 29, 1996. Richard Katsuda was elected president of the NCRR in 1995.

105. Ibid.

106. Unpublished transcripts of the CWRIC hearings, August 12, 1981, 207–8.

107. Ibid., September 10, 1981, 94.

108. Ibid., August 6, 1981, 52.

109. Ibid., September 11, 1981, 172.

110. Ibid., September 22, 1981, 146.

111. Ibid., September 9, 1981, 69.

112. Ibid., August 6, 1981, 219–20. *Gaman* refers to the internalization and suppression of anger and emotion.

113. Ibid., August 12, 1981, 151.

114. Herzig-Yoshinaga, interview by authors, October 3, 1995.

115. The *Final Report* was officially authored by General DeWitt, however, the actual author was believed to be Colonel Karl Bendetsen. In a letter from Bendetsen to Hiroshi Suzuki, dated June 11, 1976, Bendetsen claimed credit for having "prepared" the actual report.

116. Hall, suggested changes in letter of transmittal and in foreword, circa May 3, 1943. John Hall was McCloy's assistant and made these recommendations on behalf of McCloy.

117. Smith, certification regarding the destruction of "Original Report of the Japanese Evacuation."

118. Marshall, memorandum to McCloy, May 13, 1944, excerpts of which were published in Weglyn, *Years of Infamy*, 220–21. Other documents also existed that indicated the political motivation of waiting until after the November 1944 presidential elections before closing the camps. See Biddle, notes on May 26 and November 10, 1944; Bonesteel, transcript of telephone conversation with John J. McCloy, July 14, 1944; Stettinius, memorandum to Roosevelt, June 9, 1944; and McCloy, letter to General Charles H. Bonesteel, October 31, 1944.

119. E. Hsu, "War Heroes Testify on the Internment Camps," *San Francisco Chronicle*, August 12, 1981, 178.

120. "The Burden of Shame," *Time: The Weekly Newsmagazine* 118 (August 17, 1981): 32.

121. "Keep Internment Interred," *Wall Street Journal*, July 27, 1981, 16.

122. During 1982 there were mixed reactions regarding redress. Many in the community anxiously awaited the CWRIC's published findings and recommendations. Simultaneously, the financial support for redress was wavering. At the 1982 JACL National Convention John Tateishi reported that the money available to the NCR had fallen to $20,000. He stated that unless more money was quickly added to the budget, redress operations would end. Throughout the convention the delegates debated how to raise the money. Much debate centered on a proposal to provide a $100,000 line of credit each year from the JACL Endowment Fund that would be secured by having each JACL member pledge $5. JACL ultimately adopted this policy but not without great difficulty. Japanese American Citizens League, "Discussion on Use of the JACL Endowment Fund," 64–76.

123. H.R. 7383 was assigned jointly to the Committees on Agriculture; Banking, Finance and Urban Affairs; Education and Labor; Energy and Commerce; and Ways and Means. H.R. 7384 was assigned to the Committee on the Judiciary.

124. Quoted in Judy Tachibana, "Dateline: Sacramento—Rep. Robert T. Matsui Speaks Out on The Issues: Sacramento Democrat Talks of Redress Backlash, Social Security, Nat'l Deficit," *Rafu Shimpo*, February 2, 1983, 1–2.

125. Commission on Wartime Relocation and Internment of Civilians, *Personal Justice Denied*, 18.

126. Commission on Wartime Relocation and Internment of Civilians, *Personal Justice Denied, Part 2*, 5.

127. Ibid., 6.

128. Commission on Wartime Relocation and Internment of Civilians, *Personal Justice Denied*, 23.

129. Quoted in "Nikkei Legislators Are Pleased with Commission's Findings," *Pacific Citizen*, March 4, 1983, 1–2.

130. "Reaction to CWRIC Report: JACL Statement," *Pacific Citizen*, March 4, 1983, 8.

131. Commission on Wartime Relocation and Internment of Civilians, *Personal Justice Denied, Part 2*, 6.

132. Ibid., 8.

133. Ibid., 8–10.

134. Ibid., 9. This estimate was based on actuarial tables for the life expectancy of white Americans. As a result, these tables underestimated the actual number of Japanese Americans who were still alive and qualified for redress.

135. Ibid., 11–12. Commissioner Bernstein recused herself from participating in developing recommendations because of a potential conflict of interest involving her law firm.

136. Ibid., 13.

137. Ibid.

138. Cecil Suzuki, "Comments on 'Recommendations,'" *Rafu Shimpo,* June 17, 1983, 1.

139. Ibid.

140. Quoted in Lee May, "Panel Suggests $1.5 Billion for War Internees," *Los Angeles Times,* June 17, 1983, part 1, 7.

141. Quoted in "Redress Groups React to Reparations Proposal," *Rafu Shimpo,* June 20, 1983, 1.

142. Quoted in "JACL 'Extremely Pleased' with CWRIC Recommendations," *Pacific Citizen,* June 24, 1983, 4.

143. Quoted in "Redress Groups React to Reparations Proposal," *Rafu Shimpo,* June 20, 1983, 1.

144. Ibid.

145. Quoted in Fred Barbash, "Payments Backed for Internees," *Washington Post,* June 17, 1983, A1.

146. Quoted in "Comments on 'Recommendations,'" *Rafu Shimpo,* June 17, 1983, 1.

147. Marutani, interview by authors, September 12, 1994.

148. Initially, Marutani was not in favor of monetary compensation.

149. Marutani, interview by authors, September 12, 1994.

150. Daniels, interview by authors, October 5, 1994.

151. Wakabayashi, interview by authors, May 15, 1996.

Chapter 7: Other Efforts at Redress

1. Masuda, interview by authors, June 22, 1995.

2. Ibid.

3. Included among the employees was Mitsuye Endo. James Purcell, who eventually represented Endo in her Supreme Court case, was initially hired to represent the fired state employees.

4. Ouchida, interview by authors, June 22, 1995.

5. Assemblyman Mori, for whom Ouchida had been working, lost his seat in the 1980 election.

6. The actual bill has the date February 22, 1982, because of the time delay between introduction and printing.

7. Ouchida, interview by authors, June 22, 1995.

8. Ibid.

9. Ibid.

10. The vote was 6 to 0. The assembly's Committee on Public Employees and Retirement had eight members and required five votes to pass.

11. The Ways and Means Committee voted on May 20, 1982, 13 to 1 in favor of the bill. This committee had twenty-three members, which meant a majority vote of twelve members was needed to pass a bill out of committee.

12. Forty-one votes are needed to pass a bill.

13. Senator Dills authored a bill passed in the 1970s that provided state employees who were incarcerated the opportunity to purchase civil service credit for the time spent in the camps.

14. The vote was 6 to 0. The committee had eleven members and required six votes to approve a bill.

15. The vote was 9 to 1. The committee had fifteen members and required eight votes to pass a bill.

16. Twenty-one senators must vote for a bill for it to pass.

17. Formal tax legislation was needed because of inconsistencies in the interpretations by the State Franchise Tax Board. Initially, in 1982, the State Franchise Tax Board had indicated that the state redress would be tax exempt; however, by 1984 it was considering the payments as taxable income.

18. Ouchida, interview by authors, June 22, 1995.

19. Ibid.

20. Johnston, interview by authors, June 22, 1995.

21. Fiset, "Redress for Nisei Public Employees in Washington State after World War II," 30. The effort for redress in Washington was coordinated by the Washington Coalition on Redress. Cherry Kinoshita and Ruth Woo played instrumental roles in the lobbying efforts.

22. Individuals are required to file their lawsuits within six years from the time they were injured.

23. The government is protected from being sued by the doctrine of sovereign immunity. In effect the NCJAR could sue the U.S. government only if the government consented to be sued.

24. Hohri, "Thoughts on a Movement," 1.

25. William Hohri, "Chicago Nisei Critical of Nat'l 'CL Redress Drive," *Rafu Shimpo,* May 14, 1979, 1.

26. Hohri, "Thoughts on a Movement," 1, 3.

27. Herzig-Yoshinaga, interview by authors, October 3, 1995; Herzig, interview by authors, October 3, 1995.

28. Hohri, *Repairing America,* 83.

29. Hohri, interview by authors, October 12, 1994.

30. Herzig-Yoshinaga, interview by authors, October 3, 1995. Victor Stone became frustrated with the tenacity and thoroughness of Aiko Herzig-Yoshinaga's research. In a *Los Angeles Times* news article a Justice Department attorney described Herzig-Yoshinaga as "an ignoramus" and a "destructive force." Josh Getlin, "WWII Internees—Redress: One Made a Difference," *Los Angeles Times,* June 2, 1988, 1. The identity of this attorney was revealed to Herzig-Yoshinaga as being Victor Stone.

31. Ben Zelenko, "Excerpts for the Panel Discussion of NCJAR's Lawsuit," *NCJAR Newsletter,* April 7, 1982, 5.

32. Hohri, *Repairing America,* 191.

33. The plaintiffs were William Hohri, Hannah Takagi Holmes, Chizuko Omori (individually and as a representative for Haruko Omori), Midori Kimura, Merry Omori, John Omori (individually and as a representative for Juro Omori), Gladyce Sumida, Kyoshiro Tokunaga, Tom Nakao, Harry Ueno, Edward Tokeshi, Kinnosuke Hashimoto, Nelson Kitsuse (individually and as a representative for Takeshi Kitsuse), Eddie Sato, Sam Ozaki (individually and as a representative for Kyujiro Ozaki), Kumao Toda (individually and as a representative for Suketaro Toda), Kaz Oshiki, George Ikeda, Theresa Takayoshi (in-

dividually and as a representative for Tomeu Takayoshi), and the National Council for Japanese American Redress.

34. Herzig-Yoshinaga, interview by authors, October 3, 1995.

35. The twenty-two causes of action included in the lawsuit were (1) due process; (2) equal protection; (3) unjust taking; (4) Fourth Amendment's protection against unreasonable arrest, search, and seizure; (5) Article 4, Section 2, of the Constitution stating, "The citizens of each state shall be entitled to all privileges and immunities of citizens in the several states . . . "; (6) Sixth Amendment—right to a fair trial and representation by counsel; (7) Eighth Amendment—protection from cruel and unusual punishment; (8) First Amendment—freedom of religion; (9) First Amendment—freedom of speech and press; (10) First Amendment—freedom to associate; (11) First Amendment—freedom to petition for redress of grievances; (12) violation of the privacy and travel rights; (13) Thirteenth Amendment—protection from involuntary servitude (inadequate compensation for labor performed); (14) various executive orders and public laws as bills of attainder, which are "a legislative enactment against a person pronouncing him guilty without a trial"; (15) denial of *habeas corpus*—the right of a detained person to challenge the legality of his or her imprisonment; (16) conspiracy to deprive plaintiffs of their civil rights; (17) assault and battery; (18) false arrest and imprisonment; (19) abuse of process and malicious prosecution; (20) negligence; (21) breach of contract; and (22) breach of fiduciary duty. For a more detailed description of the causes of action, see Hohri, *Repairing America*, 200–202.

36. The concept of "tolling" a case became a focal part of the NCJAR's argument. The act of tolling determines the point from which the time period for the statute of limitations is initiated.

37. The "equitable estoppel" doctrine bars one party from asserting something is true and later stating that a contradictory state of affairs is true. In this case the NCJAR argued that the federal government initially claimed that persons of Japanese ancestry were excluded and incarcerated because of military necessity and that it subsequently tried to claim its actions were because of political expediency and racism. By changing its assertion, the government claimed that the statute of limitations had expired since Japanese Americans could have filed a lawsuit in the war years because the cause of action should have been clear to them then.

38. These types of losses included the loss of accrued interest from 1942 to the time they received payment under the act; losses from the confiscation of their personal property; losses incurred by those classified as "enemy aliens"; loss of collectible rent, earnings, and profits; restrictions of their rights to use various types of property; loss of vested public benefits, employment contracts, and educational programs; losses related to preparation for exclusion and resettlement after they were released from the camps; and losses incurred as a result of being imprisoned (separate from the losses due to exclusion). Hohri, *Repairing America*, 206–7.

39. Ibid., 207.

40. *Hohri v. United States*, 586 F. Supp. 769 (1984).

41. "JACL Applauds U.S. Court of Appeals Reinstament [*sic*] of NCJAR Class Action Suit," JACL press release, circa late January 1986.

42. Yasui, letter to Grayce K. Uyehara, January 28, 1986.

43. The following organizations initially joined NCJAR as friends of the court when NCJAR filed its petition for a writ of certiorari: the American Friends Service Committee; the Board of Church and Society of the United Methodist Church; the United Church Board for Homeland Ministries of the United Church of Christ; the Asian American Legal Defense and Education Fund; the Anti-Defamation League of B'nai B'rith; the JACL;

the JACL Legislative Education Committee; the American Civil Liberties Union (ACLU); the ACLU of Southern California; the National Capital Area ACLU; the American Jewish Congress; and the American Jewish Committee. The original friends of the court were joined by Fred Korematsu, Gordon Hirabayashi, Minoru Yasui, and their attorneys and by the states of Hawai'i and California. Hohri, *Repairing America*, 218.

44. The 1982 Federal Courts Improvement Act directed that appellate decisions on federal issues be heard by a federal circuit appeals court. NCJAR's first fifteen causes of action were clearly federal issues. The remaining causes of action fell under the jurisdiction of a regional appeals court. It was a mixed-issue case. In Supreme Court Justice Powell's June 1, 1987, opinion, he acknowledged that the 1982 Federal Courts Improvement Act was ambiguous in terms of the proper jurisdiction for a mixed-issues appeal.

45. Hohri, *Repairing America*, 221–22.

46. The decision was 8 to 0. Judge Antonin Scalia recused himself from hearing the case since he had ruled on it while sitting on the U.S. court of appeals. He was appointed to the U.S. Supreme Court four months after the case was heard.

47. The NCJAR considered appealing this decision but because of the legislative progress decided to help lobby the government for redress appropriations. The NCJAR then disbanded, donating its remaining money to a fund to help publish the CWRIC transcripts.

48. Irons, interview by authors, October 26, 1994.

49. Lieutenant Commander K. D. Ringle to Chief of Naval Operations, Memorandum, "Japanese Question, Report on," January 26, 1942, File BIO/ND 11BF37/A8-5, Records of the United States Navy, as cited in Irons, *Justice Delayed*, 148.

50. Quoted in Irons, *Justice Delayed*, 6.

51. Irons, interview by authors, October 26, 1994.

52. Quoted in Irons, *Justice Delayed*, 5.

53. Irons, interview by authors, October 26, 1994. The trial court for the *coram nobis* cases was the federal district court.

54. Minami, interview by authors, January 20, 1995.

55. Irons, *Justice Delayed*, 128–30.

56. Minami, "*Coram Nobis* and Redress," 200.

57. Quoted in Irons, *Justice Delayed*, 15.

58. Commission on Wartime Relocation and Internment of Civilians, *Personal Justice Denied*, 18.

59. Minami, interview by authors, January 20, 1995.

60. Quoted in Irons, *Justice Delayed*, 25.

61. Quoted in Minami, "*Coram Nobis* and Redress," 201.

62. *Korematsu v. United States*, 584 F. Supp. 1406, 1420 (N.D. Calif., 1984).

63. Quoted in Irons, *Justice Delayed*, 33.

64. *Hirabayashi v. United States*, 627 F. Supp. 1445, 1457 (W.D. Wash., 1986).

65. There is some speculation that the *coram nobis* cases had a slightly negative effect on the redress movement. Because the Department of Justice opposed these cases, it had to oppose the NCJAR case and any related legislation in order to be consistent.

66. Minami, "*Coram Nobis* and Redress," 200–201.

Chapter 8: The Continuing Legislative Battle (1983–86)

1. Roberts, interview by author, September 19, 1994.

2. Ibid.

3. Ibid.

4. Glenn Roberts interview by Calvin Naito and Esther Scott, n.d., quoted in Naito and Scott, *Against All Odds,* 12.

5. U.S. Senate Subcommittee on Administrative Practice and Procedure of the Committee on the Judiciary, *Hearings on S.R. 1520,* July 27, 1983, 66.

6. Ibid., 69.

7. Ibid., 65.

8. Ibid., 66.

9. Ibid., 67.

10. Ibid., 69.

11. Ibid., 121.

12. Baker testified about the explosion of a Japanese balloon bomb, which killed an American and his pregnant wife. She offered this story as proof that the West Coast was under military threat. Furthermore, she asserted that Japanese Americans on the West Coast posed a particular threat and at the very least needed to be evacuated for their own protection.

13. U.S. Senate Subcommittee on Administrative Practice and Procedure of the Committee on the Judiciary, *Hearings on S.R. 1520,* July 27, 1983, 351.

14. Ibid., 373, 377.

15. Ibid., 109–10.

16. U.S. Senate Subcommittee on Civil Service, Post Office, and General Services of the Senate Governmental Affairs Committee, *Hearings on S.R 2116,* August 16, 1984, 2.

17. The CWRIC had recommended the issuance of an apology on behalf of the U.S. Congress; the payment of $20,000 to eligible Japanese Americans; the creation of a civil liberties public education fund; the payment of $5,000 to eligible Aleuts; and the creation of an Aleutian Islands education and restoration fund.

18. Specifically, the bill called for individual payments of $12,000 (more than the $5,000 recommended by the commission) to be made to those Aleut citizens who had suffered personal property losses and faced unreasonable physical suffering as a result of being interned, detained, or relocated during the war. The bill also included restitution for community property losses during the war and the removal of abandoned ammunition and other hazardous material from the Aleutian Islands.

19. Initially, not all African American members of Congress were supportive of redress. Some representatives informally stated that African Americans should be the first to receive some sort of redress. Matsui, interview by authors, July 11, 1995.

20. The ten members were Miya Iwataki, Bert Nakano, and Kay Ochi from Los Angeles; Tsuyako Kitashima, Naomi Kubota, and Marlene Tonai from San Francisco; Julie Hatta and Tom Izu form San Jose; and Bill Kochiyama and Mike Tsukahara from New York.

21. The hearings were held on June 20, 21, and 27 and September 12, 1984, in the House Subcommittee on Administrative Law and Governmental Relations.

22. U.S. House Subcommittee on Administrative Law and Governmental Relations of the Committee on the Judiciary, *Hearings on H.R. 3387, H.R. 4110, and H.R. 4322,* June 20, 1984, 25.

23. Ibid., June 27, 1984, 418.

24. Ibid., 420.

25. Ibid., 439.

26. Magic cable, No. 174, from Los Angeles (Nakauchi) to Tokyo (Gaimudaijin), May 9, 1941, #067, in *The "Magic" Background of Pearl Harbor* (Washington, D.C.: Department of Defense, Government Printing Office, 1978), #D742USM27 in ibid., June 27, 1984, 496.

27. Ibid., 540.

28. *Mitchell v. Harmony*, 54 U.S. 115, 14 L. Ed. 75, 13 How. 115 (1851).

29. U.S. House Subcommittee on Administrative Law and Governmental Relations of the Committee on the Judiciary, *Hearings on H.R. 3387, H.R. 4110, and H.R. 4322*, June 21, 1984, 125.

30. Ibid., September 12, 1984, 698.

31. Ibid., 787.

32. Ibid., June 20, 1984, 32.

33. Such national religious organizations as the American Baptist Churches, USA; the United Methodist Church; the Presbyterian Church, USA; the United Church of Christ; the Buddhist Churches of America; and the American Jewish Committee passed proclamations endorsing redress.

34. These resolutions did not always endorse monetary reparations, but they did acknowledge that the incarceration was unjust.

35. The Democratic candidates were Walter Mondale, Gary Hart, and Jesse Jackson.

36. At the 1984 JACL National Convention the budget for the JACL LEC was activated with $23,200. The advance of $20,000 from Random House to John Tateishi for the book *And Justice for All* and $3,200 presented by Yosh Kojimoto, San Mateo chapter, were put into the LEC treasury. Kajihara, interview by authors, September 11, 1997.

37. Jane Kaihatsu, "Board Formally Activates LEC, Argues about JACL Role in U.S.-Japan Relations," *Pacific Citizen*, June 14, 1985, 1.

38. Ujifusa, interview by authors, September 18, 1994.

39. Wakabayashi, interview by authors, May 15, 1996.

40. Ibid.

41. Tateishi had contemplated resigning and did so in January 1986. Also in January 1986 the JACL's Redress Education Program (REP) was terminated. The JACL LEC assumed the lead in coordinating the JACL's lobbying efforts.

42. Uyehara became executive director of the JACL LEC on January 17, 1986.

43. Kinoshita, Hayashino, and Yoshino, *Redress*.

44. Ujifusa, interview by authors, November 13, 1994.

45. Ibid.

46. Quoted in J. K. Yamamoto, "Ujifusa Explains Redress Lobbying Work," *Rafu Shimpo*, November 21, 1988, 1.

47. Ibid.

48. Ibid.

49. Matsui, interview by authors, July 11, 1995.

50. Published by the JACL NCR.

51. Matsui, interview by authors, July 11, 1995.

52. Kubo was initially against monetary redress payments, but through the persuasive efforts of community members he changed his position.

53. Hirasuna, memorandum to Grayce Uyehara, March 2, 1987.

54. Hirasuna, memorandum to Min Yasui, April 29, 1985, regarding Pashayan dinner meeting on April 12, 1985.

55. "HR 442 Gets 1st Calif. GOP Backer," *Pacific Citizen*, October 18, 1985, 1.

56. Bert Nakano, interview by authors, May 29, 1996.

57. These stances included denouncing the nomination of Robert H. Bork to the Supreme Court and supporting Jesse Jackson's presidential bid.

58. Bert Nakano, interview by authors, May 29, 1996.

59. Hayashino, interview by authors, January 20, 1995.

60. Between 1985 and 1988 the JACL LEC raised approximately a million dollars. Harry Kajihara (1985–86) and Mae Takahashi (1987–88) served as fund-raising chairs during this period.

61. "No. 517. Federal Budget—Summary: 1945 to 1995, U.S. Office of Management and Budget," *Historical Tables,* annual, as cited in U.S. Bureau of the Census, *Statistical Abstract of the United States,* 333. The deficit rose to $221.2 billion in 1986 and decreased to $155.2 billion in 1988.

62. Budget categories that were exempted from automatic cuts were Social Security, interest on the federal debt, veterans' compensation, veterans' pensions, Medicaid, Aid to Families with Dependent Children, WIC Supplemental Security Income, food stamps, and child nutrition. Limited cuts would occur in five health programs, including Medicare.

63. U.S. House Subcommittee on Administrative Law and Governmental Relations of the Committee on the Judiciary, *Hearings on H.R. 442 and H.R. 2415,* April 28, 1986, 32.

64. Ibid., 54.

65. Ibid., 542–43.

66. Ibid., 543.

67. Ibid., 545.

68. Ibid., 585. Masaoka also suggested introducing an amendment to the bill that would prevent the payment from being treated as income, which might have denied eligibility for some public entitlement programs.

69. Ibid., 111.

70. Ibid., 111–14.

71. Ibid., 196.

72. Ibid., 198.

73. Ibid., 200–201.

74. Quoted in Dwight Chuman, "JAs Blast Sen. Hayakawa," *Rafu Shimpo,* March 12, 1980, 1.

75. Witnesses who appeared before the subcommittee were Representative Don Young, Arthur Flemming, John C. Kirtland, Dimitri Philemonof, John Carpenter, Alice Petrivelli, Agafon Krukoff Jr., Father Paul Merculief, Michael Zacharof, Hilda Berikoff, Perfinia Pletnikoff, and Adrian Melovidov.

76. U.S. House Subcommittee on Administrative Law and Governmental Relations of the Committee on the Judiciary, *Hearings on H.R. 442 and H.R. 2415,* July 23, 1986, 1691.

77. Saul, interview by authors, July 18, 1995.

78. Ibid.

79. Kawaguchi, letter to Harry H. L. Kitano, February 4, 1997.

80. Ibid.

81. The exclusion had special meaning to the Presidio since the exclusion orders were administered through the Presidio Army Post in San Francisco in 1942.

82. Many veterans asked to have the exhibit travel to different cities. The exhibit eventually traveled to over twenty cities.

83. The exhibition team was made up of Edward C. Ezell, project manager; Jennifer Locke, research assistant; Selma Thomas, filmmaker; and Dru Culbert, designer.

84. Crouch, interview by authors, July 11, 1995.

85. Ibid.

86. The total budget of the *A More Perfect Union* exhibit was $1.2 million. The amount appropriated by Congress was $750,000, which was appropriated on a yearly basis between 1985 and 1987.

87. Representative Mineta cites the efforts of Representative Sidney Yates (Democrat from Illinois) as very helpful. Representative Yates was chair of the appropriations subcommittee that handled the Smithsonian appropriations.

88. It had originally been planned to occupy ten thousand square feet on the main floor. The actual exhibit, however, was six thousand square feet and was placed on a side wing of the second floor. The exhibit received many accolades and awards, despite sporadic feedback on the inaccuracy of the portrayal of the barracks. A common complaint was that the barrack on display was too nice. The furniture looked like it was store-bought, and the floor was fitted too perfectly. Furniture for many incarcerated families was handmade from scraps of wood; barrack floors often had large gaps between the floorboards, which allowed dust and sand into the barracks.

89. Mineta, interview by authors, August 6, 1994.

90. Crouch, interview by authors, July 11, 1995.

Chapter 9: The Aligning of the One-hundredth Congress (1987–88)

1. No. 517. Federal Budget—Summary: 1945 to 1995, U.S. Office of Management and Budget, *Historical Tables,* annual, as cited in U.S. Bureau of the Census, *Statistical Abstract of the United States,* 333.

2. Stroebel, interview by authors, September 12, 1994.

3. Norman Mineta, as told to Susan Schindehette, "The Wounds of War: A California Congressman Recalls the Trauma of World War II Internment," *People Weekly* 28 (December 14, 1987): 175.

4. Ibid.

5. In the Ninety-seventh Congress (1981–82) the Republican party had a 53-47 seat majority. In the Ninety-eighth Congress (1983–84) this increased to a 55-45 majority. In the Ninety-ninth Congress (1985–86) the Republican party maintained its majority of 53-47 seats.

6. Quoted in Stroebel, interview by authors, September 12, 1994.

7. Frank, interview by authors, September 19, 1994.

8. Uyehara, interview by authors, August 5, 1994.

9. Ujifusa, oral comments during panel discussion at the Voices of Japanese American Redress Conference, September 13, 1997.

10. Cherry Kinoshita, "Reflections on the JACL Lobbying Experience," *Pacific Citizen,* December 22–29, 1989, sec. E, 5.

11. Matsui, interview by authors, July 11, 1995.

12. Cherry Kinoshita, "Reflections on the JACL Lobbying Experience," *Pacific Citizen,* December 22–29, 1989, sec. E, 5. Kinoshita and the Washington Coalition on Redress coordinated personal lobbying visits to each of the Washington representatives. Ultimately all eight representatives voted for H.R. 442.

13. Mineta, interview by authors, August 6, 1994.

14. Ultimately thirteen of the fourteen New Jersey representatives voted for H.R. 442.

15. U.S. House, Subcommittee on Administrative Law and Governmental Relations of the Committee on the Judiciary, *Hearings on H.R. 442 and H.R. 1631,* April 29, 1987, 1.

16. Ibid., 115.

17. Ibid., 56.

18. Ibid., 107.

19. Ibid., 132–33.

20. Ibid., 156.

21. Ibid.

22. Ibid., 159.

23. Ibid.

24. Ibid., 164.

25. U.S. House Committee on the Judiciary, *Civil Liberties Act of 1986*, 10.

26. Rodino et al., letter to their colleagues, September 10, 1987.

27. Shumway, letter to his colleagues, September 14, 1987.

28. Lungren, letter to his colleagues, September 16, 1987.

29. Ibid.

30. Commission on Wartime Relocation and Internment of Civilians, *Personal Justice Denied*, quoted in ibid.

31. Bolton, letter to Honorable Claude Pepper, September 14, 1987. In this letter Bolton claimed that H.R. 442 was too costly and that the Japanese-American Evacuation Claims Act of 1948 and President Ford's repeal of Executive Order 9066 had already remedied the losses and redressed the injustices Japanese Americans suffered as a result of the incarceration. Bolton also cited the Department of Justice's objection to compensating survivors of those Japanese Americans who voluntarily repatriated or expatriated to Japan during World War II, a group that would be compensated under H.R. 442. Bolton also warned that enactment of H.R. 442 would set an "ill-conceived" precedent for other groups.

32. Rodino et al., letter to their colleagues, September 16, 1987.

33. Henderson, interview by authors, September 17, 1994.

34. Wakabayashi, interview by authors, May 15, 1996.

35. Ujifusa, interview by authors, September 18, 1994.

36. A two-thirds vote is needed to override a presidential veto.

37. U.S. Senate Subcommittee on Federal Service, Post Office, and Civil Service of the Committee on Governmental Affairs, *Hearings on S. 1009*, June 17, 1987, 7.

38. The other individuals who testified that day were Senator Brock Adams (Democrat from Washington), Senator Alan Cranston (Democrat from California), Senator Frank Murkowski (Republican from Alaska), John Kirtland, Agafon Krukoff Jr., and Dimitri Philemonof.

39. U.S. Senate Subcommittee on Federal Service, Post Office, and Civil Service of the Committee on Governmental Affairs, *Hearings on S. 1009*, June 17, 1987, 26–27.

40. U.S. Senate Committee on Governmental Affairs, *Accepting the Findings and Implementing the Recommendations of the Commission on Wartime Relocation and Internment of Civilians*, October 20, 1987, 7.

41. Bert Nakano, videotaped interview by Glen Kitayama, June 18, 1993.

42. Ochi, interview by authors, May 31, 1995.

43. Bert Nakano, videotaped interview by Glenn Kitayama, June 18, 1993.

44. Iwataki, videotaped interview by Glenn Kitayama, June 18, 1993.

45. Tokiwa was a decorated World War II veteran who was wounded in battle. His most visible disabilities, however, were the result of a farming accident years later.

46. Tokiwa, interview by authors, September 10, 1997.

47. Matsui, interview by authors, July 11, 1995.

48. Stroebel, interview by authors, September 12, 1994.

49. Matsui, interview by authors, July 11, 1995; Stroebel, interview by authors, September 12, 1994. Both Representatives Mineta and Matsui received numerous letters and com-

ments from their colleagues that highlighted the eloquence and meaningfulness of the debate.

50. *Congressional Record,* 100th Congr., 1st sess., vol. 133, no. 141, September 17 to September 25, 1987, H 7556.

51. Ibid.

52. Ibid., H 7555–96.

53. Ibid., H 7564.

54. Ibid., H 7567.

55. This phrase had been removed in committee at the request of Representative Swindall.

56. *Congressional Record,* 100th Congr., 1st sess., vol. 133, no. 141, September 17 to September 25, 1987, H 7574.

57. Ibid., H 7575.

58. Ibid., H 7558.

59. Representatives Al McCandless (Republican from California), Ron Packard (Republican from California), Don Pease (Democrat from Ohio), Bill Frenzel (Republican from Minnesota), and Norman Shumway (Republican from California) all spoke in support of Representative Lungren's second amendment.

60. *Congressional Record,* 100th Congr., 1st sess., vol. 133, no. 141, September 17 to September 25, 1987, H 7578.

61. Matsui, interview by authors, July 11, 1995.

62. *Congressional Record,* 100th Congr., 1st sess., vol. 133, no. 141, September 17 to September 25, 1987, H 7584.

63. Ibid.

64. Ibid., H 7584–85.

65. Ibid., H 7585.

66. Ibid.

67. Verbatim transcription of videotape recording of September 17, 1987, House floor debate. Written record, which is slightly different, appears in *Congressional Record,* 100th Congr., 1st sess., vol. 133, no. 141, September 17 to September 25, 1987, H 7584.

68. Stroebel, interview by authors, September 12, 1994.

69. *Congressional Record,* 100th Congr., 1st sess., vol. 133, no. 141, September 17 to September 25, 1987, H 7587.

70. Ibid. Representative Mineta voted "present" rather than aye. He did not feel it was appropriate for him to vote for individual payments since he would stand to benefit personally from such payments.

71. Strobel, interview by authors, September 16, 1994. Strobel was the legislative aide to Representative Mineta.

72. *Congressional Record,* 100th Congr., 1st sess., vol. 133, no. 141, September 17 to September 25, 1987, H 7589.

73. Verbatim transcription of videotape recording of the September 17, 1987, House floor debate. Written record, which is slightly different, appears in *Congressional Record,* 100th Congr., 1st sess., vol. 133, no. 141, September 17 to September 25, 1987, H 7586.

74. Don Bonker (Democrat from Washington), Mervyn M. Dymally (Democrat from California), Benjamin L. Cardin (Democrat from Maryland), Barney Frank (Democrat from Massachusetts), Lawrence J. Smith (Democrat from Florida), Rod Chandler (Republican from Washington), Walter E. Fauntroy (Democrat from the District of Columbia), Barbara Boxer (Democrat from California), William J. Hughes (Democrat from New

Jersey), John Lewis (Democrat from Georgia), Mike Lowry (Democrat from Washington), and Hank Brown (Republican from Colorado) spoke in favor of the bill and against the amendment. Richard K. Armey (Republican from Texas) spoke in favor of the bill but was against the notion of payments.

75. Verbatim transcription of videotape recording of the September 17, 1987, House floor debate. Written record, which is slightly different, appears in *Congressional Record,* 100th Congr., 1st sess., vol. 133, no. 141, September 17 to September 25, 1987, H 7594.

76. Kinoshita, Hayashino, and Yoshino, *Redress.*

77. Of the 243 aye votes, 180 were Democrats and 63 were Republicans. Of the 141 nay votes, 43 were Democrats and 98 were Republicans. Of the 50 nonvotes, 34 were Democrats and 16 were Republicans. Representative Mineta was the representative who voted present. The 243 yes votes would not be enough to override a veto.

78. Matsui, interview by authors, July 11, 1995.

79. "Quiet Minority Shifts Tactics in California: Appointee Battle Reflects Asian Americans' Power," *Washington Post,* February 25, 1988, A3.

80. Included among these groups were the San Diego Urban League, Los Angeles NAACP, Friends of the River, California School Employees Association, California Rural Housing Network, Mexican American Political Association, California Congress of Seniors, Central Labor Council of the AFL-CIO/Contra Costa, California Homeless Coalition, La Raza Lawyers, and the California Democratic party.

81. "Senate Narrowly Rejects Lungren: Small Treasurer Nominee Is Backed by Assembly; Court Test a Possibility," *Los Angeles Times,* February 26, 1988, part 1, 33.

82. Quoted in "Quiet Minority Shifts Tactics in California: Appointee Battle Reflects Asian Americans' Power," *Washington Post,* February 25, 1988, A3.

83. Christopher Bond (Republican from Missouri), David Karnes (Republican from Nebraska), Mitch McConnell (Republican from Kentucky), Steven Symms (Republican from Idaho), and John Warner (Republican from Virginia).

84. Henderson, interview by authors, September 17, 1994.

85. *Congressional Record,* 100th Congr., 2d sess., vol. 134, no. 50, April 19, 1988, S 4268.

86. Ibid., S 4269.

87. Ibid., S 4280.

88. *Congressional Record,* 100th Congr., 2d sess., vol. 134, no. 51, April 20, 1988, S 4323–24.

89. Ibid., S 4327, S 4329–30.

90. Ibid., S 4333.

91. Ibid., S 4386.

92. S.R. 1009 had a safeguard provision. The Appropriations Committee would not appropriate redress funds if the budget deficit at the time made this untenable.

93. *Congressional Record,* 100th Congr., 2d sess., vol. 134, no. 51, April 20, 1988, S 4392.

94. Ibid., S 4398.

95. Senators Hecht, Helms, McClure, and Symms, all Republicans, voted against it.

96. Of the seventy-two senators (one principal sponsor and seventy one cosponsors) who sponsored the bill on the day it went to the floor, sixty-six of them voted for it. Three previously uncommitted senators also joined in voting for the bill: Senators Nancy Kassebaum (Republican from Kansas), Dale Bumpers (Democrat from Arkansas), and John Heinz (Republican from Pennsylvania). Four senators were "necessarily absent" or ill at the time of the vote: Senators Joseph Biden (Democrat from Delaware), Albert Gore (Democrat from Tennessee), Edward Kennedy (Democrat from Massachusetts), and John

Warner (Republican from Virginia). According to Elma Henderson, in a September 17, 1994, interview by the authors, three of these senators were cosponsors and would have voted yes: Senators Joseph Biden, Albert Gore, and Edward Kennedy. Three cosponsors of the bill ultimately voted against the bill: Jake Garn (Republican from Utah), Wyche Fowler (Democrat from Georgia), and Larry Pressler (Republican from South Dakota).

97. The legislators who sat on the conference committee were Representative Peter W. Rodino Jr., Representative Barney Frank, Representative H. L. Berman, Representative Patrick Swindall, Senator John Glenn, Senator Spark M. Matsunaga, Senator Ted Stevens, and Senator Warren B. Rudman.

98. U.S. Congress, Committee of Conference, *Joint Explanatory Statement of the Committee of Conference*.

99. Kemp et al., letter to their colleagues, June 14, 1988.

100. The other three Californian Republican votes came from members who had not voted on September 17, 1987. Two of these members had been cosponsors.

101. Matsui, interview by authors, July 11, 1995.

102. Stroebel, interview by authors, September 12, 1994.

103. Tateishi, interview by authors, October 25, 1996.

Chapter 10: The President's Signature and the Fight for Appropriations

1. Quoted in Naito and Scott, *Against All Odds*, 24.

2. For example, in June 1988 James Hurley, a New Jersey state Republican leader, planned to call the president; Tak Moriuchi, the Philadelphia chapter redress coordinator for New Jersey and president of the New Jersey Fruit Growers Association, persuaded several people with access to the White House to call Reagan; John Nitta of Cocoa Beach, Florida, organized hundreds of his fellow Shriners to write letters to Reagan; the Midwest district office of the JACL, directed by Bill Yoshino, sent eight hundred mailings encouraging members to lobby the president; Jo Okura (Cincinnati JACL redress chair), Tom Kometani (the governor of the Eastern District Council), Sumi Kobayashi of Philadelphia, and Terry Yamada from Portland reported that their JACL chapters sent out petitions and numerous letters to Reagan; and Sumi Kobayashi and Ida Chen organized all the Chinese American organizations in Philadelphia and the Delaware Valley Asian American Bar Association to join in the redress White House campaign. Grayce Uyehara "Grassroots Effort Gains Support of Former U.S. President: LEC Update," *Pacific Citizen*, June 10, 1988, 4.

3. Quoted in Naito and Scott, *Against All Odds*, 26.

4. "JACL-LEC Mailgram Hotline to the White House Urges President Reagan to Sign Redress Bill," *Pacific Citizen*, June 10, 1988, 1.

5. Hayakawa, letter to Howard Baker, May 5, 1988.

6. Willard, interview by authors, July 10, 1995.

7. Ujifusa, letter to Assistant Attorney General Richard Willard, May 7, 1987.

8. "Statement of Administration Policy: H.R. 442—Civil Liberties Act of 1987," September 10, 1987.

9. Karen Tumulty, "House Votes Payments for Japanese Internees," *Los Angeles Times*, September 18, 1987, part 1, 12; Duberstein, interview by authors, July 10, 1995. OMB staffers would not support $1.2 billion in payments and were concerned that the bill would create an open-ended entitlement.

10. Sutherland, interview by authors, September 19, 1994.

11. This particular limousine ride was approximately thirty minutes long. During this time Governor Kean spoke about the redress issue for about six or seven minutes. Kean, telephone interview by authors, October 18, 1995.

12. Ibid.

13. Duberstein, interview by authors, July 10, 1995.

14. Kean, telephone interview by authors, October 18, 1995.

15. Duberstein, interview by authors, July 10, 1995.

16. Kean, telephone interview by authors, October 18, 1995.

17. Kean, letter to President Ronald Reagan, February 6, 1988.

18. Kean, telephone interview by authors, October 18, 1995.

19. Quoted in "General Stilwell Pins Medal on Sister of Nisei Hero in Ceremony at Masuda Ranch," *Pacific Citizen,* December 15, 1945, 2.

20. Quoted in "3 Historically Significant Letters," *Pacific Citizen,* October 21, 1988, 5.

21. Ujifusa, interview by authors, July 9, 1995; see also "An Address from JACL-LEC Legislative Strategy Chair," *Pacific Citizen,* March 23, 1990, 5. Duberstein, also a supporter of redress, recalled talking about it a number of times with the president and his senior advisers.

22. Ujifusa, interview by authors, July 9, 1995.

23. Ibid.

24. Wright, OMB memorandum to Howard Baker, March 28, 1988.

25. Baker, memorandum to the president, March 29, 1988.

26. Quoted in "'Only Fair': Bush Says 'Yes' to Redress," *Pacific Citizen,* June 10, 1988, 1.

27. Ibid.

28. Duberstein, interview by authors, July 10, 1995.

29. Reagan, letter to Rep. Joseph Wright, August 1, 1988.

30. Duberstein, interview by authors, July 10, 1995.

31. Reagan, *Public Papers of the Presidents of the United States: Ronald Reagan, 1988–1989,* 1054.

32. Ibid., 1054–55.

33. Ibid., 1055.

34. Duberstein, interview by authors, July 10, 1995.

35. Wakabayashi, interview by authors, May 15, 1996.

36. Kinoshita, Hayashino, and Yoshino, *Redress.*

37. Meese, interview by authors, July 10, 1995; Duberstein, interview by authors, July 10, 1995.

38. Meese, interview by authors, July 10, 1995.

39. Duberstein, interview by authors, July 10, 1995; Willard, interview by authors, July 10, 1995; Meese, interview by authors, July 10, 1995.

40. Duberstein, interview by authors, July 10, 1995.

41. Assembly Bill 4087, introduced by Assemblyman Patrick Johnston (Democrat from San Joaquin).

42. Quoted in "Some People Still Don't Understand" (editorial), *Pacific Citizen,* September 2, 1988, 4.

43. Ibid.

44. Thurgood Marshall Administrative File, 88-215, Certiorari Memos, Box 454, Folder 1, 88-151 to 88-230, Manuscript Division, Library of Congress, October 19, 1988, quoted in William M. Hohri, *Epistolarian,* August 1993, 1.

45. The ORA had three executive directors during its existence: Robert Bratt (1988–92),

Paul Suddes (1992–94), and Irva "DeDe" Greene (1994–98). Deserene Worsley served as acting administrator for ORA from June 1994 to October 1994.

46. Ochi, interview by authors, May 31, 1995.

47. Rita Takahashi, JACL LEC press release, January 30, 1989, citing Bob Bratt in a January 26, 1989, public forum meeting.

48. Quoted in Tom Kenworthy, "War Internee Compensation Goes Slowly," *Washington Post,* January 11, 1989, A14.

49. Quoted in "Lawmakers Call Reparations Too Little, Too Late," *San Francisco Examiner,* January 12, 1989, A12.

50. JACL LEC press release, January 30, 1989.

51. JACL press release, January 10, 1989.

52. Quoted in Tom Kenworthy, "War Internee Compensation Goes Slowly," *Washington Post,* January 11, 1989, A14.

53. Calmes, "Budget," 3309.

54. Saiki et al., letter to President George Bush, January 31, 1989.

55. JACL LEC news release, February 7, 1989.

56. John Ota, "JA Community Shocked by No Redress Money," *Kashu Mainichi,* June 1, 1989, 1.

57. The opposition to redress was also active. At the 1989 National American Legion Convention an antiappropriation resolution was introduced. Lillian Baker led an ex-POW group in sending antiappropriation letters and resolutions to many of the major veterans organizations and to the members of the appropriate appropriations committees. Art Morimitsu, chair of JACL Veterans Affairs, was instrumental in convincing the cochair of the subcommittee of the Internal Affairs Commission to reject the bill. The bill never reached the convention floor.

In addition two court cases were filed that opposed payments to Japanese Americans. The American War Veterans Relief Association filed a suit in federal court seeking to block any payments to Japanese Americans on the grounds that the program discriminated against the Italian and German Americans who were also put into camps during the war. *Jacobs v. Thornburgh* was a suit brought by Arthur Jacobs, a German American who had been interned during World War II. The suit argued that the Japanese Americans were not victims of racial discrimination and that the redress program violated constitutional equal protection guarantees because it provided payments only to individuals of Japanese ancestry.

58. Fiscal years run from October 1 to September 30. Fiscal Year 1989 was from October 1, 1988, to September 30, 1989; Fiscal Year 1990 was from October 1, 1989, to September 30, 1990.

59. U.S. House Subcommittee on the Departments of Commerce, Justice, and State, the Judiciary, and Related Agencies of the Committee on Appropriations, *Testimony of Members of Congress and Other Interested Individuals and Organizations,* April 5, 1989, 354.

60. Ibid., 404.

61. Ibid., 389.

62. Rapp, "Appropriations," 739; "House Subcommittee: $250 Million for Redress," *Pacific Citizen,* April 14, 1989, 1.

63. Quoted in "House Votes to Approve Payment," *Rafu Shimpo,* May 27, 1989, 1.

64. The bill was entitled "Dire Emergency Supplemental Appropriations and Transfers, Urgent Supplementals, and Correcting Enrollment Errors Act of 1989" and became Public Law 101-45.

65. The increase in the appropriations in the final bill was the result of commitments by supporters in both chambers to get the $2.1 million that the Department of Justice had requested for administrative costs.

66. Quoted in JACL LEC press release, July 21, 1989.

67. On the House side the key leadership had begun to change. House Speaker Jim Wright, an unwavering supporter of redress, became embroiled in an ethics investigation. In his absence Tom Foley (Democrat from Washington), Richard Gephardt (Democrat from Missouri), and William Gray (Democrat from Pennsylvania) became more influential in the House leadership.

68. Quoted in Ed Matovik, "What it Took for the House to Pass Additional $30 Million to its '90 Redress Appropriation Bill," *Pacific Citizen,* August 4–11, 1989, 8.

69. Quoted in JACL LEC redress update, March 27, 1989.

70. JACL LEC press release, July 17, 1989.

71. Ibid., July 21, 1989.

72. Ujifusa, interview by authors, September 18, 1994.

73. Ibid.

74. Senator Daniel Inouye, "Last Full Measure," *Pacific Citizen,* August 18–25, 1989, 5.

75. Ibid.

76. Inouye, interview by authors, November 12, 1994.

77. "Senate Subcommittee Kills 1990 Redress Funds," *Rafu Shimpo,* September 12, 1989, 1; David G. Savage, "Panel Votes Not to Fund Payments for Internees," *Los Angeles Times,* September 13, 1989, part 1, 4.

78. JACL LEC news release, September 12, 1989.

79. JACL press release, September 21, 1989.

80. The proposal to create the entitlement was included in a larger bill (H.R. 2991), which sought $17.4 billion in FY 1990 for the Departments of Commerce, Justice, and State, the judiciary, and related agencies.

81. *Congressional Record,* 101st Congr., 1st sess., vol. 135, no. 128, September 29, 1989, S 12218–19.

82. Ibid., S 12219.

83. Quoted in Helen Dewar, "Exasperated Senators Rebuff Helms: His Arts, Internee Amendments Lose," *Washington Post,* September 30, 1989, A1. Amended remarks are cited in *Congressional Record,* 101st Congr., 1st sess., vol. 135, no. 128, September 29, 1989, S 12221.

84. *Congressional Record,* 101st Congr., 1st sess., vol. 135, no. 128, September 29, 1989, S 12220.

85. Quoted in Arnold T. Hiura, "Entitlement Plan Passes Congress: Hawaii Sen. Dan Inouye Engineers a Way to Guarantee Full Redress Funding," *Hawaii Herald,* November 3, 1989, 1.

86. Inouye, interview by authors, November 12, 1994.

87. Quoted in Arnold T. Hiura, "Entitlement Plan Passes Congress: Hawaii Sen. Dan Inouye Engineers a Way to Guarantee Full Redress Funding," *Hawaii Herald,* November 3, 1989, 1.

88. Among the many organizations to send letters were the American Civil Liberties Union, the National Council of La Raza, the Anti-Defamation League of B'nai B'rith, the National Urban League, and eighteen member organizations of the Washington Interreligious Staff Council.

89. LCCR, letter to Honorable Warren B. Rudman, October 13, 1989.

90. Mineta and Matsui, joint press release, October 19, 1989.

91. Ibid.

92. *Congressional Record,* 101st Congr., 1st sess., vol. 135, no. 147, October 26, 1989, H 7592.

93. Ibid., H 7627.

94. Ibid., H 7628.

95. Ibid., H 7590.

96. Bush, *Public Papers of the Presidents of the United States: George Bush, 1989, Book II, July 1 to December 31, 1989,* 1570–71.

97. This estimate, done by Price Waterhouse, is in 1986 dollars. Daniels, "Afterword," 375.

98. Canada, House of Commons, *Debates,* April 2, 1984, 2623, quoted in Daniels, "Afterword," 374.

99. Daniels, "Afterword," 376.

100. Information on payments provided by Wilma Gray, acting head of Japanese Canadian Redress Secretariat, as cited in ibid., 376–77.

101. Quoted in Arnold T. Hiura, "Entitlement Plan Passes Congress: Hawaii Sen. Dan Inouye Engineers a Way to Guarantee Full Redress Funding," *Hawaii Herald,* November 3, 1989, 1.

Chapter 11: Delivering on the Promise

1. The nine individuals who received the first redress payments were Mamoru Eto, 107, of Los Angeles, California; Haru Dairiki, 102, of Sacramento, California; Kisa Iseri, 102, of Ontario, Oregon; Hisano Fujimoto, 101, of Lombard, Illinois; Senkichi Yuge, 101, of Los Angeles, California; Sugi Kiriyama, 100, of West Los Angeles, California; Sada Ide, 90, of Arlington, Virginia; Don Hatsuki Shima, 86, of Laurel, Maryland; and Ken Yamamoto, 73, of Silver Spring, Maryland.

2. Quoted in "First 9 Japanese WWII Internees Get Reparations," *Los Angeles Times,* October 10, 1990, A1.

3. Ibid.

4. Ibid., A12.

5. Kay Ochi, "Redress and Japanese Americans," *Rafu Shimpo,* August 22, 1995, 1.

6. Ibid.

7. Wakabayashi, interview by authors, May 15, 1996.

8. Kitashima, interview by authors, January 20, 1995.

9. Two other related bills were introduced in the House during the 102d Congress. The contents of H.R. 4553 and H.R. 4570 were eventually incorporated into H.R. 4551.

10. U.S. House Committee on the Judiciary, *Civil Liberties Act Amendments of 1992,* 2.

11. The lone dissenting voice belonged to Representative Willis D. Gradison Jr. (Republican from Ohio), who expressed opposition the day after the vote in the Extension of Remarks in the *Congressional Record,* 102 Congr. 2d sess., vol. 138, no. 125, September 15, 1992, E 2628–29.

12. Ibid., 102d Congr., 2d sess., vol. 138, no. 124, September 14, 1992, H 8346.

13. Ibid., H 8349.

14. Senators Ted Stevens (Republican from Alaska), Warren Rudman (Republican from New Hampshire), Bob Packwood (Republican from Oregon), Alan Cranston (Democrat from California), John Seymour (Republican from California), Slade Gorton (Republican from Washington), Paul Simon (Democrat from Illinois), and Brock Adams (Democrat from Washington) joined Senator Daniel Akaka (Democrat from Hawai'i) as cosponsors of S.R. 2553, which was introduced by Senator Daniel Inouye. In 1990 Senator Akaka

had been appointed to the vacant senate seat from Hawai'i. The seat was vacant because of Senator Matsunaga's death on April 15, 1990.

15. Bush, *Public Papers of the Presidents of the United States: George Bush, Book II, August 1, 1992, to January 20, 1993*, 1681.

16. "Spokane Man Denied Redress Wins Case," *Rafu Shimpo*, April 22, 1995, 1.

17. Ibid.

18. "Redress: Landmark Victory for Children of Voluntary Evacuees," *Rafu Shimpo*, July 10, 1995, 1.

19. "Redress: Lawsuits Filed by Children of 'Voluntary Evacuees,'" *Rafu Shimpo*, August 3, 1994, 1.

20. Quoted in ibid.

21. The Americans in Japan were those who were stranded in Asia at the time that war broke out. Two exchanges were conducted. The first exchange involved 1,083 Nikkei and occurred during the summer of 1942 at Lourenço Marques in East Africa. The second exchange involved 1,340 Nikkei (of whom 737 were Japanese Latin Americans) and occurred during the fall of 1943 at Mormugao, India. U.S. Department of Justice, "Redress Provisions for Persons of Japanese Ancestry," June 12, 1996, 29716–19. See also Corbett, *Quiet Passages*, 56–95.

22. "Justice Dept. Proposes to Provide Redress for Minors Sent on POW Ship," *Rafu Shimpo*, June 13, 1996, 1.

23. U.S. Department of Justice, "Redress Provisions for Persons of Japanese Ancestry," June 12, 1996, 29717.

24. The lawsuit was filed by the Asian Law Caucus in San Francisco and *pro bono* attorneys from the Morrison and Foerster law firm.

25. U.S. Department of Justice, "Redress Provisions for Persons of Japanese Ancestry," June 12, 1996, 29716–19.

26. Ibid., 29717.

27. Ibid.

28. Ibid.

29. U.S. Department of Justice, "Redress Provisions for Persons of Japanese Ancestry," April 22, 1996, 17667–69.

30. Ibid.

31. Originally, NCRR and other community groups sought to have the eligibility date extended beyond June 30, 1946, so that individuals born in Crystal City and other Department of Justice camps after this date could be considered eligible. These Department of Justice camps were not closed until 1947. "Redress: Community Members Meet with Justice Dept. Officials," *Rafu Shimpo*, September 20, 1994, 1.

32. U.S. Department of Justice, "Redress Provisions for Persons of Japanese Ancestry," April 22, 1996, 17667–69.

33. Ibid., April 24, 1997, 19932.

34. Caroline Aoyagi, "Bittersweet Victory for Japanese Latin Americans," *Pacific Citizen*, June 19–July 2, 1998, 1, 3; John Lee, "Stakes Raised for Nikkei Latin Americans," *Rafu Shimpo*, August 27, 1998, 1, 5. The leaders of the Campaign for Justice included Ayako Hagihara, Fred Okrand, Grace Shimizu, Julie Small, and Robin Toma.

35. Quoted in "Court Rejects Claim of Nikkei Railroad Worker," *Rafu Shimpo*, July 20, 1996, 1.

36. Daniels, *Prisoners without Trial*, 48

37. Daniels, *Concentration Camps USA*, 72–73.

38. The detention camps were Sand Island Detention Camp in Oahu and Honouliuli Detention Camp, both in Oahu.

39. Funai and Mikami, presentation at the Japanese American National Museum.

40. Steer, letter to Whom This May Concern, January 10, 1943.

41. "Redress: Justice Dept. Announces Eligibility of Waiau Cases," *Rafu Shimpo,* June 2, 1994, 1, 3.

42. "Event: Hawai'i Japanese American Redress Topic of Lecture," *Rafu Shimpo,* June 21, 1995, 3.

43. Quoted in "Redress: Justice Dept. Announces Eligibility of Waiau Cases," *Rafu Shimpo,* June 2, 1994, 1.

44. Office of Redress Administration staff, letter to authors, July 9, 1997; "Hawaii Internees Win Redress," *Pacific Citizen,* March 6–19, 1998, 1.

45. Department of Justice, press release, February 19, 1999.

46. "Racism: Bay Area Nikkei Group Gets Hate Message." *Rafu Shimpo,* May 19, 1995, 1.

47. Ibid.

48. "Redress: Senate Committee OKs $5 Million for Education Fund," *Rafu Shimpo,* July 15, 1994, 1.

49. "Redress: Civil Liberties Public Education Fund Board Ready for Action," *Rafu Shimpo,* April 23, 1996, 1.

50. Public Law 100-383.

51. Watanabe, letter from deputy executive director of the CLPEF to authors, October 8, 1998.

Chapter 12: Lessons of a Movement

1. Herzig-Yoshinaga, interview by authors, October 3, 1995.

2. Inouye, interview by authors, November 12, 1994.

3. Ujifusa, interview by authors, July 9, 1995.

4. JACL news release, October 23, 1989.

5. Lillian Nakano, interview by authors, May 29, 1996.

6. Chizu Iiyama, telephone interview by authors, May 24, 1996.

7. Riggs, *Pressures on Congress,* 49.

8. Matsui, interview by authors, July 11, 1995.

9. Arnold T. Hiura, "Entitlement Plan Passes Congress: Hawaii Sen. Dan Inouye Engineers a Way to Guarantee Full Redress Funding," *Hawaii Herald,* November 3, 1989, 1.

Works Cited

Archival Documents

Baker, Howard H., Jr. Memorandum to the President, March 29, 1988. ID #580425, HU O13-22, White House Office of Records Management, Presidential Records. Ronald Reagan Library, Simi Valley, Calif.

Bendetsen, Col. Karl. Letter to Hiroshi Suzuki, June 11, 1976. CWRIC #3362-3364. Aiko Herzig-Yoshinaga Files, Falls Church, Va.

Biddle, Attorney General Francis Biddle. Notes on May 26 and November 10, 1944. Box 1—Folder: Cabinet Meetings, January 1944–May 1945, Francis Biddle Papers. Franklin D. Roosevelt Library, Hyde Park, N.Y.

Bolton, Attorney General John R. Letter to Honorable Claude Pepper, September 14, 1987. Redress Files. National JACL Headquarters, San Francisco, Calif.

Bonesteel, General Charles H. Transcript of telephone conversation with John J. McCloy, July 14, 1944. Record Group 338—Army Commands, Western Defense Command. National Archives, Washington, D.C.

Commission on Wartime Relocation and Internment of Civilians. Unpublished transcripts, July 14 and 16, 1981, Washington, D.C.; August 4–6, 1981, Los Angeles; August 11–13, 1981, San Francisco; September 9–11, 1981, Seattle; September 14, 1981, Anchorage; September 17, 1981, Unalaska, Alaska; September 19, 1981, St. Paul, Alaska; September 22–23, 1981, Chicago; November 3, 1981, Washington, D.C.; November 23, 1981, New York. Japanese American National Museum, Los Angeles, Calif.

Daniels, Roger. "Introduction" (prepared for the Japanese American Citizens League National Committee for Redress for Submission to the Commission on Wartime Relocation and Internment of Civilians), circa 1981. Redress Files. National JACL Headquarters, San Francisco, Calif.

Department of Justice. Press release, February 19, 1999. Mitchell T. Maki Files, Los Angeles, Calif.

Goldberg, Justice Arthur J. Letter to Stephen Nakashima, April 20, 1976. Redress Files. National JACL Headquarters, San Francisco, Calif.

Gullion, Allen W. Transcript of telephone conversation with Mark W. Clark, February 4, 1942. Record Group 389—Provost Marshal General. National Archives, Washington D.C.

Hall, Captain John. Suggested changes in letter of transmittal and in foreword, circa May 3, 1943. CWRIC #24096-24106. Aiko Herzig-Yoshinaga Files, Falls Church, Va.

Harris, Rep. David. News release, October 6, 1976. Redress Files. National JACL Headquarters, San Francisco, Calif.

Hayakawa, S. I. Letter to Howard Baker, May 5, 1988. ID #561747, HU 013-22, Japanese American, White House Office of Records Management, Presidential Records. Ronald Reagan Library, Simi Valley, Calif.

Hirasuna, Fred. Memorandum to Min Yasui, April 29, 1985. Fred Hirasuna's Papers, Fresno, Calif.

———. Memorandum to Grayce Uyehara, March 2, 1987. Fred Hirasuna's Papers, Fresno, Calif.

Hohri, William M. "Thoughts on a Movement" (presentation at University of California, Los Angeles), May 22, 1996. Mitchell T. Maki Files, Los Angeles, Calif.

Honda, Harry. Memorandum to Harry Kitano, July 28, 1994. Harry H. L. Kitano Files, Los Angeles, Calif.

Horiuchi, Wayne. "A Report on Reparations Legislation for Japanese Americans: The Capitol Hill Perspective" (confidential report for JACL), June 27, 1976. Redress Files. National JACL Headquarters, San Francisco, Calif.

JACL LEC press releases, 1989. Redress Files. National JACL Headquarters, San Francisco, Calif.

JACL LEC redress updates, 1989. Redress Files. National JACL Headquarters, San Francisco, Calif.

JACL press and news releases, 1986, 1989. Redress Files. National JACL Headquarters, San Francisco, Calif.

Kawaguchi, Tom. Letter to Harry H. L. Kitano, February 4, 1997. Harry H. L. Kitano Files, Los Angeles, Calif.

Kean, Governor Thomas. Letter to President Ronald Reagan, February 6, 1988. HU 013-22, J-A 530000-549999, White House Office of Records Management, Presidential Records. Ronald Reagan Library, Simi Valley, Calif.

Kemp, Rep. Jack, Rep. Patrick L. Swindall, Rep. Newt Gingrich, and Rep. Henry Hyde. Letter to their colleagues, June 14, 1988. Redress Files. National JACL Headquarters, San Francisco, Calif.

Kurihara, Joseph Y. Letter to Yoshiko Hosoi (entitled "Niseis and the Government"), circa 1942. Gift of Charles and Lois Ferguson, 93.3. Japanese American National Museum, Los Angeles, Calif.

LCCR. Letter to Honorable Warren B. Rudman, October 13, 1989. Redress Files. National JACL Headquarters, San Francisco, Calif.

Lungren, Rep. Daniel E. Letter to his colleagues, September 16, 1987. Redress Files. National JACL Headquarters, San Francisco, Calif.

Marshall, George C. Letter to General Delos Emmons, October 7, 1943. CWRIC #26391. Aiko Herzig-Yoshinaga Files, Falls Church, Va.

———. Memorandum to Assistant Secretary of War John J. McCloy, May 13, 1944. Record Group 107—Records of the Secretary of War, Assistant Secretary of War, and Under Secretary of War. National Archives, Washington, D.C.

Masuda, June Goto. Letter to Grant Ujifusa, August 30, 1988. Grant Ujifusa Files, Chappaqua, N.Y.

McCloy, John J. Letter to General Charles H. Bonesteel, October 31, 1944. Record Group 107—Records of the Secretary of War, Assistant Secretary of War, and Under Secretary of War. National Archives, Washington D.C.

Mineta, Norm. Letter to Shig Sugiyama, January 30, 1976. Redress Files. National JACL Headquarters, San Francisco, Calif.

Mineta, Rep. Norman, and Rep. Robert T. Matsui. Joint press release, October 19, 1989. Redress Files. National JACL Headquarters, San Francisco, Calif.

Murakami, James F. Telex to Ed Yamamoto, September 24, 1976. Redress Files. National JACL Headquarters, San Francisco, Calif.

Nakashima, S. Stephen. Internal memorandum to JACL, June 14, 1976. Redress Files. National JACL Headquarters, San Francisco, Calif.

Nishikawa, Dan T. Letter to Paul Tsuneishi, May 10, 1976. Paul Tsuneishi Files, Sunland, Calif.

Office of Redress Administration. Letter from staff to authors, July 9, 1997. Mitchell T. Maki Files, Los Angeles, Calif.

Reagan, President Ronald. Letter to Rep. Joseph Wright, August 1, 1988. HU 013-22, J-A 572800-576681, White House Office of Records Management, Presidential Records. Ronald Reagan Library, Simi Valley, Calif.

Resolution by Western Baptist State Convention of California, February 19, 1976. Redress Files. National JACL Headquarters, San Francisco, Calif.

Rodino, Rep. Peter W., Jr., Rep. Thomas S. Foley, Rep. Dick Cheney, Rep. Hamilton Fish Jr., Rep. Tony Coelho, Rep. Henry J. Hyde, Rep. Barney Frank, Rep. Dan Glickman, and Rep. Patrick L. Swindall. Letter to their colleagues, September 10, 1987. Redress Files. National JACL Headquarters, San Francisco, Calif.

Rodino, Rep. Peter W., Jr., Rep. Barney Frank, Rep. Henry J. Hyde, and Rep. Hamilton Fish Jr. Letter to their colleagues, September 16, 1987. Redress Files. National JACL Headquarters, San Francisco, Calif.

Saiki, Rep. Patricia R., Rep. Norman Y. Mineta, Rep. Frank Horton, Rep. Barney Frank, Rep. Newt Gingrich, Rep. Don Edwards, Rep. Constance A. Morella, Rep. William J. Coyne, Rep. Ben Garrido Blaz, and Rep. Robert T. Matsui. Letter to President George Bush, January 31, 1989. Redress Files. National JACL Headquarters, San Francisco, Calif.

Shumway, Rep. Norman D. Letter to his colleagues, September 14, 1987. Redress Files. National JACL Headquarters, San Francisco, Calif.

Smith, WOJG Theodore E. Certification regarding the destruction of evidence of "Original Report of the Japanese Evacuation," June 29, 1943. CWRIC #24141. Aiko Herzig-Yoshinaga Files, Falls Church, Va.

"Statement of Administration Policy: H.R. 442—Civil Liberties Act of 1987," September 10, 1987. Box 16097—Japan Internment, Dan Crippen Files. Ronald Reagan Library, Simi Valley, Calif.

Steer, Lt. Col. William F. Letter to Whom This May Concern, Office of the Assistant Provost Marshall, Honolulu Police Station, Honolulu, T.H., January 10, 1943 (declassified by authority of Executive Order 12065, Section 3-402, NNDG 745037 OSD Letter, April 12, 1974), W. G. Lewis, NARS, April 6, 1982. Hamilton Library, University of Hawai'i, Manoa.

Stettinius, Under Secretary of State Edward J. Memorandum to President Roosevelt, June 9, 1944. OF4849, Box 1—WRA. Franklin D. Roosevelt Library, Hyde Park, N.Y.

Telegram to U.S. Attorney General Francis Biddle, February 16, 1942. WB23617433 Extra, Department of Justice Enemy Control Unit File, Box 782, 146-13-7-2-0, Section 3, February 14, 1942–February 16, 1942. National Archives, Washington, D.C.

Transcripts of telephone conversations, John L. Dewitt, Allen W. Gullion and Karl R. Bendetsen, February 1, 1942. Record Group 389—Provost Marshal General. National Archives, Washington D.C.

Tsuneishi, Paul. Letter to Ed Yamamoto, June 3, 1976. Paul Tsuneishi Files, Sunland, Calif.

———. Notes and rough outline on redress for panel on October 25, 1995, at Western Wyoming Community College, October 4, 1995. Paul Tsuneishi Files, Sunland, Calif.

Tsuneishi, Paul, Sue Embrey, and Phil Shigekuni. Letter to Ed Yamamoto, April 9, 1976. Paul Tsuneishi Files, Sunland, Calif.

Ujifusa, Grant. Comments during a panel discussion at the Voices of Japanese American Redress Conference, University of California, Los Angeles, September 13, 1997. Mitchell T. Maki Files, Los Angeles, Calif.

———. Letter to Assistant Attorney General Richard Willard, May 7, 1987. Redress Files. National JACL Headquarters, San Francisco, Calif.

Watanabe, Martha. Letter from deputy executive director of the CLPEF to authors, October 8, 1998. Mitchell T. Maki Files, Los Angeles, Calif.

Wright, Rep. Joseph. OMB Memorandum to Howard Baker, March 28, 1988. ID# 576683-553999, HU 013-22, JA, White House Office of Records Management, Presidential Records. Ronald Reagan Library, Simi Valley, Calif.

Yasui, Min. Letter to Grayce K. Uyehara, January 28, 1986. Redress Files. National JACL Headquarters, San Francisco, Calif.

Newspapers, Newsletters, and Magazines

Epistolarian. 1993

Hawaii Herald. 1989

Kashu Mainichi. 1989

Los Angeles Times. 1941, 1942, 1981, 1983, 1987, 1988–90, 1998

NCJAR Newsletter. 1981–88

NCRR Banner. 1981

New York Times. 1966, 1969

Pacific Citizen. 1945–78, 1979, 1983, 1985, 1988, 1989, 1990

People Weekly. 1987

Rafu Magazine. 1988

Rafu Shimpo. 1965, 1979–80, 1981, 1983, 1988–89, 1994–96

Salt Lake City Tribune. July 23–24, 1978

San Francisco Chronicle. 1981

San Francisco Examiner. 1989

Seattle Times. 1976

Time: The Weekly Newsmagazine. 1967, 1981

Wall Street Journal. 1981

Washington Post. 1976, 1983, 1988, 1989

Interviews by Authors

Crouch, Tom. Interview by authors. Washington, D.C., July 11, 1995.

Daniels, Roger. Interview by authors. Los Angeles, Calif., October 5, 1994.

Duberstein, Ken. Interview by authors. Washington, D.C., July 10, 1995.

Frank, Rep. Barney. Interview by authors. Washington, D.C., September 19, 1994.

Furutani, Warren. Interview by authors. Los Angeles, Calif., October 3, 1995.

Hayashino, Carole. Interview by authors. San Francisco, Calif., January 20, 1995.

Henderson, Elma. Interview by authors. Washington, D.C., September 17, 1994.

Herzig, Jack. Interview by authors. Los Angeles, Calif., October 3, 1995.

Herzig-Yoshinaga, Aiko. Interview by authors. Los Angeles, Calif., October 3, 1995.

Hirabayashi, Gordon. Interview by authors. Edmonton, Alberta, Canada, August 26, 1996.

Hohri, William M. Interview by authors. Los Angeles, Calif., October 12, 1994.

Iiyama, Chizu. Telephone interview by authors. El Cerrito, Calif., May 24, 1996.

Iiyama, Ernest. Telephone interview by authors. El Cerrito, Calif., October 10, 1995.

Inouye, Sen. Daniel. Interview by authors. Los Angeles, Calif., November 12, 1994.

Irons, Peter. Interview by authors. San Diego, Calif., October 26, 1994.

Johnston, Sen. Patrick. Interview by authors. Sacramento, Calif., June 22, 1995.

Kajihara, Harry. Interview by authors. Los Angeles, Calif., September 11, 1997.

Katsuda, Richard. Interview by authors. Los Angeles, Calif., May 29, 1996.

Kean, Governor Thomas. Telephone interview by authors. Madison, N.J., October 18, 1995.

Kinoshita, Cherry. Interview by authors. Seattle, Wash., October 8, 1994.

Kitano, Harry H. L. Interview by authors. Los Angeles, Calif., October 20, 1995.

———. Interview by authors. Los Angeles, Calif., March 12, 1996.

———. Interview by authors. Los Angeles, Calif., March 14, 1996.

Kitashima, Tsuyako "Sox." Interview by authors. San Francisco, Calif., January 20, 1995.

Lowry, Governor Michael E. Interview by authors. Olympia, Wash., October 8, 1994.

Marutani, Hon. William. Interview by authors. Washington, D.C., September 12, 1994.

Masuda, Janet Nishio. Interview by authors. Sacramento, Calif., June 22, 1995.

Matsui, Rep. Robert T. Interview by authors. Washington, D.C., July 11, 1995.

Meese, Hon. Ed. Interview by authors. Washington, D.C., July 10, 1995.

Minami, Dale. Interview by authors. San Francisco, Calif., January 20, 1995.

Mineta, Rep. Norman Y. Interview by authors. Salt Lake City, Utah, August 6, 1994.

Nakano, Bert. Interview by authors. Los Angeles, Calif., May 29, 1996.

Nakano, Lillian. Interview by authors. Los Angeles, Calif., May 29, 1996.

Ochi, Kay. Interview by authors. Los Angeles, Calif., May 31, 1995.

Ouchida, Priscilla. Interview by authors. Sacramento, Calif., June 22, 1995.

Roberts, Glenn. Interview by authors. Washington, D.C., September 19, 1994.

Saul, Eric. Interview by authors. Los Angeles, Calif., July 18, 1995.

Stroebel, Carol. Interview by authors. Washington, D.C., September 12, 1994.

Strobel, Chris. Interview by authors. Washington, D.C., September 16, 1994.

Sutherland, Lisa. Interview by authors. Washington, D.C., September 19, 1994.

Tatcishi, John. Interview by authors. Los Angeles, Calif., October 25, 1996.

———. Telephone interview by authors. Kentfield, Calif., November 14, 1995.

Tokiwa, Rudy. Interview by authors. Los Angeles, Calif., September 10, 1997.

Turner, Ralph H. Interview by authors. Los Angeles, Calif., February 26, 1996.

Ujifusa, Grant. Interview by authors. Chappaqua, N.Y., September 18, 1994.

———. Interview by authors. Los Angeles, Calif., November 13, 1994.

———. Interview by authors. Chappaqua, N.Y., July 9, 1995.

Uyeda, Clifford. Interview by authors. San Francisco, Calif., January 20, 1995.

Uyehara, Grayce. Interview by authors. Salt Lake City, Utah, August 5, 1994.

Wakabayashi, Ron. Interview by authors. Los Angeles, Calif., May 15, 1996.

Willard, Richard. Interview by authors. Washington, D.C., July 10, 1995.

Other Sources

Baker, Lillian. *American and Japanese Relocation in World War II: Fact, Fiction, and Fallacy.* Medford, Oreg.: Webb Research Group, 1990.

———. *The Concentration Camp Conspiracy—A Second Pearl Harbor.* Lawndale, Calif.: AFHA Publications, 1981.

———. *Dishonoring America: The Collective Guilt of American Japanese.* Medford, Oreg.: Webb Research Group, 1988.

Ball, Howard. "Judicial Parsimony and Military Necessity Disinterred: A Reexamination of the Japanese Exclusion Cases, 1943–44." In *Japanese Americans: From Relocation to Redress,* edited by Roger Daniels, Sandra C. Taylor and Harry H. L. Kitano. Seattle: University of Washington Press, 1986.

Barone, Michael, and Grant Ujifusa. *The Almanac of American Politics, 1986.* Washington, D.C.: National Journal Inc., 1985.

Bendetsen, Karl R. "Written Statement for the Commission on Wartime Relocation and Internment of Civilians, July 8, 1981." In *Papers of the U.S. Commission on Wartime Relocation and Internment of Civilians: Part 1—Numerical File Archive,* edited by Randolph Boehm. Frederick, Md.: University Publications of America, 1984.

Biddle, Francis B. *In Brief Authority.* New York: Doubleday, 1962.

Bush, George. *Public Papers of the Presidents of the United States: George Bush, 1989, Book II, July 1 to December 31, 1989.* Washington, D.C.: U.S. Government Printing Office, 1990.

———. *Public Papers of the Presidents of the United States: George Bush, Book II, August 1, 1992, to January 20, 1993.* Washington, D.C.: U.S. Government Printing Office, 1993.

Calmes, Jackie. "The Budget—It Was Supposed to Be Easy: Where Did Good Will Go?" *Congressional Quarterly: Weekly Reports* 47 (December 2, 1989): 3309–10.

Campbell, Joseph. *How Policies Change: The Japanese Government and the Aging Society.* Princeton, N.J.: Princeton University Press, 1992.

Canada. House of Commons. *Debates.* 32d Parliament, 2d sess., April 2, 1984.

Carter, Jimmy. *Public Papers of the Presidents of the United States: Jimmy Carter, 1978, Book II, June 30 to December 31, 1978.* Washington, D.C.: U.S. Government Printing Office. 1979.

———. *Public Papers of the Presidents of the United States: Jimmy Carter, 1980–1981, Book II, May 24 to September 26, 1980.* Washington, D.C.: U.S. Government Printing Office. 1982.

———. *Public Papers of the Presidents of the United States: Jimmy Carter, 1980–1981, Book III, September 29, 1980, to January 20, 1981.* Washington, D.C.: U.S. Government Printing Office, 1982.

Castelnuovo, Shirley. "With Liberty and Justice for Some: Case for Compensation to Japanese Americans Imprisoned during World War II." In *Japanese Americans: From Relocation to Redress,* rev. ed., edited by Roger Daniels, Sandra C. Taylor, and Harry H. L. Kitano. Seattle: University of Washington Press, 1991.

Chin, Frank. Oral comments during panel discussion at the Japanese American National Museum, Los Angeles, Calif., September 21, 1996.

Chuman, Frank F. *Bamboo People: The Law and Japanese-Americans.* Del Mar, Calif.: Publisher's Inc., 1976.

Civilian Exclusion Order No. 5. In U.S. Congress, *Fourth Interim Report of Select Committee Investigating National Defense Migration,* 77th Congr., 2d sess., 1942, House Report No. 2124. Washington, D.C.: U.S. Government Printing Office, 1942.

Cohen, Michael, James March, and Johan Olsen. "A Garbage Can Model of Organizational Choice." *Administrative Science Quarterly* 17 (March 1972): 1–25.

Commission on Wartime Relocation and Internment of Civilians. *Personal Justice Denied.* Washington, D.C.: U.S. Government Printing Office, December 1982.

———. *Personal Justice Denied, Part 2: Recommendations.* Washington, D.C.: U.S. Government Printing Office, June 1983.

Congressional Record. 77th Congr., 2d sess., vol. 88, part 2, February 23 to March 25, 1942. Washington, D.C.: U.S. Government Printing Office, 1942.

———. 80th Congr., 2d sess., vol. 93, part 8, July 21 to November 17, 1947. Washington, D.C.: U.S. Government Printing Office, 1947.

———. 95th Congr., 2d sess., vol. 124, part 1, January 19 to January 27, 1978. Washington, D.C.: U.S. Government Printing Office, 1978.

———. 96th Congr., 1st sess., vol. 125, part 26, November 27 to December 6, 1979. Washington, D.C.: U.S. Government Printing Office, 1979.

———. 96th Congr., 2d sess., vol. 126, part 10, May 22 to June 4, 1980. Washington, D.C.: U.S. Government Printing Office, 1980.

———. 96th Congr., 2d sess., vol. 126, part 14, June 28 to July 21, 1980. Washington, D.C.: U.S. Government Printing Office, 1980.

———. 96th Congr., 2d sess., vol. 126, part 25, December 8 to December 30, 1980. Washington, D.C.: U.S. Government Printing Office, 1980.

———. 97th Congr., 1st sess., vol. 127, part 2, February 3 to February 23, 1981. Washington, D.C.: U.S. Government Printing Office, 1981.

———. 100th Congr., 1st sess., vol. 133, no. 141, September 17 to September 25, 1987. Washington, D.C.: U.S. Government Printing Office, 1987.

———. 100th Congr., 2d sess., vol. 134, no. 50, April 19, 1988. Washington, D.C.: U.S. Government Printing Office, 1988.

———. 100th Congr., 2d sess., vol. 134, no. 51, April 20, 1988. Washington, D.C.: U.S. Government Printing Office, 1988.

———. 101st Congr., 1st sess., vol. 135, no. 128, September 29, 1989. Washington, D.C.: U.S. Government Printing Office, 1989.

———. 101st Congr., 1st sess., vol. 135, no. 147, October 26, 1989. Washington, D.C.: U.S. Government Printing Office, 1989.

———. 102d Congr., 2d sess., vol. 138, no. 124, September 14, 1992. Washington, D.C.: U.S. Government Printing Office, 1992.

———. 102d Congr., 2d sess., vol. 138, no. 125, September 15, 1992. Washington, D.C.: U.S. Government Printing Office, 1992.

Conn, Stetson, Rose C. Engelman, and Byron Fairchild. *United States Army in World War II: The Western Hemisphere; Guarding the United States and Its Outposts.* Washington, D.C.: Office of the Chief of Military History, Department of the Army, 1964.

Conrat, Maisie, and Richard Conrat. *Executive Order 9066: The Internment of 110,000 Japanese Americans.* Cambridge, Mass.: MIT Press for the California Historical Society, 1972.

Corbett, P. Scott. *Quiet Passages: The Exchange of Civilians between the United States and Japan during the Second World War.* Kent, Ohio: Kent State University Press, 1987.

Daniels, Roger. "Afterword: The Struggle for Redress." In *The Enemy That Never Was,* by Ken Adachi. Toronto, Canada: McClelland and Stewart, 1991.

———. *Concentration Camps USA: Japanese Americans in World War II.* New York: Holt, Rinehart and Winston, 1971.

———. "The Internment of Japanese Nationals in the United States during World War II." *Halcyon, 1995: A Journal of Humanities* 17 (1995): 65–75.

———. *The Politics of Prejudice: The Anti-Japanese Movement in California and the Struggle for Japanese Exclusion.* Berkeley: University of California Press, 1962.

———. *Prisoners without Trial: Japanese Americans in World War II.* New York: Hill and Wang, 1993.

Daniels, Roger, and Kitano, Harry H. L. *American Racism.* Englewood Cliffs, N.J.: Prentice-Hall, 1970.

Duus, Masayo Umezawa. *Unlikely Liberators: The Men of the 100th and 442nd.* Honolulu: University of Hawaii Press, 1987.

Executive Order 9066. Executive order authorizing the Secretary of War to prescribe military areas signed by President Franklin D. Roosevelt, February 19, 1942. F.R. Doc. 42-1563: Filed, February 21, 1942: 12:51 P.M. *Federal Register* 7 (February 25, 1942): 1407.

Ex Parte Endo, 323 US 283 (1944).

Fiset, Louis. "Redress for Nisei Public Employees in Washington State after World War II." *Pacific Northwest Quarterly* 88 (Winter 1996–97): 21–32.

Ford, Gerald R. *Public Papers of the Presidents of the United States: Gerald R. Ford, 1976–1977, Book 1, January 1 to April 9, 1976.* Washington, D.C.: U.S. Government Printing Office, 1979.

Funai, Pam, and Jennifer Kim Mikami. Oral presentation at the Japanese American National Museum, Los Angeles, Calif., June 25, 1995.

Gulick, Sidney L. *The American Japanese Problem: A Study of the Racial Relations of the East and the West.* New York: Charles Scribner's Sons, 1914.

Hirabayashi v. United States, 320 U.S. 81 (1943).

Hirabayashi v. United States, 627 F. Supp. 1445, 1457 (W.D. Wash., 1986).

Hirose, Stacey Y. "Japanese American Women and the Women's Army Corp., 1935–1950." M.A. thesis, University of California, Los Angeles, 1993.

Hohri, William M. *Repairing America: An Account of the Movement for Japanese-American Redress.* Pullman: Washington State University Press, 1988.

Hohri v. United States, 586 F. Supp. 769 (1984).

Hosokawa, Bill. *Nisei: The Quiet Americans.* New York: William Morrow, 1969.

Ichioka, Yuji. *The Issei: The World of the First Generation Japanese Immigrants, 1885–1924.* New York: Free Press, 1988.

Inouye, Daniel K., with Lawrence Elliott. *Journey to Washington.* Englewood Cliffs, N.J.: Prentice-Hall, 1967.

Irons, Peter. *Justice at War: The Story of the Japanese American Internment Cases.* New York: Oxford University Press, 1983.

———, ed. *Justice Delayed: The Record of the Japanese American Internment Cases.* Middletown, Conn.: Wesleyan University Press, 1989.

Japanese American Citizens League. "Discussion on Use of the JACL Endowment Fund." In *The Official Minutes of the National Council Meetings 27th Biennial National Convention of the Japanese American Citizens League.* Los Angeles, California, August 10–13, 1982. San Francisco: Japanese American Citizens League, 1982.

———. *The Japanese American Incarceration: A Case for Redress.* 3d ed. San Francisco: National Committee for Redress, Japanese American Citizens League, 1980.

———. "Revised Redress Proposal." In *Visions: Official Minutes of the National Council Meetings, 25th Biennial National Convention of the Japanese American Citizens League.* Salt Lake City, Utah, July 17–22, 1978. San Francisco: Japanese American Citizens League, 1978.

Kingdon, John W. *Agendas, Alternatives, and Public Policies.* Glenville, Ill.: Scott, Foresman, 1984.

Kirtland, John C., and David F. Coffin Jr. *The Relocation and Internment of the Aleuts during World War II.* Anchorage, Alaska: Aleutian/Pribilof Islands Association, 1981.

Kitano, Harry H. L. *Generations and Identity: The Japanese American.* Needham Heights, Mass.: Simon and Schuster Higher Education Publishing Group, 1993.

———. "In Search of an Identity." In *A History of Race Relations Research: First Generation Recollections,* edited by John H. Stanfield II. Newbury Park, Calif.: Sage Publications, 1993.

———. "Japanese Americans." In *Harvard Encyclopedia of American Ethnic Groups,* edited by Stephan Thernstrom. Cambridge, Mass.: Harvard University Press, 1980.

———. *Japanese Americans: The Evolution of a Subculture.* 2d ed. Englewood Cliffs: Prentice Hall, 1976.

———. "Japanese Americans on the Road to Dissent." In *Seasons of Rebellion: Protest and Radicalism in Recent America,* edited by Joseph Boskin and Robert A. Rosenstone. New York: Holt, Rinehart and Winston, 1972.

Kitano, Harry H. L., and Roger Daniels. *Asian Americans: Emerging Minorities.* 2d ed. Englewood Cliffs: Prentice Hall, 1995.

Kitayama, Glen F. "Japanese Americans and the Movement for Redress: A Case Study of Grassroots Activism in the Los Angeles Chapter of the National Coalition for Redress/Reparations." M.A. thesis, University of California, Los Angeles, 1993.

Kohlhoff, Dean. *When the Wind Was a River: Aleut Evacuation in World War II.* Seattle: University of Washington Press in Association with the Aleutian/Pribilof Islands Associations, Anchorage, 1995.

Korematsu v. United States, 323 U.S. 214, 225–26 (1994).

Korematsu v. United States, 584 F. Supp. 1406, 1420 (N.D. Calif., 1984).

Kumamoto, Bob. "The Search for Spies: American Counterintelligence and the Japanese American Community 1931–1942." *Amerasia Journal* 6 (Fall 1979): 45–75.

Kutler, Stanley I. "Forging a Legend: The Treason of 'Tokyo Rose.'" *Wisconsin Law Review* 1980, no. 6 (1980): 1341–82.

Lipton, Dean. "Wayne M. Collins and the Case of 'Tokyo Rose.'" *Journal of Contemporary Studies* 8 (Fall/Winter 1985): 25–41.

Masaoka, Mike, with Bill Hosokawa. *They Call Me Moses Masaoka: An American Saga.* New York: William Morrow, 1987.

Mass, Amy Iwasaki. "Psychological Effects of the Camps on Japanese Americans." In *Japanese Americans: From Relocation to Redress,* edited by Roger Daniels, Sandra C. Taylor, and Harry H. L. Kitano. Seattle: University of Washington Press, 1986.

Matsumoto, Valerie. *Farming the Home Place.* Ithaca, N.Y.: Cornell University Press, 1993.

McWilliams, Carey. *Prejudice: Japanese-Americans, Symbol of Racial Intolerance.* Boston: Little, Brown, 1944.

Minami, Dale. "Coram Nobis and Redress." In *Japanese Americans: From Relocation to Redress,* rev. ed., edited by Roger Daniels, Sandra C. Taylor, and Harry H. L. Kitano. Seattle: University of Washington Press, 1991.

Mirikitani, Janice. "Breaking Silences." *Amerasia Journal* 8 (Fall/Winter 1981): 107–10.

Mitchell v. Harmony, 54 U.S. 115, 14 L. Ed. 75, 13 How 115 (1851).

Morris, Aldon D. *The Origins of the Civil Rights Movement: Black Communities Organizing for Change.* New York: Free Press, 1984.

Naito, Calvin, and Esther Scott. *Against All Odds: The Campaign in Congress for Japanese-American Redress.* Cambridge, Mass.: John F. Kennedy School of Government, Harvard University, 1990.

National Emergencies Act. In *United States Statutes at Large,* vol. 90, part 1, 1255–59. Washington, D.C.: U.S. Government Printing Office, 1978.

The New Lexicon Webster's Dictionary of the English Language. New York: Lexicon, 1987.

Nishimoto, Richard S. *Inside an American Concentration Camp: Japanese American Resistance at Poston, Arizona.* Edited by Lane R. Hirabayashi. Tucson: University of Arizona Press, 1995.

Nixon, Richard M. *Public Papers of the Presidents of the United States: Richard Nixon, 1972.* Washington, D.C.: U.S. Government Printing Office, 1974.

Ogawa, Dennis M. *Kodomo No Tame Ni: For the Sake of the Children.* Honolulu: University of Hawai'i Press, 1978.

Okamura, Raymond. "Background and History of the Repeal Campaign." *Amerasia Journal* 2 (Fall 1974): 73–94.

Ornstein, Norman J., Thomas E. Mann, and Michael J. Malbin. *Vital Statistics on Congress, 1989–1990.* Washington, D.C.: Congressional Quarterly Press, 1990.

Public Law 80-886 [H.R. 3999], Japanese-American Evacuation Claims Act of 1948. July 2, 1948, 62 Stat. 1231–33.

Public Law 100-383 [H.R. 442], Civil Liberties Act of 1988. August 10, 1988, 102 Stat. 903–17.

Public Law 101-45 [H.R. 2402], Dire Emergency Supplemental Appropriations and Transfers, Urgent Supplementals, and Correcting Enrollment Errors Act of 1989. June 30, 1989, 103 Stat. 97–131.

Rapp, David. "Appropriations—Supplemental Request Swells To $4.6 Billion in Markup: Subcommittees Add $1.6 Billion in Spending, Ignore Bush's Call for Offsetting Cuts." *Congressional Quarterly: Weekly Report* 47 (April 8, 1989): 738–39.

Reagan, Ronald. *Public Papers of the Presidents of the United States: Ronald Reagan, 1988–1989, Book II, July 2, 1988 to Jan. 19, 1989.* Washington, D.C.: U.S. Government Printing Office, 1991.

Riggs, Fred W. *Pressures on Congress: A Study of the Repeal of Chinese Exclusion.* New York: King's Crown, 1950.

Strong, Edward K. *The Second-Generation Japanese Problem.* Palo Alto, Calif.: Stanford University Press, 1934.

Takeuchi, Peter. "An Interview with Dr. Clifford Uyeda." In *The 26th Biennial Golden Anniversary JACL National Convention.* San Francisco, July 28 to August 1, 1980. San Francisco: Japanese American Citizens League, 1980.

Tateishi, John. "Interview by Eric Saul," April 15, 1986. In *National Japanese American Historical Society Oral History Project.* San Francisco: National Japanese American Historical Society, June 1986.

———. *And Justice For All: An Oral History of the Japanese American Detention Camps.* New York: Random House, 1984.

Thomas, Dorothy Swaine. *The Salvage.* Berkeley: University of California Press, 1952.

Thomas, Dorothy Swaine, and Richard S. Nishimoto. *The Spoilage.* Berkeley: University of California Press, 1946.

Truman, Harry S. *Public Papers of the Presidents of the United States: Harry S. Truman, January 1 to December 31, 1946.* Washington, D.C.: U.S. Government Printing Office, 1962.

————. *Public Papers of the Presidents of the United States: Harry S. Truman, January 1 to December 31, 1950.* Washington, D.C. U.S. Government Printing Office, 1965.

Turner, Ralph H., and Lewis M. Killian. *Collective Behavior.* 3d ed. Englewood Cliffs, N.J.: Prentice-Hall, 1987.

Uchida, Yoshiko. *Desert Exile: The Uprooting of a Japanese American Family.* Seattle: University of Washington Press, 1982.

U.S. Bureau of the Census. *Statistical Abstract of the United States.* 115th ed. Washington, D.C.: Bureau of the Census, 1995.

U.S. Congress. *Fourth Interim Report of Select Committee Investigating National Defense Migration.* 77th Congr., 2d sess., 1942. House Report No. 2124. Washington, D.C.: U.S. Government Printing Office, 1942.

U.S. Congress, Committee of Conference. *Joint Explanatory Statement of the Committee of Conference: Conference Report, Civil Liberties Act.* 100th Congr., 2d sess., 1988. House Report No. 100-785. Washington, D.C.: U.S. Government Printing Office, 1988.

U.S. Department of Justice. "Redress Provisions for Persons of Japanese Ancestry: Guidelines for Individuals Who Relocated to Japan as Minors during World War II." *Federal Register* 61 (April 22, 1996): 17667–69.

————. "Redress Provisions for Persons of Japanese Ancestry: Guidelines for Individuals Who Relocated to Japan as Minors during World War II. " *Federal Register* 61 (June 12, 1996): 29716–19.

————. "Redress Provisions for Persons of Japanese Ancestry: Guidelines under Ishida v. United States." *Federal Register* 62 (April 24, 1997): 19928–34.

U.S. Department of War. *Final Report: Japanese Evacuation from the West Coast 1942.* Washington, D.C.: U.S. Government Printing Office, 1943.

U.S. House Committee on the Judiciary. *Civil Liberties Act of 1987.* 100th Congr., 1st sess., 1987. Report 100-278 to Accompany H.R. 442. Washington, D.C.: U.S. Government Printing Office, 1987.

————. *Civil Liberties Act Amendments of 1992.* 102d Congr., 2d sess., 1992. Report 102-863 to Accompany H.R. 4551. Washington, D.C.: U.S. Government Printing Office, 1992.

U.S. House Select Committee Investigating National Defense Migration. *Hearings Pursuant to H. Res. 113.* 77th Congr., 2d sess., 1942. Washington, D.C.: U.S. Government Printing Office, 1942.

U.S. House Subcommittee on Administrative Law and Governmental Relations of the Committee on the Judiciary. *Hearings on H.R. 442 and H.R. 1631.* 100th Congr., 1st sess., 1987. Washington, D.C.: U.S. Government Printing Office, 1987.

————. *Hearings on H.R. 442 and H.R. 2415.* 99th Congr., 2d sess., 1986. Washington, D.C.: U.S. Government Printing Office, 1986.

————. *Hearings on H.R. 3387, H.R. 4110, and H.R. 4322.* 98th Congr., 2d sess., 1984. Washington, D.C.: U.S. Government Printing Office, 1984.

U.S. House Subcommittee on the Departments of Commerce, Justice, and State, the Judiciary, and Related Agencies of the Committee on Appropriations. *Testimony of Members of Congress and Other Interested Individuals and Organizations.* 101st Congr., 1st sess., 1989. Washington, D.C.: U.S. Government Printing Office, 1989.

U.S. Senate Committee on Governmental Affairs. *Accepting the Findings and Implementing the Recommendations of the Commission on Wartime Relocation and Internment of Civilians.* 100th Congr., 1st sess., 1987. Report 100-202. Washington, D.C.: U.S. Government Printing Office, 1987.

————. *Hearing before the Committee on Governmental Affairs on S. 1647: Commission on Wartime Relocation and Internment of Civilians Act.* 96th Congr., 2d sess., 1980. Washington, D.C.: U.S. Government Printing Office, 1980.

U.S. Senate Subcommittee on Administrative Practice and Procedure of the Committee on the Judiciary. *Hearings on S. 1520.* 98th Congr. 1st sess., 1983. Washington, D.C.: U.S. Government Printing Office, 1983.

U.S. Senate Subcommittee on Civil Service, Post Office, and General Services of the Senate Governmental Affairs Committee. *Hearings on S. 2116.* 98th Congr. 2d sess., 1984. Washington, D.C.: U.S. Government Printing Office, 1984.

U.S. Senate Subcommittee on Federal Service, Post Office, and Civil Service of the Committee on Governmental Affairs. *Hearings on S. 1009.* 100th Congr., 1st sess., 1987. Washington, D.C.: U.S. Government Printing Office, 1987.

Uyeda, Clifford I. *A Final Report and Review: The Japanese American Citizens League National Committee for Iva Toguri,* Occasional Monographs Series 1. Seattle: University of Washington Asian American Studies Program, 1980.

Weglyn, Michi. *Years of Infamy: The Untold Story of America's Concentration Camps.* New York: Morrow Quill Paperbacks, 1976.

Witt, Elder. "Japanese-Americans Seek Redress from Court." *Congressional Quarterly: Weekly Report* 45 (April 18, 1987): 723–27.

Yamashita, Hiroshi John. *Haiku Images.* Los Angeles: Hiroshi John Yamashita, 1981.

Yanamoto, Miwako. "Nisei WAC Has No Regrets about Enlistment." *Japanese American National Museum Quarterly* 10 (Winter 1995): 6.

Yasui v. United States, 320 U.S. 115, 63 S. Ct. 1392 (1943).

Video and Audio Tapes

House Floor Debate on H.R. 442, September 17, 1987. Videocassette. Mitchell T. Maki Files, Los Angeles, Calif.

Iwataki, Miya. Videotaped interview by Glen Kitayama, Los Angeles, Calif., June 18, 1993. In *Japanese American Internment: Oral Histories.* Videotape. UCLA Asian American Studies Center Library, Los Angeles, Calif.

Japanese American Citizens League National Committee for Redress. San Francisco, Calif., March 3, 1979. Audiocassette. Mitchell T. Maki Files, Los Angeles, Calif.

Kinoshita, Cherry, Carole Hayashino, and William Yoshino (producers). *Redress: The JACL Campaign for Justice.* San Francisco, Calif.: Visual Communications, 1991. Videocassette.

Marutani, Hon. William. Videotaped interview by Mitchell T. Maki, Darcie Iki, and John Esaki, Media, Pa., August 27, 1998. Japanese American National Museum, Los Angeles, Calif.

Nakano, Bert. Videotaped interview by Glen Kitayama, Los Angeles, Calif., June 18, 1993. In *Japanese American Internment: Oral Histories.* Videotape. UCLA Asian American Studies Center Library, Los Angeles, Calif.

Sasaki, Shosuke. *An Appeal for Action to Obtain Evacuation Redress.* Seattle, Wash.: Seattle JACL Chapter, 1975. Audiocassette.

Thill, Michael, Mary J. H. Thill, and Dimitri Philemonof (producers). *Aleut Evacuation: The Untold Story.* Girdwood, Ark.: Gaff Rigged Productions for the Aleutian/Pribilof Islands Association, 1992. Videocassette.

Index

ABA. *See* American Bar Association
"ABC" list of aliens, 27
ABC-TV 20/20, 82
Abe, Frank, 87
Abourezk, James, 72
ACLU. *See* American Civil Liberties Union
Adachi, Jeff, 215
Adams, Brock, 208, 268, 275
Adenauer, Konrad, 178
ADL. *See* Anti-Defamation League of B'nai B'rith
AFL-CIO. *See* American Federation of Labor–Congress of Industrial Organizations
African Americans, 52; churches of, 58, 76; leaders of, 66; and redress, 240, 264; as soldiers, 157. *See also* Black Caucus
Agriculture: anti-Japanese farmers in, 29; Issei farmers in, 22
Aiken, George D., 250
Akaka, Daniel, 212, 275–76
Alameda County (Calif.), 75, 146
Alaska, 91, 99, 184, 235
Alaska Defense Command, 48
Alaska Peninsula, 48
Alderson Federal Reformatory for Women, 78
Alexander, Clifford, Jr., 157
Alien Land Acts/Laws, 22, 52, 249; ruled unconstitutional, 55
Aleutian Islands, 47–48, 96
Aleutian/Pribilof Islands Association, 50, 256

Aleut Indians, 184
Aleuts and Pribilof Islanders, 7, 47, 92, 96, 155; appropriations for redress for, 199; common cause with Japanese Americans, 50, 234–35; on CWRIC, 97; CWRIC findings and recommendations on, 111–12, 264; evacuation of, 48–50, 248; investigation of wartime experiences of, 94; and Justice Department, 168; as multimillionaires, 183; and redress, 91, 139–40, 142, 153, 156, 167, 181, 185; testimony on, 142
All Center Conference, 52
Almanac of American Politics, 148, 149
Amache (Granada, Colo.), 33, 85, 118, 250
American Baptist Churches, USA, 265
American Baptist Convention, 76
American Bar Association (ABA), 146, 171
American Civil Liberties Union (ACLU), 28, 36, 145, 171, 225, 263, 274; local chapters of, 263
American Defenders of Bataan and Corregidor, Inc., 250
American Ex-Prisoners of War, 250
American Federation of Labor–Congress of Industrial Organizations (AFL-CIO), 145, 246
American Friends Service Committee, 171, 262
American Jewish Committee, 263, 265
American Jewish Congress, 166, 263
American Jews, 165–66. *See also* Anti-Defamation League of B'nai B'rith; Anti-Semitism; B'nai B'rith

Mitchell T. Maki is an assistant professor in the UCLA School of Public Policy and Social Research. He, along with Kitano and Berthold, received a Civil Liberties Public Education Fund grant and was the lead coordinator of the Voices of Japanese American Redress Conference held at UCLA in September 1997. He is the author of numerous articles on the delivery of social services to ethnic minority populations and is an active participant in the Asian and Pacific Islander American community in Los Angeles.

Harry H. L. Kitano is professor emeritus of social welfare and sociology in the School of Public Policy and Social Research at UCLA. He was the first to hold the endowed chair of Japanese American Studies. He is the author of numerous scholarly articles and books, including *Japanese Americans: The Evolution of a Subculture* (1976), *Generations and Identity* (1993), and *Race Relations* (1998), now in its fifth edition. He spent his teenage years in the Topaz Concentration Camp in Utah. He continues to teach and conduct research on the Asian American experience.

S. Megan Berthold is a senior researcher with the Center for Language Minority Education and Research at California State University, Long Beach. Her research interests include the effects of war traumas and violence on adolescents and their families, the refugee experience of Southeast Asian populations, and issues of civil and human rights. She received her doctorate of social welfare from UCLA and is a licensed clinical social worker who has practiced in the United States and in refugee camps in Asia.

Robert T. Matsui is a U.S. representative from Sacramento, California. He was elected in 1978 and established a national and international reputation as a leader on such issues as trade, tax policy, social security, health care, and welfare reform. He serves on the Ways and Means Committee. Representative Matsui was a six-month-old infant when he and his family were incarcerated during World War II. He was instrumental in the passage of the Civil Liberties Act of 1988 and its related legislation.

The Asian American Experience

Typeset in 10.5/12.5 Adobe Minion
with Gill Sans display
Composed by Jim Proefrock
at the University of Illinois Press
Manufactured by Cushing-Malloy, Inc.

University of Illinois Press
1325 South Oak Street
Champaign, IL 61820-6903
www.press.uillinois.edu